China's Use of Military Force

Beyond the Great Wall and the Long March

In this unique study of military behavior, Andrew Scobell examines China's use of force abroad – as in Korea (1950), Vietnam (1979), and the Taiwan Strait (1995–6) – and domestically, as during the Cultural Revolution of the late 1960s and in the 1989 military crackdown in Tiananmen Square. Debunking the myth that China has become increasingly belligerent in recent years because of the growing influence of bellicose soldiers, Scobell concludes that China's strategic culture has remained unchanged for decades and that soldiers, while hawkish, are not responsible for Beijing's assertive behavior. Nevertheless, the author uncovers the existence of a "Cult of Defense" in Chinese strategic culture, which, paradoxically, disposes Chinese leaders to rationalize the use of military force as defensive no matter what the actual circumstances. The author warns that this "Cult of Defense," combined with changes in the People's Liberation Army's doctrine and capabilities over the past two decades, suggests that China's twenty-first-century leaders may use military force more readily than their predecessors.

Dr. Andrew Scobell is Associate Research Professor at the Strategic Studies Institute of the U.S. Army War College and Adjunct Professor of Political Science at Dickinson College. Scobell is the editor of "The Cost of Conflict: The Impact on China of a Future War" and several monographs and reports. His work has appeared in such journals as *Armed Forces and Society*, *Asian Survey*, *Comparative Politics*, *China Quarterly*, and *Political Science Quarterly*. He holds a Ph.D. in political science from Columbia University.

Cambridge Modern China Series

Edited by William Kirby, Harvard University

Other books in the series:

Continued on page following the Index

China's Use of Military Force

Beyond the Great Wall and the Long March

ANDREW SCOBELL

U.S. Army War College

CAMBRIDGE UNIVERSITY PRESS
Cambridge, New York, Melbourne, Madrid, Cape Town,
Singapore, São Paulo, Delhi, Tokyo, Mexico City

Cambridge University Press
32 Avenue of the Americas, New York, NY 10013-2473, USA

www.cambridge.org
Information on this title: www.cambridge.org/9780521525855

First published 2003
Reprinted 2006, 2007, 2011

A catalog record for this publication is available from the British Library.

Library of Congress Cataloging in Publication Data

Scobell, Andrew.
China's use of military force : beyond the Great Wall and the long march/
Andrew Scobell.
    p. cm. – (Cambridge modern China series)
Includes bibliographical references and index.
ISBN 0-521-81979-2 – ISBN 0-521-52585-3 (pb.)
    1. China – Military policy. 2. China – History, Military – 1949– I. Title.
II. Series.
UA835.S3797 2003
355´.033051–dc21   2002041536

ISBN 978-0-521-81979-4 Hardback
ISBN 978-0-521-52585-5 Paperback

For Michele

Contents

Contents

Part IV
Use of Force in the Post-Deng Era

Preface

AS the world steps gingerly into the twenty-first century, perhaps the greatest question mark is what kind of global citizen the People's Republic of China will turn out to be. It became fashionable during the 1990s to speak of a "China Threat." Does China pose a threat to its neighbors? Will China be cooperative or confrontational? Will China be a catalyst for peace or conflict? The subject of China's use of force is a basic and important dimension in attempting to address the larger question.

This is not the first book to examine multiple cases of China's use of force. Excellent studies by Jonathan Adelman and Chih-Yu Shih *(Symbolic War)*, Melvin Gurtov and Byung-Moo Hwang *(China under Threat)*, Gerald Segal *(Defending China)*, and Allen Whiting (*The Chinese Calculus of Deterrence*) provide a wealth of data and insights. Yet, as China moves beyond what is often described as the "reform era," there seems a pressing need for a fresh and comprehensive examination of the subject. This study considers the employment of military power both outside China's borders and within; it analyzes the use of force across three eras: under Mao Zedong, Deng Xiaoping, and Jiang Zemin. Using the frameworks of strategic and civil-military culture, I seek both a better understanding of China's use of force to date and a better guide to anticipate the circumstances under which China may be likely to use force in the future.

The Great Wall is undoubtedly the most famous man-made structure in China. It is also, with the possible exception of the giant panda, the one symbol people around the world most closely associate with China. Construction of the Great Wall is widely believed to have been begun by Qin Shihuang, the emperor who first unified China in 221 B.C. For China, it is a symbol of a strong, wealthy, and united country, one with clearly demarcated and well-defended national borders. For the Chinese, the Great Wall also represents continuity between contemporary and ancient China – an unbroken historic link going back thousands of years. The Chinese are justifiably proud of this massive fortification, and its imagery is widely used in contemporary China. The People's Liberation Army (PLA) is often referred to as China's "Great Wall of Steel." Indeed, this was the phrase used by Deng to praise the commanders of the Beijing Martial Law troops at a meeting five days after the 1989 Tiananmen massacre. The Great Wall also symbolizes an enduring Chinese strategic culture that is pacifist and defensive-minded.

Historians and communist leaders alike often single out the Long March as a landmark event in twentieth century China. It ensured the survival and rejuvenation of the communist movement in the 1930s. The Long March also marked the emergence of the most important leader of the movement, Mao Zedong – the most powerful and influential figure in modern China. It is seen as symbolic of the sustained guerilla conflict that ensured the survival of the Chinese communist movement in the mid-1930s. Moreover, the expedition has taken on epic proportions in China, and participants took on the status of living legends. For decades, the Long March was de rigueur for entry into top leadership positions in the party and army, and was adopted as the label for an entire generation of leaders. The Long March can also serve as the moniker of a civil-military configuration where the distinction between soldiers and civilians is blurred and difficult to discern.

To interpret China's domestic and international behavior in the twenty-first century, observers need to look beyond the mythology associated with the Great Wall and the Long March. This book attempts to do so and thus provide a better understanding of how China uses force.

This book is a radically reoriented version of a doctoral dissertation on civil-military relations begun under the tutelage of Richard Betts and Andrew Nathan. The genesis of this project in its earliest incarnation owes much to the encouragement and support of these two accomplished scholars and mentors. I also appreciate the comments and suggestions of the other members of my dissertation committee: Randle Edwards, Samuel Kim, and Madeleine Zelin. Actually, it was Sam Kim who first suggested the rubric of strategic culture to me. I am also grateful to my *tongxue* at Columbia University in our dissertation writing group: Michael Chambers, Hsu Szu-chien, and Brian Murray, all of whom provided trenchant criticism and steadfast moral support.

Research at the dissertation stage was made possible by Foreign Language Area Studies Fellowships under the auspices of Columbia University's East Asian Institute. At the University of Louisville, the Graduate School and College of Arts and Sciences provided funding for preliminary work on the reorientation of the dissertation. A Junior Faculty Research Grant from the Smith Richardson Foundation made possible the lion's share of research and writing. The Foundation's generous support permitted me an invaluable half-year sojourn as a visiting scholar at Stanford University and made possible an extended research trip to China, Taiwan, and Hong Kong.

I extend special thanks to the late Michel Oksenberg and the scholars and staff at Stanford's Asia/Pacific Research Center (A/PARC); Cheng Hsiao-shih of Academia Sinica in Taipei; Wang Jisi, director of the Institute for American Studies at the Chinese Academy of Social Sciences (CASS) and his staff in Beijing; and Yang Jiemian, director of the Department of American Studies at the Shanghai Institute for International Studies and his staff in Shanghai. Each kindly hosted me at different times during 1998.

I am grateful to the many analysts and scholars in China and Taiwan who candidly shared with me their ideas and insights. In particular, I wish to thank three individuals who read and commented on the entire manuscript: Paul Godwin, Christopher Hughes, and Allen Whiting. The following people provided valuable input through comments on drafts of one or more chapters, reactions to research presentations, or in one-on-one conversations: Donald Boose, Monte Bullard, Cheng Hsiao-shih, Karl Eikenberry, John Garofano, Ellis Joffe, Iain Johnston, John Lewis, Lin Cheng-yi, Lin Chong-Pin, Debra Little, Andrea McElderry, Evan Medeiros, James Mulvenon, Ramon Myers, Susan Puska, Robert Ross, Charles Scobell, Robert Sutter, Larry Wortzel, Andrew Yang, Milton Yeh, Yu Bin, Yuan I, and Charles Ziegler. I received valuable feedback from audiences at the Institute for American Studies at CASS, Modern China Seminar at Columbia University; lunchtime audiences at the Hoover Institution; A/PARC; Columbia's East Asian Institute; and the Center for Nonproliferation Studies in Monterrey.

Of course, none of these individuals or organizations bears any responsibility for any errors or omissions in this work. Moreover, the views expressed in this book are solely those of the author and do not reflect the official policy or position of the Department of the Army, Department of Defense, or the U.S. Government.

Earlier versions of Chapters 2, 4, 7, and 8 appeared in *Issues and Studies, Journal of Contemporary China, Armed Forces and Society,* and *Political Science Quarterly,* respectively.

At the University of Louisville (UofL), Melissa Johnson and Mendy Dorris provided cheerful and capable research assistance. Chen Chih-hung, Lu Feng, and Zhang Amei helped with some of the translations from Chinese sources – the latter two solely out of the goodness of their hearts. Adele Collins, Gary

Cramer, and Phil Laemmle gave generously of their time on word processing–related matters. Sherry Allen and Mary Hawkesworth at the UofL also deserve the author's thanks.

This book was adeptly shepherded through the publication process at Cambridge University Press initially by Mary Child and then by Alia Winters. The author is also grateful to Andy Saff, whose skillful copyediting made all the difference.

Finally, my greatest debt lies with my closest comrade-in-arms, Michele. This project is so much the better for her frequent incisive critiques of draft chapters and her constant encouragement. This book is dedicated to her.

China's Use of Military Force

Beyond the Great Wall and the Long March

1

Introduction

SINCE the mid-1990s, the People's Republic of China (PRC) has been identified as a looming strategic threat.[1] Some have asserted that China is "on the warpath."[2] There have also been concerns about a Chinese military buildup – rising defense budgets, reported actual or attempted purchases of foreign military hardware, as well as indigenous defense research and development efforts. In terms of military capabilities, most experts contend that China poses only a modest challenge to the region and the world – at least in the short term.[3] Others see more serious problems posed by China's military modernization.[4]

Even if one goes by the modest assessments of China's military modernization, this does not mean Beijing can be written off as essentially harmless. Recent events demonstrate that China is more than capable of disrupting regional stability. During the 1995–6 Taiwan Strait Crisis, for example, troop exercises and missile tests by the People's Liberation Army (PLA) forced the rerouting of international air and sea traffic in the region. The crisis sent tremors throughout East Asia, and the United States felt it necessary to dispatch two aircraft carrier battle groups to the area. For some analysts, the strait crisis confirmed that China's military is a "nuisance threat."[5] But any threat from China is likely to be a *big* nuisance; even a weak or modestly armed China can cause major disruptions. And weak states, as Arthur Waldron notes, do start wars.[6]

Considerable attention has been given to China's assertive rhetoric and militant behavior, particularly its saber rattling during 1995–6 in the Taiwan Strait and its military moves in the South China Sea. Beijing has been depicted as increasingly belligerent, often attributed to the undue pressure of hawkish and hardline soldiers on moderate and mild-mannered statesmen.[7] This perception is in direct conflict with the earlier image of China: an ancient culture possessing a weak martial tradition (especially in contrast to Japan); a predisposition to seek nonviolent solutions to problems of statecraft, as exemplified by the thinking of sages like Sun Tzu and Confucius; and a defensive-mindedness, favoring sturdy fortifications over expansionism and invasion.[8]

Which of the two dominant images best represents China's propensity to use force? Is China more belligerent today than it was in earlier years? Are Chinese soldiers more hawkish than Chinese statesmen? And, if so, do they defer to the wishes of political leaders?

This is a study about China's use of military force. More specifically, this study is about the impact of Chinese strategic culture, civil-military culture, and military organizational culture on decisions to employ armed force at home and abroad. I contend that China's strategic culture does not reflect a single defensive, conflict-averse tradition symbolized by the Great Wall, and that post-1949 China's civil-military culture is not as harmonious or as one-dimensional as the Long March depiction suggests. China's military and civilian leaders do not approach decisions to use force at home or abroad from a single perspective. Rather, China's strategic behavior is more accurately conceived of as the outcome of the interplay between two distinct and enduring strands of strategic culture that are filtered through an evolving civil-military culture and tempered by military culture.

Earlier depictions of a nonmilitary, pacifist China, as this study will show, are more myth than reality. China has always been prepared to employ force to further policy goals.[9] It did not suddenly become bellicose in the 1990s. China's strategic disposition has not changed fundamentally; rather, its civil-military culture has shifted. It is this latter transformation that seems responsible for creating an impression among many observers that China has become more belligerent. Moreover, it is the Chinese statesman who often has been willing to use military force, and the Chinese soldier who invariably has been more reluctant.

CULTURAL LAYERS AND LINKAGES

What is China's propensity to use military force in the twenty-first century? Three concepts are particularly useful in addressing this question: strategic culture, civil-military culture, and organizational culture. Strategic culture, or the set of fundamental and enduring assumptions about the role of war in human affairs and the efficacy of applying force held by a country's political and military elites,[10] has been useful in addressing this and other questions.[11] Also central to addressing this question is civil-military relations, or "civil-military culture," defined here as the distribution of values, norms, and beliefs within a country regarding military doctrine and the identity, format, and function of the military in domestic and foreign affairs.[12] Civil-military culture is widely seen as a critical dimension for analyzing post-Deng China.[13]

Though strategic culture and civil-military culture have become central topics in China studies, both are fraught with controversy. Scholars disagree on the fundamental tradition and orientation of Chinese statecraft and on the conceptualization of military politics in the People's Republic. Related to a country's civil-military culture is the military's organizational culture that affects how soldiers act in crises. The military's values, norms, and beliefs "shape [the] collective understandings" of individuals within the institution.[14] The military tends to be a particularly cohesive corporate entity that possesses a distinct organizational culture.

The core bailiwick of the armed forces is usually defined as the "management of violence." Strategic culture entails collectively held assumptions about the nature of war. It follows therefore that strategic and civil-military cultures are closely linked. Though many scholars acknowledge that civil-military culture has an important influence on the impact of strategic culture, on defense policy, and on the employment of military force,[15] the precise nature of the relationships remains unclear.

If cultures are conceived of as complex and multilayered phenomena that can exert powerful influences on the way individuals behave and how human interactions are structured, it is very likely that in any given situation an individual or group of individuals will be influenced by more than one culture. If, for example, a military commander is ordered to employ his troops in the streets to confront his fellow citizens, he is likely to be affected by multiple layers of culture. Not only would the commander's response be conditioned by his country's political culture but also by its strategic culture, civil-military culture, and military organizational culture. These different cultures might be conceptualized as component parts of a multilayer cake, each different layer prepared as part of the same recipe. While each layer has its own distinct texture and flavor, the taste of the cake comes from a combination of all the layers. Just as it would be inaccurate to judge the taste of the cake from sampling only one layer, so it would be imprecise to analyze strategic culture and declare it the crucial element in determining when and how a country uses force. Using the layer conception, on the foundation layer one would find "political culture," on the second layer "strategic culture," on the third layer "civil-military culture," and on the fourth or top layer "organizational culture."[16]

Political Culture

Political culture comprises the patterns of behavior, values, norms, and beliefs concerning politics and society held by the people of a country.[17] Recently scholars have conceived of political culture in broader, more holistic terms and as a more interactive dynamic than earlier conceptions. This newer interpretation views political culture as very fluid, and the individual as much more than a passive subject of political socialization. Political culture now tends to be seen as an arena for and repertoire of discourse and activity for both state and societal actors. Today, manifestations of political culture include symbols, rituals, and language.[18] In each country, the political culture is the bedrock upon which the layers of strategic culture, civil-military culture, and military culture within society are embedded. This book limits its examination of Chinese political culture to understandings of the military profession.

Strategic Culture

Strategic culture is an important concept in understanding the security policies of different states. The concept was employed during the Cold War to explain national differences in the strategic outlook and behavior of the two superpowers.[19] In the 1990s, international relations theorists incorporated a cultural approach in their analyses.[20] Strategic culture has only recently been explicitly incorporated into scholarship on Chinese foreign and military policy.[21] In fact, cultural interpretations have been at the core of the majority of studies of China's foreign relations, although a few scholars use the term *strategic culture*.[22]

The Great Wall is not merely a symbol of the many glorious accomplishments of China's ancient civilization, it also epitomizes, for many scholars, Chinese preference for defense over offense, positional warfare over mobile warfare, and maintenance over expansion. The wall is held up as the prime example of a Chinese strategic tradition that is very different from that of Western countries. Waldron's research suggests that what we now call the Great Wall appears to date back not more than two thousand years but rather some six hundred years to the Ming Dynasty (1368–1644). Although Waldron's path-breaking study has gone a long way toward debunking the myth of China's cultural predilection for wall building, this perception persists.[23]

Moreover, belying China's pacifist defensive-minded reputation, research by Alastair Iain Johnston contends that China possesses a stark realist strategic tradition that views war as a central feature of interstate relations.[24] Others contend that under communism China developed into a revolutionary state more prone than other countries to resort to war to resolve conflicts.[25] These recent studies radically differ from many earlier case studies of China's use of force, which tend to highlight the moderate, defensive nature of a PRC reluctant to use military force and viewing war only as a last resort.[26] Such disparate conclusions beg the question of which interpretation best fits reality.

This study contends that two strands of strategic culture, both shaped by an ancient and enduring civilization, exist: a distinctly Chinese pacifist and defensive-minded strand, and a Realpolitik strand favoring military solutions and offensive action.[27] Both interact, and their combined impact is mitigated by a civil-military culture shared by China's soldiers and statesmen.

Civil-Military Culture

Civil-military culture transcends the boundary between comparative politics and international relations. Usually the word *relations* is used, but in this book, the term *culture* is substituted because this term suggests the inclusion of not only linkages between civil and military spheres, but also patterns of behavior, shared values, norms, and beliefs. What is civil and what is military is not so much separate and segregated but rather intertwined and enmeshed. And civil-military culture is embedded in a country's broader political culture.[28] Moreover, while the old term implied that there might be one "correct" configuration of civil-military relations, the new term suggests there may be considerable crossnational variation between civil-military cultures.

As Thomas Berger shows, "political-military cultures" are very important in determining the defense policies of states.[29] And Elizabeth Kier, despite her primary focus on organizational culture, recognizes the importance of broader cultures within society in influencing outcomes in the domestic political arena. Indeed, Kier contends, " . . . the interaction between the constraints [set by culture(s)] in the domestic political arena, and the military's organizational culture shapes the choice between offensive and defensive military doctrines."[30] In effect, Kier draws attention to civil-military culture.

Civil-military culture has been employed, particularly since World War II, initially to explain political outcomes notably in the countries of Asia, Africa, and Latin America. Attention increasingly focused on interpreting the political dynamics of communist states, and a thriving subfield emerged in comparative communism.[31] While in the post–Cold War era the subject of military politics may seem less central to an understanding of the domestic and foreign affairs of many countries, it remains critical for contemporary China.[32] Some scholars see a unique Chinese construct of civil-military culture,[33] others see a discernible variant of a communist system,[34] and still others see a Chinese military arrangement that has similar commonalities with other large countries with sizeable armed forces.[35]

The Long March symbolizes to many scholars a distinct civil-military elite configuration that either (1) firmly established the mechanism of party control over the army, or (2) forged a close-knit coalition of like-minded civil and military leaders.[36] Under the former conception, China's PLA is viewed as under the total control of the Chinese Communist Party (CCP), consistent with Mao's oft-quoted dictum, "the Party commands the gun but the gun must never command the Party." Under the latter conception, more popular with scholars of Chinese military politics, military and political leaders in the People's Republic form a single monolithic elite forged in a protracted armed struggle for power – and hold nearly identical views on most matters. Some scholars contend that the PLA does not even constitute a separate coherent interest group,[37] and Chinese soldiers do not have a perspective of organizational culture distinct from that of Chinese statesmen. When differences of opinion are evident, they are perceived as occurring along factional lines that transcend the civil-military dichotomy.[38]

The Long March does highlight the intertwining of civil and military in communist China – the overlapping of party and army leaders. Long Marchers, such as Mao Zedong and Deng Xiaoping, were often seen as both civil and military figures. Indeed, it can be difficult to label a particular individual as either soldier or civilian. Under Mao and Deng (1949–97), China's strategic doctrine and decision-making are seen as the work of one man – especially under Mao – and one elite group largely undifferentiated by bureaucratic interests or professional perspectives.

In fact, this depiction of a completely homogeneous Chinese leadership and the characterization of the party firmly controlling the gun are oversimplified and ignore the broader evolution of Chinese civil-military culture. Thus, as the Long March has been glorified and has passed into the realm of myth, so the depiction of a cohesive civil-military leadership has become increasingly irrelevant to contemporary Chinese foreign and domestic politics.

As this book will show, analyses of the attitudes of civil and military elites in the Mao, Deng, and Jiang Zemin eras reveal notable differentiation along civil-military lines and considerable numbers of leaders with career paths exclusively within military affairs after 1949. These distinctions have only become more pronounced over time. The two prime examples that blur the distinction, Mao and Deng, are both deceased now, and China's most prominent leaders in the wake of the Sixteenth Party Congress in November 2002, President Jiang Zemin and General Secretary Hu Jintao have no claim at all on military experience or identity – nor did Jiang or Hu participate in the Long March.

Organizational Culture

Military doctrines, policies, decisions, and employments are affected by cultures other than strategic and civil-military. Kier demonstrates that the organizational cultures of armed forces exert a significant impact on military doctrine.[39] Furthermore, if political culture entails the study of the "mindsets" of political actors,[40] one might expect distinctive types of belief systems based on differences in an actor's past experience, training, and organizational environment. Thus, military leaders likely hold perspectives distinct from those of political leaders. In other words, soldiers possess their own particular organizational culture or cultures.[41] There is significant variation among the military establishments of different countries as well as notable commonalities.[42]

The military is now an essential ingredient in understanding the dynamics of China's internal politics and in assessing Beijing's foreign relations after Deng. The PLA is now widely assumed to have a major impact on political outcomes, but analysts are often at a loss to demonstrate this in specific cases, particularly in foreign policy.[43] Nonetheless, in the 1990s, both individual Chinese soldiers and the military as an institution were identified as aggressively advocating harsh and bellicose policies.[44]

Some scholars argue that militaries tend to advocate offensive doctrines because doing so is in their corporate interests; a military will receive more government funding and gain greater prestige. It is the civilian political leadership that provides crucial restraints on these bellicose impulses.[45] Other studies challenge these findings and suggest that while soldiers in the United States and other countries do hold belief systems and attitudes that are distinct from those of nonmilitary officials, the former are actually far more conservative and cautious than the latter.[46] Further research indicates that soldiers do tend to respond more cautiously than their civilian counterparts to decisions to commit troops to combat.[47]

There is widespread agreement that the PLA is becoming a more significant and influential institution in China's security policy.[48] Of course, the PLA has always had substantial political clout in the PRC by virtue of its intimate relationship with the CCP (see Chapter 3). And the death, in February 1997, of Deng, Beijing's paramount leader for almost two decades, has essentially assured the military of continued influence, since his successor, Jiang, has none of the considerable military credentials of Deng and needs to cultivate a closer relationship with the PLA.

Surprisingly, given the widespread recognition of the PLA as a central institution in the PRC, studies of both China's security policy and Beijing's use of force have tended to ignore or downplay these areas as civil-military issues.[49]

In fact, broader studies of Chinese foreign policy also give little attention to the military.[50] There is a dearth of studies on the PLA's involvement in foreign policy crises where the use of force is weighed.[51] This inattention to the PLA is also evident when one examines domestic politics. There are a few important exceptions, most obviously the PLA's crushing of the popular protests in Beijing in 1989.[52] On the broader subject of the PLA's intervention in domestic politics, there is also limited coverage.[53] Most of this scholarship is focused on the Cultural Revolution, and even these studies do not address the actual use of the PLA.[54]

Research Strategies

The scholarship on China's propensity to use force seems to be shaped to a considerable extent by one's research strategy and the data one taps. To date, scholars have concentrated on one of three approaches:[55]

(1) Analyzing the influence of enduring cultural or psychocultural traditions
(2) Studying the content of Chinese military doctrines and statements
(3) Examining the actual record of military employments

The first approach studies the question from a cultural or psychocultural perspective, invariably contending that China's strategic outlook is colored by a unique cultural milieu. Typically these studies conclude that China traditionally has been pacifist and averse to conflict, resorting to war only after all else fails.[56] This research, however, tends to ignore how precisely culture impacts strategic choice and action.

The second approach examines doctrines and/or the writings and pronouncements of senior Chinese civil and military leaders.[57] These scholars reach mixed conclusions about whether China is bellicose or pacifist. Their enterprise is complicated; for those who study doctrine, it is sometimes a subjective judgment as to whether a doctrine is best labeled offensive or defensive. Moreover, the pitfall in focusing on formal doctrines is that these may be irrelevant discourses that impose apparent coherence and consistency on actions that are in reality neither coherent or consistent. The danger in relying heavily on official statements is that these may express empty, high-minded rhetoric to mask unprincipled motives and justify erratic behaviors.

The third approach examines actual cases of the employment of force. The overwhelming majority of studies are qualitative – examining the particular circumstances of one or more cases and looking for patterns. Few have used quantitative methods – but two such studies conclude that China is far more willing than many other countries to use force to resolve a foreign policy crisis.[58]

Early case studies, based on limited evidence, stress cautiousness, the aim to deter a prospective foe and avoid combat.[59] More recent scholarship, using an array of newly available Chinese sources, stresses Beijing's predisposition or willingness to use force.[60]

This book presents the first study to combine all three approaches. The goal is to gain a more comprehensive understanding of China's propensity to use force through an examination of the linkages between culture, doctrinal writings and statements, and actual military employments. First, Chinese strategic culture and civil-military culture are examined. Then, in the core of this study, a comparative analysis of five cases of the use of force by China at home and abroad is presented. Not only is the external use of military force examined, but also China's deployment of military force internally is analyzed – something other studies ignore. To consider strategic culture as a variable affecting only inter-state relations is to erect a rather arbitrary divide. The increasing incidence of intrastate warfare in the post–Cold War world dramatically underscores the need for more attention to the domestic use of force by governments (or "intrastate security").[61]

OUTLINE OF CHAPTERS

Chapter 2 argues that neither the Confucian-Mencian nor the parabellum strands of Chinese strategic culture, identified by Alastair Iain Johnston, alone is sufficient to encompass the richness and variety of China's strategic tradition. These two strands of strategic culture interact to produce what I dub a "Chinese Cult of Defense." The interplay between the two strands of strategic culture produces the paradoxical outcome of idealist, principled, high-minded logic (the Confucian school) combined with hard Realpolitik security policies and regular decisions to call out the troops (the Realpolitik school).

Chapter 3 briefly examines the status of the military in Chinese political culture and then focuses on civil-military culture as an intermediate layer of culture sandwiched between strategic and organizational cultures. An analysis of doctrine, civil-military format, military identity, and organizational function reveals dramatic changes in each dimension from the Mao era to the Jiang era.

If a Chinese military culture is present, it should be most clearly observable in times of crises. This should be particularly so in instances when a state uses force as an instrument of policy, because the concept of coercive diplomacy is at the heart of the different core beliefs of soldiers and statesmen.[62] Thus I examine as cases studies the largest troop employments in three different eras. Each instance involved the same "policy output": the use of force.[63] The use of force is defined as the employment of overt military power, including explicit, credible threats of military action backed by troop movements, exercises, missile or artillery tests, or the construction or expansion of military installations in a border area. Thus, Chinese saber rattling in the Taiwan Strait in 1995–6 and construction in 1995 of a naval station on Mischief Reef in the South China Sea – territory also claimed by the Philippines – are both examples of the use of force.[64] This is the realm of coercive diplomacy; neither actual combat nor a formal declaration of war is necessary.[65]

Five cases are selected from the fifty-year course of PRC history spanning the rule of three different leaders. Two cases are from the era of Mao (1949 to the mid-1970s), two cases are from the era of Deng (1978 to the mid-1990s), and one case from the Jiang era (since the mid-1990s). In each of the first two periods, the most significant foreign instance and domestic instance of the use of force are analyzed. The final case is the 1995–6 Taiwan Strait Crisis that occurred when Deng was still alive. Deng, however, was seriously ill and not involved in the policy-making or decision-making at all. In effect, this was the first significant use of force in the post-Deng era.

Chapter 4 examines China's decision to intervene in Korea. The challenge is to reconcile the image of an aggressive and adventurist Beijing depicted in recent accounts of the Korean War with earlier studies that stress the caution and restraint shown by Beijing in late 1950.

The PLA's role in the Cultural Revolution is examined in Chapter 5. The dual role format of China's civil-military elite meant that any intense intra-party conflict would inevitably infect the military. Yet, the slow and tortuous process by which the PLA was gradually brought in to restore order during the tumultuous Cultural Revolution is poorly understood. The PLA's strong desire to remain aloof from the turmoil eroded as the military gradually came to view the escalating societal violence as propelling China into anarchy. When Mao ultimately ordered the PLA to restore order, the military was largely united on the necessity of intervention.

Chapter 6 examines China's month-long war with Vietnam in early 1979. Many analysts regard Beijing's use of the term "self-defense counterattack" as merely a rhetorical fig leaf to cover a case of blatant aggression. Yet many Chinese leaders sincerely believed the action was defensive – that they were only driven to it by repeated Vietnamese border incursions and other hostile acts by Hanoi against Beijing.

Chapter 7 analyzes the tragic and violent end to the student-led prodemoc-racy demonstrations in Beijing in June 1989. Initially CCP and PLA leaders were divided on how to deal with the student protests. Then they adopted an approach of gradual escalating measures to deal with the protests to compel the demonstrators to withdraw. Ultimately, when the protests continued and the specter of chaos loomed, most military leaders concluded that decisive action had to be taken.

Chapter 8 analyzes the most recent crisis in the Taiwan Strait. The confrontation remains little understood, and the potential for misunderstanding and misperception between China and the United States is alarming. The hawkishness displayed by military figures during the crisis reflects fundamental differences between military and civilian approaches to the practice of coercive diplomacy. It also reflects intense PLA feelings on the subject of Taiwan, and the clear civil-military consensus that the missile tests and military exercises were a strictly controlled "show of force."

This study concludes with an assessment of the influence of cultures and a reexamination of China's use of force. Different layers of culture explain different things. Strategic culture accounts for the continuity – a fundamental propensity to use force; civil-military culture accounts for how and where force is used; and organizational culture accounts for the existence of a military perspective distinct from a civilian one.

Part I

LAYERS OF CULTURE

2

The Chinese Cult of Defense

IS China a peaceful, defensive-minded power or a bellicose, expansionist state? Has China become more belligerent in recent decades? How can contemporary depictions of a bellicose China be reconciled with earlier descriptions of a dominant pacifist tradition?

I contend that existing depictions of China's strategic culture are flawed. China's strategic disposition cannot accurately be characterized as either pacifist or bellicose. China, I argue, has a dualistic strategic culture. The two main strands are a Confucian one, which is conflict-averse and defensive-minded, and a Realpolitik one that favors military solutions and is offense-oriented. Both of these two strands are active and both influence and combine in dialectic fashion to produce what I label a "Chinese Cult of Defense."[1] Just as the "Cult of Offense" identified by Stephen Van Evera and Jack Snyder had a critical effect in precipitating World War I,[2] so the Cult of Defense increases the likelihood that China will be involved in a future war. This cult predisposes Chinese leaders paradoxically to engage in offensive military operations as a primary alternative in pursuit of national goals, while rationalizing these actions as being purely defensive and a last resort. This dualistic strategic culture has been a constant, and China has not become more bellicose or dangerous in recent years except to the extent that its military capabilities have improved and military doctrine has changed (see Chapter 3).[3]

This chapter seeks to reconcile contrasting interpretations of Chinese strategic culture.[4] First, four factors that have affected a sea change in scholarly interpretations of China's strategic culture are outlined. Next, two failings in strategic culture approaches are detailed. Lastly, a Chinese Cult of Defense is articulated.

15

A GREAT WALL IN RUINS?

A nation's strategic culture is not static or immutable. While enduring, strategic culture can evolve over time and/or undergo dramatic transformation as a result of major disruptions, such as defeat in war, invasion or occupation, and the emergence of a radically new political system, leader, or philosophical outlook. Such was the case with Japan and Germany after defeat in World War II and also with the Soviet Union in the mid-1980s after accession to power of Mikhail S. Gorbachev and the adoption of his "New Thinking."[5]

In the case of China, however, there does not appear to have been any radical change in strategic culture certainly since 1949, and probably not for hundreds – perhaps thousands – of years.[6] Indeed, if there was a reorientation of Chinese culture vis-à-vis attitudes toward violence, it occurred during the Warring States period (403–221 B.C.). Mark Edward Lewis has explained the profound changes in Chinese philosophy, state, society, and culture that occurred during this era.[7]

In spite of the leadership change from Mao Zedong to Deng Xiaoping and the resultant shift in national priorities from political to economic, one cannot discern any dramatic change in the manner or frequency with which military force is used.[8] Moreover, the People's Republic of China (PRC) does not seem to have become significantly more bellicose since the incapacitation of Deng in the mid-1990s and his subsequent death in early 1997.[9] The change seems to be more one of perception rather than reality.

Why then was the change in the thrust of scholarship in the 1990s significantly different from that of the 1960s, 1970s, and 1980s? There seem to be four main reasons. First, the change was the outcome of the increasing availability of extensive primary materials and greater opportunity for interviews. While the unit of analysis had been the unitary state actor, the focus now has shifted to individual decisionmakers. The era with the richest array of source materials is the 1950s, and the Korean War in particular. These data have enabled scholars to analyze the attitudes and actions of senior Chinese leaders. The overwhelming focus has been on the key policymaker of the time, Mao. Clearly Mao was willing to project force, and in 1950 he seems to have been predisposed to intervene in Korea early in the crisis.[10]

Until recently, most of the scholarship on China's post-1949 use of force has tended to be remarkably consistent with John K. Fairbank's interpretation of China's strategic disposition (discussed later in this section): Beijing preferred to avoid war and was cautious and deliberate in its deterrence signaling. And when conflict did occur, China's leaders made their utmost efforts to limit its scope and duration.[11] The first wave of studies of the PRC's use of force, from the 1960s until the mid-1980s, was based on extensive use of secondary works and judicious use of limited primary sources. In the late 1980s, a second wave of scholarship on China's use of force appeared. This wave, which focused on China's intervention in Korea, remained largely consistent with the first wave's depiction of a China that was extremely reluctant to intervene in Korea and did so only as a last resort with limited aims.[12]

However, the third and most recent wave of scholarship has been at odds with earlier ones. While also focused on China's intervention in Korea, this wave instead highlights China's combativeness, inclination to intervene, and the ambitious initial goal of expelling United Nations forces from the peninsula completely.[13] While the second wave of studies was primarily based on the memoirs of key military leaders and interviews, third-wave studies were grounded in painstaking analyses of a wide variety of newly available Chinese internal documents from the 1950s and recently published histories and memoirs. Other studies of multiple instances of the use of force in the 1950s, published in the 1990s, reinforce this image of an assertive, aggressive China.[14]

The second reason for the reorientation in the 1990s in studies of the early PRC is the revisionist interpretations of the nature of communism and Chinese civilization. The collapse of the communist regimes of Eastern Europe and the Soviet Union in 1989 and 1991, respectively, unleashed a slew of studies exposing the flaws of communism. The documented murderous excesses of the communist regimes of Joseph Stalin, Mao, and Pol Pot and the mass suffering they caused have swept away any remaining doubts as to the evil nature of communist dictatorships.[15] Moreover, research suggests that revolutionary regimes tend to be by nature violent, aggressive, and expansionist.[16]

The nature of ancient Chinese civilization/culture is also being reexamined. Scholars who study China tend to admire greatly its ancient culture and civilization. There is a tendency to focus on the admirable attributes of Chinese high culture and accept the generally positive accounts in official dynastic histories. Thus depictions of ancient China often romanticize the human achievements of an ancient civilization – great inventions and discoveries – while ignoring brutal and harsh aspects.

One of the most appealing aspects of ancient China is its rich philosophic tradition, particularly those elements that stress peace, harmony, and disapproval of war. The inherent positive bias of scholarship tended to nurture a monistic pacifist depiction of China's strategic tradition. Fairbank's work was particularly influential here. While his analysis of the Chinese approach to war was considerably more sophisticated and nuanced than is often depicted, he did stress the impact of Chinese culture and highlighted the influence of Confucianism. Simply stated, a fundamental assumption running through his writings is that the Chinese used violence only as a "last resort."[17]

Studies of war and violence as phenomena in traditional Chinese society and statecraft – as distinct from accounts of a particular war or rebellion – were few and far between. By the 1990s, this had changed.[18] At the same time, path-breaking scholarship on military policy in dynastic China challenged the prevailing view of a defensive-minded, conflict-averse Middle Kingdom.[19]

Third, the changes in studies of contemporary China were also the result of a growing perception that China had become a strategic threat – not merely as an economic power but also as a rising military power.[20] The perception was particularly prevalent in the late 1990s with the release of the Cox Report, with its alarming portrayal of Chinese espionage, illegal Chinese campaign contributions, and commercial sales of U.S. dual-use technology to assist a Chinese military buildup. The climate of foreboding was accentuated by the allegation that a Chinese-American physicist at a U.S. government research laboratory provided nuclear secrets to China, claims that a PLA-backed company was taking control of the Panama Canal, and the publication of a book detailing provocative Chinese views of asymmetric warfare.[21] Beijing's initial hardline stance in the aftermath of the collision between a Chinese jet fighter and a U.S. Navy EP-3 Navy surveillance aircraft in April 2001 merely served to reinforce, in the minds of many Americans, the image of a hostile China.

Fourth, interpretations of contemporary China have been influenced by significant political transformations within China. While these changes have given the appearance of a more belligerent China, they have not resulted in a significant change in strategic disposition. Historically the official Chinese version of the country's security policy has been based on ideologically correct interpretations of the world situation and has been carefully tailored to fit its intended audience.[22] Until quite recently, there have been two major audiences: the Chinese elite and foreign elites. In dynastic China, on the surface the official imperial line was that the world ought to be peaceful, orderly, and presided over by the Middle Kingdom. Thus, in this era the pervasive propaganda of sages, successive Chinese governments, and scholars – targeted at the twin audiences of China's elite and those of its tributary states – wanted to make China appear righteous, benevolent, and peace-loving.

For twentieth century China, meanwhile, the formal worldview has been of a largely dangerous – if not hostile – world in which China, as a poor and weak country, must struggle to make itself secure by becoming rich and powerful as rapidly as possible. On the threshold of the twenty-first century, there were three audiences: Added to China's elite and the leaders of foreign states were the ordinary Chinese people – in Western terminology, "public opinion" – who are much more aware, informed, and opinionated about foreign and security policies.[23]

In the second half of the twentieth century, official propaganda aimed to project the image of a tough, hardline, and vigilant China. Somewhat paradoxically, in the 1990s, just as the country had grown stronger economically and militarily, significant portions of Beijing's rhetoric became harsher and its perception of the global situation became more alarmist. Many other policy pronouncements are, by contrast, more pacifist, stressing China's peaceful disposition and the positive trends for peace around the globe. The propaganda, aimed at several different audiences, has become more difficult to decipher. Which message is meant for which audience? The more militant rhetoric meant for internal elite and mass consumption often gets mixed up in the milder pronouncements meant for foreign consumption. The situation became even more complicated in the 1990s with the emergence of ultranationalism combined with a lively quasi-official publishing scene. Books written by conservative intellectuals aimed at a mass Chinese audience with the goal of becoming best sellers are not uncommon. Significantly, these volumes have been widely cited by China threat proponents.[24] The result is a seemingly confused, jumbled, and inconsistent stance, but one that actually reflects reality. Therefore, someone perusing party documents, statements by leaders, and official histories is likely to pick up one (or more) of several "party lines" depending on which sources are tapped. And a researcher's own biases are likely to play a key role in her interpretation.

Thus better data, new interpretations of scholarship, changing geopolitical perceptions of the Middle Kingdom, and China's more complex and confusing political environment all combined during the 1990s to challenge the prevailing scholarly wisdom on the nature of China's strategic culture.

RETHINKING CHINESE STRATEGIC CULTURE

Both of the two main interpretations of China's strategic tradition tend to assume its strategic culture is monistic and make no attempt to link it to domestic policy. But it would be a mistake to assume that a country's strategic culture can be subsumed within a single tradition or to focus exclusively on interstate violence. Indeed, there are likely to be multiple strands of strategic culture. Furthermore, by ignoring intrastate and societal violence, one risks overlooking important values and beliefs about the use of force and violence.

Presumption of Monism

Most of the strategic culture scholarship, as Alastair Iain Johnston observes, "allows no room for the possibility of ... multiple strategic cultures."[25] The work of Fairbank and others stresses the pervasive influence of Confucianism and downplays China's substantial body of strategic writing. Various scholars highlight Confucianism's impact on Chinese strategic thinkers; the tendency is to focus on Sun Tzu's *Art of War* and to emphasize the "winning without fighting" theme in this tome – that is, to defeat your opponent through ruse and stratagem rather than brute force.[26]

In contrast, the scholarship of Arthur Waldron and Johnston highlights the important discrepancy between articulated Confucian values and the substance of military texts, and between assumed cultural proclivities and actual state defense policies. Yet Johnston seeks to explain away the presence of a "Confucian-Mencian" strand in strategic writings. Contrary or conflicting evidence is glossed over or summarily dismissed. While Johnston detects the presence of two strands of strategic culture, he contends that the "Confucian-Mencian" paradigm is purely for "idealized discourse," and only the parabellum (Realpolitik) paradigm exerts real impact on policy and how force is used.[27]

Johnston, as Waldron notes, is far too dismissive of Confucianism.[28] How can one brush aside as largely irrelevant a philosophical tradition that for thousands of years has constituted the bedrock legitimizing ideology of the Chinese polity? I argue, on the contrary, that both strands of strategic culture are operative, and that the "Confucian-Mencian" one reflects deeply held beliefs.

Supporters of a distinct Chinese Confucian tradition abhorring violence tend to treat this culture as a monistic one. But Confucianism itself encompasses a broad spectrum of approaches.[29] While Confucianism is often depicted as a philosophy that does not condone violence and has "harmony" as one of its core values, different strands of Confucianism were not totally opposed to violence. In fact, the writings of Confucius, Mencius, and their disciples explicitly recognize that violence was necessary. The use of force was sanctioned, particularly in certain circumstances including defense of the honor of one's family and ancestors.[30] Confucius clearly recognized that armed force was a necessary instrument of state power and, according to one scholar, "implicitly admits that war is inevitable."[31] Confucius said, "The requisites of government are that there be sufficiency of food, sufficiency of military equipment, and confidence of the people in their ruler."[32]

In fact, certain types of violence were accepted. Violence by the state and by authority figures in society was culturally sanctioned. However, violence against authority figures from below was condemned.[33] It was the intent or motive of the violence that was important. If a battle or war was waged in order to educate, punish, or "restore the correct order of things," then the war was "righteous" *(yi)*.[34]

20

Confucius did not criticize war per se but rather the improper use of war. He said:

> When good government prevails in the empire, ceremonies, music, and punitive military expeditions proceed from the son of Heaven. When bad government prevails in the empire, ceremonies, music, and punitive expeditions proceed from the princes.

Confucius explained that improperly motivated statecraft, violent or otherwise, led to ruin for the dynasty in a matter of generations.[35] Furthermore, Confucius said, "Let a good man teach his people seven years, and they may then be employed in war." What the sage condemned was a leader sending his "uninstructed people *(bujiao min)* into battle."[36] If the conflict was simply gratuitous or merely for material gain, then it was wrong. Confucius viewed force used to unite the empire as proper.[37] Some Confucianists approved of violence for vengeance – indeed, it was considered "a highly moral act."[38]

Simply because Confucius did not discuss military matters in great detail does not mean that he was a pacifist. Indeed it is only natural that he made "scanty mention of war" since his calling, as a teacher of a moral philosophy, was to inculcate religiouslike principles that governed idealized patterns of harmonious behavior.[39] In fact, while aspiring to an ideal world, Confucius supported the use of war and violence under certain real-world conditions. Many scholars of China's strategic tradition are guilty of seeing Confucianism as virtually completely pacifistic.[40] In short, we are presented with something of a false Confucian–Realpolitik dichotomy.

The existence of other traditional and contemporary schools of thought – particularly those that strongly support the use of domestic (and foreign) state-sanctioned violence – is often overlooked. In addition to Confucianism, there are numerous philosophical traditions in China: Legalism, Daoism, Mohism, Buddhism, and Islam, to name the major ones. Each of these, or at least offshoots or sects of them, offered rationales/justifications for violence and rebellion under certain conditions.[41]

The various strands of thinking on war and violence are evident from the central myths about the origins of Chinese civilization that emerged during the Warring States period. The myth of China's founding involves the powerful figure of the Yellow Emperor *(Huang Di)* – revered as the progenitor of the Chinese race. The legend of the emperor's gargantuan struggle to vanquish his two main foes is crucial to delineating the role of sanctioned violence in subsequent Chinese culture. The Yellow Emperor's first adversary was the Divine Husbandman *(Shen Nong)*, an avowed pacifist farmer, while his second adversary was the Fiery Emperor *(Chi Yan)*, who was the bellicose inventor of weapons of war.

The symbolism of the three main protagonists in the epic is strong. The Divine Husbandman represents the narrow utopian dream of a world where evil, violence, and even scholarly pursuits have no place. The Fiery Emperor by contrast represents the harsh reality of man's brutish animal nature, which, if unchecked, leads to constant violence and mayhem. The Yellow Emperor represents the middle way between the unrealistic and very dangerous extreme of complete pacifism and the all-too-real and terrifying extreme of unrestrained violence. Thus, violence that is focused, disciplined, and limited can be a force for good: "The historical Chinese culture and polity began with the 'invention' or cultural innovation made by the Yellow Emperor, and that innovation was *the use of correct violence to establish political authority.*"[42]

The Yellow and Fiery Emperors also provided the justification for a government to rule by laws. The laws were administered by Heaven's earthly representative – the Emperor. And law, as Lewis notes, was synonymous with punishment. Punishments were invariably harsh, originally entailing either physical disfigurement or death. Enforcement of the law was "the precondition of good government and social order."[43]

In Chinese criminal justice policy, the two main philosophical influences have been Confucianism and Legalism. The former stresses education, reform, and benevolence, while the latter emphasizes punishment, retribution, and harshness – including vigorous use of the death penalty. Both have impacted on China's criminal justice system, and this dual influence can also be seen in post-1949 China.[44] If China's criminal justice policy has historically been shaped by the interplay between two divergent philosophies, then surely this is also possible in the case of defense policy. Indeed, Johnston has been criticized for not recognizing the similarities between Legalism and the Realpolitik or parabellum strand of strategic culture.[45]

The more recent ideology of Marxism-Leninism in its Chinese variant has encouraged the use of repression and violence against perceived enemies of the state. New research highlights the importance of making linkages between domestic and foreign policies in communist party-states. Stephen Morris draws attention to what he calls a "revolutionary political culture" in these regimes that tends to nurture excessive paranoia and the perception of antiregime conspiracies at home and abroad. With class enemies everywhere who are constantly scheming to overthrow or undermine the regime, a constant state of war exists. And these enemies must be destroyed, or they will destroy the regime.[46]

Traditional Chinese philosophies tend to receive little if any attention. Johnston, for example, is dismissive of other traditions, although he does acknowledge in passing the influence of Legalism and Daoism on the *Seven Military Classics*.[47] Indeed, contrary to Johnston's overall conclusion, his detailed analyses of these seven tomes reveal evidence of more than one strand of strategic culture. Inconvenient themes keep appearing in the texts Johnston examines that need to be explained away, and specific textual interpretations and coding of some key terms are problematic. The most important and most obvious inconvenient fact is the continual appearance of a Confucian paradigm in addition to the Realpolitik one.[48]

Proponents of the Realpolitik and Confucian approaches both tend to ignore other philosophical and religious schools of the "great" tradition as well as the "little" tradition. In China, as in other civilizations, there is a "great tradition" at the elite level and a "little tradition" of folk religions, ancestor cults, superstitions, and local deities at the grassroots level. Parts of the little tradition could either be consistent with orthodox state Confucianism *or* in direct conflict with it, depending on the circumstances. The realm of popular culture, for example, although less formally or explicitly articulated, certainly exerts an important influence on elites as well as the masses. And the little tradition was particularly influential among soldiers. The depictions of war and violence were passed along through the media of popular culture, especially traditional myths, folk tales, and opera.[49]

A rich and colorful mythology, including the myth of China's founding by the victorious Yellow Emperor, glorified war, violence, and the exploits of brave and brilliant generals. Perhaps most importantly, these myths sanctioned violence.[50] All Chinese, particularly soldiers, were aware of this legacy, and it exerted a powerful influence on them.[51]

In short, one cannot assume outright that only one cultural tradition is influential.

Exclusion of Intrastate Violence

Another neglected dimension in the study of strategic culture is the frequency of intrastate violence. Adherents of strategic culture, who have tended to be international relations scholars, focus on the use of force between states, and usually exclude any consideration of the use of force within states.[52] One would expect significant correlation between the traditions that guide the way a state employs military force against other states and the way a state employs violence against individuals and groups within society. Therefore, one might find that China's strategic culture was consistent with the position of conflict and violence within Chinese society – that is, strategic culture should overlap with Chinese political culture generally. In other words, whatever the place and frequency of violence in Chinese foreign affairs, it should be consistent with the prevalence of the state's use of internal force and coercion. How does Chinese society view violence? How common are violence and conflict in Chinese culture?

State-on-society violence can be divided into that inflicted against individuals and small groups and that committed against larger and more disruptive groups. The former tends to be handled within the scope of a criminal justice system, while the latter, which usually constitutes far more serious threats, is handled by a constabulary or military. Criminal justice policy in China has been influenced by two major traditions: Confucianism and Legalism. The first of these tends to stress education and reform in dealing with criminals, while the second emphasizes punishment, often advocating harsh penalties. Legalism and Realpolitik seem to be intertwined[53]; Lewis has traced the common origins of warfare and punishment in Chinese culture and mythology.[54] This is not surprising since they are the dual faces of state-sanctioned violence – one aimed at protecting the state from external challenges, and the other from societal challenges.

Collective violence and internal warfare have been features of Chinese society for thousands of years. Studies of domestic armed conflict in China tend to focus on nonstate forces – the rebels, revolutionaries, and mutineers – rather than the state's response to them.[55] Strategic culture scholars, meanwhile, focus on China's foreign wars.[56]

Do the Chinese consider collective violence in society and domestic wars to be completely different from wars conducted against foreign states and violence inflicted upon foreigners? Many scholars argue that there is a blurred distinction between internal and external national security in Chinese thinking.[57] Therefore, Chinese leaders may not differentiate to any great extent between civil wars and foreign wars. And many scholars observe that historically, most Chinese conflicts have been civil wars.[58] Certainly a considerable amount of fighting in twentieth century China has been between Chinese combatants.[59]

Civil wars (in Chinese, *neizhan*, literally *internal war*) in any country tend to be particularly vicious and hard-fought. They are often very bloody and costly in terms of casualties, largely because they are more likely to be viewed in zero-sum terms – a struggle to the death. Wars between states, by contrast, can be more limited and tend to be resolved short of total annihilation.

A considerable amount of violence is evident in Chinese society. While Chinese culture is probably no more or no less violent than many other cultures, it begs the question of why such a variety and frequency of physical conflict occur in a society that officially abhors conflictual behavior and places high value on harmony and order.[60] What is the connection between conflict and violence among individuals and groups within Chinese society and war waged by China against another country?

The interstate armed conflicts of the Warring States period, according to Lewis, grew out of violent clan feuds of the Spring and Autumn period. The militant well-organized lineages that battled for material gain, scarce resources, and the honor of their ancestors against perceived slights and insults of another lineage evolved into disciplined mass armies controlled by Chinese states.[61] It is significant that the modern Chinese word for state or country is comprised not only of the character for *kingdom (guo)* but also of the character for *family (jia)*.[62] In ancient China, an emperor was viewed as a father, and his subjects as part of his extended family.

The sort of clan violence identified by Lewis in the early imperial era seems to be an enduring – if not endemic – feature of certain regions in China, which is traceable across historical periods, in imperial China and on into the late twentieth century. For example, lineage violence in parts of Fujian and Guangdong provinces continued unabated in the Qing dynasty, lasted through the Republican era, and remains a problem in post-Mao China.[63]

Banditry and piracy were also regular features of Chinese society. Normally both were kept under control, but in periods of state decline or when China was divided, these activities tended to flourish. This was true during the waning years of the Qing dynasty as well as during the warlord era that followed. Banditry, piracy, and crime in general again became problems in late twentieth century China.[64]

Rebellions were not infrequent events in dynastic China. If the Chinese people considered the emperor their father, how could rebellion against him be justified? According to Lewis, "The problem of rationalizing and ritualizing the forcible overthrow of the legitimate ruler remained a basic issue in the use of violence through Chinese history."[65] Such a step was justified if the emperor was considered to be a bad father. If the empire was racked with disaster and turmoil, then the direct implication was that the emperor was not doing his job properly and could lose the Mandate of Heaven, grounds for deposing him through force of arms. Indeed, an antidynastic rebellion was one of the three kinds of "righteous war" acceptable in imperial China.[66]

In sum, the omission of studies of the employment of domestic force in China seems particularly surprising and indeed problematic given that internal warfare has been central to the genesis and evolution of the People's Liberation Army (PLA). Scholars of Chinese strategic culture cannot afford to ignore the use of military force within China and the prevalence of societal violence in their analyses of its nature and impact on state policy and behavior.

THE CHINESE CULT OF DEFENSE

I contend that there is a Realpolitik strand of Chinese strategic culture and along-side it a Confucian-type strand. The two strands of strategic culture combine in such a way as to imbue a distinct set of beliefs held by many Chinese leaders and researchers. I label this set of beliefs the "Chinese Cult of Defense."[67] I assert that Chinese elites believe passionately in the existence of a unique defensive, conflict-averse Chinese military approach to interstate relations. Coexisting alongside this – but rarely explicitly acknowledged by leaders and researchers – is a realist outlook that readily sanctions the use of violence in statecraft. The resultant mixture of these two outlooks is a worldview that rationalizes the use of force, even when used in an offensive capacity, as a purely defensive measure. The combined effect is paradoxical: While most of China's leaders, analysts, and researchers believe profoundly that the legacy of Chinese civi-lization is fundamentally pacifist, they are nevertheless very willing to employ force when confronting crises.

Intellectual Groundwork

The concept of a Cult of Defense owes intellectual debts to the work of Stephen Van Evera, Jack Snyder, and Shu Guang Zhang. First, the strength and preva-lence among Chinese elites of the beliefs articulated in this chapter have signifi-cant parallels with the "Cult of the Offensive" dominant among elites in Europe on the eve of World War I, so vividly described by Van Evera and Snyder. In contrast to this European phenomenon, the Cult of Defense affects only one country, and has deep cultural roots rather than ideological or organizational ones. Moreover, the effect of the present Cult of Defense paradoxically is not a preference for what are clearly defensive military policies and actions but rather those that are actually offensive. Nevertheless, the upshot of each cult is the glorification of flawed strategic assumptions and the increased likelihood of a state or states resorting to war.

Zhang uses the concept of "Mao's Military Romanticism" to help explain why China resorted to the use of force in October 1950 and intervened in Korea despite the daunting military challenges involved and widespread opposition and reluctance among Chinese leaders. Zhang contends that the Chinese Com-munist Party's (CCP's) reliance on military solutions and its remarkable record of success created a romanticized view of war as a preferred solution when confronted by a foreign or domestic crisis.[68] A major contribution of Zhang's conception is that it readily explains how a deeply held idealist belief is not nec-essarily inconsistent with a realist belief that war is a central means to resolve the crises that confront a regime.

But Zhang's adoption of the term – originally formulated by Stuart Schram – does not fully capture the scope or depth of the conviction.[69] Zhang attributes the belief to one man. Zhang also, if anything, understates its significance. This romanticized view of war was held not only by Mao – it was widespread among other CCP leaders as well and, judging from the evidence presented in this chapter, continues to exist a quarter of a century after Mao's death. Further, there is considerably more to this view than a simple romanticizing of military solutions to China's problems. Rather, there is a whole set of beliefs (see the following section). These beliefs reflect an abiding reverence for an ancient Chinese strategic tradition averse to the use of armed force while, at the same time, rationalizing a purely defensive war for a righteous cause.

These beliefs were readily detectable in the 1990s, as veneration for the glory of China's past civilization was more evident on the eve of the twenty-first century than they were during Mao's time, when China's past was condemned as being feudal or backward. Yet Chinese soldiers have long studied the strategy and tactics outlined by military thinkers of ancient times. Only in the 1990s did many Chinese researchers openly embrace the importance of culture in influencing how their government handles matters of war and peace. Moreover, the concept of strategic culture has enjoyed considerable popularity in China (see the following section). The Chinese are intensely proud of the past achievements of their once magnificent civilization. At the dawn of the twenty-first century, the veneration among elites for China's philosophical and metaphysical traditions borders on worship. The religiouslike fervor that Chinese seem to have for a unique strategic tradition is akin to the way many Americans believe the Founding Fathers made an unparalleled contribution to establishing universal political principles through the sacred texts of the Declaration of Independence and the Constitution. Just as many Americans are justifiably enamored of their heritage of political philosophy and the resilient democratic system it spawned, so the Chinese are particularly smitten with what they view as China's special gifts to the theory and practice of statecraft and international relations. In each case, the elites concerned tend to feel smugly and sincerely that in this particular arena their country possesses a monopoly on the truth.

The Cult of Defense

The Cult of Defense comprises three core philosophical elements and six guiding strategic principles. The core elements of this military tradition are that the Chinese: (1) are a peace-loving people; (2) are not aggressive or expansionist; and (3) only use force in self-defense. This set of beliefs seems quite consistent with the stereotype of a Confucian pacifistic, defense-minded civilization averse to the use of force identified in this chapter. And yet China's high-minded ideals have not prevented its leaders from waging war against their neighbors or using lethal force against their own people. Nor did core American beliefs in the fundamental rights of man prevent the United States government from oppressing African Americans, through slavery and later segregation, and rolling westward to conquer native Americans.

While the leaders of most countries tend to believe they use military power in a strictly defensive manner,[70] this cluster of beliefs seems to be particularly inviolable among the Chinese. In the broad realm of security policy (both internal and external), two guiding principles counter the fundamental tenets noted previously: (1) a strong reverence for national unification, and (2) a heightened sense of threat perception. In confronting foreign threats, the three fundamental tenets noted previously are countered by two guiding principles: that China (1) fights only "just wars," and (2) adheres faithfully to the strategic concept of "active defense." In addressing domestic threats, these three tenets are countered by two other principles: (1) a deep-seated fear of internal chaos, and (2) a heavy emphasis on the primacy of community over individual.

The extent to which these ideas are prevalent throughout Chinese society, while important to ascertain, is not central to my analysis. Here I concentrate on China's civilian and military elites. Nevertheless, as John Garver has observed, such beliefs seem widespread within China: "The self-perception of China as a pacific, non-threatening country that wishes nothing more than to live in peace with its neighbors is extremely common in China, both among the elite and ordinary people."[71]

The cluster of beliefs outlined in the following subsections appears to be held by a significant number of leaders in China. The cult of defense articulated here is derived from writings published primarily in the 1980s and 1990s and from interviews conducted in the 1990s.[72] These beliefs are widely held but they are not universally held within the Chinese defense or foreign policy communities. Significantly, however, such beliefs are so prevalent among Chinese elites that it is extremely rare to find civilian and military leaders who do not hold some or all of these beliefs.[73]

Peace Is Precious. A deeply held belief in elite circles is that China possesses a pacifist strategic culture. Certainly a majority of people in most countries, including the United States, say they love peace – indeed it seems a near universal human desire. What is striking in the case of China, however, is the extreme degree to which this is stressed – to the extent that Chinese civilization is viewed as being completely pacifistic, quite distinct from other strategic traditions in the world. One of the most recent official articulations of this appears in China's 1998 Defense White Paper:

> The defensive nature of China's national defense policy . . . springs from the country's historical and cultural traditions. China is a country with 5,000 years of civilization, and a peace-loving tradition. Ancient Chinese thinkers advocated "associating with benevolent gentlemen and befriending good neighbors," which shows that throughout history the Chinese people have longed for peace in the world and for relations of friendship with the people of other countries.[74]

Numerous Chinese leaders and researchers in the People's Republic of China contend that the Chinese people value peace. Lt. General Li Jijun, at the time deputy director of the Academy of Military Sciences, told an American military audience in July 1997 that "the Chinese are a peace-loving people."[75] And in 1995, Admiral Liu Huaqing, then a vice chair of the Central Military Commission, told a pro-communist Hong Kong newspaper:

> China has consistently pursued a foreign policy of peace and insists that various countries should, in line with the charter of the United Nations and the Five Principles of Peaceful Coexistence . . . maintain a peaceful international environment and that disputes between countries should be settled through negotiations.[76]

Military researchers trace this preference for peace and harmony back in history. According to General Xing Shizhong, the commandant of the National Defense University: "The Chinese people have always dearly loved peace. . . . This historical tradition and national psychology have a profound influence on national defense objectives and strategic policies of the new socialist China."[77] According to Li Jijun: "China's ancient strategic culture is rooted in the philosophical idea of 'unity between man and nature' *(tian ren he yi)*, which pursues overall harmony between man and nature and harmony among men."[78] Researchers also frequently mention the Confucian saying, "Peace is precious" *(he wei gui)*.[79]

Contemporary leaders and researchers stress that China pursues peaceful solutions rather than violent ones. Chinese civilian and military leaders repeatedly stress China's adherence to the "Five Principles of Peaceful Coexistence" as Liu does in the preceding quote. The five principles, first outlined by Zhou Enlai in the 1950s, are mutual respect for sovereignty and territorial integrity, nonaggression, noninterference in internal affairs, equality and mutual benefit, and peaceful coexistence. According to one civilian scholar, the ancient principle of "trying peaceful means before resorting to force" *(xianli houbing)* has been a major influence on post-1949 China. Thus, while the "leaders of Mao's generation were willing to use force to serve China's security, and more broadly, foreign policy goals whenever necessary . . . in most cases China sent strong warnings or protests or engaged in negotiations" prior to employing armed force.[80]

In a discussion of the military thought of Deng, two scholars observed, "For many years we employed the thinking that, in whatever method we adopt to solve a problem, we should not use the means of war [but rather] peaceful means."[81] Note that Deng also stressed that one of China's three main tasks for the 1980s was supporting world peace.[82] Of course, the flip side of this mission was actively "opposing hegemonism" (see the next section), certainly not consistent with a pacifist stance. Nevertheless, Chinese researchers regularly seek to bolster the assertion that China is by nature peace-loving. A prime example given is Beijing's policy on reunification with Taiwan: China's preferred means of unifying China since 1979 is by nonmilitary means.[83] It is true that under Deng, China's policy altered dramatically from liberation by force to peaceful unification. It is also important to note, however, that the change is more tactical than strategic. Indeed, Beijing has refused to renounce the use of force.[84]

Never Seek Hegemony. A second deeply held belief is that China has never been an aggressive or expansionist state. According to many leaders and researchers, China has never fought an aggressive war throughout its long history. Neither has China threatened other countries. In post-1949 China, this belief has taken the form of constant pronouncements to the fact that "China will never seek hegemony."[85] Senior soldier Liu told a Hong Kong interviewer in 1995: "China is opposed to the use of force and to threatening with force. . . . China is against hegemonism and power politics in any form . . . China does not seek hegemony now, nor will it ever do so in the future."[86] And Deng asserted in 1980 that one of the main tasks for the decade of supporting peace was intimately linked to "opposing hegemony" *(fandui baquanzhuyi)*.[87] Of course, at that time, *hegemony* was code word for Soviet domination. Since the end of the Cold War, it has come to mean U.S. domination. But the term *hegemony (ba)* has a deeper meaning in Chinese political thought. *Badao*, or "rule by force," has extremely negative connotations in contrast to *wangdao* or "kingly way" or "benevolent rule."[88]

According to many Chinese analysts, China goes to war only in "self-defense." These analysts assert that virtually all of the wars China has fought have been waged to protect itself from external threats or to unify the country. According to one prominent Chinese military scholar, virtually all of the approximately thirty-seven hundred to four thousand wars that China has fought in more than four thousand years of dynasties (ending with the collapse of the

Qing in 1911) have been civil wars or wars to unify the country. Moreover, all of the eight "military actions" since 1949, the scholar asserts, have been waged in "self-defense."[89] When Chinese forces have ventured abroad, they have done so for a limited time and for nonexpansionist purposes. According to one analyst, "The facts are: There are no records showing that China invaded other countries or that China stations any soldiers abroad."[90] Researchers regularly cite Mao's statement, "We [China] do not desire one inch of foreign soil."[91]

Examples often cited to support this interpretation include the famous voyages of Ming dynasty admiral Zheng He. Chinese researchers emphasize these expeditions were nonmilitary in nature, and that the Chinese armada made no attempt to conquer or colonize the lands it visited. The imperial eunuch's travels to East Africa and South Asia seem to have been purely voyages of exploration. According to several scholars, unlike Western adventurers such as Christopher Columbus and Vasco Da Gama, Zheng did not attempt to establish colonies or use force against peoples with whom he came in contact.[92]

If Someone Doesn't Attack Us, We Won't Attack Them. The third central tenet of the Cult of Defense is that China possesses a purely defensive strategic culture. According to Li, "The Chinese are a defensive-minded people."[93] The classic illustration of this tendency regularly cited by Chinese scholars is, not surprisingly, the Great Wall. According to Li, "China's Great Wall has always been a symbol of a defense, not the symbol of a national boundary."[94] In the 1990s, some Chinese researchers have sought to validate this point by citing Western scholarship, notably the work of Fairbank and Mark Mancall.[95] They also seek to make their case by drawing a direct comparison between Western and Chinese strategic traditions. According to one military researcher, China's military tradition places "complete stress on a defensive stance" whereas, in contrast, Western military tradition "emphasizes offense."[96]

Another example of the defensive nature of China's strategic posture is the "no first use" pledge regarding nuclear weapons.[97] Chinese officials also point to the military reforms that China has undertaken over the past two decades as proof of China's purely defensive stance. Liu said in 1995:

As is known to all, China possesses a strategy of active defense, and cut its troops by 1 million several years ago, something no other country has thus far achieved. Our present military strength is of a defensive nature and the Chinese Government strictly limits defensive expenditure to the minimum level necessary to ensure national security.[98]

Perhaps the most commonly touted evidence is Mao's admonition, "If someone doesn't attack us, we won't attack them; however if someone does attack us, we will definitely [counter] attack" (*Ren bu fan wo, wo bu fan ren; ren fan wo, wo bi fan ren*).[99] This quote appears in China's 1998 Defense White Paper. The phrase also appeared in a key *People's Daily* editorial in December 1978. The editorial contained a stern warning to Vietnam that China would retaliate if Hanoi did not end its aggressive behavior (see Chapter 6). Significantly, PLA soldiers widely used the slogan during the Cultural Revolution and in Beijing during the weekend of June 3–4, 1989.[100]

Marshal Xu Xiangqian cited this slogan in an August 1980 interview with an Italian journalist. Xu mentioned it in practically the same breath that he discussed Vietnam's invasion and occupation of Cambodia.[101] Significantly, China's largest military conflict in the post-Mao era – an attack against Vietnam in February 1979 – was triggered by Vietnam's invasion of Cambodia. Although China had in fact invaded Vietnam, Beijing officially labeled this war a "self-defensive counterattack" (*ziwei huanji*). According to two military thinkers, "...[A] strategic counterattack implies a strategic offensive." The strategists continued:

> [In]...the February 1979 self-defense counterattack against Vietnam, from the military operational standpoint, offensive actions were employed. Nevertheless, the essence of this kind of offense was a self-defense counterattack.

Of course, as the authors also noted, the choice of terms had political advantages too, since China could avoid being branded as the aggressor.[102] Moreover, China's intervention in Korea in October 1950 was also a counterattack, since in Beijing's view the United States had made the first aggressive moves against China on the Korean Peninsula and in the Taiwan Strait.[103] The same logic applied to China's brief but bloody border wars with India in 1962 and with the Soviet Union in 1969. Both conflicts are labeled "self-defense counterattacks" (*ziwei fanji*).[104]

Guiding Principles for General Security

Counteracting these core elements at the overall security level are two guiding principles that justify military force: (1) efforts to achieve national unification or protect national unity, and (2) heightened threat perceptions that tend to produce a siege mentality among China's leaders.

Primacy of National Unification. National unification is a core value in China's national security calculus on which no compromise is possible. It is an immutable principle in part because of China's history of division and inability to stop exploitation and oppression by foreign powers. However, this is also probably an emotional and unwavering public stand precisely because the leadership of the PRC in the reform era seems to lack any other inviolable principles.[105] According to Li:

> The most important strategic legacy of the Chinese nation is the awareness of identification and the concept of unification, and this is where lies the secret for the immortality of . . . Chinese civilization . . . [S]eeking unification . . . [is] the soul of . . . Chinese military strategy endowed by . . . Chinese civilization.[106]

According to another analyst, "[the] principle of unification hoping for unification, defending unification is a dimension of the Chinese people's . . . thought culture and is a special feature of its strategic thought."[107]

Heightened Threat Perceptions. China's political and military leaders see threats everywhere. The full extent of the siege mentality of China's leaders is not always appreciated. This paranoia results in elites viewing the foreign as well as domestic environments as treacherous landscapes filled with threats and conspiracies.[108] The ongoing campaign against corruption in China and the crackdown on the Falungong sect suggest the depth of the regime's fear of domestic threats.[109] This tendency reinforces and exacerbates the features of the military mind – the pessimism and negative views of human nature.[110] Moreover, China confronts a post–Cold War paradox: While the PRC has the most secure external security environment in its history, Beijing's leaders, particularly military leaders, have heightened threat perceptions. They see a world that is complicated and filled with uncertain challenges and threats.[111]

This mindset may explain the need of the Chinese authorities during the Maoist era to come up with the seemingly innocuous phrase "China has friends all over the world."[112] By the same token, one would expect that China had also at least some enemies in the world. Indeed, one is tempted to conclude that the slogan itself was prompted by Chinese insecurities. If a country has friendly states around the world, why is it necessary to recite this ad nauseum? The reality in the late Maoist era was that China actually had few staunch friends: the handful that come to mind are Albania, North Korea, and Pakistan. The fact of the matter is that Maoist China believed itself to be surrounded by enemies. This was true of Deng's China, and also holds true for China in the post-Deng era.

Traditionally, Chinese governments have viewed with greatest alarm the combination of internal disturbance and foreign aggression *(neiyou waihuan)*. In particular: "In the view of PRC leaders, the greatest danger to the regime exists when there is collaboration between internal and external hostile forces." This was clearly why, for example, Deng and other senior leaders viewed the popular protests in the spring of 1989 with such seriousness.[113] In the last decade of the twentieth century and the first decade of the twenty-first century, there are three sources of security threats to regime security and all are viewed as especially serious because of internal/external linkages: peaceful evolution, bourgeois liberalization, and social instability.[114]

Guiding Principles for External Security

Counteracting these three core elements are two key strategic constants that justify the external use of military force. The concepts of "just or righteous war" and "active defense" in practice negate the pacifying effects of the preceding core philosophical elements.

Just War Theory. The idea of just war *(yi zhan)* is an ancient one. Confucius adopted this idea, and Mao absorbed it.[115] The distinction is simple: just wars are good wars and unjust wars are bad ones. Just wars are those fought by oppressed groups against oppressors; unjust wars are ones waged by oppressors against the oppressed. Since China has long been oppressed – enduring more than a century of humiliation – it follows that any war China wages is a just one, even a war in which China strikes first.[116] The principle of just war seems to be a crucial element of China's traditional approach to war in the view of many contemporary military researchers.[117]

Active Defense. The idea of "active defense" *(jiji fangyu)* is a more recent concept in Chinese strategic thought. This concept crops up frequently in spoken and written material by Chinese strategic thinkers – it is mentioned in the 1995 interview with Liu quoted previously, for example. While Johnston dismisses active defense as mere propaganda,[118] the strategy appears to have real significance. In fact, active defense was a key guiding principle in Mao's day, in Deng's time, and remains important at the dawn of the twenty-first century.[119] Indeed, it figures prominently in China's 1998, 2000, and 2002 Defense White Papers.

In 1957, then Defense Minister Peng Dehuai explained China's attachment to active defense:

> ... in military matters our country has had a guiding principle of strategic defense, not a guiding principle of launching strategic offensives. This kind of defense, however, ought not be passive defense; instead, it should

be guided by the strategic principle of active defense. . . . Our country's nature, mission, and foreign policy all very clearly show our strategic guiding principle should be defensive.[120]

According to Deng " . . . active defense is not merely defense per se, but includes defensive offensives. Active defense includes our going out, so that if we are attacked we will certainly counter attack."[121]

Senior Colonel Wang Naiming explains:

[active defense] . . . emphasizes that the nature of our military strategy is defensive, but also active in requirements. It requires the organic integration of offense and defense, and achieving the strategic goal of defense by active offense; when the conditions are ripe, the strategic defense should be led [sic] to counterattack and offense.[122]

This "organic integration" between offense and defense is very much consistent with the idea of "absolute flexibility" *(quanbian)* highlighted by Johnston.[123] In a real sense, then, the line between offense and defense is blurred. In the final analysis, *"Active defense strategy does not acknowledge the difference . . . between defense and offense."*[124] In fact, according to a researcher at the Academy of Military Sciences, active defense does not rule out a first strike: "Our strategic principle of 'striking only after the enemy has struck' certainly does not exclude sudden 'first strikes' in campaign battles or counterattacks in self-defense into enemy territory."[125] Peng articulated the logic of such a move in the late 1950s:

Launching a war first offensively against another country is in violation of our country's nature, mission, and our foreign policy fundamentals.

. . . Under the strategic guiding principle of active defense, are we permitted to gain the initiative by striking first? That is to say, when we are expecting an imminent large-scale offensive attack by the enemy against our country, are we permitted to act first and launch an offensive strike against enemy territory or not? We may consider this unacceptable. Yet, in such a situation, the chief criminal culprit is the enemy who originally schemed to launch the war. The peace loving people of the entire world can only be suddenly threatened if the enemy is allowed to instigate war. However, if we don't wait for the enemy to move first, then we can strike first offensively into enemy territory. In this case our war in defense of the motherland would be completely just. . . .

Peng cited China's intervention in Korea against the United States as an example.[126]

Guiding Principles for Internal Security

The two guiding principles that tend to predispose the Chinese state to resort to force internally are a fear of turmoil, and an emphasis on the community over the individual.

Chaos Phobia. Chinese strategic culture places great emphasis on internal security and in particular on the survival of the regime in power.[127] There is a deep-seated cultural fear of chaos and turmoil. Since ancient times, Chinese leaders have attached great importance to domestic stability. Western concepts of security, by contrast, have focused on external threats, according to Chinese researchers.[128]

Domestically, the stress has tended to be on nonlethal force to maintain stability. Under Mao, and to a lesser extent under Deng, a powerful system of controls was in place that operated through an individual's work unit *(danwei)*. The factory, office, school, or commune held an inordinate amount of power over members of the *danwei* even in the most basic decisions in life, such as whom one could marry and where one could live.[129] Therefore, there has been little need for a modern centralized police force in the PRC. Members of the Public Security Bureau are normally not armed, and it was only in the early 1980s with the decline of controls – including the power of the work unit – that a new national constabulary was established. Decommissioned PLA units, who merely swapped uniforms, staffed the People's Armed Police. In communist China, only two types of people are armed: soldiers and criminals. Possession of firearms was a key defining feature of the PLA.[130]

When officials determine that China has lapsed into chaos or is on the verge of chaos, resorting to deadly force is a natural step. This is particularly true when ordinary instruments of control break down or weaken, as they did during the Cultural Revolution and the Tiananmen Square protests in 1989. Not surprisingly, Chinese leaders have a near obsession with maintaining stability at all costs. Deng argued in early 1980: "... it is clear that without stability and unity we have nothing [*meiyou anding tuanjie, jiu meiyou yiqie*].... [We] cannot afford further chaos [that is another Cultural Revolution] and [we] will not permit it to recur."[131]

Community over Individual. In China, as in many cultures, the interests of the community are considered paramount, and the interests of the individual take a back seat. This focus on the collective over the individual means that authorities in China are likely to turn swiftly and harshly against persons and groups perceived as threatening social order and stability. Mao reportedly considered the most important purpose of the legal system was to obtain the "greatest benefit for the greatest number of people." Hence, according to one legal scholar, "The people's benefit is our highest law." Significantly this discussion of China's "highest law" occurred in a paper on the subject of China's use of the death penalty.[132]

Fear of chaos and a belief in the primacy of the collective majority – "the People" – contributed to the communist party-state taking particularly repressive and violent actions against those identified as "enemies of the people." Despite the emphasis on nonlethal force and on the educative and rehabilitative role of punishment, the system seemed paradoxically to mete out brutal treatment to those suspected of being enemies of the state.[133] Communist China has consistently experienced extreme and terrifying episodes of lethal violence. During the campaign against landlords in the early 1950s, Mao claimed that more than eight hundred thousand people were killed. It is conservatively estimated that during the Cultural Revolution half a million people were killed. More recently, during the reform era, I estimate that China leads the world in the number of judicial executions carried out: at least tens of thousands of prisoners have been executed in China during the past twenty years.[134]

Extremely harsh punishments are rationalized as being necessary to educate the offender and/or society – a major goal of China's criminal justice system – but at the same time are tempered by mercy. The communist authorities, like their Confucian predecessors, emphasize correct thinking and the power of education to inculcate proper attitudes and beliefs, hence the institutions of reform through labor and reeducation through labor. Employing the concept of general education and making an example of serious criminals can serve as a deterrent to the rest of society. Petty crimes involving "nonantagonistic contradictions" among the people can be dealt with fairly simply and with mild penalties. More serious crimes that involve antagonistic contradictions represent more critical challenges to order. According to Deng:

> We should distinguish between antagonistic and non-antagonistic contradictions. We should educate the overwhelming majority of persons who disrupt public order, all those who can be educated, and take stern legal steps against those who are beyond education or who prove incorrigible.... We must continue to strike resolutely at various kinds of criminals, so as to ensure and consolidate a sound, secure public order. We must learn to wield the weapon of law effectively.[135]

Deng continued: "By dealing sternly with these criminals now, we will be giving some kind of education not only to the overwhelming majority of offenders, but to the whole party and people."[136]

Even, for capital punishment, a prime rationale has been its educative role – in terms of a lesson for the individual and/or society. The category of punishment called "death penalty, suspended for two years," is especially noteworthy. According to several Chinese officials, the measure reflects the strong humanitarian current in their country's criminal justice system.[137] The suspended death sentence is roughly equivalent to life without parole and appears to have been widely used in China since the early 1980s. The measure seems to have deep roots in Chinese tradition.

In the final analysis, however, the extensive use in the reform era of anticrime campaigns characterized by the vigorous use of harsh penalties, such as capital punishment, underscores the depth of fear of social disorder and the paramountcy of collective interests over those of the individual.

CONCLUSION

China's strategic behavior is influenced not just by a Realpolitik strand but also by a Confucian one. The combined effect is what I have dubbed a Chinese Cult of Defense, in which realist behavior dominates but is justified as defensive on the basis of a pacifist self-perception. The key point is that the defensive-mindedness and preference for nonviolent solutions to interstate disputes are not merely empty rhetoric or symbolic discourse, but rather are part of a belief system that has been deeply internalized by Chinese civilian and military elites. The outcome of these two strategic cultures interacting is a China that assertively protects and aggressively promotes its own national interests, up to and including acts of war, but that rationalizes all military moves as purely self-defensive.

Beijing's dramatic switch from preoccupation with revolution under Mao to economic modernization under Deng did transform civil-military culture (see Chapter 3), but this had no moderating effect on China's disposition to use armed force. In other words, the reorientation from an emphasis on political struggle to a stress on economic development *does not* seem to have decreased the frequency and intensity of China's use of force. This is surprising considering that one would logically expect that such a change in national priorities would result in a greater reluctance to use force – that China would tend to place a greater value on a peaceful international environment so that it could concentrate all its efforts on rapid economic growth. The consistency might be attributed to an enduring Chinese Cult of Defense.

Clear, irrefutable proof of a causal link between strategic culture and deployment of armed force, however, is probably impossible. This is so, I suggest, because it is mediated by other variables such as civil-military culture. To use

the conception of layers suggested in Chapter 1, other levels of culture miti-
gate the impact of strategic culture on behavior. For Johnston and Waldron, the
dependent variable is military policy rather than military employment. While
policy obviously affects strategic behavior, it remains at least one step removed
from the actual employment of military force. In this study, the dependent variable is the use of armed force. The intervening layer, civil-military culture, is
the subject of Chapter 3.

3

Bringing in the Military

IS the Chinese People's Liberation Army (PLA) separate and distinct, or is it indistinguishable from the Chinese Communist Party (CCP)? Is the PLA completely dominated by the CCP, or is the PLA an autonomous actor in its own right? In other words, how accurate is the Long March conceptualization of Chinese communist civil-military culture identified in Chapter 1? The military's influence in modern China is frequently overlooked, and David Shambaugh has rightly called for "bringing the military back in" to the study of China.[1] In this chapter, I "bring the military in" to the study of Chinese strategic culture.[2]

This chapter analyzes the evolving nature of Chinese political culture and civil-military culture and then evaluates its impact on a state's disposition to use force. While China's strategic culture has remained constant for a hundred years or more, Chinese civil-military culture has been altered over the course of the twentieth century. The shift in political culture in 1978 from a preoccupation with revolution to an obsession with modernization and reform triggered a thoroughgoing transformation of military doctrine, format, identity, and function. The major shifts in these four dimensions of China's civil-military culture within the last half of the twentieth century have affected how and where China is most likely to use force. They have also altered the manner and milieu in which decisions about the use of force are made. These changes have tended to make China appear more militant and aggressive, whereas the actual inner workings have simply become less shrouded in mystery, with soldiers' viewpoints becoming more distinct from and autonomous of the civilian party elite, and China's leaders focusing more on addressing external threats.

First the fluctuating image of the soldier in political culture across the broad sweep of Chinese history is considered. Then the doctrinal shift from People's War to Limited War under High Technology Conditions is examined. Next the civil-military format, which alternated between dual role and functional differentiation configurations, is considered. Third, the identity of the military is examined within the core context of personal and political loyalties. Lastly, the functions of the armed forces are examined – the extent to which these missions are external or domestic, combat or noncombat.

A SOLDIER'S STATUS IN CHINESE CULTURE

Whether a soldier's image is positive or negative is largely determined within the broader realm of political culture. Whether the soldier holds a negative or positive image is significant because of what this implies about Chinese thinking regarding violence and war. It also makes society more or less favorably disposed to the military as an institution or soldiering as a profession, and it may encourage or discourage the best and the brightest from aspiring to a military career.

It is often assumed that in traditional China the soldier was universally despised. China is widely believed to possess an antimilitary ancient culture in which soldiering was looked down upon and warfare was considered barbaric.[3] One oft-cited saying asserts that "good iron does not make nails, good men do not make soldiers."[4] However, this is a gross generalization and serious distortion of the record.[5] In fact, the image of the soldier has fluctuated dramatically over time in Chinese history.[6] Indeed, in many periods of Chinese history, soldiers have enjoyed a very positive image.[7] Moreover, it is essential to distinguish officers from enlisted men: The rank and file has tended to be viewed with some scorn, while officers are often accorded more respect and deference. Chinese military leaders in particular have benefited from the colorful and largely positive depiction of martial heroes from Chinese history and mythology.[8]

The Soldier in the Communist Era

Thanks to the victory of the communists in the Chinese Civil War in the late 1940s and the identity projected by the men and women of the PLA, the Chinese people held the military in high esteem for much of the last half of the twentieth century. The image of the patriotic, decent, and well-mannered peasant soldier promoted by Chinese communists had a profound impact on the image of the military in political culture. Mao Zedong and his colleagues soon recognized the tremendous value of communist soldiers holding boy scout reputations. Hence the genesis of the "Three Main Rules of Discipline" and the "Eight Points for Attention" in 1928. Among other things, these admonished soldiers

41

to always "speak politely," and "pay fairly for what you buy."[9] Mao recognized this was a very basic but crucial dimension of "political work" – in winning the hearts and minds of the Chinese masses. Anecdotal evidence, backed by scholarly research, supports the thesis that treating ordinary people with respect and living as one of them was important in winning support among Chinese people for the communist cause. Theodore White recounts how, in late 1939, a detachment of Kuomintang troops that he was accompanying masqueraded as communists when they entered a village. The puzzled journalist asked the commander why he had told the villagers they were communist forces. The officer explained that he had done so in order to take advantage of the far better reputation communist soldiers enjoyed among the peasantry.[10]

This reputation for dedication to the people earned during the Civil War and unflinching patriotism earned in the Anti-Japanese War was reinforced by the exploits of the Chinese People's Volunteers (CPV) in the Korean War. The image was particularly powerful and endured due to the timeless popularity of a newspaper article titled "Who are the most beloved people *(zui ke'ai de ren)*," published in the April 11, 1951, issue of the *People's Daily*. This moving account of CPV troops in Korea struck a deep cord with many people and was reprinted numerous times.[11]

This image continued in the 1960s when the heroic soldier Lei Feng was trumpeted as a model worthy of national emulation. In the early 1980s, public admiration for soldiers was evident from such things as the enormous popularity of a novel, *Wreaths of Flowers at the Foot of the Tall Mountains (Gao shan xia de huahuan)*, about a company of soldiers who fought heroically against Vietnam in the short border war of 1979. The book was turned into a very successful movie that exploited the emotions of cinemagoers across China.[12]

Of course, negative images of Chinese communist soldiers have also emerged. The heavy-handed intervention of the PLA during the Cultural Revolution produced negative reactions among people. And, during the 1980s, growing corruption within the military tarnished the reputation of the PLA.[13] The most serious blow to the Chinese military in the late twentieth century was its use of deadly force to suppress the massive popular protests of 1989 in Beijing (see Chapter 7). But the PLA seems to have recovered from the damage this caused to its own self-esteem and its public image. Chinese military leaders appear to be trying to ride the crest of the tidal wave of strident nationalism that emerged in the 1990s and remake their identity from the butchers of Beijing to the vigilant protectors of the motherland.[14] The PLA adopted high-profile stances in episodes of high drama and patriotic appeal, such as the return of Hong Kong to Chinese control in July of 1997, and the Taiwan Strait Crisis of 1995–6.

The Soldier in Late Imperial and Republican China

For much of the nineteenth century, Chinese soldiers were not held in very high esteem. The standing armies of the late Qing were in considerable disrepair: Bannermen had become demoralized, poorly trained, and equipped with broken or antiquated weaponry; the Green Standard forces were slovenly, ill disciplined, and incompetent. In fact, the Banners became useless and troublesome parasites.[15]

This sorry state of affairs changed slightly in the mid-1850s when imperial scholar officials resorted to raising temporary forces to deal with local violence and insurrections. These forces tended to be better disciplined and more effective. And serving in these forces did hold the promise of adventure and loot.

By the twentieth century, however, this perception had changed dramatically. China's gradual slide into chaos and dismemberment prompted diligent imperial officials to establish modern-style military schools and academies throughout China, and bright young Chinese began to seek training at foreign military academies, mostly in Japan. A catalyst seems to have been China's humiliating defeat in 1894–5 at the hands of Japan. The loss of Korea and Taiwan to a nominal Chinese tributary state was particularly galling. The upsurge of patriotism led more and more of China's best and brightest to "switch from the pen to the sword," or from pursuing a career as a scholar-official to one as a military officer. In the aftermath of the First Sino–Japanese War, applications to military academies in China shot up significantly.[16] Growing interest by the gentry and the acceptance of soldiering as a scholarly undertaking greatly enhanced the prestige of the armed forces.[17]

The collapse of the Qing dynasty in 1911, triggered by a mutiny of ordinary soldiers in units of the New Army in the central city of Wuchang, further raised the stature of the military profession.[18] China lapsed into a period known as "warlordism" because the new Republic, inspired and then briefly led by Sun Yat-sen, failed to function as a national government. The warlord era is typically considered to have lasted from the death of President Yuan Shikai in 1916 to the Northern Expedition of 1926 led by Chiang Kai-shek. The outcome of a regional approach to military modernization followed by the declining Qing dynasty had led to the formation of multiple modern-style provincial forces rather than a single unified national army. During the warlord era, China was divided into fiefdoms each controlled by a general who held political power by virtue of the army he commanded.[19]

Over the span of about seventeen years (1911–28), the number of Chinese males in military service quadrupled from less than half a million to about

2 million. What accounts for the dramatic increase in the number of soldiers? There was growing demand for soldiers from the warlords who ruled China – men were needed not to fight China's external enemies but rival warlord armies. Why did Chinese men enlist to fight their countrymen? Most enlistees were volunteers; conscription and the press gang enjoyed extremely limited usage. Why did they enlist of their own free will – especially at a time when, according to Diana Lary, the military was held in nearly universal contempt? Lary says that, given the lack of attractive alternatives, these men enlisted for the assurance of a full stomach, regular income, and the promise of loot. In short, the primary motive was material gain. As a consequence, Lary labels these men "mercenaries." Nevertheless, despite the many important practical reasons for becoming a soldier, it seems implausible that the number of enlistees increased at a time when a soldier's reputation was allegedly so appalling.[20] There must have been other considerations, and indeed, Lary hints at some: the prospect of adventure and glory. At least the latter motive does not seem consistent with the perception of soldiering as a disdained occupation.[21] Of course, the officer was held in higher esteem than the enlisted man.[22] Still, even an ordinary "mercenary" foot soldier has his self-respect.

Actually the image of the soldier in this era was not as negative as some historians claim. As noted previously, after the First Sino–Japanese War (1894–5), the status of the military was enhanced. Modern-style soldiers were seen as patriots capable of rescuing China from its predicament. Still, fighting essentially civil wars against fellow Chinese does not on the surface appear to be a patriotic activity. However, many of the best warlords attempted to inculcate some kind of basic patriotic spirit in their soldiers. They often claimed to be fighting to unify China and make it strong. But equally important was the inspiration and example provided by the warlord himself. Was he brave and heroic of stature? Did he show concern for the welfare of his men? Did he declare himself committed to unifying and strengthening China? In other words, did he inspire admiration among his men? Donald Munro has highlighted the significance in Chinese philosophy and culture of "model emulation." This was very important not only in Confucianism, but also in other philosophical traditions, and was a lasting feature of Chinese political culture well into the Maoist era.[23]

The increased appeal of a military career owed much to the presence of colorful and charismatic warlords such as Feng Yuxiang, Zhang Zuolin, and Li Zongren.[24] Many consciously modeled themselves on ancient heroes and deliberately fostered cult worship of mythical martial figures such as the God of War, Guan Yu.[25] Later, generals such as Chiang, Zhu De, He Long, and Peng Dehuai provided additional models for emulation, more powerful and appealing because these men could more plausibly lay claim to being patriots.

Chinese officers continued to be held in high esteem until the early 1920s. According to Arthur Waldron, it was not until the Second Zhili–Fengtian War of 1924–5 that society began to heap scorn on military leaders. The massive scale and scope of warfare between the two sides in this conflict repulsed people, especially since it seemed that Chinese soldiers were interested only in their own personal power and wealth while the country was internally divided and humiliated by foreign powers. In fact, the term *warlord* (*junfa*) did not enjoy widespread usage until after 1924.[26] Thus Chinese military leaders were rarely called warlords or even viewed in the negative light that this term connoted until toward the latter part of the period historians later labeled the "warlord era."

Indeed, prior to the mid-1920s, soldiers seem to have been viewed in a very positive light. The Chinese, for example, celebrating the end of World War I – and China's participation as one of the victorious Allies – did not seem to hold military leaders in contempt or low esteem. High-spirited students in Tianjin in late 1918 marched in a parade with a mock-up of a boat labeled "national spirit boat" *(guohunzhu)*. Inside were two youths, one costumed as Guan Yu, the God of War, and the other dressed as a military hero of the Southern Song. The celebration:

> ... drew upon a traditional Chinese vocabulary of martiality ... by refer-ring to the age of chivalry and knighthood, [and] ... saw nothing inherently wrong with warfare or the military: they were only concerned that their cause and their nation should be victorious.[27]

In sum, the military profession has not been viewed in totally negative terms by Chinese political culture. Rather, a soldier's bravery, patriotism, and dedication to the Chinese people determined his status.

MILITARY DOCTRINE

Military doctrine provides the integrative framework for the formulation of civil-military format, identity, and function. Both doctrine and security policy tend to be determined by trends in the larger political culture of a country and its security environment. Security policy identifies a state's national security objectives and the potential military threats it confronts. Consequently, mili-tary doctrine is devised to prepare for the kinds of wars that the armed forces anticipate from the threat environment and national objectives defined by the security policy.

Military doctrine, however, is one part of a multilayered architecture for the application of military force. The most abstract level is the broad political-military strategy of a state determined by the political elite. Below this is basic military doctrine: the core principles by which the armed forces guide their actions in planning the employment of military force to support national objectives. The next level is military strategy: the use or threat of military force to achieve the objectives of national policy. The following level is operations: the campaigns planned and conducted to achieve the objectives of a military strategy. The lowest level is tactics: the planning and conduct of battlefield engagements.

While doctrines are often labeled "defensive" or "offensive," in practice they frequently contain elements of both at different levels. Contemporary Chinese doctrinal, strategic, and operational concepts can be particularly challenging to label because they are extremely broad and interpreted very flexibly and pragmatically by political and military leaders. The concept of active defense (discussed in Chapter 2) is a case in point. Chinese doctrine, at least in the twentieth century, has tended to be malleable and open-ended rather than rigid and constraining.[28]

The Early Communist Era: Security Policy and People's War

While circumscribed by ideological tenets, early Chinese communist security policy was dominated by pragmatic considerations. From the temporary alliance with the Nationalist Party or Kuomintang (KMT) in the early 1920s to the switch to rural insurrection and resistance when turned upon by their erstwhile KMT allies in 1927 and beyond, the CCP has been very much guided by practical matters. On foreign policy, Mao's thinking was ever evolving, from rudimentary and ill-informed conceptions in the 1920s and 1930s to more sophisticated and better-informed perspectives in the 1940s and 1950s. Up until 1949, he was remarkably receptive to an improvement in relations with the United States. Mao's thinking about the United States was actually surprisingly nuanced, flexible, and eclectic.[29] This is the exact opposite of how he is often depicted – as doggedly anti-American and pro-Soviet for ideological as well as experiential reasons.[30] In sum, the theories and policies of Mao, the principal – but not sole – strategist of the CCP, are studies in determination to concentrate on long-term ideologically inspired goals while employing flexibility and opportunism in the short and medium terms.

A prime example of this element is Mao's doctrine of People's War, often heralded as one of the major strategic innovations of the twentieth century.[31] With its emphasis on guerilla warfare, it became a blueprint for wars of national liberation fought by peasant irregulars around the world. It has received considerable attention because it was, first of all, extremely successful in the Chinese case, and second, because it was promoted by a very effective propaganda offensive.[32] Mao's strategy of protracted guerilla warfare was described as "the latest and most publicized manifestation of over two thousand years of Chinese strategic thought."[33] For these reasons, People's War is viewed, like ancient Chinese military thinking, as a series of stratagems and ruses aimed at achieving victory in the long run with minimal use of violence. When employed by a revolutionary movement, it has tended to be characterized as a solely rural insurgency strategy; and when adopted by a revolutionary party-state, it has often been characterized as a strictly defensive doctrine.[34]

In fact, People's War is a far more flexible and broad strategic outlook, encompassing a wide variety of approaches at the levels of political-military doctrine, military strategy, operations, and tactics. While People's War borrowed from Chinese traditional conceptions of warfare and Marxism-Leninism, it was a logical response to contemporary conditions.[35] First of all, People's War is not simply concerned with lightly armed peasant irregulars waging insurgency. It is based on a holistic and pragmatic approach of adopting policies to fit changing circumstances and includes the use of regular warfare. Mao's writings on strategy by a revolutionary movement outline three phases of warfare.[36] First comes classic guerilla conflict waged just as most conceptions of People's War have described it. It is largely a defensive, opportunist strategy that made virtue out of necessity. Indeed, Mao's conception of the peasantry as a revolutionary class was a Marxist-Leninist ideological deviation demanded by a revolutionary movement that had been forced to abandon the cities or face extinction at the hands of the KMT. But as the strength of revolutionary forces increased, the conflict enters a second phase in which the military wages a guerilla struggle, but this is supplemented by conventional fighting wherein the enemy can also be engaged on equal terms in mobile warfare. Then, in the third and final phase, the revolutionary armed forces, now superior, launch conventional strikes combined with positional warfare, supported by continued guerilla struggle.[37]

Moreover, People's War cannot simply be classified as a defensive doctrine; it can be offensive, defensive, or difficult to determine. Certainly, Mao was not the originator of many of the concepts he described so vividly, practiced so adroitly, and popularized so effectively. Some of these concepts come from Sun Tzu,[38] others from popular martial lore in popular culture,[39] and still others from games of strategy such as *weiqi*, or one variant of Chinese chess better known as "go."[40] Employing *weiqi* to understand contemporary Chinese strategy underlines the blurring of what is offensive and what is defensive, since the precise nature of a move is difficult to determine until the game progresses. Also, since the purpose of the game is to surround rather than to attack directly or destroy enemy pieces, *weiqi* – and by extension Chinese military tradition – is easily labeled as being averse to actual combat.

For the People's Republic of China (PRC), People's War was actually at least two doctrines: one was a defensive military strategy for China to counter external threats; and another was an offensive political-military doctrine for exporting revolution.[41] The first was certainly defensive in nature at least at the strategic level. The presumption was that if China were attacked, the armed forces would not attempt to hold the aggressor at the borders, but rather retreat and "lure the enemy deep" into the country where the PLA and militia forces would at the operational level carry out protracted guerilla warfare and wear the invader down gradually. The second doctrine, the export of revolution, was more obviously offensive. Yet, Beijing's support for foreign communist insurgency movements was more symbolic than real. While the rhetoric of revolution and communist fraternal solidarity was there, in actual practice China was very selective and limited in providing material support for indigenous struggles, preferring to cultivate good relations with ruling regimes.[42] Still, China's threat to assist other communist movements was taken seriously by many countries, including the United States.[43] In retrospect, the effectiveness of the doctrine was more as a successful model of People's War for others to take heart from and seek to emulate.[44] Its potency in this regard can be seen from the Maoist-type insurgencies in India (Naxalites), Malaya, Angola, Mozambique, Peru (Sendero Luminoso), and Nepal, not to overlook the successful ones in Vietnam and Cambodia (Khmer Rouge). While only a handful of these struggles have been victorious, what is remarkable is that the model has proved so broad in its appeal and so flexible in application. Moreover, these insurgency movements have often proved enduring.

Both the "offensive" political-military doctrine and the "defensive" military strategy of People's War espoused by post-1949 China were born of necessity – the logical military policies to be pursued by a weak, revolutionary state. This point is very clear from the importance that Mao attached to obtaining nuclear weapons. While publicly Mao called atomic weapons "paper tigers," he soon concluded that it was essential for China to develop its own nuclear capability. In the wake of the 1954–5 Taiwan Strait Crisis, Mao made the acquisition of nuclear weapons a national priority and lavished considerable resources to ensure that China would join the nuclear club sooner rather than later.[45] This is not to say that the trumpeting of the superiority of man over weapons and political consciousness over military expertise was merely rhetoric. These things were what Maoists believed based on the victories achieved by relying on the largely illiterate masses.

The Post-Mao Era: Toward Limited War under High-Tech Conditions

After Mao's death in 1976, PLA leaders began a soul-searching reassessment of China's military situation. Some influential figures voiced concern that the strategic posture and capabilities were totally inadequate to deal with changing global realities. Thus a revised doctrine dubbed "People's War under Modern Conditions" was adopted in the late 1970s. Recognition that cities had become vital production and communication centers to be protected, the People's War strategies of "luring the enemy deep" and relying on mobile warfare to defeat the invader were modified to include such features as a more active border defense and positional warfare.[46] But forward-thinking leaders also saw much more than just doctrinal flaws. Not only did strategy need to be overhauled, but also PLA training, equipment, and personnel needed to be upgraded, bureaucracy streamlined, and manpower trimmed.[47]

The man who was able to articulate these problems and give them a sense of great urgency was the same one who proved able to tap into the popular groundswell among members of the CCP and society who yearned for more moderate policies: Deng Xiaoping. Starting in the late 1970s, China under Deng undertook market-oriented economic reforms and a dose of political liberalization, while the PLA commenced gradual but thoroughgoing reforms. More dramatic rapid change within the PLA was evident in 1985: A one million strong force reduction was announced, the command structures of eleven existing military regions were consolidated into seven, main force units became integrated combined group armies, military ranks were restored, and new, smarter uniforms were introduced.[48]

Providing coherence to these transformations was a "strategic transformation" made by China's senior leaders in meetings of the Central Military Commission in May and June 1985. There was pragmatic recognition that war with the Soviet Union, or at least a major war, was unlikely in the near term. Indeed, there was no longer the threat of an early, major, protracted global military conflict. Many Chinese leaders reached the conclusion that an era of sustained overall peace was likely. But this did not mean there would be no wars. In this era, the threat to China would come in the form of multiple, small, limited, regional wars.[49] These limited wars would be fought on China's periphery – the jungles of southern Yunnan and Guangxi, the mountains of Tibet, the deserts of Xinjiang, or off the coast in the East China or South China seas. This called for smaller, specially trained mobile units with high-tech weaponry and significant force projection capability. Particular emphasis was placed on upgrading the PLA's air and naval arms.

Since the stunning success of the U.S.-led coalition forces in the Gulf War in 1991, credited to the use of technologically sophisticated weaponry, the suffix "under high-technology conditions" was added to the doctrine of "Limited War."[50] Greater attention was given to addressing how China would adapt to the Revolution in Military Affairs (RMA) – the application of advanced information and computer technology to the conduct of warfare.[51] In the post-Deng era, even more emphasis has been given to technological innovation and a corresponding focus on reducing unnecessary manpower and shedding distracting if financially lucrative commercial pursuits. In 1997 a planned troop cut of half a million men was announced, and in mid-1998 a directive was issued ordering PLA organs to divest themselves from business enterprises.

What did these changes mean? On the one hand, China was no longer preparing for a world war and anticipated an era of peace, which suggested that China was less likely to be bellicose. On the other hand, the changes in force configuration, improved capabilities, and doctrinal shift intimated that China might be more willing to employ force in pursuit of foreign policy aims.

The PLA's new doctrine of "Local, Limited War under High Technology Conditions" certainly made the possibility of war a more attractive and acceptable option to China's leaders. The earlier doctrine of People's War envisioned a protracted conflict – a cataclysmic all-out struggle that would devastate much of China and result in the deaths of tens of millions of Chinese. This new doctrine anticipated a short conflict, limited to a single region and likely fought at or beyond China's borders. Therefore, conflict would result in minimal casualties and cost to China. Moreover, whereas under People's War China would be forced to assume a strategic defensive posture in hostilities and fight a protracted war of attrition, under limited high-tech war China would seize the offensive and quickly emerge victorious. In Chinese strategic thinking about modern, limited, local war under high-technology conditions, the initial engagement in a contemporary conflict was seen as critical. In contrast, under Mao's strategy of protracted war, Chinese forces should bide their time absorbing enemy offensives and preparing for a counteroffensive when the time was right. According to one military thinker, "In a local high tech war, the first battle is the decisive battle, which will decide the outcome of the entire war."[52] Thus the idea of a preemptive strike was increasingly attractive to Chinese strategic thinkers all the while being viewed in their minds as a defensive measure (see Chapter 2). Beijing also appeared ready to use tactical nuclear weapons in such circumstances.[53]

In sum, doctrine is an important determinant of whether a military is offensively or defensively disposed. Certainly, military doctrine in communist China provides a framework for organizing and preparing for war-fighting, influencing how and where the PLA is employed. Nevertheless, Chinese doctrine remains broad and flexible, encompassing elements of both offense and defense at different levels of strategy. Moreover, in China, doctrine can also provide a coherent framework for the country's civil-military culture.

CIVIL-MILITARY FORMAT

Civil-military format refers to the institutional structure of the military in relation to political organs and society. The two ideal types of civil-military formats are dual role and functional differentiation. In the format of the former, political leaders double as military leaders (or vice versa), and ordinary people serve as soldiers; in the latter, political elites are clearly distinguished from military elites, and civilians are distinct from soldiers. In fact, even in the dual role configuration in contemporary China, the most senior political position or positions were restricted to civilian leaders.

These two formats tended to alternate over time in a kind of Hegelian dialectic with one of the two dominating for a time only to be replaced by the other, often corresponding to the cyclical nature of dynastic rise and fall. For much of the Spring and Autumn period (722–481 B.C.), for example, the dual role format prevailed, while during the Warring States era (403–221 B.C.) which followed, the functional differentiation model had become dominant.[54] In late imperial China, the dual role model was clearly dominant for most of the Qing dynasty; emperors and imperial civil scholar-officials were expected to double as generals when circumstances dictated it.

Civilian Supremacy: Chinese Theory and Practice

The Long March depiction of a seamless monolithic civil-military elite or a military under firm institutional civilian control did not reflect reality. Even under the dual role format, when the civil-military divide could be fuzzy, most military leaders could be distinguished from civilians. Nevertheless, because of the overlap between elites and the history of persistent military domination of politics, there was considerable concern about soldiers wresting power. To counter this threat, communist leaders went to great lengths to stress the inviolability of the principle of civilian control and enforce concrete rules of the game in order to limit the power of military leaders.

Indeed, Maoist ideology was central to providing the logic to check the power of the army and restrict its autonomy. In 1927, the year that the forerunner to the People's Liberation Army was established, Mao made his famous assertion about political power growing out of a gun. But Mao was equally adamant in asserting that the "party commands the gun, and the gun must never be allowed to command the party."[55]

Confucianism also has had considerable instrumental value in limiting the power of the military. Political leaders in imperial China constantly emphasized Confucianism's strong strands of antimilitary bias and its implicit championing of the core principle of civilian supremacy as a powerful normative weapon to forestall domestic challenges by soldiers. This effort was made all the more urgent because the nuts and bolts of maintaining tight control of the military were a perennial problem in Chinese history.[56] While scholars frequently recognize the value of Confucianism to legitimize dictatorial rule, the ideology's significance for civil-military culture is not widely appreciated. Confucianism provides a key rationale for attaching lower status to military leaders.

It was vital that the important normative abstract notion of civilian supremacy be translated into concrete "rules of the game" in civil-military culture. These rules would tend to check the power and limit the autonomy of the armed forces.[57] In communist China, two fundamental rules have been (1) prohibitions against soldiers assuming the position of paramount political leader, and (2) limitations placed on the decision-making and policy-making roles of senior soldiers, particularly in nonmilitary affairs.

Because of a legacy of praetorianism in the Republican era and the close ties between the CCP and PLA, Mao (like other Chinese communist leaders) took it as an article of faith that the paramount party leader should be considered a civilian. In 1955 Mao was insistent about not being awarded the honorific title of marshal. He was also opposed to other senior members of the party – many of whom like Mao had an extensive record of military service or experience serving with the military – being given such a title.[58] As a result, only ten individuals, at the time all totally absorbed with PLA affairs, were given the title of marshal.

It is noteworthy that a soldier has never served as the chair of the CCP Central Military Commission (CMC). The most senior post with responsibility for military matters has always been occupied by the de facto or de jure paramount political leader of the day: Mao (1935–76), Hua Guofeng (1976–80), Deng (1981–November 1989), and Jiang Zemin (1989–present).

And top soldiers tended to be concentrated in certain functional areas and to remain distinct from nonmilitary career personnel. As William W. Whitson and Chen-Hsia Huang have noted, there are at least three identifiable functional elites in the Chinese communist movement: "military commanders," "party and government administrators," and "ideologues"; the third group refers to the propaganda bureaucracy.[59] Thus, even in a dual role format, soldiers and statesmen tended to be readily distinguishable.

Functional specialization of personnel existed at the highest level: Members of the Politburo serve as gateways *(kou)* each responsible for a specific functional bureaucratic system *(xitong)* in the party-state. One member supervises the legal/internal security system, another economics, another foreign affairs, another party organization, yet another propaganda and education, and still another military affairs. This distribution of portfolios within the highest echelon has been done since the earliest days of the PRC.[60]

Military men did not tend to serve as policymakers in functional areas outside of defense matters in the PRC – a tradition dating from the warlord era.[61] While the minister of national defense is by convention a career military officer, few senior soldiers have been appointed to serve in other functional spheres. A succession of soldiers have held the post of defense minister, including Marshals Peng, Lin Biao, Ye Jianying, and more recently General Chi Haotian. While soldiers have served as policymakers in the areas of public security and foreign affairs, they have remained largely absent from other spheres, most notably economic policy.[62] Thus, for example, Marshal Chen Yi served as minister of foreign affairs and Luo Ruiqing served as minister of public security.

Maoist Dual Role Elites

With the rise of the communist movement, a dual role civil-military format emerged in China.[63] Mao saw the essence of revolutionary war as the unity of the army with the people. He could see no reason why officers and enlisted men could not be meshed with the masses, and vice versa:

> There is a gap between the ordinary civilian and the soldier, but it is no Great Wall, and it can be quickly closed. . . . By saying that civilians can very quickly become soldiers, we mean it is not very difficult to cross the threshold.[64]

Chinese soldiers and statesmen over the centuries have regularly been difficult to differentiate from each other. Indeed, at times soldiers and statesmen have been one and the same. This fusion has been most apparent in the founding of a new dynasty. All imperial dynasties have come to power through force of arms, meaning that the first emperor has invariably been a general with considerable martial skills. Such a blurring of identities was also a feature of Mao's China and Deng's China.[65] According to two military researchers, in the pre-1949 era Deng himself was "a concentration of political and military expert all in one leader."[66] If the PRC is viewed as a new dynasty and Mao as the founding emperor, then it is no wonder he and his top lieutenants, including Deng, are difficult to label strictly military or civilian.

Such a situation is not unusual and had strong roots in Chinese history – leaders who excelled both in refined scholarly pursuits *and* in the art of war were highly esteemed.[67] The personification of this ideal blend of civil skills and martial prowess, *wenwu shuangquan*, is the mythical Yellow Emperor. And the Yellow Emperor is credited with being the founder of Chinese civilization – not just of proper violence, but strategy, organization, and ritual.[68] In this tradition, it was presumed that warfare was an art, and that a political ruler could master its strategic, organizational, technological, and ritualistic dimensions in addition to the civil affairs of state.

Post-Mao Functional Specialization

Under Deng, the emphasis shifted from continuing the revolution to moderniz-ing China. Two of the "Four Modernizations" identified by Deng were science and technology, and national defense. China's leaders desired a better-educated and more technologically competent PLA, one that would be better able to de-fend the country against the sophisticated and mechanized armies of China's adversaries and potential adversaries. This meant a stress on a more special-ized or professional military. Hence the civil-military format developed along functionally differentiated lines.

Political and military leaders tend to become differentiated and distinct when soldiering is viewed as a specialized endeavor requiring more education and training, as well as a career commitment.[69] While political and military elites are functionally separate, soldiers may continue to play major political roles without much hesitation.[70] Over time, however, attitudes change such that it becomes less acceptable for military men to play major political roles with-out first becoming "civilianized." That is, military men must demonstrate that their interests, skills, and frame of reference go beyond strictly defense matters.

It was in the Warring States period that the role of the general first became distinct from that of the statesman. Whereas before the Warring States era "there was no difference between those who commanded the state and those who commanded the army," during this period they became two separate elites.[71] This was the beginning of China's scholarly tradition of military affairs: strategic treatises, technical handbooks, and histories of campaigns of conquest and battles.

Civilianization

In the PRC, many soldiers became "civilianized," as they departed the PLA for civilian bureaucracies to focus on nonmilitary affairs.[72] New supreme political leaders in China who had attained political power through force of arms had long sought to legitimize their new positions by "civilianizing" themselves. That is, they sought to establish their credentials as civilian leaders, since civil affairs were considered far weightier than military matters. The founders of new dynasties and their successors sought to demonstrate their abilities as morally upright rulers, learned men, and skilled administrators. They would go to considerable lengths to "civilianize" themselves.[73] These leaders included twentieth century figures such as Chiang, Mao, and Deng.

Moreover, soldiers in any culture tend to have difficulty making good their claims to permanent political legitimacy.[74] This holds for China: A conquering general could not expect to retain the Mandate of Heaven until he had transformed himself into an upright civilian ruler who diligently administered the empire, performed all the appropriate rituals, and ensured the material and spiritual well-being of his subjects. While he was expected to be able to protect his people from external military threats and domestic insurrection and banditry, this was merely a portion of his larger duties. China's supreme leaders were also expected to be poets and philosophers. Mao, for example, wrote poetry and gave discourses on a wide variety of topics, which is reflected in the broad spectrum of subjects discussed in his *Selected Works*.

A prime candidate for civilianization is a potential successor as paramount leader – Deng being the case in point. Deng became sufficiently civilianized by the late 1950s that he was seen as a senior nonmilitary leader and a potential successor to Mao. Prior to the establishment of a proper central government in the early 1950s, Deng's career, like that of many other Communist Party leaders, had been centered for some three decades on the military. Deng served primarily – but not exclusively – as a political commissar, eventually attaining the position of first political commissar for the Second Field Army. After several years of working as an administrator in southwest China following the establishment of the PRC, he was summoned to Beijing to assume the posts of vice premier, vice chair of the Finance and Economic Committee, and member of the State Planning Commission. Deng then served as general secretary of the CCP Secretariat and director of the CCP Organization Department. In the early 1960s, Deng was selected as acting state premier before his purge in 1967. Deng's civilianization is evident in the classic study of the PLA by Whitson and Huang. Whereas in the 1920s and 1930s Deng was identified as a "military leader," by the late 1960s he was described as a "prominent party member."[75] In the mid-1970s, following his first rehabilitation, he was appointed PLA chief of General Staff. After a second purge, Deng was rehabilitated by Mao's successor, Hua, and he took advantage of the situation to engineer Hua's ouster and install himself as China's paramount political leader.

Deng's extensive military experience and his wide knowledge of defense matters are evident from the number of speeches devoted to PLA affairs in the second and third volumes of his selected works. Moreover, he was recognized as one of the thirty-three most "prominent military figures of the People's Liberation Army" in the military volume of the *Chinese Encyclopedia* published in late 1989.[76] Nevertheless, it is a tribute to the thoroughness of his transformation from soldier to civilian that a 1990s treatment of Deng's soldierly status tends to play down his military credentials.[77]

In short, one can usually distinguish between civilian and military leaders even during the dual role configuration of the Mao era. The civil-military divide, while not impermeable, tended to be accentuated by Mao, who remained sensitive to the potential for military domination of the party.

MILITARY LOYALTY AND IDENTITY

Loyalty is a critical dimension that both defines a soldier's identity and determines his obedience and motivation. The significance of loyalty in civil-military culture tends to be overlooked.[78] Loyalty is arguably the most highly valued trait in a soldier. A good soldier is a loyal one. The military man who is bonded to his comrades, devoted to his immediate superior, and pledged to a noble cause will possess good morale and perform well.[79]

Loyalty, however, is not singular – a soldier tends to have multiple objects of loyalty. It is useful to conceptualize a soldier's allegiance as possessing two components: a political element that is abstract and institutional, and a personal element that is proximate and particular. A soldier holds a higher alliance to a noble cause, entity, or individual superior, but also another more immediate loyalty to his or her military comrades, to a particular civilian, and/or to his or her military superior. Both types of loyalty tug on a modern soldier's heart and mind, and both must be firm for high morale, which is itself a precondition for the functioning of an effective military force. These loyalties, however, can either reinforce each other or compete.

This distinction regarding allegiances may become clearer when one considers the subject of combat motivation. Military officers and researchers have found that soldiers do not expose themselves to life-threatening situations simply out of a sense of patriotism. Rather, they perform acts of heroism largely because of the strong affinity they feel with their fellow soldiers and immediate military superiors. It is this emotional bond of comradeship or group loyalty that translates itself into unit cohesion and high morale that drives troops to commit acts of bravery and sacrifice.[80] Still, patriotism and/or allegiance to a noble cause or paramount leader is also important.[81] Thus, for soldiers to sustain military effectiveness, whether in combat or noncombat situations, both personal and political loyalties must not only be present but also fused.

Loyalty is a core aspect of a soldier's identity; to whom the armed forces owe allegiance is a key determinant of how the military views itself and is viewed by society. Is it the general's army or the emperor's army? Is it the party's army, or the people's army? An examination of the evolution of military loyalties underscores the predominance of personal over political allegiances throughout the broad sweep of Chinese history. Over the course of the twentieth century, however, political loyalties have become increasingly important.

Loyalty is considered an extremely important trait in Chinese political culture. Generation upon generation of Chinese revere Qu Yuan, an official and poet in the ancient state of Chu, as an "exemplar of political loyalty, [and] a paragon of public dedication."[82] Despite being wronged by his sovereign and ostracized by his state, he remained loyal to both. When calamity befell the kingdom, Qu committed suicide as the ultimate act of dedication.

PLA Soldiers and Loyalties

To what or whom do soldiers in the PRC owe their allegiance? The tendency among scholars has been to focus on the abstract political loyalties of a soldier. A soldier is ideally supposed to owe his paramount loyalty to the state, and most academic treatments stress a special relationship between the two, bordering on mythical proportions. Perhaps best exemplified by the title of Samuel Huntington's trailblazing book *The Soldier and the State*, this approach has dominated the literature, including the study of military politics in the PRC.[83] The fixation on this special relationship between the soldier and the state is understandable because it is the foundation upon which a soldier's "apolitical ness" is set: When a soldier owes loyalty to the state, he or she stands above the political fray. Rather than be bound to a particular political leader, party, or cause, a soldier has a sacred duty to uphold the sovereignty of the state.

Of course, under certain conditions, soldiers owe their allegiance to entities other than the state. Indeed soldiers may have "contradictory loyalties" – to a revolutionary movement, regime, ethnic group, tribe, nation, or the armed forces itself rather than to the state.[84] Nevertheless, for soldiers the most potent political loyalty in modern times has been nationalism. The state furnishes the soldier with both the focus of his loyalty and the resources with which to perform his duties. The rise of the centralized, bureaucratic state provided the soldier with a concrete entity with which he could readily identify and to which he could pledge his allegiance. In addition, the state provides the concentrated financial support, manpower, matériel, and direction required to develop and sustain a standing army. While scholars of civil-military relations disagree on many things, they are unanimous in the opinion that the one characteristic trait of the modern soldier is that he is highly nationalistic.[85]

Soldiers in communist states are generally seen as owing their primary allegiance to the communist party. In fact, since in these countries many high-level officials were also senior party members, they tend to function as the "party in uniform."[86] While the alignment of civil-military culture can vary from country to country, depending on factors such as whether the regime was established indigenously or not and the degree of unity within the party, the fundamental dynamic according to many experts is the nature of the army's allegiance to the party.[87]

Among scholars of the PLA, one group stresses its political loyalties, asserting the military owes its allegiance to the party (CCP),[88] the Chinese Revolution,[89] the state (PRC), or some combination thereof. Paul H.B. Godwin argues that PLA soldiers at times direct their loyalty toward the state, but usually owe their allegiance to the party.[90] This suggests there are competing loyalties.

A second group that studies PRC military politics emphasizes personal allegiances.[91] Some argue that shifting, factional groupings, which cross-cut civil-military boundaries, form the primary basis for military loyalties.[92] Others contend that officers channel their primary loyalties according to field army affiliations – bonds to comrades and superiors cemented during the prolonged military struggle prior to the establishment of the People's Republic in 1949.[93]

Personal Trumps Political

From the inception of the PLA, under its original name, the Worker's and Peasant's Red Army, the dominant principle stressed by party leaders was that the armed forces owed its complete loyalty to the CCP. There was no possibility for equality between the two or for military dominance over the party. Hence Mao insisted that "the Party commands the gun," and not vice versa. Given the country's long history of soldiers playing dominant political roles in Chinese affairs, it is not surprising that the principle of unquestioned loyalty of the army to the party has been stressed. Mao's admonishment is found in such key party documents as Deng's 1983 volume of selected works, and in the 1981 resolution reassessing CCP history.[94] Such repetition typically provokes the question: "How loyal is the army to the party?" A more appropriate and useful question may be: "To whom in the party does the army owe its loyalty?"[95] This question essentially recognizes the distinction between the loyalty a soldier might feel toward "the party" as a political entity and any personal allegiances the same soldier might hold. Indeed, the principle of unquestioned loyalty and obedience of the PLA to the CCP was never institutionalized, and military loyalty to the party has remained heavily dependent on the loyalties of individual soldiers to the paramount political leader: first Mao, then Deng, and later Jiang.

Historically in China the strongest military loyalties are based on personalistic ties of kinship, geographic locale, or military service. Soldiers in the armies of imperial China tended to owe their strongest allegiance to individual commanders. Their political loyalty to the emperor or an entity called "China" was far weaker. These "soldiers belonged to the generals" *(bing wei jiang you)* rather than to the emperor.[96]

The establishment of new Western-style regional armies in the late 1800s resulted in stronger bonds of loyalty within each army and deeper provincial loyalties. The armies of Li Hongzhang, Zeng Guofan, and Zuo Zongtang were militia forces in the tradition of peasant armies assembled to meet a temporary emergency, rather than modern-style standing armies. While commanders of these forces were all imperial civilian officials who obeyed instructions from the throne, nevertheless, a soldier's strongest bond of loyalty continued to be to his immediate superior. The militia forces raised by imperial officials, such as Li, have been aptly described as "semi-personal,"[97] since their primary allegiance lay with their creators and commanders, but formally they were soldiers of the emperor and fought in that capacity. Thus, as Chinese historian Wang Erh-min argued, it is wrong to consider the Xiang and Huai as merely regional armies.[98] Still, commanders such as Li deliberately promoted a "narrow personal loyalty" among their subordinates, which effectively sabotaged efforts to build a nationwide military with a sense of allegiance to the whole country.[99]

The Rise of Modern Military Academies

Provincial Western-style military and naval academies attracted students from across China and also managed to instill gradually among soldiers a nascent sense of identification with the nation. These schools became hotbeds of nationalistic activity. Prior to the establishment of these academies, there was little sense of Chinese nationalism. Out of this growing feeling of patriotism to the Chinese nation grew a sense of dedication to a Chinese revolution and vanguard political party: the Tung Meng Hui or Revolutionary Alliance, then the KMT, and later the CCP. These burgeoning political loyalties often fused with personal loyalties to individual political and military leaders serving as mutual reinforcers. As a result the armed forces of the KMT and CCP became more politically reliable than their Chinese predecessors. Nevertheless, personal allegiances continued to dominate.

Whampoa Academy. In 1924, when Sun, the frustrated leader of the KMT, spoke of the unfulfilled promise of the revolution and the scourge of warlordism, he concluded that the Chinese revolution had failed so miserably because it lacked a loyal army.[100] With the assistance and encouragement of Soviet advisors and his eager protégé Chiang, Sun sought to rectify this deficiency by establishing the Whampoa Military Academy *(Huangpu junxiao)* in May 1924 in an isolated locale some fifteen miles from Guangzhou on the grounds of former army and navy schools. The establishment of the Whampoa Academy represented the last-ditch effort of Sun's Republican government to build real state power and authority. Sun realized, especially after talks with Soviet representatives, that to establish any kind of authority and power, the state had to have its own military force that owed complete loyalty to the KMT. Reliance on warlord armies proved a fiasco and Sun's government exerted control only in the area around Guangzhou. The academy was based on the Bolshevik model and was heavily influenced by the Soviet Union, and Soviet aid and expertise were critical to the establishment and initial development of the institution.

The aim of the Whampoa Academy was to provide the KMT with a well-trained, dedicated, and politically indoctrinated military arm to implement the will of the party. What distinguished Whampoa – and its successor institution, the Central Military Academy – from earlier Chinese academies, even the modern Baoding schools of Yuan Shikai, was its emphasis on "spiritual and ideological education" *(jingshen jiaoyu).*[101] "Politically indoctrinated armies," as John K. Fairbank noted, "were a new thing in modern China."[102] In addition to training, drilling, and instruction in activities traditionally considered military matters, and academic courses in "revolutionary warfare," politics, economics and propaganda were offered.[103] Cadets also were indoctrinated with Kuomintang ideology: Sun's "Three Principles of the People" *(sanminzhuyi).* They were taught to believe a proper spirit and organization were essential – a selfless dedication to the Chinese people and the revolution. In short, in addition to receiving technical training, cadets were instilled with a patriotic mission: to unify and modernize China under the Kuomintang.[104] At Whampoa and its successor KMT and CCP institutions, messianic Chinese nationalism became the dominant theme. This was true from the start, when Sun told Whampoa cadets that they were the saviors of the nation and the vanguard of a new party-army – a nucleus that would rescue the floundering Chinese revolution.[105]

In terms of political indoctrination, KMT military education had much in common with communist military education. Both condemned warlords and imperialists and appealed to nationalist sentiments to motivate students to realize the Chinese Revolution. While this ideological training was an important element in the success of the Northern Expedition, this propagandizing work proved more significant later when employed by the PLA with the invaluable experience they had gained as expedition participants. Though the Northern Expedition was primarily a military victory rather than a political one,[106] the military victory was made possible by political indoctrination of officers and troops of the National Revolutionary Army who believed they were in the service of a great cause and should act accordingly. They were an army of the people and should serve the people and treat them decently and humanely.[107] This image predates communist propaganda about the PLA and was an important model for the latter.[108]

But more potent than the dedication to a cause or larger entity – the Chinese Revolution and a vanguard revolutionary party, the KMT – were the dominant personal allegiances to Sun, Chiang, and each other. While the Whampoa Academy was a landmark development for civil-military relations in China, its graduates' primary loyalties remained personal ones. Sun was named the nominal president *(zongli)* of the Whampoa Academy, but the day-to-day administration of the school was to be divided between Chiang, the military commandant, and Liao Zhongkai, the party representative. Despite the formal division of labor, in practice Liao was absent much of the time and served in this position only for fifteen months until his death in August 1925. He gave only half a dozen lectures to Whampoa cadets and constituted a "symbolic" presence at the academy.[109] As a result, much of the power and responsibility for the day-to-day running of the school fell into the hands of Chiang. His influence was everywhere. It was Chiang who constantly lectured and admonished the cadets, and it was Chiang to whom many increasingly looked for leadership and inspiration in military as well as political instruction.[110] His influence remained pervasive at the academy even after its move to Nanjing.[111]

Moreover, the 7,399 cadets in the five classes that graduated from the Whampoa Academy between 1924 and 1927[112] established strong bonds of personal loyalty to their classmates. Whampoa cadets were instilled with a strong sense of esprit de corps that has been called the "Whampoa spirit." This feeling of camaraderie or corporateness was highlighted by the school motto: "love your comrades with the utmost sincerity" *(qinai jingcheng)*.[113] Whampoa faculty members and graduates who later became top CCP civilian and military leaders included Zhou Enlai, Ye Jianying, Lin Biao, and Xu Xiangqian.

Although the Whampoa Academy preached political loyalties, it tended to transmit personal ones. In the final analysis, while the rhetoric was of selfless dedication to the Chinese people, in practice the stress was on proximate loyalties to fellow cadets and military superiors. For all of Chiang's talk of noble principles, and similar assertions by cadets, Chiang's message was absolute loyalty to your leader, and the students' unflinching loyalty was directly to him, based on Chiang's "indefinable force of personal magnetism."[114]

From Mao's Army to Jiang's Army?

The collapse of KMT–CCP cooperation in 1927 deprived the communists of a formal military academy. Only dogged determination by key CCP leaders ensured that their military establishment continued to train loyal and competent soldiers. Once again, personal loyalties were stronger than political ones, but, unlike in the past, these tended to complement each other. The Anti-Japanese War and the unity of the CCP leadership greatly contributed to this fusing of loyalties.

Even with declarations of nationalism and dedication to serving the people of China, it was personal loyalties that were of paramount importance to members of the PLA. Of the three main military ethics identified by Whitson and Huang as influencing the Chinese communist military elite, two – the "Warlord" and the "Peasant" ethics – heavily stressed personal loyalties to colleagues and superiors with no attention to political ones. Only one, the "Russian" ethic, emphasized a more abstract or institutional loyalty – to the communist party. According to one early communist leader, Zhang Guotao, during the difficult days of the 1920s, soldiers such as Peng Dehuai, He Long, and Zhu De were "motivated more by personal loyalty than by consideration of ideology . . . ." A Chinese soldier, according to Whitson and Huang, had a "disdain for any authority beyond his immediate chain of command," and "a personal interpretation of obligations and loyalty characterized every military organization . . . ."[115]

The CCP did not establish a worthy successor institution to the Whampoa Academy until 1937, when the Anti-Japanese Political and Military University, or *Kangda*, opened in the communist capital of Yanan. While temporary training schools had been set up in various locations, a proper Red Army academy was not established until 1936. *Kangda* was formally inaugurated the following January and soon became the most important educational institution for the instruction of both civilian and military communist officials.[116] Many key communist figures served in leadership positions at *Kangda*. Mao served as chairman of the education department, Lin served as the principal of *Kangda*, Luo served as vice-principal and political commissar (and as acting head during Lin's many absences), and Zhu was a member of the faculty.[117]

Indeed it is the deep bonds of loyalty many soldiers personally felt toward senior party figures like Mao and Zhou forged over years of direct contact, shared hardships, and habits of obedience that reinforced and made more tangible the abstract principle of military allegiance to the party. But when conflicts arose among top party leaders, then competing personal loyalties called political loyalties into question. The dilemma was even greater when senior military leaders with substantial loyalty networks within the PLA clashed with senior party leaders.

In terms of personal loyalties, PLA officers owed allegiance to particular military leaders, often superiors they had served under for decades in the same field armies. These men also felt strong bonds of loyalty to certain civilian leaders who also had served in military capacities, often as political commissars in these same armies. But until the 1970s these conflicting personal loyalties were subsumed by an overriding personal allegiance to paramount leader Mao. After Mao's death, these bonds of loyalty were eventually transferred to Deng, who dominated China's politics from the late 1970s until his incapacitation in the mid-1990s (and subsequent death in 1997).[118] Deng's successor, Jiang, seemed to command the loyalty of most PLA leaders, although these ties were not as strong as those enjoyed by either Mao or Deng.[119]

Perhaps a good indication that soldiers transferred their loyalty from Mao to Deng is that the only confirmed episode of praetorianism occurred during the interregnum. I refer to the military-initiated and -implemented coup d'etat of October 1976 against the Gang of Four.[120] The ouster of the paramount political leader who presided over China, Hua, by Deng barely two years after Hua's accession, further highlights the fact that Hua proved unable to gain the unwavering loyalty of PLA leaders. Hua holds the distinction of being the only one of four paramount leaders in the more than fifty years of PRC history to be deposed. Deng emerged as the new paramount leader in large part because he could build on existing loyalty networks not just from his experience in the party and state bureaucracies but also from his extensive service in the armed forces.

Following the Tiananmen Square massacre in 1989, China's leaders appeared to be, on the one hand, ignoring the problem of conflicting loyalties while on the other hand unwittingly exacerbating it.

Two instances highlight this predicament. First, Deng, in November 1989, after stepping down from his last formal political post as chair of the CMC, blithely urged Chinese soldiers to pledge their loyalty to four distinct entities. He told senior PLA officers, "Our Army is an army of the party, the socialist state, and the people which should always remain loyal to the party, the state, socialism, and the people."[121] In the Long Marcher's mind, the four elements were synonymous, but to some PLA members they represent different and possibly competing allegiances. The essence of Deng's statement has also been repeated by then PLA Chief of General Staff Chi Haotian.[122]

Second, the National Defense Law, approved by the Fifth Session of the Eighth National People's Congress (NPC) in March 1997, focused almost exclusively on the role of the state and state institutions in controlling and providing for China's armed forces. This legislation, promulgated by the NPC a month after Deng's death (in February 1997), stressed the roles of the State Central Military Commission, the State Council, and the NPC, but only mentions the "leadership" of the Chinese Communist Party once (in Article 19).[123] This legislative "footnote" was given special emphasis a month later (in April 1997) at a high-level conference of military and civilian leaders. Chi, minister of national defense, vice chair of the CMC, and chair of the committee that drafted the Law on National Defense, gave the keynote speech stressing the importance of CCP leadership of the PLA. Apparently, Chi, like the late Deng, saw no obvious conflict between military obedience to the state and to the party.[124]

However, there is implicit official acknowledgment that there are PLA soldiers who have multiple loyalties of both the personal and political variety. This much is evident from articles in the mainland press. Perhaps the most blatant was a commentary in the *Liberation Army Daily* in late 1992. The unsigned piece was entitled "The Army Should Obey the Party." The article not only cited Mao's admonishment on the importance of the party commanding the gun and not vice versa, but also quoted Deng reiterating Mao's statement. The commentary went on to emphasize specifically that the PLA should obey the Central Committee and the CMC, and identified Jiang as the key individual to which the army should be loyal.[125] Such statements imply, of course, that there are other entities and individuals to which soldiers might pledge their allegiance.

The most obvious implication, in political terms, was that the PLA could shift the main focus of its loyalty to itself or the state, rationalizing that the army or state, better than the CCP, represents the best interests of the country. As the PLA developed a sense of its own history, tradition, and institutional interests, soldiers felt a growing sense of allegiance to their units, branch of service, and the military as a whole. This development created a loyalty that could compete and even conflict with a soldier's allegiance to the CCP or the PRC. Indeed, historically the standing army was the earliest form of government bureaucracy – a distinct and specialized administrative structure more institutionalized than previous military organizations. Hence, as Max Weber observed, soldiers were the "pioneers in organization of the modern type of bureaucracy."[126] The officer corps represented the prototype of the new officials emerging to staff the state bureaucracies, which acquired vested interests and often instilled strong organizational loyalties on the part of their members.

There has also been a strong groundswell within the PLA in the 1990s to make it an army of the state rather than an army of the party. Pressure for "nationalization" or "statification" *(guojiahua)* is evident from the continuous propaganda barrages condemning the idea and insisting that the PLA must remain the party's army.[127] In terms of personal loyalties, military personnel could decide they owe greater allegiance to other individuals within the party or army than to Deng's designated heir.

Nevertheless, there were signs that Chinese soldiers increasingly thought of themselves as loyal to Jiang. By the first decade of the twenty-first century, virtually all the top brass owed their appointments to Jiang. Jiang has also made a point of cultivating the PLA's rank and file, seeking to depict himself as the champion of the common soldier. Reportedly very concerned that ordinary soldiers get good food and amenities, Jiang visited military installations in all seven of China's military regions at least once.[128] And Jiang used the 1995–6 Taiwan Strait Crisis to bolster his standing further among the troops. Certainly, at the outset, the army was the most enthusiastic constituency urging that China make a strong show of force (see Chapter 8), and initially the crisis had the effect of highlighting Jiang's lack of military credentials. But Jiang shrewdly turned the situation to his advantage and used it as an opportunity to play to the hilt his role as commander-in-chief of China's armed forces. During the air and naval exercises of October 1995 off the coast of Fujian, for example, Jiang manned the bridge of the PLA Navy command vessel for three hours observing joint air and sea maneuvers. Thus the crisis provided the equivalent of a baptism of fire for China's putative paramount leader and had the effect of raising his stature within the military.[129]

Changing Modes of Influence

In the early 1950s and to a lesser extent in the 1960s and 1970s, the dual role elites in the PRC made their views known in direct, informal discussions in closed meetings. There was little or no public debate or discussion. By contrast, military leaders of the 1990s made their case more vocally, energetically, and in very visible ways. In the past, holding positions at the highest levels of political power – the Politburo and Politburo Standing Committee – and functioning as both party and army leaders, these senior soldiers made their views known in "smoke-filled rooms." Today, with the passing of the Long March generation, the military elite is more separate and distinct from the civilian elite. The passing of this older generation is underlined by the deaths of Deng in 1997 and Yang Shangkun in 1998, and the retirement of Liu Huaqing (b. 1916) from his posts on the Politburo Standing Committee and Central Military Commission in 1997. PLA leaders increasingly make their views known through lobbying by their military representatives in the National People's Congress, in letters to top political leaders, and in books, journal articles, and newspaper opinion pieces.[130] In short, the PLA has become more of a formal bureaucratic actor.[131] While to a considerable degree the most outspoken generals identified in this study have been from the older generation, the voices of a new generation also have been heard – a prime example being Deputy Chief of General Staff Xiong Guangkai (b. 1939).

In sum, historically Chinese armies have identified themselves in terms of allegiance to a particular civilian or military leader. As the twentieth century progressed and while personal loyalties remained strong, Chinese soldiers increasingly defined themselves in terms of political allegiances.

FUNCTION: MULTIDIMENSIONAL MILITARY MISSIONS

The readiness of an army to take on various functions is influenced by the types of missions it has had historically and the traditional duties an army has shouldered. Most armies have had important domestic duties as well as responsibility for defense against foreign foes, but over time other bodies assumed the primary responsibility for domestic missions. Internal security, for example, was taken over by national police and/or paramilitary organizations. In the PRC, this transformation did not take place until the 1980s. However, even after these transfers of responsibilities, militaries tend to retain a support function in the event of serious civil unrest.

In China the dualities of internal security and external defense, and combat and noncombat missions, reflect the influence of tradition and the impact of the functional imperative. Chinese troops have rarely been deployed beyond China's borders for long. While military expeditions have been launched and wars waged at the farthest reaches of the empire, soldiers were not garrisoned abroad. The system of tributary states obviated this need. Of course, in some periods of dynastic decline or weakness, China did not have the capability to launch expeditions or wage wars anyway. This was true for the latter part of the Qing, as well as for the Republican era. Prior to 1950, the PLA had "no horizon beyond Chinese territory." And, even after this, the "consistent focus [was] . . . on the application of military force either within or on the immediate periphery of China's borders."[132] In Mao's day, the PLA "devoted its best energies to internal problems."[133]

There has long been an important internal dimension to the security mission of the Chinese armed forces, as well as what are, strictly speaking, nonmilitary duties. Without effective, well-trained police forces, the army automatically took up the responsibility for internal security. Moreover, Chinese armies have long performed social, cultural, and economic tasks. In Ming China, for example, soldiers cultivated their own food.[134] And in Qing times, the Armies of the Green Standard served as escorts for state property in transit, protected government buildings, delivered the imperial post, and served as a ready pool of labor for state construction projects.[135] This tradition continued in Mao's China, as, in addition to being "a fighting force," soldiers were called upon to be "a working force, a production force, a propaganda force.... [and a force for] doing mass [political] work."[136]

The legacy was reenergized under Deng.[137] The PLA was encouraged to become a greater economic force; to compensate for the shortfall in defense outlays, Chinese soldiers became free market entrepreneurs. The military was heavily involved in the production of key civilian consumer items such as motorcycles and refrigerators. The PLA managed hotels, restaurants, and nightclubs all for profit and targeted at civilian customers. The Chinese military was also active in the international arms trade with clear bias toward deals that earned significant amounts of foreign exchange.[138]

A concerted effort was under way early in the post-Deng era to divest the PLA of its business empire. President Jiang issued a directive in mid-1998 ordering the PLA and People's Armed Police (PAP) to end their commercial activities. The directive appeared to have the support of the PLA's most senior generals.[139] It was a controversial directive that proved extremely difficult to enforce.[140] But there appeared to have been a consensus among senior civilian and military leaders that these business ventures were detracting from the PLA's combat-readiness. While a valuable source of extrabudgetary income, such ventures bred corruption and PLA involvement in other illegal activities, notably smuggling. The key issue for the military almost certainly was how it would be compensated for this loss of income. Premier Zhu Rongji reportedly assured the military members of the CMC that this loss would be offset by an increase in the defense budget.[141] The defense budgets did rise but initially not as steeply as the PLA or outside analysts had anticipated. A large rise eventually came in March 2001, when the biggest annual increase in defense spending in more than a decade – 17.7 percent – was announced.[142]

Diminishing Domestic Missions

In the early years of state building, an army plays an especially significant role in domestic affairs. This is because other institutions of state power have yet to be established. Thus the army is often called upon to carry out a broad variety of basic tasks at the state's behest. However, as time goes on, new, larger, bureaucracies develop in response to specific challenges or problems faced by the state. These departments, bureaus, and other apparati of state control tend to be charged with specific missions and responsibility for particular spheres of activity. While the military was for many years a catchall force to implement state policies, its domestic duties were gradually taken over by other organs.

Army, Police, and Paramilitary

Important factors curtailing internal security functions for the military were the creation of public security and paramilitary organizations. According to one scholar, "Of all the numerous changes in civil–military relations in the nineteenth century, the most important was the establishment of police forces."[143] Perhaps the most important development of the twentieth century was the widespread proliferation of paramilitary units in countries around the globe.[144] While many countries seem to follow a similar trajectory in the development of a security apparatus, the rate of change can vary widely according to specific national contexts and conditions.[145]

Morris Janowitz has documented a dramatic increase in the number and size of paramilitary forces, most notably national police forces, in many countries between the mid-1960s and mid-1970s.[146] The purpose of these formations is primarily to control civil unrest, relieving the regular military from frontline responsibility for this distasteful mission. A major concern driving the establishment of paramilitary organs was the radicalization of student protest in many countries during the 1960s.[147]

By the late twentieth century, most states possessed three main types of coercive forces with a division of labor for internal security functions.[148] First, the local police are on the frontline of the mission to ensure basic day-to-day law and order throughout the land. Second are paramilitary forces, composed of national police forces and militias, with special responsibility for dealing with civil unrest.

The third component of a state's coercive apparatus is the regular armed forces, whose principal focus is defense against external enemies. These military formations of the state can be further divided, according to their level of war-readiness and areas of responsibility, into active duty forces and reserve forces. Active duty units are composed of full-time soldiers who are kept at a high state of combat-readiness, with their overarching mission being to defend against foreign threats. In the event of serious civil disturbances, however, such units constitute the last resort of civil authorities. In contrast to active duty units, reserve force units – which may or may not be staffed by full-time soldiers – are at a much lower state of combat-readiness and can be used for either foreign or domestic missions. While reserve forces are part and parcel of a country's armed forces, they can be mobilized to wage war against the armies of other states, to handle domestic unrest, revolt, and natural disasters, or even to participate in economic construction work.

The Chinese Military and Internal Security

The main responsibility for domestic security in imperial China fell to the military forces. Indeed maintaining public order was an important part of their mission. Modern-style police forces were not established in China until the first decade of the twentieth century. Police forces did exist in large cities prior to this, but they functioned under direct military auspices. The numerous, well-organized and -deployed police in Qing dynasty Beijing, for example, were closely supervised by officials of the Manchu Banners or Armies of the Green Standard.[149]

Qing military forces were garrisoned throughout the empire to serve primarily a police function: They were used in bandit suppression and to put down rebellions.[150] And the Qing navy's raison d'être was combating piracy. There were some impressive large-scale antipirate campaigns; however, generally the navy served as a coastal force, and piracy tended to be met by evacuation of the population of coastal areas.[151]

When Green Standard forces and the Manchu Banners proved largely useless against the most serious nineteenth century revolts, local imperial officials took the initiative to recruit and train militia armies that were better drilled, disciplined, equipped, and led. These new armies, which adopted piecemeal elements of Western armies, including drills and weapons, proved generally quite effective in suppressing rebellion. The most significant of these were the Xiang Army of Zeng (established in 1853), the Chu Army of Zuo (established in 1860), and the Huai Army of Li (established in 1862). These militia forces replaced the Banners and the Green Standard Armies as the "regular army of China."[152] The armies of Zeng, Zuo, and Li were the first to adopt in any systematic fashion Western elements in the Chinese military mainstream.

Modern-style police forces and paramilitary organs were developed under Yuan and Chiang.[153] As was the case in many other countries, many of the police officers in Republican China were former soldiers. Yuan, for example, took entire military units and established police forces with them – a trend that continued under the KMT and CCP. Modern police forces existed mostly in urban centers, first established in cities such as Beijing, Baoding, Tianjin, and Shanghai,[154] and rural areas had to rely on peasant militias, private armies, or the presence of national troops. It was under the KMT that China first attained what could be called a nationwide police force. Although a Department of Police Administration *(Jingzheng bu)* was created in the last years of the Qing dynasty, this organ did not assume much central administrative control until the late 1920s, when it became part of the KMT Ministry of the Interior. Chiang was avidly interested in police matters, and in 1935 a proper Central Police Academy *(Zhongyang jingguan xuexiao)* was formally established. Despite the existence of these law enforcement organs, since military conflict was a constant affliction of the Republican era, particularly in the final decades – the Anti-Japanese War (1937–45) or Civil War with the CCP (1927–36 and 1946–9) – the KMT military retained substantial overall responsibility for domestic order.

With the establishment of the PRC in 1949, the PLA assumed basic responsibility for maintaining law and order across China. However, with the exceptions of the early 1950s and the decade following the launching of the Cultural Revolution, the public security bureaus (PSBs) were charged with basic day-to-day policing activities. The KMT police apparatus was coopted by the communists, but most former Nationalist officials were eventually ousted. Gradually during the 1950s, sizeable numbers of troops were demobilized, and some staffed the PSBs that had been established across the land. These men underwent little if any training for their new jobs. While overall the Ministry of Public Security (MPS) in Beijing maintained supervision, there was loose central control, and provincial and local PSBs came under the control of regional, county, or municipal authorities.

For most of this era, the public security apparatus remained a significant arm of state power. However, public order was assured less by the PSB than by self-policing efforts of the local populace, carried out in cities by residents' committees *(jumin weiyuanhui)* and in rural areas by militia. Each was supervised by PSB organs and backed by the PLA. The police function was considered so basic that little or no special training was necessary. Little thought was given to having the possible need for specialized units or organs at the national level. Although the PRC had a feared secret police under the leadership of Kang Sheng, the victims of its surveillance and repression were elites, not ordinary

Chinese.[155] For the first three decades of its existence, the PRC did not develop a Chinese version of the Soviet Committee for State Security (KGB) or Ministry of the Interior (MVD).

Throughout the first three decades of the PRC, the PLA was considered the bedrock guarantor of public order. In addition to having the mission of protecting the country against external threats, the army had a domestic mission. According to an article in the March 27, 1990, issue of *Liberation Army Daily*:

> The Army of any country . . . [is] an important component part of state power and must perform its dual functions in dealing with external and domestic affairs. . . . [The PLA] . . . must perform the following two functions: guarding against and resisting aggression by external enemies, and defending the security and territorial integrity of the state; preventing subversion by the hostile forces to safeguard the peaceful labor of the people, and give peace and stability to our country. . . . [A]lthough the external functions of our Army are essential, its domestic functions are also very important.[156]

In fact, according to article 29 of the 1982 PRC state constitution, the duties of the PLA are not just "to strengthen national defense, resist aggression, [and] defend the motherland," but also to "safeguard the people's peaceful labor, participate in national reconstruction, and work hard to serve the people."

This internal security mission fell largely to the PLA's regional forces, freeing main force units to concentrate on external threats to China's security. For regional forces, internal security was "one of their primary duties since 1949."[157] The regional PLA units, which were controlled and continue to be controlled by regional military commanders, are lightly armed, trained only sporadically, and maintained at a low level of combat-preparedness. These included the PLA Security Army, charged with maintaining domestic order, which had briefly been controlled by the MPS.[158] Aside from their internal security mission, regional forces are often involved in construction projects, agriculture, and other "nonmilitary" pursuits. Main force PLA units, which are directly under the command structure of the Central Military Commission and the General Staff Department, are, by contrast, well armed, well trained, and combat-ready.

After the chaos of the Cultural Revolution, during which the effectiveness of the PSBs proved generally abysmal, the issue of the most appropriate way to maintain domestic law and order underwent serious reappraisal. Following months of unrest in 1966 and 1967, basic law and order collapsed as PSB organs were unable to cope with the turmoil. The People's Police Army – the reincarnation of the PLA Security Army of 1950 – was responsible for trying to restore order. The force was under the control of the PLA's Second

Artillery,[159] underlining the military's perceived responsibility for ensuring domestic order. The People's Police Army could not fulfill this function, as the body itself was racked by internal divisions and not trained or equipped to handle civil unrest, let alone the pitched battles waged between well-armed rival Red Guard groups. The PLA was the only force up to the task and was charged with restoring and then maintaining order.

Only in the Deng era did Beijing finally establish distinct specialized national-level internal security organs. The PRC's first truly national police force, the People's Armed Police (PAP) *(Renmin wuzhuang jingcha)*, was organized in the early 1980s. Although a paramilitary force existed since 1949, its mission was vague, it did not have much of an identity separate or distinct from the PLA or MPS, nor did it have a separate chain of command. According to Tai Ming Cheung, between 1949 and 1972 the PAP's precursor entity switched operational responsibility between the MPS and PLA a total of six times, with a corresponding number of name changes. These changes represent not only an ongoing bureaucratic turf war but also a schizophrenic approach toward the appropriateness of the PLA holding such responsibilities. In its 1983 incarnation, the PAP was placed under military control but under the operational oversight of the MPS. Shortly thereafter, the government also established a Ministry of State Security (MSS) *(Guojia anquan bu)*.[160] The mission of the former was to take up the internal security role previously held by the PLA.[161] A senior PAP official explained that the PLA and PAP are: "both armed forces of the state but they have a division of labor. The PLA is responsible for the exterior. The Armed Police is responsible for internal security."[162]

Actually the officers and ranks of the PAP are composed primarily of former soldiers. Entire army units switched emblems and uniforms and became PAP as part of the much hyped one million strong cut of the PLA during the mid-1980s. At first the force was composed of guard details and "economic construction" units.[163] Elements of the PAP were trained and equipped for riot control duty. Others took responsibility for frontier patrols, passport inspection, and the security of foreign diplomatic missions and key government buildings and institutions.[164] In the late 1980s and early 1990s, the PAP was mobilized to deal with unrest in rural and/or remote areas such as Tibet, Qinghai, and Xinjiang. Units were also used to combat organized crime and the smuggling of narcotics and weapons in Yunnan.[165] The PAP was also called up for crowd control duty in Beijing in May 1989. Significantly, in Tibet, Qinghai, and Beijing, the performance of PAP units was at best slightly deficient and at worst, as in the case of Beijing, incompetent and ineffective. In all these places, intervention by the PLA was also required. The MSS, meanwhile, was charged with counterintelligence duties, including surveillance of foreigners living in China.[166]

Thus, the PRC did not witness the proliferation of a differentiated and specialized internal security apparatus that developed in the Soviet Union and other communist states until the 1980s – decades after the communist state was founded.[167] Paradoxically, this occurred not in the Maoist era when China was considered by some to be a more authoritarian – if not totalitarian – state, but during a period of reform and liberalization.[168]

Despite the establishment of these new coercive organs, the PLA still retains ultimate responsibility for domestic order in times of crisis. In the aftermath of June 4, 1989, military and civilian leaders have stressed that the PLA has a legitimate domestic role. In early 1991, State Council Spokesperson Yuan Mu, reportedly speaking on behalf of State President Yang Shangkun, told a veteran American journalist that the PLA has important domestic missions. Apart from actively participating in social projects and economic construction, the army also had a basic responsibility to ensure the "state's security and social stability." Yuan noted that the PLA now serves a backup function, with day-to-day law and order remaining the primary responsibility of the police.[169]

The press continued to stress the importance of the PLA's domestic responsibilities in a crisis. According to a 1990 article in *Liberation Army Daily*:

> Under general conditions, public security cadres and policemen and the Armed Police Forces undertake the task of maintaining stability and normal social order. There is no need for us to use the Army. However, once serious turmoil occurs, and especially when counter-revolutionary rebellion happens, the social order is undermined, and our state power is seriously threatened. When this problem cannot be solved by simply relying on public security forces and legal and administrative means, the Army must be directly used.[170]

Three months later in a front-page article in the same army newspaper, then Chief of General Staff Chi referred to the "dual functions" of the PLA.[171] The commanders of two military regions also stressed these same domestic responsibilities in mid-1992. In separate articles in the same issue of *People's Forum*, Commander Fu Quanyou of the Lanzhou Military Region and Commander Gu Gui of the Nanjing Military Region stressed the importance of the army in guaranteeing domestic order and fulfilling its constitutional responsibility to "safeguard the people's peaceful labor."[172]

In mid-1992 the CMC reportedly issued regulations governing the conduct of soldiers in dealing with domestic unrest. These instructions addressed matters of basic discipline and deportment and aimed to improve soldiers' knowledge of military regulations and civilian laws. They also outlined the appropriate steps that units of the armed forces should follow before opening fire on civilians.[173] Laws promulgated in the late 1990s – the Law on Martial Law (1996), the National Defense Law (1997), and the Defense White Papers of 1998 and 2000 – indicate that, in the eyes of China's senior leaders, the military retains critical responsibility for internal security. The PLA has a key role either as the backup to the PAP or as frontline troops in a particularly acute crisis.[174]

Certainly China's political leadership hopes to avoid domestic deployment of the PLA to deal with future protests, but it remains prepared to do so as a last resort; the PLA has established and trained rapid response units also drilled in riot control tactics. Indeed, PLA troops have been employed to deal with domestic disturbances in recent years. A case in point was in February 2000, when the PAP proved ineffective for dealing with unemployed miners in Yangjiazhangzi, Liaoning Province, and the PLA had to be called in.[175]

Meanwhile the PAP has been revamped. PAP manpower has doubled (from about half a million), it has been placed firmly under the control of the Central Military Commission, and its funding has increased substantially. Indeed, the PAP's budget in 1990 alone was almost 50 percent higher than in 1989, with most of the increase going to purchase nonlethal riot control equipment. The PAP's manpower and budget continued to grow throughout the 1990s.[176]

CONCLUSION

An overview of Chinese political culture reveals a fluctuating attitude toward the military: At times the soldier has enjoyed a positive image, while during other times the soldier has held a poor one. An analysis of Chinese civil-military culture also reveals a pattern in frequent flux. Military doctrine, format, identity, and function in China have also fluctuated over time. These changes indicate a complex but generally coherent civil-military culture.

In the Maoist era, the doctrine of People's War served as the linchpin for the entire civil-military culture. People's War highlighted the dual role concept: the crucial importance of a soldier's loyalty to the party and its leader, and the extramilitary roles for the PLA so that the army would serve as a boon to the people rather than a burden.

In the Deng era, People's War was gradually replaced with "People's War under Modern Conditions," and then by the concept of "Limited War." While these changes did make significant breaks with People's War, PLA doctrine was largely in flux during the late 1970s and for most of the 1980s.[177] In the post-Deng era, on the threshold of the twenty-first century, "Limited War under High-Technology Conditions" became the PLA's doctrine. The stress has been on elite forces that could wage war beyond China's borders.

Era	MAO	DENG	POST-DENG
Doctrine	PEOPLE S WAR	PEOPLE S WAR UNDER MODERN CONDITIONS/ LIMITED WAR	LIMITED WAR UNDER HIGH-TECHNOLOGY CONDITIONS
Format	EVERYONE A SOLDIER	ELITE TROOPS	ELITE TROOPS
Identity Who s army?	PARTY S ARMY/ MAO S ARMY	PARTY S ARMY/ DENG S ARMY	PARTY S ARMY?/ JIANG S ARMY?
What Kind of army?	RED	RED AND EXPERT	EXPERT (AND RED?)
Function	DOMESTIC, NONCOMBAT	FOREIGN/DOMESTIC COMBAT/NONCOMBAT	FOREIGN, COMBAT

Figure 1. Dominant Themes in Civil-Military Culture in China since 1949.

An examination of format reveals that the Long March conception of communist leadership is somewhat misleading and outdated. In Mao's day, the emphasis in format was on unity and overlap between the military and society, captured by the slogan "everyone a soldier." But even then, at the elite level there tended to be separate career paths for military and nonmilitary leaders. Moreover, unwritten but implicit rules of the game were in place to limit the potential for military figures to dominate the party-state. By the 1990s, in place of the permeability of the line between soldier and civilian and a mass army, the PLA stressed a clear divide and a relatively small, superbly conditioned force of elite troops *(jingbing)* who are equipped with the most technologically sophisticated weapons (see Figure 1).[178]

The PLA's identity in the Mao era was inseparable from total obedience to the CCP. This is illustrated by the preoccupation with "redness" (that is, complete loyalty to the party) and the corresponding dismissal of "expertise." While Deng and others continued to stress the importance of political loyalty to the party, equal emphasis was given to competence in technical knowledge and military training. Hence the PLA's Dengist identity was both "red" and "expert."

In the Jiang era, the PLA's identity became increasingly defined by expertise in war fighting and the application of advanced technologies ("expert") and less so by devotion to communism ("red"). Political education now largely consists of hammering home the principle of army obedience to the party rather than adhering to the "specific philosophical tenets" of Marxism-Leninism or Maoism.[179] As for personal loyalties, while Jiang has proven quite adept at cultivating the allegiances of senior soldiers, one cannot call the PLA "Jiang's army" as confidently as one could proclaim it "Mao's army" or "Deng's army" in earlier eras.

In the post-1949 era, the military's orientation has been gradually shifting toward greater emphasis on external missions over domestic ones. The domestic noncombat preoccupation of Mao's time was replaced in the Deng era by increasing attention on deployment beyond China's borders – to project force quickly and efficiently and sustain it. However, attention to the deployment of PLA units to deal with domestic contingencies was not overlooked.

The transformation in civil-military culture does not seem to have fundamentally altered the frequency or intensity of China's resort to the use of force. Nevertheless, the major changes in civil-military culture discussed in this chapter do hold significant implications for how China will use armed force at home and abroad. The changes in military doctrine of the 1980s and 1990s have served only to increase the likelihood that the PLA will be deployed at or beyond China's borders. The change in format has altered the process by which decisions to use force are made; these have become more complicated, visible, and raucous. The PLA's identity has shifted: from unshakable allegiance to the party and its paramount leader (perceived of as one and the same in the Mao and Deng eras), to one on the threshold of the twenty-first century questioning where the army's ultimate loyalty lies. Orders from party leaders may be challenged or even disobeyed, especially if they involve domestic deployment. Changes in function suggest that in the new century the PLA will be somewhat less likely to be deployed internally but more likely to be used externally.

Part II

USE OF FORCE IN THE MAO ERA

4

Lips and Teeth: China's Decision to Intervene in Korea

THIS chapter analyzes the attitudes of civilian and military leaders toward China's 1950 decision to intervene in Korea. The analysis aims to determine how these two groups compare in their basic orientations toward the initiation of hostilities. The Korean case is particularly valuable not only because analyses of China's strategic disposition in this instance vary radically, but also because the perspectives of soldiers and statesmen have not been fully examined, and the primary focus has been on the dominant figure of Mao Zedong. In the twenty-first century, with no single leader as dominant as Mao or Deng Xiaoping, such an approach is of limited utility. The richest and most extensive sources now available on the views of military and civilian leaders regarding the PRC's use of force are those on the Korean intervention.[1] Indeed, scholars have studied Beijing's path to the Korean War far more thoroughly than any of the other cases examined in this volume. Hence the circumstances of China's intervention in Korea can be readily discerned elsewhere, and this chapter does not go into the degree of detail of the chapters that follow.

Although it took place half a century ago, the Korean conflict remained a defining experience for many individuals who at the dawn of the twenty-first century were China's most senior military leaders. Moreover, lessons of the conflict continue to be carefully studied by younger generations.[2] These leaders included General Chi Haotian, who until the Sixteenth Party Congress in November 2002 was concurrently a member of the Politburo of the Central Committee of the Chinese Communist Party (CCP), a vice chair of the Central Military Commission (CMC), and minister of national defense.

Each decision to commit troops has its own specific context, and the case of China's entry into the Korean War is no exception. In 1950 a single paramount leader dominated the decision-making apparatus: Mao. Beijing's leaders perceived a major threat to China from the considerable military might of the United States.[3] The purpose of this chapter is to assess the views of individual

Chinese soldiers and statesmen regarding the use of force – most of the recent English-language literature on the Korean War does not consider this – rather than focus exclusively on Mao or study the decision-making process.[4] The fundamental goal is to determine whether a pattern of attitudes among political and military elites is discernable.

Interpretations of the logic behind China's decision to enter the Korean conflict have shifted from emphasizing Beijing's reluctance and caution to stressing Beijing's enthusiasm and recklessness. Until the late 1980s, studies of Chinese intervention in Korea highlighted Beijing's attempts at deterrence and gradual escalation leading ultimately to the Chinese People's Volunteers (CPV) crossing the Yalu River.[5] In stark contrast, however, studies published in the 1990s – utilizing the wealth of newly available primary sources – underscore Beijing's impetus to pursue armed conflict.[6] Moreover, the views of political and military officials tend not to be examined in any systematic fashion.[7] In fact, all these studies tend to be Mao-centric, giving limited attention to the thinking and influence of other Chinese leaders.[8]

The context of China's intervention in Korea in October 1950 is briefly sketched. The attitudes and actions of senior Chinese civilian and military leaders are then examined, and, finally, the pattern of results obtained is evaluated. The rubric of coercive diplomacy is not highlighted in this chapter, largely because the elements of deterrence and compellance and of carrot and stick did not prove a significant civil-military issue. Moreover, discussion of coercive diplomacy has already been well covered especially as regards the significance of mutual misperception and miscommunication between China and the United States over Korea.[9] The momentous decision confronting and dividing China's civilian and military leaders was not whether to escalate by increments in order to deter United Nations Command (UNC) forces from crossing the Thirty-Eighth Parallel or approaching the Yalu River. There was widespread agreement that this was the correct policy. What was at issue was whether or not Chinese forces should intervene in Korea in strength and rescue the teetering regime of Kim Il Sung.

THE CONTEXT

When the first units of CPV troops crossed the Yalu River into North Korea under the cover of darkness on the night of October 19, 1950, it marked the culmination of a protracted and deliberative decision-making process. Beijing had been caught by surprise when forces of the Korean People's Army (KPA) launched a dramatic strike against South Korea across the Thirty-Eighth Parallel on June 25. The Chinese were aware of Kim Il Sung's goals, having provided him with some fifty-thousand to seventy-thousand Korean troops from the People's Liberation Army (PLA) between late 1949 and mid-1950. However, Pyongyang did not keep Beijing appraised of its invasion plans or notify Beijing of the attack across the Thirty-Eighth Parallel until June 27.[10] Still the Chinese had months to assess the significance and threat posed by the presence of U.S. troops on the Korean Peninsula and the positioning of the U.S. Seventh Fleet in the Taiwan Strait. The Chinese responded prudently in mid-July by creating a Northeast Frontier Defense Army (NEFDA) with headquarters in Manchuria. Initial Chinese indignation over the insertion of the U.S. fleet and the awareness of the involvement of U.S. ground forces in the Korean conflict turned to considerable alarm by early September. Even before the Inchon landings in midmonth, intelligence reports indicated KPA units were overextended and in danger of being destroyed by an enemy counteroffensive.[11]

After the overwhelming success of the Inchon operation in mid-September, UNC troops under the direction of General Douglas MacArthur continued northward beyond the Thirty-Eighth Parallel toward the Yalu River. In late September and early October 1950, Beijing issued stern public warnings to Washington and transmitted other private warnings via New Delhi that China would intervene if these troops did not pull back. Beijing's gradual escalation of rhetoric and military preparation appears evident – particularly the explicit warnings to UNC forces not to cross the Thirty-Eighth Parallel – up until the time the Chinese actually intervened in mid-October.[12] However, while Chinese leaders considered the possibility of intervention as early as August,[13] this is not to say that the decision was solidified at an early date, that intervention was inevitable, or that the leadership in Beijing spoke with one voice.[14]

THE DECISION

The Political Elite: Sustained Ambivalence

In fact, China's civilian leadership pondered the matter of whether to enter the Korean conflict for months before finally acting. The process was tortuous, and there was widespread reluctance as well as significant opposition within the Chinese elite to becoming embroiled in Korea. Nevertheless, as key leaders became convinced of the necessity of intervention, dissenters were gradually won over or silenced.

The Paramount Leader. The opinion of China's top civilian leader, Mao, was critical in Beijing's decision to dispatch troops to Korea. Evidence of the extent of the chairman's preoccupation with the situation in Korea and his considerable involvement in the most minor details of Beijing's response is overwhelming.[15] The decision was a difficult one for Mao, who, although having reached a decision in August that in principle China would probably have to intervene in Korea,[16] wavered on the actual decision until virtually the last minute. According to acting Chief of General Staff Nie Rongzhen, Mao "pondered deeply for a long time and from many different angles before he finally made up his mind."[17] According to many accounts, the chairman had all but made up his mind on October 1 after receiving an urgent telegram from North Korean leaders Kim and Pak Hon Yong requesting that Chinese troops intervene. At an enlarged Politburo Standing Committee meeting the following day, Mao stated that China should intervene but left undecided the timing of the operation and the appointment of a military commander.[18]

But it was another week before Mao finally issued the formal order (on October 8) after convincing himself and other top officials, following days of deliberation and discussion with Chinese civilian and military leaders, that China had no choice but to intervene. It was also on this date that Mao informed Kim of China's decision to assist Korea.[19] Nevertheless, after receiving an October 10 telegram from Zhou Enlai in Moscow reporting that Joseph Stalin had decided against providing air support for the intervention, on October 12 Mao instructed Commander Peng Dehuai of the CPV to postpone the intervention. Mao directed Peng and Gao Gang, the CCP boss of Manchuria, to hurry to Beijing for urgent consultations.[20] During the period October 11–13, Mao did not sleep, pondering "a most difficult decision."[21] Finally, on October 13, Mao reaffirmed his decision.[22]

The Diplomat. China's foremost diplomat, PRC Premier and Foreign Minister Zhou, firmly supported intervention.[23] Judging by his statements to India's ambassador in China, K. M. Panikkar, and his speeches about Korea, Zhou consistently took a hawkish view.[24] While it is debatable whether these words actually reflect Zhou's own thinking, it is very likely that these views were his own.[25] According to CCP Central Committee member Bo Yibo, as early as August 1950 Zhou strongly favored intervention in Korea.[26] A military attaché named Chai Chengwen reports briefing Zhou in Beijing on September 1, 1950, upon the former's return from Korea. According to Chai, he gave the premier a sober and ominous assessment of the military situation. After listening attentively, Zhou asked him pointedly, "In case the situation suddenly worsened – if we had to dispatch troops to intervene in Korea – what difficulties do you envision?" Chai took this to mean that Zhou was favoring intervention and would enter China in the conflict if the military situation deteriorated.[27]

Another account, citing an unnamed high-level communist source, notes that Zhou firmly supported intervention in the face of serious opposition from others.[28] Still, one can discern even in Zhou hints of reservations about the prudence of dispatching Chinese forces to Korea. The foreign minister seemed to harbor some degree of doubt about the prospect of a Korean adventure.[29] It was Zhou who reportedly insisted on issuing a final warning to the UNC via Ambassador Panikkar in the early morning hours of October 3.[30] Certainly, this was in part a propaganda ploy, but it also held out the last-minute possibility of averting Chinese military action if the UNC heeded the warning.

Doubts in the Party. There is evidence of considerable opposition within the CCP leadership about the wisdom of sending Chinese troops to Korea. The PRC had barely celebrated its first anniversary on October 1, 1950. Five months earlier, the CCP Central Committee ordered the demobilization of 2.4 million soldiers to be accomplished in two phases.[31] Many Chinese looked forward to a period of peace at last, in which the country could focus on economic development after decades of protracted armed struggle.

There appears to have been nothing short of a "high-level policy debate" on the merits of intervention.[32] According to one account, "some comrades" feared that China was completely unprepared for war with the most powerful country in the world and would probably be defeated. At a Politburo meeting on October 4, these individuals argued that it would be best to postpone intervention for a few years so that China could properly prepare itself.[33] When the meeting resumed the next day, these opponents of intervention remained but seem to have been won over by the shrewd arguments of Peng and Mao.[34] The prospect of a relatively unsophisticated peasant army with little armor or artillery and no air force or navy to speak of against the most technically advanced armed forces in the world possessing nuclear weapons was extremely daunting. Accordingly, for China's top leaders, "... the policy decision to dispatch troops to resist America and aid Korea was one of the most difficult ... of their lives."[35]

One bloc of opposition identified by many scholars is the economic bureaucracy.[36] Chen Yun, an economic planner and Politburo member, seems to have opposed a war. The tone and content of a November 15, 1950, report about the country's finances, made to a national economic conference on the impact of China's involvement in Korea, supports the notion that Chen opposed the war. Chen's mood is noticeably unenthusiastic and matter-of-fact.[37] Still, economists appear to have been convinced eventually by Mao, Zhou, and others that China must intervene.[38]

"Most of the old Communists," including senior CCP leader Dong Biwu, reportedly opposed China's entry into the war until the PRC was more firmly established.[39] Liu Shaoqi, a member of the Politburo Standing Committee, and Rao Shushi, the leader of China's eastern region, were also reportedly against intervention.[40] There was allegedly opposition from some other civilian leaders – including Gao. It appears that Gao initially opposed sending troops to Korea but eventually decided to support the move.[41]

The Military Elite: Deep Reluctance

Military men proved extremely reluctant to commit troops to the peninsula and were ultimately convinced as to the wisdom of the move only after the sustained and forceful arguments of Mao and later by CPV Commander Peng.

Peng Dehuai. General Peng had strong reservations about the wisdom of intervening in Korea. After the outbreak of war in June 1950, Peng saw Korea mainly as a conflict between the Soviets and the Americans, a confrontation that the Chinese should keep an eye on but not get involved in. In August 1950, he told top party and army leaders in the northwest region:

> The Korean peninsula is divided in two, both mutually antagonistic, the problem is relatively complicated, related to problems in bilateral relationships between the Soviet Union and the United States. [As] the North Korean People's Army is fighting in the south, the U.S. will not sit back and ignore it. This possibly creates a problem, and our country also ought to be prepared.[42]

In early October 1950, Peng was urgently summoned to Beijing from Xian, where he was engaged in reconstruction work in northwest China. He came straight from the airport on October 4 to the top leadership compound at Zhongnanhai, arriving at about 4 P.M. to attend a Central Committee meeting, already in progress, where the merits of sending Chinese troops to Korea were being debated. Peng, who was probably expecting to be quizzed about his work on the northwest frontier, seemed to have had no inkling that the subject would be Korea. He sat and listened in silence to the debate. When the meeting adjourned for the day, he found it impossible to sleep in his comfortable hotel room with the possibility of war with the United States on his mind. While he later told his military subordinates in Shenyang on October 10, shortly after arriving to assume command of the CPV, that he believed the decision to intervene in Korea was correct, Peng clearly had serious reservations about the move and agonized over his decision.[43]

Peng wrote in his memoirs that, although he said naught during the October 4 meeting, his inclination at the time was that "troops should be *(yinggai)* sent to rescue Korea." But this was a tentative, preliminary reaction. Peng goes on to explain it was only during the course of a sleepless night that he concluded intervention was "essential *(biyao)*." He recalled: "Having straightened out my thinking, I gave my support to the Chairman's wise decision."[44] Having made up his mind that China had no choice but to intervene, Peng acceded without hesitation to Mao's request that he assume command of the troops being readied to go to Korea.[45] When Mao asked Peng's opinion on October 5, Peng replied:

> Chairman, last night I got almost no sleep. I couldn't stop thinking about what you said. I realized this was a question of fusing internationalism with patriotism. If we only stress the difficult aspect, don't consider the critical implications of American troops bearing down on the Yalu River, not to mention the uncertainties this holds for the Democratic Republic of Korea – which are linked – then can we not see that the defense of our country's northeast frontier is also directly threatened. Is dispatching troops advantageous or not? After thinking it over, I endorse Chairman Mao's wise policy decision to send troops to Korea.

Peng continued:

> ... if [we] allow the enemy [the United States] to occupy the entire Korean peninsula the threat to our country is very great. In the past when the Japanese invaded China they used Korea as a springboard. First they attacked our three eastern provinces, then using these as a springboard, they launched a large-scale offensive against the interior. We cannot overlook this lesson of history. We must fight the enemy now, we cannot hesitate.[46]

Once he had convinced himself of the necessity of intervention, Peng could without hesitation accept Mao's October 5 offer to make him commander. He later told staff officers in Shenyang, "I, Peng Dehuai, do not know how to say the word 'no.'"[47] Once convinced, Peng took on the role of a key advocate of intervention in the face of continued opposition at the October 5 meeting.[48] Given Peng's reputation for forthrightness and frankness, if the general had concluded that intervention was wrong, he would undoubtedly have stated his opinion, as he did on other occasions much to his detriment.[49]

Peng's deliberations highlight what seems to have been a considerable dilemma for many senior officers: Their political loyalty was torn between a sense of "Chineseness" on one hand and a sense of global class-consciousness on the other. Many senior soldiers remarked that important to their support of intervention was the linkage of patriotism with the cause of global communism. Peng remembered lying awake on the night of October 4–5, 1950 pondering whether it was in China's best interests to intervene in Korea or not. He recalled: "Again and again I turned over in my mind the Chairman's remarks....I came to realize that his instruction combined internationalism with patriotism."[50]

Phrases linking the two appear frequently in military memoirs on Korea. While the repetition could be dismissed as the parroting of official propaganda, judging from the context in which "internationalism and patriotism" is mentioned, it is no mere platitude. The words seem to have great significance to the Chinese veterans of that war. It is usually mentioned reverently, sometimes emotionally.[51] Initially many soldiers were either opposed to or very reluctant to get involved in Korea; they viewed intervention as counter to China's best interests. Their feelings of "proletarian solidarity" with the oppressed people's of the world, particularly the strong ties forged with the Korean communist troops who fought side by side with them during the Anti-Japanese War and the Chinese Civil War,[52] did not seem sufficient at the outset of hostilities on the peninsula to dispose them toward intervention. Rather, the basic rationale behind China's eventual involvement came down to defense of the motherland. Mao shrewdly linked the two concepts so as to make support of the war not just a patriotic crusade to stir every Chinese heart but a politically correct cause that would satisfy dedicated communists.[53]

Nie Rongzhen. Others, including acting Chief of General Staff Nie, also had reservations about intervening in Korea. While Nie does not specifically say in his memoirs that he opposed the idea of intervention, neither does he say he vocally endorsed it from the start. Implicit in his discussion of the deliberations is his own ambivalence. Nie wrote vaguely of the doubts of unnamed "comrades" and alludes to his own doubts: "Whether to fight that war was a question on which no one could easily make up his mind."[54] By the end of September, he was convinced if U.S. forces kept advancing toward the Yalu, China would have no alternative but to intervene. On September 25, during a dinner in Beijing with K. M. Panikkar, Nie told the Indian diplomat, "in a quiet and unexcited manner that the Chinese did not intend to sit back with folded hands and let the Americans come up to their border." He continued soberly, "We know what we are in for, but at all costs American aggression has to be stopped."[55]

Zhu De and Xu Xiangqian. By October, PLA Commander in Chief Zhu De had also apparently decided that China must intervene.[56] During the critical period when the debate over whether to enter Korea raged, PLA Chief of General Staff Xu Xiangqian was at a sanitarium in the coastal resort of Qingdao recuperating from an illness. Because of his incapacitation, his deputy Nie assumed his duties. When Xu returned to Beijing in late October, he labeled the policy on Korea "wise."[57]

Determined Military Dissent

Some soldiers openly opposed China's involvement in a war on the Korean Peninsula. One such general was Lin Biao.

Lin Biao. Until very recently, Lin was in official disgrace. Many scholars agree that Lin was a shrewd and clever – if not brilliant – tactician who appeared to suffer from self-doubt and a "strong streak of pessimism."[58] Although claims that he opposed Mao on Korea suggest character assassination, this stand is consistent both with what we know about Lin's character as well as circumstantial evidence, and is corroborated by many different sources.[59] While one account speculates that Lin was "an enthusiastic proponent" of intervention in Korea, this view was based on fragmentary and faulty evidence and the erroneous assumption that Lin had served as the first commander of the CPV before being replaced by Peng in 1951.[60]

The evidence suggests that Mao first asked Lin to command the CPV.[61] An important question is why Mao waited so long before deciding to select Peng (on October 2), and waited several more days before actually asking him (on October 5). This delay is understandable if Mao had assumed that Lin would take the job but at the last minute begged off on grounds of ill health. Lin declined Mao's request to lead the CPV but left open the possibility of stepping in later if he recuperated quickly.[62] Only in late September did Mao learn that Lin would not be available and spent two "days and nights" before selecting Peng. Mao apparently also considered selecting General Su Yu, who had been charged with masterminding the invasion of Taiwan, to lead the CPV.[63]

Chai, a military attaché posted to the hastily activated Chinese embassy in Pyongyang, gives an account of a conversation with Lin in early September. Chai had just returned with an ominous sounding report on the military situation in Korea indicating that while on the surface things appeared to favor the KPA, North Korean forces were overextended and would be particularly vulnerable to a sudden American counteroffensive. According to Chai, Lin asked him "bluntly": "If we don't dispatch troops and tell them [North Korea's leaders] to head for the mountains and wage guerilla warfare, would that be okay?"[64] Mao reportedly told the October 2 Politburo meeting that, in a conversation several days earlier, Lin had raised serious doubts about the wisdom of intervention. Indeed, Mao said, Lin insisted that involving the country in Korea would only hurt China.[65] Foremost among Lin's concerns was the possibility that the United States would use nuclear weapons.[66] Another account states that Lin opposed dispatching troops both at the Central Committee meeting chaired by Mao on October 4 and also at a meeting of the Central Military Commission chaired by Zhou two days later. At this second meeting, Lin reportedly declared: "The United States is highly modernized. Furthermore, it possesses the atomic bomb. There is no guarantee of achieving victory [against the United States]. The central leaders should consider this issue with great care."[67] Zhou criticized Lin's attitude, saying the matter had already been decided. Zhou and Lin were eventually selected to go to the Soviet Union to facilitate arms transfers – the latter since Lin was already scheduled to travel there to receive medical treatment.[68]

Lin's reaction to Mao's request that he command the Chinese forces in Korea contrasts dramatically with Peng's response. Lin, pleading illness, declined his superior's request. Many accounts report Lin "said he was ill" *(shuo bing)*, or used sickness as "an excuse" *(jiekou, jiegu, or tuoci)*.[69] It is likely that he was feigning illness to shirk duty in Korea, although it is also possible that he really was sick.[70] The refusal to obey, which could have been considered insubordination, was necessarily couched in terms of poor health since this offered an honorable out, short of flat refusal. Despite Mao's polite phrasing, his "request" was actually an order.

Where the likelihood of character assassination comes into play is over the scornful tone of many accounts suggesting that Lin was using sickness as an excuse to avoid a difficult mission that he personally opposed. There is the clear inference in several accounts that Lin acted out of cowardice.[71] Far from qualifying as shameful behavior, however, this was accepted face-saving etiquette for a senior official (military or civilian) strongly opposed to a major policy. From Mao's words and actions, he seemed to have believed Lin was really ill. Mao was deeply concerned and went so far as to order personally a top physician to treat Lin.[72] Mao told the October 2 meeting of a conversation in which Lin insisted he was ill and suffered from insomnia. Lin was "afraid of wind, light, and noise, aiya!" Mao exclaimed. He continued: "he [Lin] has the three afraids – how could he possibly command troops!" Mao later recounted this story to Peng.[73]

Indeed Lin, like several other military figures including PLA Chief of General Staff Xu, had a record of chronic ill health, and others, including Nie, suffered serious bouts of illness at different times, probably brought on by overwork.[74] In the final analysis, Lin's affliction is best viewed as a "political illness" *(zhengzhi bing)*, and this is the way many senior Chinese leaders perceived it.[75] Thus Lin's response was a convenient and time-honored excuse to avoid an escalation of intra-elite conflict over policy.

Other Military Opposition. General Ye Jianying, like Lin, also reportedly opposed dispatching troops to Korea. Even after UNC successes following Inchon, Ye appeared to believe that it was unnecessary for China to become involved. He told a gathering in Guangzhou that the KPA should take to the mountains and gave no indication that he believed China should consider dispatching troops.[76] Generals He Long and Su allegedly also opposed intervention in Korea.[77] Su, the man charged with masterminding the invasion of Taiwan, appeared to be an extremely cautious commander. Speaking in February 1950, Su was circumspect about the prospects for the invasion of Taiwan; he was adamant that China needed more time to prepare.[78] Liu Bocheng reportedly opposed intervention in Korea because it would mean postponing indefinitely the invasion of Taiwan.[79]

Despite initial reservations, most military leaders became convinced that intervention was the best course of action. Many were persuaded by Peng after he became adamantly convinced of the correctness of this course. Even those skeptical or opposed concurred with the decision out of strong personal loyalty to Mao and Peng, or they kept silent.

Officers in the Field

Field commanders in the northeast initially seemed genuinely enthusiastic about the prospect of fighting in Korea, but they soon exhibited extreme caution and sought to postpone intervention. Some units had been moved to the northeast as early as mid-July 1950 after the NEFDA had been formed in response to the American military involvement in Korea. Deng Hua, commander of the Thirteenth Army Corps, and his deputy, Hong Xuezhi, had been preparing for action since they received orders on August 5 to be ready to move by early September. These orders were superseded by orders dated August 15 to be ready before the end of September.[80]

After the rapid deterioration in the military situation following the Inchon landings, Pak Hon Yong, KPA commander and North Korean interior minister, arrived in Andong, China, near the Yalu, to brief local PLA commanders on the military situation in Korea. He reportedly asked the officers for Chinese troops, and the NEFDA commander Deng Hua and others sought to reassure him saying they would pass the request on to Beijing and stood ready to move as soon as they received the order to go to Korea. Deng Hua, Hong, and the other commanders all agreed that the advancing American troops posed a direct threat to China and expressed a readiness to confront this threat head on.[81] Hong recalled thinking on October 2:

> The circumstances of the Korean military situation had already swiftly worsened, requiring China to assist promptly by dispatching troops. Our Thirteenth Corps leaders and troops were already well prepared. All we needed was the order from CCP Chairman Mao and we would immediately move into Korea.[82]

The units preparing to cross the Yalu were from the Fourth Field Army and had been under the command of Lin. Yet officers such as Deng Hua and Hong gave no indication that they were disappointed at not being led by their former commander. In fact, Deng Hua and Hong were both enthusiastic about the news that Peng had been selected to lead them. Peng's reputation for being a no-nonsense, battle-hardened general directly affected their outlook on the impending mission.[83] On October 10, Peng, after arriving in Shenyang to assume command of the CPV, asked Deng Hua what he thought about intervention. Deng Hua replied that he agreed completely with Peng's viewpoint, China had no choice but to dispatch troops. Hong also told Peng he believed, "We should resolutely dispatch troops."[84]

Nevertheless, many troop commanders in the prospective field of operations were deeply concerned about the nuts and bolts of the actual intervention. Their concerns reveal a large measure of doubt as to the wisdom of prompt intervention. At a meeting of commanders at and above the corps level in Shenyang on October 9, Peng and Gao explained Beijing's order to dispatch them to Korea. After the briefing, there was a chorus of concerns: "... various officers raised questions, they were most worried that troops were being sent abroad to fight without air support."[85] General Liu Zhen, commander of the infant air arm of the CPV, stated candidly that after being appointed commander, he surveyed the years of his military career and acknowledged that while he had commanded infantry, artillery, and armored units, he had never commanded air units. Liu admitted air warfare and organization were a "mystery." He continued: "Neither I nor any of the other cadres had any experience organizing or commanding air combat operations and there was no shortage of problems." Liu Zhen also noted the obvious: "... in our levels of tactics and technology we were way, way below those of our enemy."[86] Considering the enemy that China was facing and the paltry resources available, building an air force was a daunting task. Liu Zhen could only draw strength from the fact that the PLA had long struggled successfully against overwhelming odds learning military strategy, tactics, and combat through trial and error in battle. Liu Zhen recalled: "I nevertheless had a resolute thought running through my mind over and over again. The cause of the revolution had all along developed out of nothing, gone from small to big, developed as a brutal, difficult, death-defying struggle."[87]

Chai, the first military attaché at the fledgling PRC embassy operating in Pyongyang in mid-1950, enthusiastically supported intervention. He was excited about the prospect. On September 1, 1950, after Chai briefed Zhou on the Korean situation, Chai recalls thinking: "... sending Chinese troops was the correct move – all that remained was the question of the order."[88]

Despite these pro-interventionist opinions, Deng Hua, Hong, and their fellow officers in the theater of operations soon grew ambivalent about engaging in a mission beyond China's borders – something with which they had no experience. During a meeting with Peng on October 10, Deng Hua, Hong, and other senior officers from the Thirteenth Army Corps all insisted that Peng query Beijing's decision to send on two army corps across the Yalu. They argued that these units were simply "too few" *(tai shao)*, and urged Peng to ask Beijing to approve a doubling of the initial expeditionary group to four corps. Peng agreed and requested the increase in troop strength, and Mao approved it. But the next day (October 11), Deng Hua and Hong warned Peng:

> Even if we initially send four corps into Korea, this still would be insufficient manpower. If we advance these four corps, who will protect the rear? We don't have any troops to protect the rear area, [so] how can our supplies be guaranteed? We must designate another corps to protect our rear.

And again Peng concurred.[89]

Then on October 17, Deng Hua and Hong sent a cable to Peng and Gao suggesting that intervention be postponed until the spring of 1951. The CPV field officers were growing increasingly perturbed; the lack of air support and the onset of winter raised grave concerns about the wisdom of entering Korea in late 1950. The telegram from Deng Hua, Hong, and other commanders declared: "It is our opinion that we are not yet fully prepared, and our troops have not undergone thorough political indoctrination. We suggest it would be more suitable with the onset of winter to postpone the operation until the spring...."[90] Peng and Gao transmitted these concerns to Mao, who ordered Peng and Gao back to Beijing and put the operation on hold for twenty-four hours.[91] A final hurdle, the extreme caution of CPV leaders, was overcome during an October 18 meeting in Beijing when Mao and Zhou – the latter just returned from Moscow with promises of Soviet military assistance and air support from Stalin – insisted on forging ahead with intervention.[92] Mao promptly issued orders for CPV units to cross the Yalu the following evening, and Peng returned to his headquarters to inform his commanders that the decision to enter Korea was final.[93]

CONCLUSION

While Mao clearly dominated the decision-making on Korea in 1950, other figures, including soldiers, played major roles. Moreover, focusing on individual leaders cautions against viewing intervention as preordained or China's path toward Korea as inexorable once the subject of possible entry was raised. It is clear that despite key factors that favored Chinese intervention – including Mao's underlying propensity to dispatch troops – many senior leaders, Mao included, still harbored great ambivalence, and others, such as Lin, were adamantly against such a move. While Mao's thinking was undoubtedly critical and his resolve carried the day, the considerable discussion regarding intervention constituted nothing less than a major policy debate in which the views and concerns of many leaders were aired and weighed. Particularly important in winning over doubters and preserving party unity were Zhou and Peng. Moreover, soldiers (such as Peng, Lin, and Nie) seemed to have been more reluctant than their civilian counterparts (such as Mao and Zhou) to intervene in Korea. Indeed, Jong Sun Lee concluded that on Korea military men tended to be consistently dovish throughout the deliberation and preparation for intervention.[94]

The quite different perspectives between military and civilian leaders suggest the existence of a military culture above and beyond a civil-military culture in spite of the dual role elite format. Indeed it was because of this leadership format – and the towering figure of Mao, who epitomized it – that soldiers had great difficulty in opposing the decision to intervene in Korea. The other three elements of civil-military culture seemed to indicate that intervention was unlikely. The doctrine of People's War had been pursued largely in a defensive manner, the PLA's function until 1950 had been exclusively domestic, and the PLA's identity was narrowly nationalistic – it was an army of the Chinese people. In sum, these factors strongly pointed toward nonintervention.

The fact that China did not "sit idly by," however, implies that the country's strategic culture had a considerable impact on the decision. Indeed, the Cult of Defense appears to have fostered the belief among China's leaders that U.S. forces advancing northward on the Korean Peninsula gravely threatened the PRC's national security. Use of the metaphor of "lips and teeth" to describe the intimate relationship between Korea and China underscores the degree of alarm felt in Beijing.[95] Civil and military leaders felt particularly vulnerable to a threat from this direction because, as Peng noted, Korea had been the steppingstone to China for the Japanese only decades before. In Beijing's view, first it had tried unsuccessfully to deter the U.S. advance through warnings. From the leadership's view, the PRC looked to military means as a last resort. Active defense, as Peng later explained with particular reference to

Korea, permitted offensive measures in pursuit of a broadly conceived defense strategy (see Chapter 2). Despite the overwhelming challenges confronting them, such daunting situations were nothing new to military men such as Liu Zhen. In addition, the cause was just; not only was it in defense of the motherland but also to rescue a fledgling socialist neighbor from an aggressive imperialist foe.

5

"Support the Left": PLA Intervention in the Cultural Revolution

THE intervention of the People's Liberation Army (PLA) in the People's Republic of China (PRC) in 1967 has received considerable attention by scholars.[1] The use of PLA units during the Great Proletarian Cultural Revolution (CR) (1966–9) has been viewed as a negative step that proved detrimental to both Chinese politics and the PLA itself.[2]

Chinese scholars have not mirrored the attention given by foreign analysts to the extensive intervention of the PLA in the internal affairs of China during the Cultural Revolution. Indeed, official Chinese documents and histories tend to ignore the PLA's significant domestic role during the Cultural Revolution.[3] In one sense, the lack of treatment is nothing short of remarkable since there is widespread consensus that military intervention literally rescued China from the brink of civil war and complete collapse. The price of this rescue was military rule *(jun guan)* at the local and provincial levels throughout China. However, the PLA never assumed control over the operations of the central government in Beijing. The dearth of coverage of this aspect of a troubled period in PRC history reflects the extreme sensitivity of China's political leaders to the domination – real or perceived – of the military vis-à-vis the civilian (party and state) authorities.[4] Despite this sensitivity, in no way can this intervention be considered a military coup d'etat. The PLA intervened only at the behest of China's top political leader, Mao Zedong, and never took control of the national government. Nevertheless, this begs the question of why there was no military coup in 1967. (The point will be addressed later in this chapter.) Here the process by which the decision was reached to deploy the PLA – the euphemism "support the left" was used rather than the term "restore order" – is examined as a case study in coercive diplomacy.

Launched by China's paramount political leader Mao in the summer of 1966, the Cultural Revolution was an attempt to shake up the Chinese Communist Party (CCP), purge those officials Mao viewed as disloyal to him, and reinvigorate the Chinese Revolution.[5] He thus called upon the youth of China to attack the CCP and "bombard the headquarters." By circumventing the bureaucratic chain of command and appealing directly to China's youth to make revolution, Mao set the stage for a mass movement of unparalleled scope and momentum in post-1949 China. These mobilized youths formed themselves into paramilitary units called Red Guards, which quickly split into factions. Initially these groups merely vied energetically but relatively tamely to prove the superiority of the revolutionary ardor of their own particular group vis-à-vis others. Eventually this zealous competition, fed by elite factions in Beijing jockeying for power, escalated into deadly armed conflict between rival groups. Other groups formed by workers, former soldiers, and party members joined them. The emergence of these paramilitary formations virtually autonomous from Beijing's control and largely independent of local civil or military authorities resulted in a particularly volatile and complex state of affairs.[6]

The Exasperated PLA

The exasperation of the PLA grew as the destruction and violence escalated and chaos loomed. In the late summer of 1966, youthful Red Guards throughout China got caught up in the enthusiasm of the movement and looked for ways to demonstrate their dedication to Mao, much to the frustration of soldiers. Red Guards vigorously sought to eradicate the "Four Olds" (old ideas, old culture, old customs, and old habits). PLA consternation at the antics of high-spirited youths is typified by the response of a unit commander in a small village in Hebei Province who attempted to protect the Buddha at the local temple from destruction. After drawing up his men in front of the temple, he tried to dissuade the students from their mission. But while he and his men were thus distracted, another group of youths had surreptitiously entered the grounds and succeeded in toppling the statue. Horrified at the act and momentarily at a loss for words, the officer eventually blurted out: "You – You – What kind of Red Guards are you?"[7]

By October 1966, the turmoil of the Cultural Revolution had spread to PLA academies. Military cadets formed Red Guard groups and engaged in the same violent, destructive behavior as their civilian counterparts. Detachments of military cadets assailed their teachers and other authority figures and also traveled to Beijing to be received by Mao. Groups of PLA Red Guards even seized the Ministry of Defense and the headquarters of the PLA Air Force.[8]

The concerns of senior officers can be gauged by the admonition of Marshal Ye Jianying in November 1966 to students of military academies: "... [Y]ou must not take part when struggle or confiscation of personal property is carried out in a place. If you take part, they [the masses] will think that the PLA is involved, and this is undesirable."[9]

By the end of 1966, many of China's top leaders felt that the Cultural Revolution had spun out of control and that order had to be restored. The time was ripe to have the radical factions across the country bring the conflict to an end by ousting incumbent conservative officials and assuming control themselves. In early January 1967, Mao and the members of the Central Cultural Revolutionary Group (CCRG) instructed loyal Maoists to make "seizures of power." After the mobilization of hundreds of thousands of Red Guards from across China for massive rallies in Tiananmen Square, Mao and other leaders seemed confident that they now possessed a loyal, dedicated, and politically reliable force with which to oust conservative leaders and functionaries in the party and state hierarchies.

By the second half of January 1967, however, few "seizures of power" had been successfully carried out and most regions of the country remained in turmoil. Many of China's political leaders were alarmed that the situation did not seem to be stabilizing, and they were becoming concerned that the country might descend into complete chaos. According to an account of the period written by the CCP Political Research Institute's Teaching and Research Office for Party History:

> After the "Cultural Revolution" had entered the "power seizure" stage in January 1967, local-level party and government organs were paralyzed, and the power seizures of "rebel factions" had resulted in conflict. The chaotic situation only worsened by the day. [Therefore] Mao Zedong ordered the People's Liberation Army to intervene locally to support the Cultural Revolution.[10]

While at this stage the intent of Mao and other political leaders as to what the army should do in practice is unclear, Mao seems to have wanted the military to supervise the process of ousting conservative leaders, installing radicals, and ensuring a basic level of stability.[11] He feared that the Cultural Revolution had spun completely out of control.[12] Mao realized it was impossible for the army to remain aloof, and he did not want the PLA to continue to find itself paralyzed in the midst of the conflict. Thus he ordered PLA regional forces across China to intervene.[13] On January 23, 1967, the "Decision Concerning the People's

Liberation Army Resolutely Supporting the Masses of the Revolutionary Left" was officially issued jointly by the CCP Central Committee, the State Council, the Central Military Commission (CMC), and the CCRG. The decision stated:

> The so-called "[policy of] noninterference [by the PLA]" is bogus: [the PLA] has already been involved for some time. Thus the issue is not intervention versus nonintervention; rather the issue is where to stand. The issue is whether to support the revolutionary factions or to support the conservatives, or even the rightists. The People's Liberation Army should actively support the leftist revolutionary faction.[14]

By mid-January, in the midst of the additional turmoil prompted by Mao's orders to radical groups to seize power, military leaders became more and more concerned. On January 23, senior soldiers, including Marshals Xu Xiangqian, Lin Biao, Ye Jianying, and Nie Rongzhen, and Chief of General Staff Yang Chengwu, put forward six suggestions on moderating the excesses of the Cultural Revolution and clarifying the position of the PLA. The session ended when Lin, apparently feeling unwell, abruptly departed. The meeting reconvened the next evening at the defense minister's residence and later shifted to the Diaoyutai complex, with the CCRG also present. Together the officials hammered out a nine-point directive that included an order forbidding assaults on the PLA. After the CMC released a seven-point version on January 28, with an additional point added by Mao, the situation stabilized somewhat.[15]

Lin, defense minister of the PRC since 1959, tends to be reviled by scholars mirroring official Chinese accounts, where he is identified as one of the chief villains of the Cultural Revolution – status confirmed by his alleged aborted coup attempt against Mao in 1971.[16] However, in light of recent evidence and scholarship, it seems that Lin has been overly maligned and, along with Jiang Qing and the other members of the Gang of Four, was set up to take the blame for the machinations and failures of Mao himself. In the revisionist interpretation of Lin, he comes across as reclusive, shy, and eccentric, with a host of ailments both real and imagined.[17] Lin appears not to have sought out power and privilege but to have had it unwillingly thrust upon him by Mao. However, once promoted by Mao, he strove to secure his position with the support and encouragement of his family and supporters. Seen in this light, Lin is more a tragic figure, manipulated by Mao, goaded by his family, and appalled by the destructive impact of the Cultural Revolution on his beloved PLA.[18]

Indeed, Lin seems to have been as concerned about the destructive impact of the Cultural Revolution on the military as other top PLA leaders: " . . . a major concern of Lin Biao . . . was how to minimize chaos in the army."[19] Lin was personally disturbed by Jiang's hare-brained schemes for the army and sought to thwart them at every opportunity. Even his rival Marshal Xu acknowledged that Lin, as the most senior military leader in the PLA, did not want to see the army in disarray. And while Xu was the driving force behind the promulgation of the "eight-point order" in January 1967, Lin seems to have been a key figure also. Thus while it was Xu who took the initiative to burst into Maojiawan on the evening of January 24, to press upon Lin the urgency of the task, it was Lin who seized the moment. Lin promptly summoned members of the CMC for an impromptu meeting at his residence and followed up immediately with an enlarged meeting with members of the CCRG in the early morning hours of January 25. In fact, Xu quotes Lin as telling him on the evening of January 24, "Disorder can't be allowed in the army."[20]

The level of frustration and confusion felt by military officials at the provincial and local levels in late January and early February 1967 can be gauged by the following telephone call to Lin's office by a staff officer from the Jilin Military Region commander's headquarters:

Chairman Mao advocates supporting the broad Revolutionary masses of the left. We will follow this firmly. But, who are the rightists? In the Changchun area there are many mass organizations with different viewpoints. Who should we support? Because of this matter . . . the provincial military commander asked me to telephone you and ask for your instructions. . . .[21]

Lin's secretary recalls:

This telephone call troubled me. They didn't know "who the leftists were," and I didn't know either. . . . The military in locales across the country were also in a similar quandary. They anxiously awaited more explicit instructions from higher authorities. However, at that time no level, even the central authorities, was able to give this kind of directive. At the time the central authorities, owing to the Cultural Revolution, were unable to exercise the function of issuing directives. Probably only the CCRG was capable because the Politburo had already become irrelevant.[22]

This dilemma also confronted small PLA work teams dispatched to implement the directive. An officer and two enlisted men arrived at Xibu, an agricultural brigade some forty miles north of Tangshan in Hebei Province in mid-February 1967. The three soon became "very confused." They were unable to answer the question "[W]hich of the two mass organizations was a true proletarian revolutionary organization, and which was an organization that protected the capitalist-roaders?"[23]

Unfortunately, there was no respite to ease the level of frustration felt by many soldiers. The directions by Mao issued in early February did little to alleviate their anxiety:

> The gist of Mao's written instructions is [as follows]: Attacks on troops by rightist mass organizations cannot be tolerated, but incidents should be handled in an appropriate manner. First try to persuade them; if persuasion is ineffective and they obstinately attack, let them enter. If they occupy the first floor, troops can retreat to the second floor and continue to use persuasion. If they forcibly occupy the second floor, troops can retreat to the third floor. If they take Liberation Army forbearance as a sign of weakness and proceed to occupy the third floor by force, troops can open fire in self-defense. But shoot only the rightist ringleaders; for the majority, they should criticize and educate them and then let them go.[24]

Marshal Ye, in his capacity as a vice chair of the CMC, read Mao's instructions to a meeting of exasperated top PLA brass, including representatives from the military regions. Ye tried to present an upbeat assessment of Mao's message, but the level of frustration by participants was high.[25]

Three Groups and the February Adverse Current

In mid-February, there were three opinion groupings within the CCP leadership on the issue of the PLA and the Cultural Revolution. First, there was the conservative faction that favored swift, massive military intervention to restore order. Second, there was the radical group concentrated around the CCRG and led by Jiang, which opposed such intervention. Holding a position between these two extremes was a third group led by China's paramount political leader Mao and his faithful premier Zhou Enlai. The conservatives were adamant in their view because if current trends continued, not only would China descend into full-scale civil war but also they would be purged from power. The radicals were equally adamant in confronting the conservatives over this issue because their position and influence depended heavily on continuing the Cultural Revolution. They were quite willing to permit unrest in order to allow radical groups to attempt power seizures across China because this would strengthen their authority and influence. Wholesale intervention by the PLA, however, would be potentially disastrous for them. Such a move would undercut their position and destroy their power base: the revolutionary Red Guard and worker militia organizations. Mao and Zhou, meanwhile, wanted to strike a balance in order to ensure that neither group became too powerful and China did not lapse into complete anarchy. Hence they advocated limited PLA intervention.

As a result of divergent interests and priorities, the confrontation between the leaders of the radicals and conservatives was inevitably incendiary. The heated elite clash between the two groups took place in mid-February 1967 at Zhongnanhai and became known as the February Adverse Current. Mao, Jiang, and Lin were present for few, if any, of the meetings, which were chaired by CMC Vice Chair Zhou. It was Zhou who sought to mediate between the two factions and keep the two sides talking. The struggle between the two groups became "white hot" in two meetings of the CMC on February 13 and 16. On the side of the conservatives was Vice Premier of the State Council and Vice Chair of the CMC Tan Zhenlin, Marshal and Foreign Minister Chen Yi, Li Fuchun, Li Xiannian, Yu Qiuli, Gu Mu, and several top soldiers. On the other side were radicals including Chen Boda, Kang Sheng, Guan Feng, Qi Benyu, and Vice Premier Xie Fuzhi.[26]

The core of the conservative group that faced the CCRG at CCP meetings in mid-February 1967 was composed of old marshals, including Chen Yi, Ye, Xu, and Nie.[27] With industrial and agricultural production drastically curtailed or at a complete halt, groups of Red Guards traversing the country, and armed factional violence breaking out across the land, China seemed in dire straits. Marshal Nie later summed up the concern felt by these soldiers at the time in his autobiography: "Our motherland was in peril."[28] By mid-February 1967, top military officials had become fit to be tied because they felt the chaos was harming the corporate interests of their beloved army, and of even greater concern was the threat posed to the unity and very existence of the PLA. This concern was paramount in the minds of senior military officials. One of the three critical issues debated in February 1967:

> ...was whether or not there would be stability in the military. On this issue, several old comrades were unanimous in the view that whether or not there was stability in the army, the army would not be permitted to degenerate into chaos....[29]

At a February 13, 1967, meeting in Zhongnanhai, it was Marshal Xu who spoke up forcefully:

> "The army is the mainstay of the dictatorship of the proletariat. If the army descends into chaos like this, how can it remain the mainstay? ....
> Are we going to allow people like Kuai Dafu to step in and command the army?"
>
> At this time Kang Sheng remarked: "The army is not your personal force, Xu Xiangqian. What makes you think you're so special?"

Xu Xiangqian replied: "We've devoted our whole lives to this army. Do you think the soldiers of the People's Army will simply let a few of you destroy it?"[30]

At another meeting of the CMC in mid-February, Marshal Ye displayed the clear frustration of the army with the rollercoaster course that the Cultural Revolution was taking. Ye asked Zhang Chunqiao, "The Shanghai power seizure, the name change to Shanghai Commune, these kinds of major questions which affect the state structure were never discussed by the Politburo – just what do you want?"[31] Ye then turned his attention to Chen Boda, saying in a contemptuous tone:

We don't read books or reports, and we don't understand the principle of the Paris Commune. Please enlighten us a little: what is the principle of the Paris Commune? Can revolution be made without the leadership of the party? Without the army?[32]

Ye finally exploded in anger, telling Chen Boda and the other radicals: "You have made a mess of the Party, government and industry. But even that doesn't satisfy you, so now you want to wreck the army."[33] Marshal Nie and other top soldiers were particularly incensed that the residences of high-level military leaders had been ransacked.[34]

A particularly heated exchange took place in mid-February between Tan and Zhang Chunqiao. Zhang was scornful of the CCP, asserting that the masses could function well on their own and that the party's leadership was unnecessary. Tan accused the radicals of trying to destroy the party and let the masses make revolution without guidance from the party. Tan grabbed his briefcase and coat and was about to storm out of the conference room when Zhou convinced him to stay.[35] On February 16, Zhang Chunqiao, Yao Wenyuan, and Wang Li, with the assistance of Jiang, secretly sent a collection of materials to Mao condemning their opponents for instigating a "February adverse current."[36]

By late February 1967, as the chaotic results of the attempted power seizures became apparent, the PLA was given more explicit instructions and a broader mandate to curb the excesses. Mao decided that the military had to play a greater role in stabilizing the situation and he ordered the launching of the "Three Supports, Two Militaries" Campaign *(sanchi, liangjun)*. On March 19, the CMC issued the "Decision Concerning Concentrating Efforts on Carrying Out the Task of Supporting the Left, Supporting Agriculture, Supporting Industry, Military Control, and Military Training."[37]

The orders were frustrating, however, because although they gave the PLA the authority to broaden the scope of intervention, they also hamstrung the army with severe restrictions that inhibited its mission. Because of this, the PLA became a bigger target for the increasingly agitated and heavily armed Red Guard factions. Indeed, the measures Mao approved for the PLA were severely circumscribed: A CMC order issued on April 6, 1967, virtually forbade the use of force and firearms and circumscribed powers of arrest. The emphasis was on "political work" or the PLA's powers of persuasion.[38] Soldiers on patrol usually carried not firearms but one of Mao's "little red books" instead.[39] The role of soldiers was essentially one of peacekeeping with an extremely limited mandate. For any peacekeeping mission to have a real chance of success, there must first be a desire for peace on the part of all the warring factions. This condition had not been met in most areas of China by the spring of 1967. According to one bystander in a southern Chinese city in late 1966 or early 1967, the PLA exercised enormous restraint:

> They [the soldiers] were slapped repeatedly in the face but stoically held their hands in front of their chests to show they wouldn't fight back. The soldiers were black and blue from the beatings, with swollen lips and bleeding noses.[40]

As it became increasingly clear to the radicals that the PLA regional forces, by their actions and nonactions, were favoring local government and party incumbents and conservative Red Guard groups and inhibiting radical ones, the CCRG pushed for placing greater restrictions on the PLA. Indeed, PLA regional forces suppressed many radical organizations and took control of many public security bureaus (PSBs) between late January and mid-March 1967.[41] Mao too became unhappy with the performance of regional forces, which generally had not supported the radical left but backed local party leaders with whom they had close ties. The activation of the regional forces intensified rather than calmed the conflict. And the solution to such problems, as in Wuhan, was the activation of main force units, a measure Mao turned to as a last resort in a growing number of incidents after March 1967.[42]

The Wuhan Incident

The situation in the central Chinese city of Wuhan was typical in many ways of the chaos that was enveloping most of the country's urban centers in the summer of 1967. Wuhan Military Region Commander Chen Zaidao and First Political Commissar Zhong Hanhua sided with local party leaders and a conservative mass organization called the Million Heroes, composed largely of workers and local party officials. Violence simmered and escalated across China during the months of June and July, with the regional military forces blatantly favoring the Million Heroes. The most glaring indication of this was the Wuhan Affair or "7–20 Incident" in mid-July of 1967. These events highlight the complex interplay between competing elite factions at the national level and mass organizations at the local level.

The Wuhan Incident of mid-July 1967 highlighted the growing sense of exasperation felt by the regional PLA, which was given the job of restoring order but at the same time was hampered and obstructed by the meddling of central party and military leaders. Although the incidents of July 20–23 were quickly termed a "mutiny," the events of these tumultuous days are more appropriately described as a showdown between the PLA and the CCRG.[43] But even this description does not entirely capture the complexities of the situation. The events in Wuhan were complicated by three factors: Mao's presence in the city, unruly mobs beyond the control of national or local elites, and competing loyalty networks within the PLA.

The first complicating element was the presence of Mao in the eye of the storm. Sequestered in virtual anonymity and apparently oblivious to the chaos around him, Mao reportedly harbored no concern that he might be kidnapped or harmed by anyone, least of all Chen Zaidao.[44] Still the knowledge of Mao's precarious state affected the calculi of both Chen Zaidao and Beijing. Chen's response to the mass unrest in Wuhan was guided by a desire not to do anything that might worsen matters and endanger Mao.[45] Similarly, concern over Mao's safety influenced Beijing's reaction to the crisis and contributed to the decision not to send in PLA main force units to resolve the crisis in Wuhan until Mao had been moved.

Officials in Beijing took news of the turmoil in Wuhan extremely seriously, especially radical leaders such as Jiang, Chen Boda, Zhang Chunqiao, and Yao.[46] Not only had two official envoys from the capital – Vice Premier and Minister of Public Security Xie and CCRG member Wang – been seized, but paramount leader Mao also appeared to be in imminent danger. To deal with the situation, Beijing pursued a two-pronged approach: Zhou was promptly dispatched to try and negotiate a solution, while a military official, Qiu Huizuo, was sent to find and extricate Mao.[47] A combination of luck and the efforts of Zhou and Qiu resulted in an easing of the crisis: Xie and Wang were returned to Beijing, and Mao was moved to Shanghai.[48]

Another factor complicating the situation was that while mass organizations in Wuhan, including Red Guards, supported certain national and local leaders and took their cues from these figures or their personal representatives, the organizations were not under the direct control of these individuals – or any civil or military entity, for that matter. The Million Heroes organization, for example, although it backed the Wuhan Military Region establishment led by Chen Zaidao and Zhong, did not obediently follow orders from either of these soldiers. These groups were essentially autonomous paramilitary formations.

Groups of both conservative and radical political persuasions sought to arm themselves either by demanding weaponry from the PLA and militia or simply seizing guns and ammunition outright. By mid-1967, China had plunged deeper into chaos, with basic law and order seriously eroding in many areas and totally collapsing in others. The Ministry of Public Security proved inept or powerless.

The level of violence and disorder in southern provinces, such as Sichuan, Yunnan, and Hubei, was of particular concern to Beijing. Xie and Wang were dispatched on an investigative tour of southern cities. Mao and Zhou also headed south in an effort to end the turmoil. All four men arrived in Wuhan on July 14, although they did so separately and at different times of the day.[49]

Over the next few days, Wang and Xie met with various groups in the city. The sympathies of the two men and those of the different mass organizations quickly became evident. Wang and Xie received a boisterous welcome from radical groups, and they in turn stoked the reservoir of bad feeling against the leaders of the Wuhan Military Region and the conservative mass organizations. Xie and Wang then presented their one-sided findings to Zhou and Mao on the mornings of July 15 and 16. Zhou meanwhile conducted his own investigation, meeting with local and regional party and military leaders on four consecutive afternoons (July 15, 16, 17, and 18). In these meetings, Zhou insisted that the official assessment of the situation in Wuhan was as follows: The leaders of the military region had made "serious mistakes" in implementing central directives, but these could be rectified without purging Chen Zaidao and Zhong. On the evening of July 18, Zhou departed Wuhan for Beijing.[50]

Late on the evening of July 18, Mao, with Xie and Wang present, met with Chen Zaidao. Mao told Chen Zaidao that while he (Mao) supported him, Wang and Xie wanted to oust him.[51] The two radicals interpreted Zhou's ruling and Mao's remarks to Chen Zaidao as a green light to escalate their attacks against the commander of the Wuhan Military Region. Xie and Wang continued their rhetorical blasts against the conservative Million Heroes organization and Chen Zaidao, raising the level of tension.

Military tolerance of the antics of Wang and Xie reached the breaking point after the two men addressed a meeting late on the evening of July 19 attended by military cadres at the divisional level and above. The audience was particularly incensed over the tone and content of the remarks by Wang, who addressed the gathering condescendingly, much like a primary school teacher scolding a class of mischievous students.[52]

Following the meeting, groups of rogue soldiers and thousands of workers converged on the Dong Hu guesthouse where Xie and Wang were staying. Mao was also staying at the Dong Hu complex but was apparently not disturbed because he was housed in a different building and the crowds were unaware of his presence.[53] The mob stormed the guesthouse to seize Wang and Xie. Chen quickly appeared on the scene, but his attempts to rectify the situation were fruitless. While supportive of Chen Zaidao, the mob was not under his total control. Indeed, according to Chen Zaidao, the crowd disregarded his appeals to curb their riotous behavior.[54] For his trouble, he was beaten by the mob, receiving the same treatment as the crowd's intended quarry.[55] According to another account, Chen Zaidao was assaulted because he was mistaken for Wang.[56]

A third aspect of the situation in Wuhan that exacerbated the crisis was the tension that existed between different factions within the PLA, specifically between those of Lin and Xu. Marshal Xu, who had been named to succeed Marshal He Long as head of the PLA's Cultural Revolution Small Group in early 1967, and Defense Minister Lin viewed each other as rivals. Xu's prestige, his opposition to many of the CCRG's extreme policies, and his own extensive network of supporters within the PLA resulted in Xu becoming a prime target of Cultural Revolution radicals. Chen Zaidao, as a Xu man, also became a target for the radicals.[57] Chen had strong ties of loyalty to Xu, having served under him in the Second Field Army, and the two continued to have a close relationship that lasted until the marshal's death in the early 1990s.[58] In 1967, Xu was generally considered to be Chen Zaidao's patron. As such, the Wuhan regional commander was targeted by the CCRG. The marshal was repeatedly accused in wall posters, the press, and finally by Lin himself of being the "behind-the-scenes manipulator of Chen Zaidao."[59]

Lin's faction certainly took advantage of the situation to purge Chen Zaidao in the process of resolving the Wuhan crisis. The defense minister's strongest base of support was to be found in the Air Force, and Air Force commander Wu Faxian and Wuhan regional Air Force chief Liu Feng were instrumental in solving the crisis to Lin's satisfaction. Naval officer and Lin supporter Li Zuopeng recommended deploying main force units in Wuhan.[60] Whatever the motive behind the decision to introduce outside naval, air, and ground units, these formations succeeded where the forces of the Wuhan garrison had failed: in disarming local mass organizations and reestablishing basic order.[61] Before calm was restored "more than six hundred people" had been killed and "more than sixty-six thousand" persons had been injured.[62]

Chen Zaidao and Zhong, although roundly labeled by radicals as military mutineers, were recalled to Beijing and relieved of their posts, but beyond this were subjected to only cursory punishment. Mao and other top party leaders recognized that the actions of Chen Zaidao and Zhong were the result of the immense pressure placed on the military by the chaos of the Cultural Revolution.[63] Indeed, Mao's telegram to the newly formed Wuhan Military Region Party Committee on July 25 described the efforts to oust Chen Zaidao as "serious mistakes committed by cadres."[64]

In the Aftermath of Wuhan

The radicals considered the resolution of the Wuhan crisis a victory, and Wang and Xie were treated like returning heroes when they arrived back in Beijing. In late July, the head of the CCRG, Jiang, issued a communiqué ordering Red Guards to "attack with reason, defend with force."[65] Radicals widely interpreted this order as a call to arms against conservative groups, including those in the army. In the wake of the Wuhan Incident, violent attacks on the PLA increased. The situation only seemed to worsen in early August with the *Red Flag* editorial written by Chen Boda and Wang introducing the slogan "Pull out a small handful in the Army." The result was a further escalation of the violence against the PLA and seizures of firearms and ammunition.[66]

CIVILIAN ELITE

As the level of violence continued to escalate across the country, a consensus emerged in late August among most of China's top political leaders that the situation had deteriorated substantially, and it was necessary to utilize the PLA to restore order. The level of concern among China's top political leadership can be gauged by the flurry of official notices *(tongzhi)* and decisions *(jueding)* aimed at curbing the excesses of the Cultural Revolution, and ensuring continued production and the reestablishment of basic order issued by various top bodies between January and August of 1967.[67]

Most importantly, of course, Mao reached the conclusion that the PLA must intervene to restore order, and other leaders of various political stripes quickly came around to this view. Between February and September, Mao toured extensive areas of northern, eastern, and south-central China and became concerned about the extent of the chaos across the land.[68] By September Mao was disappointed by the results of the PLA's performance to date, but at the same time he had become convinced of the necessity of massive PLA intervention to restore law and order.[69] For the "three supports and two militaries" policy to be successful, Mao declared, "There must be no chaos in the army."[70] Explaining his decision to himself and the nation, Mao rationalized it thus in the *People's Daily* in early 1968: "Soldiers are just workers and peasants wearing uniforms."[71] In other words, the military was not some elite, privileged socioeconomic class in Chinese society to be the target of attack but ought to be revered as part of the good revolutionary classes. Further evidence of Mao's determination to end the anarchy was his decision in late August 1967 to arrest key radical leaders such as Wang and Guan. The incarceration of these men had an immediate and noticeable impact on the level of disorder.[72]

Premier Zhou was greatly concerned about the chaos being wrought by the Cultural Revolution. Although wary of crossing Mao, by his words and deeds Zhou was clearly desperate to blunt or limit the destructive impulses of the movement and eager to have the PLA intervene to put an end to the chaos once and for all. But he strongly favored a resolution with minimal use of force.[73] Zhou also tried to protect the PLA as an institution from harm and shield individual military leaders from persecution – much as he tried to buttress other ministries and shelter civilian officials. Zhou, as can be seen from the preceding discussion of the Wuhan Incident, was instrumental in mediating between different factions, including radical mass organizations and regional PLA commanders. In fact, he was engaged in exhaustive Kissingeresque shuttle diplomacy both in Beijing and in cities across China. There is little doubt that Zhou was the busiest senior party leader during the Cultural Revolution.[74]

CCP General Secretary Deng Xiaoping saw the situation in China as critical and in need of military intervention. Although he was to be purged shortly, in mid-1967 Deng was an important voice supporting PLA employment. Deng later noted that "...at that time the army could not but intervene to stabilize the situation, intervention was proper...." Nevertheless, although "the 'three supports and two militaries' proved extremely useful," said Deng, intervention "inflicted great harm to the army [because it] brought many bad things...greatly damaging the army's prestige."[75]

On September 5, 1967, the Central Committee, State Council, CMC, and CCRG, reflecting a surprising degree of unity, jointly issued orders to the PLA giving it sweeping powers to use force to reestablish law and order.[76] Ultimately even radicals like Jiang and Yao were of the opinion that full-scale military intervention was necessary. Jiang, in an address to a delegation from Anhui Province on September 5, urged support for the Central Committee's order issued that same day. She backed away from criticizing the PLA and urged a return to order. Jiang said: "Sometime earlier, there was this wrong slogan: Seize a 'small handful in the army.' As a result, 'a small handful in the army' was seized everywhere and even the weapons of our regular troops were seized."[77]

In addition to taking the reins of government in cities, towns, and villages across China, the military also assumed judicial powers and duties. By the end of 1967, Minister of Public Security Xie could report that "most of the public security organs have been put under military control."[78] Commencing in late summer, mass trials were held in many cities for the first time in China since the early 1950s. These trials were staged by the PLA, presided over by the PLA, the defendants were sentenced by the PLA and had sentences – including executions – carried out by the PLA.[79]

The use of the PLA to restore order after the Red Guard movement had spun out of control was an act of desperation by China's top political leaders. They had nowhere else to turn; there was no other disciplined, cohesive force capable of restoring order across the land. The communiqué on party history issued in June 1981 can be read as an authoritative assessment of the PLA's intervention in the Cultural Revolution. It states:

> The chaos was such that it was necessary to send the People's Liberation Army to support the left, the workers and the peasants and to institute military control and military training. It played a positive role in stabilizing the situation, but it also produced some negative consequences.[80]

THE MILITARY ELITE

The leadership of the PLA was extremely reluctant to permit the army to get involved in the upheaval. In the early days of the Cultural Revolution, when the movement was confined to a purge of party elites, many of the top military brass lent their support. But as the scope expanded to include mass participation and hence threatened to disrupt social order and attack the organizational unity of the PLA itself, the military leadership became less supportive.[81]

When the military finally got the go-ahead in September 1967 to restore order by force if necessary, it was a relief to most soldiers. General Xu Shiyou's frustration was still detectable eleven years later in a talk to other senior party and military leaders. It was only "[i]n September 1967," recalled Xu Shiyou, "when Chairman Mao let me subdue the turmoil" in Nanjing and Jiangsu.[82]

At each stage, the senior officers sought to keep the army out of the line of fire. When the arena of conflict was enlarged with the mobilization of Chinese youth, the PLA remained reluctant to get involved. Although the military was instructed to provide logistical support to the Red Guard detachments that traversed the country to "exchange revolutionary experiences," and to exercise extra vigilance in guarding key installations during the January power seizures,[83] it tried to maintain a neutral and aloof posture as long as it could.[84]

This is not to say that military units did not try to provide assistance surreptitiously wherever possible to more conservative Red Guard factions in order to give them an edge over the more radical ones. Nevertheless, even when battles broke out between opposing factions, the PLA tended to refrain from getting involved. In Changsha in August 1967, soldiers stood aside as Red Guards used hand grenades, machine guns, and artillery to inflict heavy casualties on each other. The only violations to the scrupulous neutrality observed in this particular instance were words of advice shouted to combatants on the side taking the most punishment.[85]

Radical Red Guard groups were often angry at local PLA headquarters because they clearly tended to favor conservative groups, and in many places radicals stormed military installations, sometimes repeatedly. Despite instructions to remain strictly neutral, troops such as those in Guangzhou by late February had had enough and launched a concerted crackdown on the most radical group, imprisoning thousands. Two weeks later, Guangzhou soldiers officially established a military control commission.[86]

Some regional military leaders exercised more restraint than others. At one extreme was General Wei Guoqing in the Guangxi Zhuang Autonomous Region, who brutally suppressed leftist radicals who had tried unsuccessfully to seize power in early 1967.[87] At the other extreme was Shanghai Garrison Commander Liao Chengguo, who showed considerable skill and initiative in averting the use of deadly force by quickly disarming the factory militias and swiftly aligning himself with Zhang Chunqiao in January 1967.[88]

In late summer, Lin grew increasingly alarmed by a spate of weapons seizures by radical mass organizations across China. As Lin wrote to Mao:

> The major problem is the confrontation between the two factions [and] armed conflict is escalating, especially the seizures of weapons from the army, which have taken place in five southern provinces. The trend is spreading and demands immediate attention.[89]

Local and regional military leaders, while all along preferring to remain completely removed, became increasingly frustrated as they were severely restricted by the limitations of their orders and found themselves the butt of criticism from Beijing for performing poorly. But by August factional warfare between Red Guard groups had grown fiercer and more deadly as most were armed with weaponry stolen from armories or donated by sympathetic soldiers or militia members. Moreover the PLA had become fair game as a target for radicals. Radicals rallied under the slogan "strike down a handful of military leaders taking the capitalist road."[90] Even Jiang noted in a major speech in early September 1967: "Everywhere we seized their guns, beat them up, and scolded them. But they did not strike back, nor did they argue. Is there such an army in other part[s] of the world?"[91] In the eyes of most soldiers, the situation had become intolerable and something had to be done.

Moreover, the tension and frustrations of the Cultural Revolution resulted in factional struggles within the PLA at both the highest and lowest echelons. At the top level there were power struggles between Lin and others, including Marshals Xu and Nie, whereby Lin tried to purge his rivals in the PLA. Lin was allegedly behind the persecutions and eventual deaths of Marshals He and Peng Dehuai.[92] Intra-PLA conflict also led to the deaths of more junior officers. An officer attached to the Beijing Military District, for example, was seized from his home and imprisoned. He was murdered – reportedly beaten to death with steel bars at the hands of PLA enlisted men.[93] The level of intensity in the Cultural Revolution even resulted on rare occasions in battles between different combat units and between military cadets and regular army units.[94] Usually, however, PLA units preferred to intervene indirectly through proxy mass organizations to which they provided weapons and assistance.[95]

On August 9, Lin gave a pep talk to military personnel from the Wuhan, Shenyang, and Jinan Military Regions. There were two elements that ensured China would successfully weather the turmoil, said Lin: Chairman Mao and the PLA.[96] This speech was important not only in raising the morale of soldiers but also in rallying support among the party leadership for a more proactive role for the PLA. And by late August, Lin was able to broker an agreement with regional military chiefs during a meeting of the CMC. The soldiers agreed to participate in the establishment of "Revolutionary Committees," which would be led by PLA members, and the central party leaders agreed to give the PLA full authority to deal with the Red Guards.[97] On September 5, the PLA received formal authority to reassert control by force if necessary. The process of restoring order, suppressing armed groups, and disbanding the Red Guards continued for months – well into 1968 in many areas. The autumn trade fair in Guangzhou even had to be postponed a month (from mid-October to mid-November).[98] The restoration of basic order and the reestablishment of effective power centers in each province, autonomous region, and municipality were officially signified by the formal declaration of the creation of a "Revolutionary Committee." Although composed of party officials, representatives of mass organizations, and soldiers, these organs were dominated by the PLA. Some two-thirds of these committees (twenty of twenty-nine) were not formed until 1968, the last two in September of that year.[99]

The September 1967 announcement marked the culmination of a consensus decision by political and military elites to approve full-force employment of the PLA to deal with the chaos created by the Cultural Revolution. Despite this massive intervention, violence continued to flare up across China in 1968. But the worst was over, and the employment of the PLA ensured that the party-state would not totally collapse.

THE COUP THAT NEVER WAS

The Cultural Revolution was a tumultuous and turbulent event that dramatically affected virtually every institution in the PRC. Aside from the CCP itself and China's educational system, perhaps no institution was so adversely affected as the PLA. The military became increasingly confused and frustrated because the Cultural Revolution seemed to push China closer and closer to the brink of anarchy. As social order broke down across the country and mass organizations grew more and more unruly and violent, even daring to launch attacks on PLA installations and personnel, soldiers' morale dropped lower and lower. Not only did the PLA find itself assailed by society, but it also was torn by factionalism within.

The majority of military leaders were opposed to the Cultural Revolution because of the chaos it had unleashed on China and the havoc it wrought on the army. Despite the level of anguish among senior soldiers, such as that expressed previously by Marshals Ye and Xu Xiangqian in February 1967, these soldiers somehow tolerated the situation without choosing to rebel against the party. The blame for the anarchy produced by the Cultural Revolution, as other scholars have noted, lay squarely with Mao and the top party leadership and, as such, provided ample grounds and justification for a military coup d'etat.[100] Yet there was no coup at the height of the Cultural Revolution. Of course, there was the sensationalized military coup allegedly hatched by Lin in September 1971. However, this purported attempt occurred years after China was on the brink of anarchy. While the well-worn answer for the absence of a military coup is the PLA's total loyalty to the CCP – the "party commanded the gun" – the real answer is more complicated. Four dimensions are important in understanding why a coup did not occur. First, there was a fusion between party and army leaders – a dual role elite structure. Second, there was the strong personal loyalty that most senior soldiers felt to Mao – that the PLA was essentially Mao's army. Third, the military never questioned its internal security mission. Fourth, the PLA did not see itself as autonomous and distinct from the

111

party-state or society. These factors ensured that the crisis did not lead to a complete rupture between the party and military.

The Dual Role Elite

When a country lapses into chaos because of the ineptitude or bumbling of political leaders, a powerful military often views this as justifying the overthrow of the civilian leadership. Rationalizing that it has no choice but to rescue the country from disaster, the armed forces either seize power themselves or, after ousting one set of civilians, install another set of civilians.[101] This did not happen because the civil-military leadership configuration in the late 1960s remained dual role. That is, the key figures of the Long March generation remained in both the CCP and PLA hierarchies. Particularly important, of course, were paramount leader Mao and his dedicated premier Zhou, who, although best classified as civilians, each had impeccable military service credentials. PLA commanders considered both to be honorary soldiers. Similarly, CCP leaders viewed Marshals Lin and Xu Xiangqian as senior CCP members. Thus, it was not easy to separate the party from the army, or vice versa.

Mao's Army

When armies launch coups against civilian authorities, the act is frequently justified by the claim that soldiers are loyal not to any specific civilian leader or the incumbent in a particular formal office but to an abstract entity such as the state, nation, or constitution.[102] In the case of communist China, army allegiance to the "party" was no guarantee against a coup: Any number of individuals or groups of the dual role elites among Chinese military leaders could have attempted to seize power in the name of the party. However, a major reason there was no military coup in 1967 was because of the strong bonds of personal loyalty that most of these PLA men felt to Mao. This special allegiance to the paramount leader that many senior officers held reinforced the more abstract political loyalty to the CCP that PLA commanders had drummed into their heads. In short, to these soldiers, the party was synonymous with Mao.[103] As General Xu Shiyou remarked to Mao adamantly in 1967 and on several subsequent occasions:

> I object to making the Cultural Revolution, but if someone wanted to kill the Chairman, go against the Central Committee, usurp power, and fight civil wars, then I would fight all the way to Peking [Beijing] to protect you.[104]

In other words, for many military leaders, the PLA was Mao's army. While most soldiers were extremely frustrated at the degree of chaos in the country and its negative impact on the PLA, senior military leaders and most junior officers maintained an unwavering personal loyalty to Mao. Furthermore, this hallowed bond was identified as being synonymous with military loyalty to the party. While there appear to have been instances of military units battling each other, the most serious crisis in civil-military relations was the Wuhan Incident in July 1967.

Nevertheless, issues of allegiance and identity were confused by the tangled web of personal loyalty networks of different military leaders. The PLA was deeply divided within itself. In large part this was due to the tug of multiple and competing, if not conflicting, loyalties. Even though the PLA was by far the most unified and cohesive national institution in China during the Cultural Revolution, it was highly factionalized. Factions, such as Lin's family, sought to expand their own influence at the expense of other soldiers. Nevertheless, these ties of personal and political loyalty were severely tested by the words and deeds of radical party leaders, such as Jiang and Wang Li. Still these bonds of allegiance to Mao endured largely because they were undergirded by loyalty networks between junior and middle-ranking officers and respected senior party and military leaders, such as Premier Zhou and Marshal Xu Xiangqian, who remained completely faithful to Mao.

Internal Security and Noncombat Missions

It is often argued that military coups are more likely when an army is heavily involved in internal security duties and/or noncombat-related roles such as economic construction or rural development.[105] In Mao's China, most soldiers considered internal security and other noncombat duties as integral to the PLA's mission. Consistent with the doctrine of People's War, in the mid-1960s the PLA was very much domestically oriented and internally focused on defense in depth in anticipation of external invasion. Furthermore, the PLA had long had internal, noncombat responsibilities that for many years did not seem in conflict with combat-readiness.

Noncombat functions, though ever-present for the PLA, became exceedingly demanding by the late 1960s. Not only did the PLA virtually take over complete responsibility for law and order, but it also took on the actual business of day-to-day administration of local, county, municipal, and provincial jurisdictions, and some 2 million soldiers assumed hands-on supervision of work units across the country.[106] The country was in such shambles that the PLA was even prepared to play police officer – a particularly distasteful task for soldiers that can increase the likelihood of a coup d'etat.[107] Shanghai was a significant exception to the heavy involvement of the PLA evident in other Chinese cities.[108]

The mass civil unrest of the Cultural Revolution was a source of considerable alarm for the PLA. It was a significant distraction for the military that diverted attention from external threats – the Soviet Union to the north and west, and the United States in Vietnam to the south. The long Sino–Soviet border was heavily fortified, and the PLA had tens of thousands of "volunteers" serving in engineering and anti-aircraft artillery units in North Vietnam. The domestic turmoil made supplying the frontlines difficult – especially since the PLA relied heavily on the railways, a mode of transportation used heavily by Red Guards traveling around the country. While the Cultural Revolution forced the PLA to focus on internal security, it was not this role per se that was an anathema. Rather, it was the distraction from concentrating on the grave external threats that China faced and, more fundamentally, the threat that domestic turmoil posed to the PLA as an institution that most concerned military leaders (see the following section).

The Limited Corporateness of the PLA

Soldiers are likely to launch a coup if they believe that the survival of the military as an institution is threatened or its monopoly of the use of force is being usurped.[109] With the paramilitarization of Chinese society during the Cultural Revolution, quasimilitary societal groups, such as Red Guards and factory militias, emerged prepared to wage urban warfare. Not only was the PLA under direct attack from mass organizations, but also by August 1967 it could no longer claim to have a monopoly on the legitimate use of armed force. Paramilitary groups armed with homemade weapons as well as firearms taken from PLA armories were engaged in pitched battles with each other and in some cases at war with the PLA itself. Zhou estimated that during the turmoil of the Cultural Revolution, "hundreds of thousands of casualties were inflicted" upon the PLA.[110]

Whereas in most countries the frenzy and chaos of a Cultural Revolution and the destruction it unleashed on the armed forces might have triggered a coup or at least numerous mutinies, in China no such reaction was forthcoming. In large part, this was because the corporateness of the military, while strong in many ways, was limited. While infused with a staunch esprit de corps, the PLA did not see itself as autonomous of the party-state or society. Chinese soldiers were imbued with the idea that they were the party's army *and* the people's army. The army's link with the party was cemented by dual role elites and the belief that the PLA was Mao's force. The PLA was indoctrinated into believing it was an army of the people comprised, in Mao's words, of "workers and peasants in uniform." Furthermore, the PLA did not see the existence of paramilitary groups as challenging the functional prerogatives or corporate interests of the army. Under the doctrine of People's War, the defense of China was predicated on arming and training the masses to wage protracted struggle against any invader. However, when these groups sparked a civil war by waging war against each other and even the PLA, military attitudes changed. Moreover, when a group such as the worker militia that backed the Gang of Four was seen as a rival power center, the PLA could be prompted to act.[111]

CONCLUSION

There was considerable reluctance among China's political and military elite to employ the PLA in order to restore law and order in 1967. The party leaders opted for incremental moves whereby the extent of military involvement escalated gradually as the previous step proved to be inadequate. In late January, the military was given vague orders to "support the left"; in early 1967, it was directed to enforce order but was forbidden to use force; by the end of summer, the PLA was essentially given carte blanche to restore normalcy. The remarkable tolerance and forbearance displayed by most PLA units in the face of turmoil and indignities during the initial part of the Cultural Revolution were near the breaking point by the autumn of 1967. Within the military, there was not just enormous frustration with the mounting street violence but also tremendous dissatisfaction with the party's series of low-key and ineffective prescriptions.

When the warnings and threats to get mass organizations to end their mischief were ignored and law enforcement organs failed to quell the disturbances, Mao and other party leaders called out the PLA. At first soldiers were directed to use only their powers of persuasion and under no circumstances to use force. When this had negligible effect, an escalation of the military response was ordered: The army was permitted to use force as a last resort. When the intervention of regional forces failed to restore order, then PLA main force units were dispatched. These active-duty units were far more successful than the reserves because they were better disciplined, had no allegiance to local political factions, and were seen by most parties as impartial.

By September 1967 there was fundamental agreement about the need to end the turmoil among political radicals, moderates, and conservatives, but this coalition was tenuous. The Central Cultural Revolution Group was fearful that wholesale military intervention would completely undermine the group's power, as evident by CCRG's various statements and actions prior to September.

The political leaders led by Mao insisted on a policy of gradual escalation of threats and warnings. Many hoped that the presence of PLA units would intimidate the extremists and deter them from continuing to create mayhem. The PLA leadership was not keen to see their troops inserted into the turmoil with vague orders and a weak mandate. When limited intervention proved to be totally ineffective and PLA units found themselves the target of attacks, senior officers began to conclude that it was impossible for the PLA to remain aloof. Implicit recognition that Beijing's gradualist policy – what amounted to a policy of coercive diplomacy – had failed came in the form of the September 1967 directive for swift, massive, and unrestricted PLA intervention.

The military itself – although far more cohesive and unified than the party and government – was also poisoned by factionalism. The result was some battles between different military units. The complexities of the Chinese situation are more understandable when one recognizes the transgroup linkages at work, especially between political elites and paramilitarized mass organizations. As a result, the PLA had to fight bloody battles for many months in some locales to reestablish basic order. This was followed by years of PLA administrative work until effective party and government institutions at the provincial and local levels were rebuilt across China.

Part III

USE OF FORCE IN THE DENG ERA

6

Half-Hearted Coercive Diplomacy: China's 1979 Attack on Vietnam

THE ferocious artillery barrage and subsequent massed infantry assault on Vietnam by the Chinese People's Liberation Army (PLA) on February 17, 1979, should not have come as a complete surprise to anyone.[1] While the precise timing of the attack might have been unexpected, the military assault itself had been anticipated for months. After a month of fighting, China unilaterally announced it would withdraw and the PLA pulled back across the border into China, leaving scenes of total devastation behind it. The Vietnamese proved themselves tough adversaries, and the PLA performed worse than Beijing had anticipated.[2]

Why did Beijing initiate the war? What did Chinese leaders hope to accomplish from the conflict? This, the largest military operation conducted outside China's borders since the Korean War, has been carefully studied by a handful of scholars, with the primary focus being its international causes and consequences.[3] Monographs have studied China's foreign policy goals, emphasizing that Beijing's decision was triggered by the strengthening of ties between Vietnam and the Soviet Union – China's major adversary at the time. In addition, Vietnam allegedly committed numerous incursions into Chinese territory and adopted a policy of forcing hundreds of thousands of ethnic Chinese residents to flee Vietnam. The final straw was Vietnam's all-out invasion of Cambodia – officially the Democratic Republic of Kampuchea – launched on December 25, 1978. However, little attention has been given to the domestic political dimensions of the conflict. Even less attention has been focused on the debate among Chinese leaders over whether to use military force against Vietnam.[4]

I contend that Beijing practiced "half-hearted coercive diplomacy" toward Vietnam in the six months leading up to China's largest military conflict of the post-Mao era. The Chinese action was not only a response to changes in the international environment but also reflected a civil-military culture in the throes of radical change in terms of leadership, doctrine, and identity. This chapter examines the roles of senior PLA and Chinese Communist Party (CCP) leaders in order to determine the attitudes of various individuals toward the use of military force. First the background and circumstances leading up to China's decision to attack Vietnam are reviewed, and then the positions of different leaders toward an attack are analyzed.

THE CONTEXT

In the late 1970s, Beijing felt extremely vulnerable. The Soviet Union loomed menacingly along China's long northern border. Newly unified Vietnam, a budding Soviet client state, was flexing its considerable military muscle in the south and seeking to dominate Indochina. This sense of vulnerability was exacerbated by the sequence of events that occurred on China's periphery in 1978, which led many in Beijing to feel at once surrounded by foes and bereft of friends. Concerns over the Soviet connection and Vietnamese expansionism, especially Hanoi's designs on the Khmer Rouge regime in Phnom Penh, were compounded by Vietnam's treatment of its ethnic Chinese residents, border incidents, and Vietnam's increasingly vocal claims to territory that China considered its own.

But the decision to attack Vietnam was made not only within the context of the geopolitical environment, it was influenced also by the sense of outrage at what Beijing felt was Hanoi's deceitful betrayal of a steadfast friend. The Chinese viewed the Vietnamese as ingrates who reciprocated decades of Chinese aid and sacrifice with backstabbing. Vietnam had received more economic and military assistance from China than any other country, with the possible exception of North Korea. Certainly in terms of sustained military aid provided during more than two decades of war in Indochina, Beijing's support to Hanoi is without parallel for the PRC. The CCP actively assisted Viet Minh forces in their struggle to win independence from France virtually from the start. Then, during the struggle to unify Vietnam waged against South Vietnam and its main ally, the United States, China provided additional aid. During the 1960s, hundreds of thousands of troops served in Vietnam and Laos in engineering and anti-aircraft artillery divisions. Inevitably Chinese soldiers were killed in Indochina in American air attacks.[5]

The Strategic Dimension. However, during the 1970s Hanoi became gradually more estranged from Beijing and drew closer to Moscow. The culmination of these trends was the formal establishment on November 3, 1978, of an alliance between Vietnam and the Soviet Union – a twenty-five-year Treaty of Friendship and Cooperation. The Soviets established a naval base in Camh Ranh Bay in the south, and by the late 1970s provided Vietnam with considerable economic and military aid. Moreover, Hanoi appeared to harbor ambitions to become the hegemon of Indochina. Battle-hardened from decades of combat and well equipped with American, Soviet, and Chinese hardware, the Vietnamese People's Army had become one of the world's most effective and largest military machines. Hanoi sought to expand its influence in Vientiane and Phnom Penh. And its aggressive moves toward Cambodia particularly alarmed China. Commencing in July 1978, official pronouncements emanating from Beijing began to refer to Vietnam scornfully as the "Cuba of the Orient" – a not-so-subtle reference to the significant role that Cuban troops played in Africa as Soviet proxies.[6]

With the downward spiral of Sino–Vietnamese relations seemingly beyond repair – and the complete failure of Hanoi's efforts to speedily establish full diplomatic relations with Washington – Vietnam decided to go full speed ahead with closer ties with the Soviet Union.[7] As early as February 1978, the Communist Party of Vietnam (CPV) seems to have decided that an attack on Cambodia would probably be necessary and that some kind of military response from China would be forthcoming.[8] In June Vietnam formally joined COMECON, and General Vo Nguyen Giap traveled to Moscow to begin negotiations on a Treaty of Friendship and Cooperation. The Soviets promptly began sending weaponry to Vietnam in August, although the treaty was not formally signed until some three months later.[9] In addition, on December 25, 1978, China was confronted with a full-blown Vietnamese invasion of Cambodia. And then some two weeks later, on January 6, 1979, China's embassy in Phnom Penh was evacuated hurriedly as Vietnamese troops approached the Khmer Rouge capital. In Chinese eyes, these developments merited a swift and forceful response.

The Overseas Chinese Factor. Hanoi had long considered the Hoa – the ethnic Chinese inhabitants of Vietnam – a latent security concern. The Chinese of Vietnam, as in so many other countries in Southeast Asia, were disproportionately concentrated in the commercial and financial sectors. As such, many were some of the most prominent and wealthy members of Vietnamese society. Because of their high visibility, there tended to be considerable resentment among the indigenous Vietnamese toward the great success and material well-being that some in the Chinese community enjoyed. Thus the CPV began a crackdown on private enterprise in the recently liberated south. This crackdown slipped into high gear in March 1978 and quickly became a witch hunt directed at Chinese businesses. In response to the crackdown, Chinese merchants and financiers lay low, hoarded their goods, and/or operated on the black market. As a result, Vietnam's economy went into a tailspin. Both the authorities and many ordinary Vietnamese tended to blame the Hoa for the economic crisis. In this extreme political climate, attacks on and discrimination against Vietnamese residents of Chinese descent became more severe, particularly from March 1978 onward.[10]

Nevertheless, the initial exodus of Hoa that also began in March 1978 seems to have been unrelated to the crackdown on the one million strong Hoa community in southern Vietnam. The first wave of departees, numbering some two hundred thousand, arrived in southern China from northern Vietnam.[11] Their departure seemed to have been triggered by rumors of impending war between China and Vietnam and the circulation of pamphlets of mysterious origin urging ethnic Chinese to return to the motherland and contribute to economic modernization. These moves are not likely to have been the result of any coordinated policy by Hanoi. Indeed, Hanoi would seem to have had little to gain from the exodus of these northern residents, many of whom were vital workers in critical industries. Thus the blame for the initial outflow of ethnic Chinese residents cannot be placed solely on Hanoi, although Vietnam's policy toward the Hoa contributed to the outflow. And after the emigration began, the exodus took on a logic and momentum all of its own.[12]

Later on, the Hanoi regime seems to have made an explicit policy decision to encourage the departure of Hoa from the south. Local authorities on the coast were instructed to build and/or make available boats of various descriptions and permit ethnic Chinese to exit the country in exchange for fees and taxes. Many of these refugees were forced to pay high prices for boats of dubious seaworthiness and sizeable bribes to Vietnamese officials to look the other way. While this outflow of humanity – dubbed "Boat People" – caused tremendous consternation in the international community, it enraged Beijing's leaders who saw it as a direct affront to China.[13] In April 1978 the PRC official with primary responsibility for overseas Chinese affairs, Liao Chengzhi, expressed concern at the plight of the Hoa and stated that Beijing opposed any foreign government that forced overseas Chinese to take up a foreign nationality. The temperature rose considerably the following month. In mid-May China announced the suspension of twenty-one Chinese aid projects in Vietnam and stated that the funds allocated for these projects would be redirected to assist ethnic Chinese refugees from Vietnam. Then, on May 24, the Overseas Chinese Affairs Office formally condemned Vietnam's persecution and expulsion of ethnic Chinese residents in strong terms. The statement made it clear that Beijing would hold Hanoi responsible for any mistreatment of the Hoa.[14] On May 26 China escalated the war of words by announcing it would send two ships to rescue "persecuted Chinese." Four days later, China canceled more aid projects.[15]

Territorial Disputes. Vietnam had paid little attention to territorial claims until the mid-1970s. Until 1975 its priority had been reunification with the south.

Vietnam's common land border with China, almost eight hundred miles of very rugged mountainous terrain, like so many national borders in Asia, had never been properly demarcated to everyone's satisfaction. The wording of an 1887 Sino–Vietnamese treaty was extremely vague, water courses referred to in the treaty had altered over the decades, and the location of the stone markers that delimited the border became a matter of dispute, further complicating the situation. Moreover, Vietnam and China also put forward competing claims to maritime locations: coastal waters in the Gulf of Tonkin as well as archipelagos in the South China Sea, notably the Paracel and Spratly islands.[16]

The Dilemma

China's leaders were confronted by a dilemma.[17] If they sat back and did nothing, China would look weak and impotent and such inaction might encourage Vietnam to take further action. But China had to be careful not to provoke a Soviet military response. What could China do? How could China come to the aid of the embattled Khmer Rouge? Since China did not share a land border with Cambodia, all aid had to go either by sea, air, or overland via a sympathetic third country (that is, Thailand).

It was the invasion of Khmer Rouge–ruled Cambodia, a Chinese ally, that by most accounts infuriated China's top civilian and military leaders. The subject of Chinese military action against Vietnam was first raised in connection with Cambodia. Discussion of a military response to a Vietnamese invasion of Cambodia reportedly was first raised at an enlarged Politburo meeting in May 1978. The consensus was that such a move by Hanoi would merit a forceful response by Beijing.[18]

Out of this meeting came a decision to prepare for a limited war on China's southern border to "hit back" at Vietnam. Beijing thus dispatched more troops to the frontier regions of Yunnan and Guangxi. This was done reportedly for two reasons. First, the move was taken to guard against a surprise attack – a possibility raised by the buildup of Vietnamese forces detected across the border. Second, the step was aimed to "[i]f possible . . . reduce . . . pressure on Cambodia," according to the text of an internal speech by a senior State Council official in early June 1978. The official went on to specify the mood of the leadership:

If the confrontation escalates, we don't mind engaging in a localized war. *The party leadership has made a clear decision: If Vietnam tries to engage in military adventure, we are determined to fight.* If Vietnam imposes war on the people of Cambodia and invades the country in force, we will support Cambodia with material and money and we don't mind making national sacrifices.[19]

Beijing escalated the rhetoric in late May when it announced China would dispatch two ships to pick up any persecuted ethnic Chinese who wished to leave Vietnam. That summer, two Chinese freighters waited off the coast of Vietnam for clearance that never came to enter Vietnamese waters and collect Hoa. The move by Beijing has been interpreted either as a "test" of Vietnam's willingness to compromise or as a publicity stunt by a frustrated Chinese government.[20] The step was virtually guaranteed to anger Hanoi and make China look impotent to resolve the crisis. The incident marked the beginning of a hardline approach by Beijing toward Hanoi; prior to this, China had sought to resolve issues in a conciliatory and moderate manner. For example, Beijing had worked tirelessly to moderate the rhetoric and actions of Phnom Penh toward Hanoi in late 1977 and early 1978. The Chinese hoped to forestall a Vietnamese invasion of Cambodia. Moreover, in seeking to resolve the ethnic Chinese issue, Beijing at first tried a low-key and confidential diplomatic initiative in early 1978.[21]

After the rescue ship incident, the Chinese leadership redoubled its efforts to support the Khmer Rouge. Consultations with Cambodia's defense minister during a visit to Beijing in July 1978 led to China stepping up its military aid to Phnom Penh; by December, there were some five thousand Chinese military advisors in Cambodia. Commencing in August 1978, U.S. intelligence detected heightened Chinese military activity near the border with Vietnam.[22]

Then in early November Chinese leaders were dispatched to the region to get a firsthand look at the overall situation. Vice Premier Deng Xiaoping made a tour of Southeast Asian states to explain China's position on Cambodia and Vietnam. From accounts of Deng's discussions in Bangkok and Singapore, it seems clear that the Chinese leader was trying to gauge the thinking of Association of Southeast Asian Nations (ASEAN) leaders on the situation in Indochina and prepare them for the possibility of Chinese military action. At the same time, Politburo member Wang Dongxing led a delegation, which included Hu Yaobang and Yu Qiuli, to Cambodia. Pol Pot appealed to the delegation for direct Chinese military intervention. In the aftermath of these trips, the Beijing leadership gathered to consider carefully the evolving situation and China's appropriate response.[23]

THE DECISION

The Central Work Conference in the winter of 1978 was without a doubt the most important meeting of the post-Mao era. Indochina was only one of a number of critical issues discussed at the meeting, which stretched from mid-November until mid-December. The series of decisions reached at this meeting by China's leaders, and formalized at the Eleventh Party Central Committee that immediately followed, had enormous ramifications for the direction that the country would take in its domestic and foreign affairs for the next two decades. Domestically, the decisions committed China to a reform agenda encompassing both thoroughgoing economic and political reforms. Externally, the decisions wedded China to a more pragmatic approach to strengthen the country's geopolitical position – through the forging of a new international alignment with the United States – while modernizing the economy by expanding foreign trade and encouraging foreign investment in China. The most immediate impact was on China's foreign policy: a decision to normalize relations with the United States at the earliest possible date, and to prepare to launch a limited, carefully calibrated attack on Vietnam in early 1979.[24]

Why did China decide to attack Vietnam? The decision was made because, as Chinese leaders stated repeatedly, commencing in very late December 1978, they wanted to "teach Vietnam a lesson." The phrase was used only after the fully fledged Vietnamese invasion of Cambodia.[25] The decision, although calculated, was an emotional response to Vietnam's all-around "anti-China" *(fan-Hua)* actions. The phrase "teach Vietnam a lesson" is itself filled with emotion and tinged with arrogance. The contempt and venom for Hanoi among Beijing's leaders was patently evident in the way they spoke about Vietnam to officials from other countries, including Thailand, Singapore, and the United States.[26] The attack was deemed necessary because Beijing's efforts at coercive diplomacy had failed. China had failed to stop Vietnam from victimizing its citizens of ethnic Chinese origin, and had also failed to deter Vietnam from invading Cambodia.[27] In principle, the decision for a military move was made quite easily because there seemed to be considerable agreement in Beijing that some kind of forceful Chinese response was in order. However, there were significant differences of opinion as to the appropriate size and scope of China's action as well as some opposition.

The PLA began its preparations for the attack months before, starting in mid-November, if not earlier.[28] Beijing gave much thought to the decision. Deng assured U.S. reporters during his visit to the United States in early 1979, "We Chinese do not act rashly."[29] China issued plenty of warnings and threats prior to its attack. China also made it clear to the Soviet Union and Vietnam at the outset of the attack and repeatedly during the conflict that the war would be strictly limited in scope and duration.[30]

Chinese leaders viewed the attack on Vietnam as similar in style and scope to Beijing's brief but fierce 1962 clash with India in the Himalayas.[31] In fact, this parallel is flawed in several important respects. First, as Gerald Segal observed, there was "no consistent escalation of Chinese warnings" the way there was for India in 1962 (and Korea in 1950).[32] An analysis of statements made by Beijing in the months before the attack bears this out: While China issued stern, ominous warnings in late December 1978 – on the heels of Vietnam's invasion of Cambodia – China's pronouncements in January and early February 1979 were, by comparison, innocuous.[33] While from Beijing's perspective the three "strong protests" issued by the Foreign Ministry on January 18, February 10, and February 16, were clear and unequivocal warnings, this does not appear to have been the message that Hanoi received.[34] Second, China's opponent in 1979, Vietnam, was militarily far stronger and more competent than India was in 1962, as Beijing belatedly realized to its chagrin.[35]

China also held consultations prior to the attack with friendly states, notably the United States, Japan, and Thailand. Of the three, it was Bangkok that provided the strongest support and closest cooperation to Beijing. Politburo member Geng Biao and Deputy Foreign Minister Han Nianlong were dispatched on a secret mission to Thailand in mid-January to meet with Prime Minister Kriangsak Chomanan. The result of several days of intense negotiations was the formation of a de facto alliance against Vietnam.[36] Deng also talked bluntly about a Chinese attack on Vietnam during his momentous visit to the United States in late January and early February of 1979, following on the heels of the establishment of full diplomatic relations between Beijing and Washington on January 1. In two separate meetings with President Jimmy Carter, Deng made China's intention to attack Vietnam very clear.[37] Deng also made pointed remarks to this effect to other political leaders in Washington. While the Carter administration did not give the Chinese leader its firm support for the move, neither did it publicly oppose it. Beijing was satisfied with the ambiguity because it left Moscow and Hanoi guessing as to the degree of Washington's backing for the eventual attack and the level of U.S. coordination with China.

A day after Deng's return from the United States and Japan, a meeting of the Central Military Commission (CMC) convened. In a session lasting from February 9 until February 12, top civilian and military leaders reached general agreement on the parameters of an operation against Vietnam. They agreed that there should be no direct PLA Navy participation in order to minimize the chances of drawing in Soviet naval forces in the region. The decision not to use aircraft was also made with the aim of avoiding escalation. There is no doubt that the fact that China possessed a very limited air capability, one quite likely inferior to that of Vietnam, figured in the decision.[38] Nevertheless, both Chinese air and naval units in the vicinity were reinforced and placed on alert as a precaution. PLA Air Force aircraft patrolled the border and protected Chinese air space.[39] These limits and China's intention to withdraw swiftly after any attack were communicated in a variety of ways to China's friends and foes. Deng was named as overall commander-in-chief of the operation, and Marshals Nie Rongzhen and Xu Xiangqian were named his deputies. Then, on February 16, on the eve of the attack, Deng articulated the basic rationale for the attack on Vietnam at a meeting of central party leaders.[40]

Despite the repeated warnings that some kind of military action would be forthcoming, Beijing sought to maintain an element of surprise as to the exact timing of the attack. While China was clearly massing troops along its border with Vietnam, it tried to mask the impending assault. On December 22, 1978, China informed Vietnam that service on the international rail line between the two countries would be suspended because of dangerous track conditions resulting from damage inflicted by Vietnamese attacks. Certainly, this reason for halting passenger and freight traffic could be taken at face value but, more likely, that announcement was meant to mask the main reason for closing the line: stepped up preparations for a February attack.[41] More significant was that the actual attack began during the visit to China of Foreign Minister Atal Bihari Vajpayee of India. Vietnam had not anticipated any attack to come during this visit (neither had India; an irate Vajpayee cut short his visit and returned to New Delhi). Deng was deliberately vague when Indian journalists, who were in Beijing for Vajpayee's visit, asked him what kind of lesson China intended to give Vietnam. His response led some correspondents to conclude that an attack on Vietnam was not in the cards for the immediate future.[42]

The eventual attack on February 17, 1979, consisted of heavy artillery bombardments and fierce fighting by PLA infantry units. The assault consisted of coordinated advances on two fronts: from Yunnan in the west and from Guangxi in the east. After some initial successes, Chinese troops got bogged down because of the rugged terrain and the stubborn defense put up by Vietnamese defenders. As a result, the PLA's advance was much slower and casualties were far heavier than Beijing had anticipated. An indication of Beijing's displeasure at the way things were going was the demotion of Xu Shiyou. By one account, Xu Shiyou was replaced as operational commander by Yang Dezhi.[43] Whether or not this occurred, we do know that less than a year later, in January 1980, Xu Shiyou was ousted from his position as commander of the Guangzhou Military Region. On March 5, after sixteen days of brutal fighting, the offensive portion of the operation was concluded following the capture of Lang Son, the last major border town held by Vietnamese forces. On the same day, Beijing announced that Chinese troops would be withdrawn from Vietnam. And the departure of Chinese troops was completed eleven days later.

CIVILIAN LEADERS

While some analysts report that the war did not seem to be a major "divisive issue" in Beijing, others insist there were significant "disagreements among the leadership" about whether or not to launch an attack. Most analyses assert that a major concern seemed to be that such an attack would divert valuable time and resources away from China's top priority: economic reform and development.[44] In addition there were fears that the attack would escalate out of control, quite possibly provoking a Soviet attack on China.

Strong Proponents

By December 1978 Deng, the de facto paramount leader, was the strongest advocate of an attack on Vietnam. Deng was one of five deputy chairs of the CCP, and a vice premier of the State Council. Deng took the initiative from the start, at the May 1978 enlarged Politburo meeting where the matter of what to do about an increasingly assertive Vietnam was first raised. Deng reportedly said: "We should deal a head-on heavy blow at the anti-Chinese adverse current stirred up by Vietnam. Our policy is ... to make a head-on confrontation and to struggle over every inch of land."[45] While he is classified here as a civilian, at the time Deng was also director of the PLA's General Political Department and had extensive experience in military affairs. Actually, Deng seemed to view himself on a par with Mao – that is, as a top civilian party leader with extensive military expertise and a special talent for matters of strategy. Deng did not regard himself a mere soldier.[46]

Deng looked at things in broad geopolitical terms. The growing assertiveness of the Soviet Union indicated by the invasion of Afghanistan in December 1978, and the cementing of a de jure alliance between Moscow and Hanoi a month earlier, raised considerable alarm in Beijing. These developments made swift progress on normalization with Washington all the more urgent and some kind of forceful Chinese response to the upheaval in China all the more important. In Deng's mind, China needed to demonstrate resolve – that it was not all bark and no bite. Thus, the shifting international balance of power seemed to require a Chinese display of force. And this foreign policy position was an important and integral part of a domestic "policy package" being promoted by Deng and his reformist allies.[47] For Deng it demonstrated his resolve vis-à-vis a client state of Beijing's number one threat (Moscow), accentuated the danger posed by Hanoi, and highlighted the logic of improved ties with Beijing's erstwhile foe, Washington.[48] A small war would tend to win over potential moderate allies and silence vocal conservative critics. It would also simultaneously give Deng ample opportunity to demonstrate his considerable military expertise and draw attention to Hua Guofeng's glaring lack of the same. Moreover, the operation would provide valuable combat experience for the PLA, and, even if highly successful, undoubtedly reveal shortcomings and increase calls for fundamental reforms in the military – a cause near and dear to Deng's heart.[49]

This does not mean that Deng threw caution to the wind; he was very concerned about the conflict escalating into a larger conflagration involving the Soviet Union. Deng advocated a limited war because he thought it would greatly minimize the possibility of Soviet intervention. A major attack from the Soviet Union was unlikely in Deng's view, and China was well prepared for a medium or small-scale military response from the Soviets. In addition, Deng believed there would not be a negative international response. He also argued that a limited conflict of relatively short duration would not adversely affect China's economic modernization. In the final analysis, Deng argued, while it was unlikely that China would achieve a great military victory in such a war, it was equally unlikely that China would suffer a major defeat. Deng was strongly opposed to more adventurous souls who advocated direct military intervention in Cambodia.[50]

Another advocate of an assertive response to Vietnam's actions was Wang. Because he was one of the most powerful men in China by dint of his post as commander of the Central Guards Regiment – the praetorian unit responsible for the security of China's top leaders – Wang's opinion was important. He had been in charge of protecting Mao and was instrumental in the successful arrest of the Gang of Four in October 1976. Here Wang is classified as a public security official rather than as a soldier since his primary organizational affiliation and career were within the public security apparatus.[51] His influence was reflected in his appointment as a deputy chair of the CCP and the fact that it was he who headed a Chinese fact-finding delegation to Phnom Penh in early November 1978.[52] During his visit, Wang received an urgent appeal from Khmer Rouge leader Pol Pot for Chinese volunteer troops to be sent to Cambodia. At the month-long Central Work Conference in late 1978, Wang advocated doing just this.[53] In remarking that Vietnam might continue to "run wild for a while," Wang seemed to realize that, even if China did intervene militarily in Cambodia, transporting Chinese soldiers to the country would take some time and whatever force was dispatched would likely be limited in size.[54] Since he seems to have given some thought to the potential problems, logistical and otherwise, connected with such an operation, he was probably fairly receptive to a less risky compromise proposal: attacking Vietnam directly.

Li Xiannian, also a deputy chair of the CCP, a vice premier of the State Council, and the leader of the Foreign Affairs Leading Group, appears to have supported the attack. This conclusion is based on Li's forceful statements about the military operation both before and after the fact. On February 11, during a conversation with a Pakistani military delegation, Li said:

> ... Vietnam has launched wanton aggression against Kampuchea [Cambodia] and at the same time stepped up its military provocations along the Sino–Vietnamese border and occupied some Chinese places. The Chinese people are very indignant at this. We have time and again warned the Vietnamese not to turn a deaf ear to what we have said.[55]

He told a Japanese newspaper reporter on March 4, 1979, that the operation had been a great success and that the PLA was being withdrawn because it had achieved its objective of establishing a "secure border."[56] While usually a moderate person, Li's strong views in this case may be explained by his key role in the Beijing foreign policy establishment and his long history of active involvement in Sino–Vietnamese relations. Li was likely to be highly indignant at the way Vietnam seemed to be repaying decades of Chinese friendship and considerable economic and military assistance.[57] Thus, he probably viewed an attack on Vietnam as a move that would boost China's stature in the world, particularly vis-à-vis the two superpowers. Nevertheless, a month later, in a report to a central work conference, Li's emotions gave way to a cooler assessment of the conflict in terms of the financial drain it took on state funds. Li's bureaucratic responsibilities in financial work greatly influenced his outlook.[58]

Moderate Support

Hua, chair of the CCP, premier of the PRC, and chair of the CMC, appeared to cautiously support military action. Although nominally the highest-ranking leader in China by dint of his troika of top posts, his position was far from secure. In fact, Deng and his supporters were gradually undermining Hua's formal authority. Hua was much younger than Deng and did not possess the prestige, depth of experience, or extensive personal networks enjoyed by Deng and other members of the Long March generation. Moreover, Hua had no military expertise and very limited international exposure and foreign policy experience. As such Hua did not openly oppose the attack on Vietnam, although he was probably against it.[59] It is worth quoting the innocuous but restrained remarks attributed to Hua at the May 1978 Politburo meeting. We should "be courageous and skillful in our struggle with Vietnam," he told his colleagues.[60] Hua gave the opening speech at an important national meeting to explain the rationale for an attack on Vietnam to central and provincial leaders. He spoke briefly at the February 16, 1979, meeting, stating that the Politburo had decided to launch an attack on Vietnam the following day. He then turned over the podium to Deng, who provided details on the scope, objectives, and risks associated with the operation.[61] Hua's peripheral role in the decision is underlined by his virtual omission from the group of top leaders who oversaw the course of the operation. As the nominal head of the party organ charged with direct responsibility for the PLA, such an omission is surprising.[62] Either Hua deliberately kept his distance from the war because he opposed it or was prevented from becoming more involved by Deng and his allies.

Opposition

It seems that Chen Yun, another deputy chair of the CCP and China's top economic expert, opposed the war. After the war, Chen Yun reportedly said: "We didn't break their fingers, but merely hurt them. In some respects we actually helped them."[63] He is said to have issued a "scathing indictment" of the conflict after the fact in a report he delivered at a work conference in April 1979. Chen Yun remarked that the war had been halted none too soon. If the conflict had continued several more months, he insisted, the economic burden to the country would have been extremely heavy.[64] Chen Yun implied that PLA troops had failed to achieve their military objectives and were withdrawn in early March for economic reasons.[65]

MILITARY LEADERS

There are conflicting reports about the views of PLA leaders toward military action in Indochina. At least one analyst contends the military were opposed to an attack on Vietnam, and it was a more hawkish civilian leadership that carried the day.[66] Others argue that military figures were prime advocates of an attack. At the Politburo meeting in May 1978, a group of senior soldiers reportedly pushed for direct military intervention in Cambodia. "Some of the military leaders" advocated sending "Chinese volunteers" to Cambodia to prop up the Khmer Rouge government.[67] At an enlarged Politburo meeting held as part of the Central Party Work Conference of November–December 1978, military figures were reportedly hawkish, much more so than civilians.[68] The actual situation seems to have been mixed: While some PLA officers advocated war, other soldiers proved unenthusiastic about military action, whether directed at Cambodia or Vietnam, and still other military men were adamantly opposed to any attack.

Support

Some Chinese soldiers had strong emotional ties to the Vietnam People's Army, going back to the 1950s when the CCP and Viet Minh cooperated closely. Some Chinese were veterans from the Viet Minh's campaigns against the French. Such soldiers appeared to be particularly bitter about Hanoi's actions and especially vehement about a forceful response to Vietnam's hostile actions toward China. Wei Guoqing, the director of the PLA's General Political Department (GPD), was head of the Chinese Military Advisory Group to the Viet Minh established in 1950 and present at the historic victory over the French at Dien Bien Phu.[69] Wei reportedly made a rousing speech to PLA officers in Nanning on December 11, 1978, arguing that China must "teach Vietnam a lesson."[70] Wei was a Deng ally who had succeeded Gang of Four member Zhang Chunqiao as director of the GPD in September 1977.

Xu Shiyou, another PLA veteran, strongly supported an attack on Vietnam at the Politburo meeting in late 1978. Indeed, he volunteered personally to lead the Chinese forces. He did command troops in the eastern sector. Operations in the eastern theater of the conflict, adjacent to Guangxi, proved to be far less successful than those in the west, where Yang commanded the forces. Xu Shiyou's uninspiring performance was not evident from the upbeat speech he gave to honor soldiers who had distinguished themselves in the war. He said, "In this self-defense counterattack war against Vietnam we performed very well and achieved a great victory – demonstrating our national power, demonstrating our martial prowess."[71] Su Zhenhua, first political commissar of the PLA Navy, was another strong advocate of dispatching ships off the Cambodian coast to support the Khmer Rouge.[72] Su died ten days before the February attack was launched.

Deputy Chief of the PLA's General Staff Department General Wang Shanrong seemed to support the war. At a banquet for Phnom Penh's ambassador to Beijing in honor of the anniversary of the Kampuchean Revolutionary Army, in mid-January 1979, Wang Shanrong declared, "All commanders and fighters of the Chinese People's Liberation Army . . . will . . . resolutely support the Kampuchean Revolutionary Army and people in their war against Vietnamese aggression and for national salvation."[73] As Deng's deputy, he could say no less on such an occasion. In any event, Wang Shanrong likely supported his superior's position on the conflict.

Moderate Support

Marshal Xu Xiangqian, minister of national defense and a Politburo member, seems to have supported the attack, though perhaps not overly enthusiastically. A year and a half later, in August 1980, Xu Xiangqian alluded to the Vietnam war in an interview with an Italian journalist. He noted that, while China sought a peaceful international environment in order to concentrate on economic modernization, this did not mean that China would turn the other cheek if threatened militarily. And he observed a number of regional conflicts were being waged around the globe, including in Indochina. It was in practically the same breath that he reiterated Mao's dictum: "If someone doesn't attack us, then we won't attack them; but if someone does attack us, we will definitely attack them."[74] But speaking to a military audience only a few weeks after the war, Xu Xiangqian was far more reserved in his assessment of the conflict. He said:

> [In] this military operation against Vietnam we have gained experience in all aspects [and this] will lead to a very good postmortem. We can analyze which things went well and which things went wrong – all beneficial to our future work.[75]

Xu Xiangqian, also a vice chair of CMC and deputy commander-in-chief of the Vietnam operation, spelled out some of these lessons later in his speech.[76] His official biography states that he took a central role in "policymaking and decisionmaking about the Sino–Vietnamese self-defense counter-attack war." He "participated in the drawing up of the battle plans, choosing his words with great care and carrying out his investigation with scrupulous attention to detail."[77]

Geng, the head of the CCP's international liaison department and a vice premier, seems to have backed a limited attack on Vietnam. Although he also served as a diplomat, here Geng is classified as a soldier. He had an extensive military career and saw himself as a soldier first and foremost.[78] Two years after the war, in March 1981, he was appointed minister of national defense. He told a Swedish delegation in Beijing on February 21, 1979, that China's attack was limited "in terms of space and time."[79] Geng appears to have strongly opposed military intervention in Cambodia and took the lead in arguing against such a move. He contended that as a matter of principle and for pragmatic considerations it would be extremely imprudent. If China did intervene militarily in Cambodia, it would violate some of its own Five Principles of Peaceful Coexistence, namely noninterference in the internal affairs of other states and nonaggression. And from a purely pragmatic standpoint, such action would be detrimental to China's interests and pose considerable risk of escalation. The war would probably nix the chances of the Khmer Rouge taking the Cambodian seat at the United Nations. Furthermore, intervention was likely to bog down China in an Indochinese quagmire with little hope of a quick exit and raise the real danger of direct Soviet intervention.[80]

Opposition

Marshal Ye Jianying, at the time a CCP deputy chair and chair of the National People's Congress, had advocated a purely defensive strategy against Vietnam. Until March 1978, Ye had served as minister of national defense. In late October 1978, he reportedly urged careful defensive preparation in the south against a possible attack from Vietnam.[81] In his speech at the Central Party Work Conference in December 1978, Ye made no mention at all of tensions with Vietnam or the drama developing in Indochina. It is possible that his views may have changed in late December, after Vietnam's invasion of Cambodia. However, judging by a major speech he made to commemorate the thirtieth anniversary of the founding of the PRC in late September 1979 – seven months after China's attack – this does not seem to have been the case. In the address, Ye made no mention at all of the recent war with Vietnam. He did reiterate China's support for Cambodia in the same breath as expressing support for other causes around the globe, and he gave token acknowledgment to the PLA's role in safeguarding the "sacred territory" of the motherland.[82]

Wang Zhen, vice premier and another old soldier, was probably either opposed to or neutral about the proposed attack, although I cannot say for sure. However, two years later, Wang was the coauthor of a *Workers' Daily* commentary published on February 4, 1981, opposing an adventurous foreign policy. According to the commentary, "China should guard against diverting a local war to our country, and avoid being taken as the main target for attack." The article was coauthored by fellow soldier Xiao Jingguang, military strategist Wu Xiuquan, and foreign policy advisor Liao.[83]

ANALYSIS

An analysis of China's road to the war with Vietnam reveals that, while Beijing was spoiling for a fight, it acted in a deliberate and controlled fashion. Especially after Vietnam's invasion of Cambodia in December 1978, China wanted to punish Vietnam militarily. The official rationale for China's attack given in

Beijing pronouncements at the time and in subsequent accounts of the war even two decades after the fact is that Vietnamese forces intruded on Chinese territory on literally thousands of occasions during a five-year period (from 1974 until February 1979).[84]

The Failure of Coercive Diplomacy?

When one examines the eighteen-month period leading up to China's attack on Vietnam, two phases are discernible: one before December 25, 1978, and one after this date ending with the outbreak of war on February 17, 1979. The full-scale Vietnamese invasion of Cambodia is the watershed event. The overarching goal of China's policy before Christmas Day 1978 was to deter an invasion, and after this date China's ultimate objective was switched to teaching Vietnam "a lesson." Vietnam's invasion of Cambodia dramatically demonstrated the failure of China's first attempt at coercive diplomacy.

Did China's attack on Vietnam demonstrate the failure of its second attempt? Coercive diplomacy tends to be seen as ending when actual war breaks out; the emergence of the latter indicates the failure of the former. According to this logic, China's coercive diplomacy failed. A key reason given for the failure was the "asymmetry of motivation": Vietnam was far more committed to keeping Cambodia as a sphere of influence than China was at preventing this from happening, and Hanoi undoubtedly calculated this. It is highly unlikely that Beijing was ready to commit Chinese ground forces to defend Cambodian soil. Moreover, China's tone was inconsistent and lacked credibility; until mid-1978, China for the most part avoided inflammatory rhetoric and actions in its dealing with Vietnam over Cambodia and overseas Chinese. Not until the summer of 1978 did China begin to talk tough and, even then, China did not back its talk with resolute action. Vietnam probably also concluded that China lacked the military capacity to protect Cambodia – in terms of providing either sufficient weaponry and aid to the Khmer Rouge or airlift capabilities. Another reason for the failure of coercive diplomacy was poor signaling by China and the absence of a "carrot." As James Mulvenon notes, China was not clear and unambiguous in its messages to Vietnam about its goal; there was too much background "noise." Further, China did not provide any incentive for Vietnam to comply, let alone offer a face-saving way out.[85]

Yet phase two of coercive diplomacy should not be so quickly dismissed as a failure. Beijing had multiple goals and motivations in launching its attack in February 1979. Certainly China wanted Vietnam to halt persecution of Hoa and end its armed provocations along the nations' common border. The war did not achieve the specific official military goal articulated: It did not bring an end to Vietnamese armed provocations along the border with China. China's actions did not dislodge Vietnam from Cambodia – a desirable outcome. It was in the context of Hanoi's invasion that the first serious discussion of possible military action emerged in Beijing. In January 1979, China's rhetoric did escalate. Chinese leaders began to talk publicly of "teaching Vietnam a lesson." Whether this was simply meant to supply a clear ex post facto justification for China's eventual attack or to compel Vietnam to withdraw from Cambodia cannot be said with complete certainty. The only step by Hanoi that would have satisfied Beijing would have been an immediate withdrawal from Cambodia or the announcement of a timetable for a full withdrawal of Vietnamese forces. But short of this highly improbable complete about-face by Hanoi, Beijing seemed unlikely to be swayed from some kind of show of force.

In sum, it seems safe to say that China was intent on taking some "punitive action" against Vietnam. Beijing also had a broader deterrence effort in mind: to deter the Soviets or Vietnamese from launching any kind of major military operation against China in the future. There was no major border clash or war fought with Moscow or Hanoi for another decade (although border skimishes with Vietnam continued into the 1980s), until a brief naval engagement with Vietnam in the disputed Spratly Islands in March 1988. Viewed from this perspective, China's coercive diplomacy can be judged a qualified success.

Following the December invasion, while China certainly desired a Vietnamese withdrawal from Cambodia, it was viewed as more of a medium- or long-term goal. China did not realistically expect a withdrawal to happen in the immediate future. That this was an important foreign policy goal for Beijing is evident from the inclusion of a Vietnamese-occupied Cambodia as one of "three obstacles" identified as hindering a Sino–Soviet rapprochement repeatedly articulated during the 1980s.

China's leaders were also very much concerned with status. In late 1978, in the face of Soviet intervention in Afghanistan and the emergence of a Soviet–Vietnamese alliance, China wanted desperately to show it was a major power that did not issue warnings and threats idly. In late December, a strongly worded editorial in the *People's Daily* warned:

> There is a limit to the Chinese people's forbearance and re-
> straint. . . . [China] will not attack unless it is attacked. But if it is attacked,
> it will certainly counter-attack. China means what it says. We wish to warn
> the Vietnamese authorities that if they, emboldened by Moscow's support,
> try to seek a foot after gaining an inch and continue to act in this unbridled

fashion, they will decidedly meet with the punishment they deserve. We state this here and now. Don't complain later that we've not given you a clear warning in advance.[86]

In short, China wanted to be taken seriously.[87] Indeed, on March 30, 1979, Deng claimed that the conflict had enhanced China's "international prestige."[88]

Games People Play

Beijing's leaders were practicing what one might call "half-hearted coercive diplomacy" during late 1978 and early 1979. China's leaders did not just have coercive diplomacy on their minds; they also had multiple goals on the domestic front both before and after Vietnam's December invasion of Cambodia. Prestige was an important commodity both for Deng himself and the PLA generally. As for Deng, he sought to use the crisis to enhance his own stature vis-à-vis his political rivals both in and out of the military. His position as chief of the General Staff Department and prime mover behind the war emphasized his extensive military experience and patriotism while underlining at the same time Hua's lack of the same. Deng hoped to stir up a storm of patriotism that would solidify support for reforms.[89] He hoped that the war would draw attention to the popular slogan of an earlier generation of Chinese reformers: "rich country with a strong army" *(fuguo qiangbing)*.[90] Whether the PLA's prestige in domestic circles was enhanced is another matter. Certainly Deng proclaimed it was so.[91] As for the PLA, it emerged from the Cultural Revolution with a rather tarnished image. The extensive involvement of the military in domestic affairs that lasted from the late 1960s well into the next decade meant that the reputation of the PLA as the staunch defender of the motherland had suffered. A short but significant engagement with a traditional enemy of China might boost its flagging reputation. And in Deng's opinion, it did.

Civil-Military Culture in Flux

Explaining the varied reactions of Chinese leaders and ordinary people to the 1979 war with Vietnam requires attention to China's civil-military culture. On the one hand, the consensus that surrounded the decision to attack was the result of the persistence of the Long March civil-military leadership configuration. On the other hand, the doubts, controversy, and opposition arose because of conflicts over PLA doctrine, function, and identity. The PRC had just begun tentatively the first steps toward a difficult paradigmatic shift in its civil-military culture (see Chapter 3).

Dual Role Elites

The key figure in Beijing's decision to attack Vietnam was without a doubt Deng. He was clearly the biggest booster of the war. Indeed, it is quite likely that without Deng's active and determined efforts, there would not have been a war in the first place.[92] The ease with which Deng was able to bring around his colleagues, both civilian and military, to this point of view is attributable in part to his being a prominent member of the Long March generation with strong political and military credentials as one of the "dual role elites." This was underlined by the fact that he held not only the position of vice premier but also was chief of the PLA's General Staff. He was able to work both sides of the aisle. Deng stepped down from his military post in March 1980. In fact Deng's tenure in this key military post is highly unusual: Although Deng had impeccable military credentials, he was *not* a career military man, and the chief of general staff post was invariably held by a senior serving military officer.[93] Deng's central involvement, then, was not only critical in making the military operation happen but was also crucial in ensuring that a civil-military consensus swiftly developed. Similarly, the dual role nature of men such as Geng and Ye further blurred the civil-military distinction. Despite the opposition of certain military figures, such as Marshal Ye, to the proposed invasion, it was extremely difficult for military leaders to articulate a unified viewpoint challenging the attack.

From People's War to What?

As Beijing deliberated the pros and cons of intervention in Vietnam, debate over military doctrine was heating up.[94] Marshal Xu Xiangqian was at the forefront of soldiers pressing for a revision of doctrine. The issue was politically charged because it became intimately caught up in questions of Mao's legacy and the political platforms of different factions. Of particular importance was Hua, the leader of what were dubbed as the "Whateverists," a faction that advocated adhering to whatever policies Chairman Mao advocated. Advocates of changes in military doctrine were directly challenging the credibility and legitimacy of the "Whateverists." Furthermore, this became a serious political life-and-death struggle between factions because the demise of the entire status quo platform – including the key national defense dimension – would signal total defeat in the battle to succeed Mao as paramount leader of China. Thus, it is not surprising that Hua did not enthusiastically support the attack on Vietnam.

Doctrine was such a controversial subject because it struck at the heart of the identity and function of the military in post-Mao China. Some opposition to the war arose precisely because the operation ran counter to existing doctrine – the conflict was alien to People's War – and counter to the domestic focus of the PLA – the conflict was beyond China's borders. The prevailing doctrine of People's War, which stressed a strategy of "defense in depth," had a decidedly domestic orientation for the military and represented an extremely egalitarian ideal for Chinese soldiers – they were an organic and integral part of the common people of China. Thus, when some influential military figures, such as Xu Xiangqian, advocated updating Maoist doctrine – what became known as "People's War under Modern Conditions" – they were challenging the entire existing system. Indeed, Deng was pressing for a complete overhaul of civil-military culture. The kind of war that China fought against Vietnam in 1979 called for radical reforms in defense: more attention to advanced technology and a smaller, more highly trained PLA with significant air and naval arms rather than a large, rudimentarily trained light infantry force. Marshal Xu Xiangqian and other progressives used the war to press for "raising our army's combat capabilities to the modern level."[95] Deng himself, in a key speech on military reform a year after the war, sought to use the conflict to his advantage:

Is our army combat effective? Can it deal with a real problem? I'm not talking about a situation like the self-defense counterattack on Vietnam. That kind of situation is relatively easy to cope with. What I mean is: If we should be faced with a more powerful adversary than Vietnam, how combat effective would we be?

Deng acknowledged the bravery of PLA soldiers in the war but stressed the serious deficiencies in the level and training of personnel. In a remark almost certainly prompted by an actual incident from the war, he asked rhetorically during the same speech, "If a soldier doesn't know how to use maps, what good is he!"[96]

In the aftermath of the war, Deng and his pro-reform allies took concrete steps to purge military leaders opposed to rapid modernization and/or those who were just plain incompetent. Some actions were swift, while others were more gradual. Within a year of the war, for example, Deng had engineered the ouster of Xu Shiyou, one of the key field commanders in the attack on Vietnam. Xu Shiyou and Deng had reportedly blamed each other for the PLA's less than stellar performance.[97] Then, starting in 1983, reformers used a rectification campaign to identify Maoist traditionalists and radical leftist holdovers from the Cultural Revolution. Many of these were pushed into retirement as part of the massive PLA force reduction of the mid-1980s.[98]

There were secondary aims in launching the war. One was to give the army practical experience. Deng purportedly told the February 16 gathering that one goal of the attack was to conduct a "military exercise."[99] Given the PLA's existing doctrine, domestic orientation, and lack of combat experience, serious deficiencies would inevitably become apparent. The upshot would probably be increasing calls for a radical rethinking of the identity, format, function, and doctrine of China's military establishment. Indeed that appears to be precisely what happened. Marshal Nie, a CMC vice chair and pro-Deng man, reportedly criticized the tactics used in the war on Vietnam in a speech to the CMC in February 1980.[100]

Confusion over the PLA's Identity, Format, and Function

What is one to make of the distinct lack of enthusiasm for the war among many Chinese and the disparaging remarks about the PLA? To take the second part of the question first, some Beijingers expressed glee to one foreign scholar over the military's abysmal performance in 1979.[101] This feeling might be explained as representing the views of some of China's most sophisticated elite – individuals who were well informed about domestic politics and resentful of the PLA's huge political influence and the high-handed behavior of the military in the Cultural Revolution. On the first part of the question, many Chinese do seem to have had a rather muted response to the war.

The mixed views of the public likely reflected the fact that the PLA's identity, format, and function were very much in flux (see Chapter 3), and the people's expectations of the PLA were confused. In Beijing, intellectuals reportedly "expressed varying opinions" on the conflict. Some intellectuals expressed opposition to the war, with comments such as one to a European correspondent that "China had enough problems without having to fight a border war."[102] Another foreign correspondent noted a clear lack of public enthusiasm for the war, especially in the provincial capitals of Yunnan and Guangxi, during a visit in August 1979.[103] This reaction in part reflects the realization that the war was not an overwhelming success and that the PLA had not performed that well, suffering heavy casualties. Some Chinese probably feared the war might become a protracted affair and sap the energy and resources of the country. Certainly, the majority of Chinese supported the war for reasons of patriotism. Indeed, strong expressions of patriotism and pride in China's soldiers were evident among the Yunnanese who were living near the border in early 1979, and these expressions were recounted to the author five years later. Villagers vividly recalled watching PLA units marching smartly through their towns and villages on their way to the front. Several referred to the soldiers as "most beloved people" *(zui ke'ai de ren)* – a phrase popularized during the Korea conflict more than a quarter century earlier.[104]

Negative comments and remarks about the war and the PLA should also be viewed in the context of the more relaxed political atmosphere of the time. Because the war came on the heels of the Democracy Wall movement of winter 1978–9, and because China's leaders deliberately had played down the war, some people probably felt it was permissible to express their opinions freely and question the wisdom of the attack. Moreover, in contrast to the Korean War, there was no mass movement launched to whip up popular support for the war. Except for frequent editorials condemning Vietnam and regular upbeat news dispatches from the border, there were no emotional speeches by leaders seeking to exhort the masses. An extremely low-key approach to the war pervaded Beijing throughout the course of the hostilities.[105] A newspaper reporter from the *Liberation Army Daily*, reporting from the front, told a radio audience several days into the war not to be fearful. He recounted how PLA fighters in the war zone had asked him to tell the Chinese people, "... not to worry ... [and remain] at their posts to contribute to the ... four modernizations."[106] The same generally mild tone is evident when reading later accounts of the war, as well as in the speeches and writings of key participants. In short, the war never became a crusade to the Chinese people or Chinese soldiers the way the Korean conflict did. Significantly, many of the official biographies of the key participants published since 1979 contain no reference to their roles in the conflict.

A Passive/Aggressive PLA

Opposition by military figures was also likely linked to ambiguity over the precise military objectives of the operation. Such ambiguity is inherent in the practice of coercive diplomacy, and the civil-military distinction is often exacerbated when a state resorts to such behavior.[107] As Alexander George explains:

> In contrast to ... traditional military strategy ... coercive strategy focuses on affecting the enemy's will rather than upon negating his capabilities. It does not rely on ample or quick use of force to achieve political objectives. Rather, if threats alone do not suffice and force is actually used, it is employed in a more limited, selective way. ...[108]

The reason for this tension is that soldiers and diplomats see coercive diplomacy from very different perspectives. While both invariably prefer a solution short of war, statesmen favor subtle signals and gradual increases in the pressure applied to an opponent in order to deter or compel them. Soldiers, by contrast, prefer to send a strong, direct, and unambiguous message promptly – a rapid, massive show of force to bring an opponent swiftly to his senses.

While the political objectives were more or less straightforward, the military goals of the attack were never fully spelled out. The general political goal was to force Vietnam to respect China's resolve, and more specifically to put an end to the persistent border provocations as well as force Vietnam to divert military resources away from Cambodia. All these aims were mentioned either in Beijing's formal policy statements or remarks by top leaders. By contrast, China was unlikely to reveal the military goals prior to or even during the actual war because this would provide valuable intelligence to the enemy. And these precise goals were not revealed afterward so that China could claim victory no matter how unsuccessful the outcome. Indeed, the closest China came to giving a military objective was the formally stated goal of ending Vietnam's harassment along the nations' common frontier and improving border security generally. Deng also gave this as the primary aim of the action in a discussion with U.S. Treasury Secretary Michael Blumenthal during the latter's visit to China in late February 1979.[109] Still it was never explained precisely how these objectives would be achieved.

Available evidence suggests that military objectives were never properly specified.[110] Deng was extremely vague on this subject during a meeting with Indian journalists on February 14, three days before China's attack. When asked what he meant by "teaching Vietnam a lesson," Deng replied, "Well, you see it depends on how the situation develops."[111] Certainly Deng was in part being deliberately cagey in order to deceive Vietnam (as noted previously). But the vagueness also probably reflected the imprecise military goals of the operation. At a February 26 meeting in the midst of the conflict, Deng was asked by the president of the Kyodo News Agency what precise lesson the Chinese had in mind for the Vietnamese. Deng responded: "We would not mind military achievements. Our objective is a limited one, that is to teach them they could not run about as much as they desired."[112] Such vagueness likely contributed to opposition by some military figures to the operation. Without a clear idea of what was to be accomplished, many PLA men were reluctant to support such a risky attack. In this regard, Chinese soldiers tend, like soldiers in some other countries, to be conservative, pessimistic, and more reluctant than their civilian counterparts to resort to force.[113]

The soldiers who did seem very eager to "teach Vietnam a lesson" were those with a strong anti-Vietnam sentiment. Most such soldiers were involved in assisting the Vietnamese communists in their wars against the French and Americans. China provided a considerable amount of arms to Vietnam between 1957 and 1974. In the 1960s, Beijing provided an estimated U.S. $60 million in weaponry to Hanoi, which constituted almost two-thirds of China's entire foreign military assistance during this decade.[114]

CONCLUSION

China's 1979 attack on Vietnam was relatively moderate in terms of the spectrum of military options entertained by Beijing. While the strong support among some military figures for an attack on Vietnam may suggest a bellicose PLA, the action chosen constituted one of the more restrained and moderate among all the alternatives considered.[115] Both civil and military leaders seemed divided on the merits of the war. In any event, it was the top civilian leaders, Deng in particular, who carried the day.

Finally, the analysis in this chapter suggests that the succession struggle between Deng and Hua did not end with the Third Plenum in December 1978. While the plenum did represent a significant victory for Deng, it was only one battle in a larger political contest between the two men and their supporters. Further, given that Deng's ambitious economic reform program had to be scaled back in the spring of 1979 after suffering setbacks, he was not in the strongest of positions. While the conventional scholarly wisdom is that the war was a political setback for Deng,[116] it seems that, on the contrary, the conflict might best be viewed as a mixed blessing for the tenacious reformer who otherwise found himself in a tight spot in early 1979. Some analysts have argued that the war had no impact on domestic politics, and little, if any, impact on military affairs, including doctrine.[117] This chapter suggests that the war helped rather than hurt Deng. The war enabled Deng to claim some measure of success in the rough and tumble of pressing for political and economic reform. Moreover, it allowed him to advance his ambitious agenda of transforming the Maoist civil-military culture – one that in terms of leadership format, military doctrine, and army identity was already in considerable flux. In this context, the 1979 war looms as a far more critical event in launching China firmly on the path of reform than has been recognized heretofore.

7

Why the People's Army Fired on the People: Beijing, 1989

THE flowering of the student protest movement in the People's Republic of China (PRC) in April 1989 and its bloody suppression by the People's Liberation Army (PLA) some two months later have been widely documented.[1] The use of lethal force to crush a largely peaceful protest movement has been almost universally condemned. What is rarely discussed or understood, however, are the factors that led to the PLA opening fire with live ammunition on the citizenry of Beijing on June 3–4, 1989.

This chapter charts the rise of the protest movement and the response of CCP leaders. The decision to impose martial law and orders to the PLA to intervene are examined. Next the genesis of the orders to use deadly force and the military response are examined. Finally, the factors leading to this violent outcome are assessed.

Civil-Military Culture in Flux

In 1989, China's civil-military culture was in a state of transition, particularly civil-military format. Specifically, critical to understanding the outcome of the crisis are the role of a small but enormously influential group of elderly communists and the relationship between the military and the Chinese Communist Party (CCP).

First, although China's aging paramount leader Deng Xiaoping insisted that the reins of power had been successfully handed over to a new, younger generation of leaders, the events of 1989 proved this had not yet occurred.[2] By the end of 1988, the PRC's political elders, all veteran communists of the Long March era, were ostensibly either retired or on the verge of retirement. A new younger core of leaders had supposedly stepped to the fore – at least they occupied the most visible positions of authority in the formal hierarchy of the power structure. In fact, this generation administered the day-to-day affairs of the state, but major policy decisions were still made by the elders. A small circle of influential octogenarians still held unparalleled prestige by virtue of their association with the communist movement since its earliest days. The most important of these men numbered some half a dozen. Most easily recognizable was Deng (b. 1904). Though he was the dominant figure, as the events of 1989 clearly show, Deng was far from being the unchallenged ruler of China. Also extremely powerful were two former generals: State President Yang Shangkun (b. 1907), and Vice President Wang Zhen (b. 1908). Other elders included conservative economist Chen Yun (b. 1905), retired National People's Congress (NPC) Chair Peng Zhen (b. 1902), Chinese People's Political Consultative Conference Chair and former general Li Xiannian (b. 1909), Central Advisory Commission Deputy Chair Bo Yibo (b. 1909), and the sole woman – the widow of Zhou Enlai – Deng Yingchao (b. 1904). Chinese often referred to this group as the Gang of Elders. Here they are referred to as "the Elders."[3]

These elders were dual role elites, a reminder that CCP and the PLA hierarchies, especially at the higher echelons of leadership, remained inextricably intertwined. Over time it has become easier to distinguish between the civilian and military hierarchies and the leaders – especially at the lower levels of the PLA – but the distinction between the two remained blurred at the highest level of political power. Military figures who traced their careers and networks as far back as the 1920s still existed. Old soldiers, such as PRC President Yang, retained strong followings within the PLA and held top-level posts in both party and state bodies with direct responsibility for the PLA. Like Yang, Deng also retained tremendous support and prestige among China's soldiers. Thus, although they held top posts in the party and state apparatus, both could be logically classified as "military men." During the critical months of April, May, and June, Deng and Yang were chair and vice chair, respectively, of both the party Central Military Commission (CMC) and the state CMC.

THE CONTEXT

The reform program of paramount leader Deng that had proceeded relatively smoothly and successfully for almost a decade began to produce unwanted and unpopular results. By early 1989, urban Chinese were growing increasingly disgruntled with inflation, flagrant official corruption, and glaring inequities in the distribution of the fruits of the economic reform program. As 1988 drew to a close, China's leaders vacillated on difficult economic decisions, and reformers were unable to offer quick or easy solutions. The elders blamed CCP Secretary Zhao Ziyang for the deteriorating economy, and Zhao's patron, Deng, considered the party chief a mounting political liability. By March 1989, a concerted effort spearheaded by Chen and Bo was under way to topple Zhao from power. Old soldiers Li and Wang also opposed him, and Zhao's sole backer within the group was Deng.[4] Senior PLA officers such as Chief of Staff Chi Haotian, although far from being staunch supporters, respected Zhao for his efforts as vice chair of the CMC to help modernize the PLA.[5]

It was beneath this protracted round of elite conflict that the student protest movement developed. Sparked by the death of former CCP Secretary Hu Yaobang on April 15, the spontaneous student demonstrations rapidly gained momentum. Unrest also spread to other parts of China: Protests were held in many other cities, and rioting erupted in Changsha and Xian on April 22. After students began a boycott of classes on April 24, Deng issued a stern warning: a strongly worded editorial in the *People's Daily* of April 26 condemning the demonstrations.[6] The editorial, through its use of vocabulary, drew implicit parallels with the Cultural Revolution. The intention of the document was, combined with other moves, to compel the students to end their protests.[7] Rather than intimidating the students, however, the editorial served only to invigorate the movement. The following day saw the largest crowd since the beginning of the crisis: More than 150,000 students forced their way past police cordons into Tiananmen Square, cheered on by a crowd of some half a million onlookers.[8] Other steps were taken to underline the seriousness of the warning: dispatching party cadres to the streets of the capital to urge an end to the demonstrations and increasing the number of soldiers around the square. Other more conciliatory steps were taken to balance the "stick" with a "carrot" dimension.[9]

The intensity of the movement and the breadth of support it attracted caught the leadership of the CCP and the PLA off guard and divided. One of the main splits was along generational lines. Many younger midlevel officers were very critical of elderly senior officers or recent retirees who abused their powers and insisted on being coddled in luxury. Some publicly voiced their complaints. Chen Xianhua, the commander of the 42nd Group Army, openly disdained the "empty politics" and outdated management of his superiors.[10] Another group of officers indicated their discontent in an open letter to the CMC several days prior to the imposition of martial law. The authors, who remained anonymous, urged support for CMC Vice Chair Zhao's calls for moderation in dealing with the demonstrations. The letter also called for the defense budget to be lowered, military organizations to be "streamlined," and senior officers to give up luxuries such as "imported cars." The funds saved from these cuts would be put toward education.[11]

The situation was complicated by two high-profile international events scheduled for May. The Asian Development Bank (ADB) convened its first-ever meeting in Beijing, and the city hosted the first Sino–Soviet summit in thirty years. World attention focused on the Chinese capital, yet both events were overshadowed by the mass demonstrations. The protests disrupted scheduled activities. The official welcoming ceremonies for Mikhail S. Gorbachev on May 15, for example, were held at the airport instead of Tiananmen Square, which was awash in a sea of demonstrators.[12]

As the weeks went by, the demonstrations did not subside, although the number of participants and spectators fluctuated considerably over time. Token displays of strength by public security officers and units of the People's Armed Police (PAP), aimed at intimidating the students, seemed only to revitalize the protests. Meanwhile, a consensus began to emerge among the Elders: In their eyes, negotiation and restraint had failed. Student demands were growing progressively more radical and rebellious. As the protests continued, the party elders grew increasingly frustrated and restless. Their anger was directed not just at the student demonstrators but at the younger leaders of the party and government who, in the Elders' opinion, were proving incapable of rapidly resolving the crisis.

The Elders seem to have been willing to use military force to crush the protests from the early days of the demonstrations. Deng reportedly remarked on April 25 that the shedding of blood – even tens of thousands of lives – was an acceptable price to pay to avert chaos. Deng said defiantly, "I am not afraid because I have millions of troops."[13] Then, on June 9, four days after the massacre, Deng spoke in all seriousness, of a full-blown "rebellion" confronting martial law enforcement troops.[14] What constituted a rebellion in his eyes? Anything that conflicted with the Four Cardinal Principles declared by Deng in 1979 and enshrined in the 1982 PRC Constitution – namely, adherence to the socialist road, leadership of the CCP, Marxism-Leninism and Mao Zedong thought, and the people's democratic dictatorship. Indeed he was right: During the final days of the protests, at least some activists did call for the overthrow of the CCP. However, there is no evidence of a well-organized plot, and very few dissidents explicitly advocated the violent overthrow of the CCP.[15]

The student demonstrations confronted a leadership divided over economic policy and embroiled in a power struggle in which Zhao was fighting for political survival. Further, hordes of foreign journalists were in Beijing to cover the ADB meeting and Sino–Soviet summit. Deng and other top leaders were furious about the prolonged student occupation of Tiananmen Square – which demarcates both the city center and the symbolic heart of China – but were unwilling to evict them forcefully while the international media recorded the event.

Martial Law Is Declared and a Standoff Results

After Gorbachev's visit, the leadership made an attempt at compromise: Premier Li Peng held a dialogue with student leaders in the Great Hall of the People on May 18. When Li Peng failed to convince the students to end their protests, the Elders decided to impose martial law in the capital and suppress the demonstrations. The premier declared martial law on state television in the early hours of May 20 at the conclusion of an "extraordinary" meeting of the CCP Central Committee and the State Council with Beijing municipal party, government, and military cadres.[16]

Martial law, which officially went into effect in the central area of the capital at 10 A.M. on May 20, had never been imposed in Beijing before – not even during times of major upheaval. Of course, martial law had been declared in the Tibetan city of Lhasa two months earlier after bloody ethnic riots had broken out. Its imposition in the capital was an attempt both to intimidate the students and to pay token heed to constitutional law. Martial law in Beijing was formally declared by Li Peng – as had been the case in Lhasa in March 1989 – in his capacity as premier of the State Council, under the authority of the 1982 PRC Constitution.[17] President Yang spoke briefly after Li Peng, announcing that troops had already been dispatched to the city to restore order. Shortly afterward, Beijing Mayor Chen Xitong issued three martial law orders that, among other things, instructed troops and police to enforce martial law by "whatever means necessary."[18]

The actual decision to impose martial law had apparently been made at a Politburo Standing Committee meeting a few days before. Deng reportedly called the meeting at his residence on the morning of May 17, and all five members of the Standing Committee – Li Peng, Zhao, Security Chief Qiao Shi, Vice Premier Yao Yilin, and Propaganda Chief Hu Qili – attended. In addition, Deng, Yang, and Bo were present. These Elders were there despite the fact that none was a member of the Standing Committee. After heated discussion, Deng announced that he was in favor of imposing martial law and bringing in the PLA. The Standing Committee adjourned and resumed its meeting later the same day in Zhongnanhai minus Deng. The vote on whether to impose martial law was reportedly deadlocked two to two, with Zhao and Hu dissenting and Qiao abstaining. The session ended inconclusively and another meeting was held the following morning (May 18), attended by all Standing Committee members except Zhao, all the Elders – including Deng – and three of the most senior uniformed members of the Central Military Commission: Hong Xuezhi, Liu Huaqing, and Qin Jiwei. All fifteen were in favor of martial law and agreed to impose it formally in central Beijing on May 21 (the date was later moved forward one day).[19]

Shortly after Li Peng declared martial law, troops began maneuvers in the vicinity of the city center. In a show of force, small units – some armed, others without weapons – tried to convince demonstrators to disperse. Instead of weakening the resolve of the demonstrators, these efforts seemed to galvanize student protestors and spur public sympathy for them. Citizens began almost immediately to impede the progress of troops; military trucks were halted and their tires slashed. These acts of defiance quickly multiplied as hundreds of thousands of Beijing residents spontaneously poured out onto the streets to block the roads leading to the square when troops approached. The soldiers, many of whom were unarmed, were stopped in their tracks, surrounded in a sea of civilians.

To the Elders and other CCP leaders, China seemed on the brink of chaos, and swift, decisive action had to be taken; the protests had to be suppressed, and order had to be restored. Traditionally, Chinese governments have felt it necessary to claim a monopoly on morality. The students directly challenged this claim by capturing the moral high ground. A critical event in this regard was the hunger strike that began on May 13. In a political culture that values symbolism, the demonstrators' carefully worded, moralistic appeals and scrupulously nonviolent deeds paradoxically raised the stakes in the eyes of China's leaders. The contest soon escalated "from moralizing to revenge," with both student leaders and the Elders viewing the protests as a symbolic battle to the death.[20] The Elders also came to fear they might be physically overthrown. They were apparently worried about the threat of a coup d'etat; the palace coup that toppled the Gang of Four in 1976 had also been preceded by huge demonstrations in Tiananmen Square. Elder Li Xiannian reportedly remarked at the May 18 meeting previously mentioned, "If we don't put Beijing under martial law we'll all end up under house arrest."[21] In their minds, the specter of civil war also loomed. At the very least they recognized that there was clearly tremendous sympathy and support for the youthful protesters not only among the common people but also within the ranks of the CCP and the PLA.

Military Dissent

Many officers publicly declared themselves against using troops to suppress the student movement. The public letters and pronouncements issued by both senior military leaders and highly respected retired veterans are the most glaring evidence of the depth and breadth of opposition to using force against the students. Retired Marshals Nie Rongzhen and Xu Xiangqian also spoke out against the use of the army.[22] On the evening of May 21, student representatives visited the residences of Nie and Xu to appeal for them to oppose the use of military force against the students. Nie met with the delegation and assured them that the PLA would not move against the students. Xu did not meet with the students but he conveyed through members of his staff that the army should not be used to suppress the students. However, the reports of these meetings – broadcast on May 21 – noted that both veterans also strongly urged the students to end their protests and return to classes.[23] This aspect of the marshals' statements tends to be overlooked.

There were at least several other open letters from military leaders. Defense Minister Qin and Chief of Staff Chi along with more than one hundred other military figures, including former Defense Minister Zhang Aiping, former Chief of Staff Yang Dezhi, former Higher Military Academy Director Xiao Ke, and former Naval Chief Ye Fei, reportedly signed a letter urging that the PLA not be sent into the capital. Their letter to the party CMC and the Martial Law Enforcement Command stated: "The PLA belongs to the people. It should not confront the people, much less suppress them."[24] PLA commanders also knew that CCP leaders were divided over how to respond to the crisis, and they were unwilling to become pawns in a factional struggle.

As the extent of popular discontent became clear, Zhao sought to champion the movement's cause. In mid-May, he publicly criticized Deng and openly voiced support for the student movement.[25] Zhao disappeared from public view after a tearful meeting with students in Tiananmen Square just before martial law was declared. Rumors circulated of pro-Zhao plotters within the CCP or PLA or both who might try to seize power.[26] Although there is no hard evidence of such a plot, the Elders apparently feared that troops loyal to Zhao might be preparing to topple them.[27]

Obvious and alarming signs of public discontent and protest appeared throughout Beijing and in virtually all major Chinese cities. Intellectuals and members of nearly all organizations within the capital, including the party newspaper, the *People's Daily*, and Public Security Bureau personnel, joined the student demonstrators. Demonstrations occurred across China, and the nightmare most feared by the octogenarians was also looming: a fledgling workers' movement independent of CCP control. PLA troops also marched publicly in support of the students. On May 16, a group of approximately one thousand soldiers in camouflage combat fatigues marched arm in arm along Chang'an Avenue to show their solidarity with the student protestors. A week later, a group of some one hundred PLA naval cadets marched through Tiananmen Square in full uniform shouting, "Down with Li Peng!"[28] In addition to these visible signs, Beijing was rife with rumors of plots.

THE DECISION

The call to the PLA to disperse the demonstrators in central Beijing was a logical step for the Elders. In their eyes, police efforts, dialogue, and finally threat and intimidation had failed to break the resolve of the protesters. Indeed, it is not unusual for a government faced with civil unrest to resort to calling out the troops. It is a common knee-jerk reaction by governments to riots or demonstrations – even when a riot control capability is present.[29] Although national and regional police usually possess crowd control equipment and training, many factors lead governments to bypass this choice. Ideally, police riot control units should be ready on short notice; however, there is often a significant lag between when they are called on and when they are ready to be deployed. Also, the numbers of riot police available may be wholly inadequate to deal with huge crowds. This was the case in China in 1989. The riot control units of the PAP were dispersed throughout China under the commands of provincial governments, each of which had its own demonstrations to deal with.[30] The use of armed troops also promised a final solution. Even if sufficient numbers of antiriot units are effectively deployed, crowds dispersed one day can reassemble the next day.[31] Further, riot squads are not always successful in dispersing crowds, and their presence can actually stimulate violence. Indeed, in some instances riot police seem to provoke crowd violence – witness the almost ritualized street warfare between riot police and radicals in Japan and South Korea in the late twentieth century.

On the morning of June 2, Deng and four other Elders met with the three remaining members of the Politburo Standing Committee: Li Peng, Qiao, and Yao (Zhao and Hu Qili had been purged by this time). The group decided that the situation had become intolerable and order had to be swiftly restored; the PLA and the PAP were instructed to clear the square promptly.[32] But the situation seemed to deteriorate overnight and the armed forces were thwarted. The turning point for the leadership came late on the evening of June 2 with an unsuccessful attempt by a crowd to storm the main gate of Zhongnanhai and the popular indignation triggered by a tragic traffic accident involving a PAP jeep. The latter incident reenergized the protest movement, and crowds prevented troops from moving to Tiananmen Square.[33]

Following aborted efforts by large numbers of troops on June 2 and in the early morning on June 3 to advance toward the city center, the fateful decision was made to restore normalcy to the capital with deadly force if necessary. The decision appears to have been made at an enlarged Politburo Standing Committee meeting held midafternoon on June 3 called by Yang Shangkun.[34] The decision to crack down itself had already been made by Deng alone, and Yang was relaying this information to the Li Peng, Qiao, Yao, Beijing's Mayor Chen Xitong, Beijing's party secretary Li Ximing, and senior military men, including Hong Xuezhi, Chi, and the Commander of the Beijing Military Region and Martial Law Enforcement Command Deputy Commander Zhou Yibing. The group concluded that the crisis had escalated to the point where a counterrevolutionary rebellion had broken out in Beijing. The PLA and PAP were ordered to begin to suppress it that evening. The absolute deadline for the armed forces to clear Tiananmen Square would be 6 A.M. on Sunday, June 4.[35]

China's paramount leader, in a talk to senior military veterans more than a year later, accepted full responsibility for the decision to crush the protests.[36] No other individual could match Deng's level of prestige or authority.[37] Had any lower authority issued the order, other members of the CMC or midlevel officers almost certainly would have challenged it. It is unlikely that any of the Martial Law Enforcement Command officers could have made the decision. No such officer, no matter how senior, would have been willing to take responsibility for the drastic order, given the clear reluctance to such a move at all levels of the PLA noted previously.

Whereas the specific wording of the order itself was ambiguous, the content of the decision was clear. The vague language was probably deliberate, as no one wanted to assume direct responsibility for the decision and any resulting bloodshed. Troops were simply instructed to empty Tiananmen Square of demonstrators by 6 A.M., June 4, at the latest.[38] According to the minutes of the June 3 Politburo Standing Committee meeting, Yang Shangkun stressed: "we must do everything we possibly can to avoid bloodshed. . . . The Martial Law Command must make it quite clear to all units that they are to open fire only as a last resort." Andrew Nathan underscores this apparent desire by Deng to avoid lethal force and places blame for the killings on the shoulders of the PLA. The fact is that Deng (and the other Elders) anticipated civilian deaths and were willing to pay this price. Certainly the orders given to the Martial Law Enforcement Command by the Politburo Standing Committee stressed reaching and clearing Tiananmen Square without delay and "using any and all self-defensive means that may be required." By entrusting the task of dealing with what they viewed as "counterrevolutionary rebellion" to heavily armed troops, the Elders had to expect there would be significant bloodletting.[39]

Radio, television, and loudspeaker announcements starting late afternoon on June 3 warned Beijing residents to stay indoors. The bulletin stated that soldiers and police officers had "the right to use all means to forcefully dispose of [those who defy martial law regulations]."[40] Such orders, according to a Hong Kong newspaper, were tantamount to telling troops and police that they could "kill on the spot with the authority of the law."[41] Under the circumstances, the Elders felt a little blood was an acceptable price to pay for clearing the streets and reestablishing their authority.

Evolution of Thinking within the PLA

Between May 20 and June 3, all efforts by the army to enter the center of the capital and clear the square failed. These rather halfhearted and generally peaceful attempts contrast dramatically with the determined and bloody crackdown of June 3 and 4. How can the two be reconciled? The short and simplistic answer is that the army was following orders – that is, prior to June 3, troops had not received orders to shoot so they did not do so; when on the evening of June 3 they received such orders, many of them did so. While this is true, the full story is more complex. When troops were first ordered to enter the city center and end the protests on May 20, there was substantial dissent within the military on this issue. This public dissent continued until early June, by which time there had emerged a general consensus among the PLA that the country was on the brink of chaos and that the army should restore order as quickly as possible. Of course, there was limited but continued dissent within the army during the weekend (discussed later in this section), but by June 3 the thinking of the vast majority of soldiers converged with that of the most senior party leaders.

This continued dissent within the PLA did not translate into widespread mutinies and revolts, let alone civil war. The military proved far more unified than many demonstrators and members of the foreign media at the time wanted to believe.[42] Many officers sympathized with the students' goals but opposed their methods. A senior officer serving with martial law troops in Fengtai District told a German journalist in late May:

I personally think that they [the students] are right in criticizing the privileges and corruption of many officials. For that reason, we consider the demands of the students patriotic. However, I cannot approve of the students resorting to hunger strikes and large demonstrations.

Zhu Zengquan, a political commissar in the Twenty-Seventh Group Army, probably spoke for many soldiers when he expressed support for student grievances while stressing concern over the specter of chaos spreading across China.

The following excerpt from an interview he gave to the German newsmagazine *Der Spiegel* seems to capture the perspective of many soldiers:

DER SPIEGEL: The government speaks of a small minority of trouble-makers. It is difficult to understand why the military should be used against a handful of people.

ZHU (laughing): China's affairs are difficult to comprehend for foreigners. You want to know why so many people joined the protest? They have criticized the work of the party and the government, they are upset about the mistakes of the leadership.

DER SPIEGEL: If a state of emergency were declared after every anti-government demonstration in our country. . . .

ZHU: You must understand Chinese peculiarities. The Chinese people have had to endure a lot of hardship in the past because of unrest and chaos. We want to prevent another big chaotic scene in China.

DER SPIEGEL: You are referring to the Cultural Revolution?

ZHU: The Cultural Revolution is the most recent chaotic event in our history. It is the event we regret most.

DER SPIEGEL: This means that demonstrations will never again be permitted because they always involve the danger of creating chaos.

ZHU: We do not want unrest in China. Our young students do not want that either. As far as this is concerned, the government and the citizens are in agreement. However, the students lost control of the movement. They see things from their angle, but our party and our government know what is going on and see the consequences. The consequences are certainly chaotic.

DER SPIEGEL: The unrest consisted only of a demonstration of students, workers, and employees, and the occupation of Tiananmen Square. Do you need the military for this?

ZHU: You must understand this. Beijing is our capital, the center of our government, economy, and culture. Tiananmen Square is the center of Beijing, all of China is looking to this square. However, it is not only this square that was affected. There was also unrest in Changsha, Xian, Chongqing, and Wuhan. Railroad lines were blocked. There were tumultuous scenes everywhere in front of government and party buildings. If this had continued, the consequences would have been unforeseeable. China is still a developing country with many contradictions, controversies and problems. The party and government have also made mistakes. However, if we allow unrest, we would have to bury China, a country with so many problems. For this reason we declared a state of emergency.

When Zhu was asked why his command had not yet moved into the city center, he replied: "We have not received an order [to do so] yet. We are currently on standby status." He also said he had not been given orders to move against the students. Commenting on the failure of other units to break through crowds and penetrate the square, Zhu said: "Of course, it would have been possible for us to reach the center of Beijing – naturally with consequences that nobody wanted. We would have had to apply violence; we would have had to injure people."[43] Thus, soldiers were following orders and were prepared to use force if ordered to do so.

By the evening of Saturday, June 3, when people berated troops: ". . . the sympathy [for the demonstrators] that had characterized the troops last week had gone; the soldiers seemed to have a certain resolve." When members of the crowd blocking the soldiers' advance asked the troops whether they would shoot if they were so ordered, the soldiers gave "weak assurances" that they would not. One soldier replied, "We have to obey orders because we are soldiers." An officer told the crowd what the army feared most was its weapons falling into the wrong hands: "We just fear that our guns will be taken and then we will have chaos."[44]

Therefore, in the minds of many in the officer corps, the ongoing protests, the indignities and injuries suffered by their troops, and the standoff in the streets disposed them to favor prompt decisive action to end the deadlock. Even though many officers and men obviously sympathized with the protesters, a consensus developed among the soldiers that China was drifting toward chaos and this had to be checked at all costs. Even the May 21 statements of retired marshals Nie and Xu, while suggesting that the military should not be used against the students, also urged the students to end their protests for the good of the country. Their comments as reported in the Chinese media clearly indicate that these men, while sympathizing with the students, also felt that their actions constituted a threat to stability and social order. As time went on, the intensity of the latter feelings grew. According to Yang Shangkun's secret speech of May 24, these two distinguished old soldiers supported the decision to impose martial law.[45] Indeed, a week after the June 3–4 weekend, both reportedly wrote letters expressing "sympathy and solicitude" *(weiwen)* to martial law troops. In a letter dated June 11, Marshal Nie commended their performance and "saluted" them. Marshal Xu, in a separate letter dated June 13, offered his condolences for the losses suffered during the operation and expressed "lofty tribute to all the officers and men of the Martial Law Command."[46]

According to Yang Shangkun, Deng also consulted top military leaders, including Minister of National Defense Qin and CMC members Liu and Hong, before concluding martial law was necessary.[47] Although it is thought Qin and Hong had reservations about the move – the two reportedly signed a letter, made public shortly after the imposition of martial law, that was written by serving officers opposing the use of force – they appear to have backed the crackdown during the June 3–4 operation and its aftermath. On June 9, Qin, Hong, and Liu all visited PLA soldiers and PAP troops in Beijing area hospitals recovering from injuries received during the weekend.[48] PLA Chief of General Staff Chi, who reportedly had been one of the one hundred officers who signed a letter of dissent, apparently changed his mind. In an interview given months after the crackdown, he explained:

> The People's Liberation Army intervention was a matter of necessity. It is understandable that some students were resentful of party corruption, official profiteering and inflation. But a small minority of people with evil ambitions instigated the turmoil and spread rumors to provoke the masses.[49]

While the PLA is by no means of one mind on many matters, "... on the most basic issue of supporting domestic political order," the army is united.[50]

The General Military Response

Why were many units clearly reluctant to move against the demonstrators? Why did some officers insist outright that turning the army on the people was inappropriate or wrong? The issue came down to one of identity: Was the PLA the people's army, the party's army, and/or Deng's army? The troops were extremely reluctant to move against civilians because they had been indoctrinated into believing that the PLA was truly an army of the people.[51] In the unlikely event that troops might overlook such propaganda, they were constantly reminded of it by Beijing crowds; civilians told soldiers that they were the people's army, and they should not move against the people.

A crucial point in understanding how the officers of the PLA responded to their orders is to distinguish between hesitation and disobedience. Many PLA officers and troops initially questioned their orders because they found them distasteful and possibly illegal.[52] At his court martial trial, Xu Qinxian commander of the 38th Group Army, reportedly defended his decision to disobey orders; he argued they did not bear the signatures of more than three members of the CMC as was required by military regulations.[53] Yet, in the end, Xu Qinxian remained the exception, as the vast majority of officers and troops obeyed orders to suppress the demonstrations with force.[54]

For several days in the aftermath of June 3–4, numerous stories circulated that individual units or whole armies were battling each other, some supporting the people and others carrying out the crackdown. Most of the stories concerned clashes between the Twenty-Seventh and the Thirty-Eighth Group armies.[55] But there were also rumors that Deng was dead or dying. There was even one elaborate report that a soldier – later amended to be an officer of the PAP – had attempted to assassinate Li Peng.[56] Many people wanted to believe such rumors, and yet most of them proved to be false. Most likely the rumors about clashes among military units divided along political lines were of the same general nature. They have yet to be substantiated by hard evidence.[57]

This leaves the question as to why there were so many troops and so much sophisticated weaponry brought into Beijing at the time. Estimates of troops in the capital range from 150,000 to 350,000.[58] Some were equipped with tanks, antiaircraft guns, and heavy artillery. One explanation is that the Elders were uncertain about the reliability of any units and so erred on the side of caution by bringing in as many as possible. Divisions from at least thirteen of the twenty-four PLA Groups throughout China, including the Fifteenth, Twentieth, Twenty-Fourth, Twenty-Sixth, Twenty-Seventh, Twenty-Eighth, Thirty-Eighth, Thirty-Ninth, Fortieth, Fifty-Fourth, Sixty-Third, Sixty-Fifth, and Sixty-Seventh, participated in the crackdown.[59] Obviously the presence of so many different units discouraged the officers of any one unit from contemplating a coup d'etat. As for the heavy equipment, it may have been brought along simply because soldiers will not readily leave it behind.

The very delay in using troops to enforce martial law probably helped to form a consensus among key military officers once the decision was made. Some may have favored strong decisive action so that their troops could be withdrawn from the city and return home. Even younger, reform-minded officers who sympathized with the student movement may have begun to fear that China was moving toward chaos.[60] To many, the option of not intervening no longer seemed viable.[61] To be sure, Xu Qinxian, commander of the Thirty-Eighth, feigned illness and refused to order his troops against the protesters, as we have seen.[62] Moreover, Lu Xiansheng, commander of the Twenty-Eighth, may also have refused to order his troops into Beijing, and this may have been the reason for his subsequent removal.[63] But most others, from Defense Minister Qin to Chief of Staff Chi on down to officers at the regimental level, eventually fell into line. In the aftermath, very few officers were actually punished for their activities in support of the demonstrations beyond receiving cursory reprimands.[64] Once again the army assumed, however reluctantly, the task of preserving basic order.[65] The clarification of the role of the army may even have come as a relief to many of the soldiers who had not known what to think for the past several weeks.[66]

The Operational Response

Once units of the PLA began the serious business of crushing the protest movement, the sudden and uncontrolled release of passions by both civilians and soldiers took its toll. After weeks of remarkable civilian self-control and military discipline, pent-up feelings of anger and frustration finally broke to the surface. Speaking at the enlarged Politburo Standing Committee meeting of June 3, Zhou Yibing remarked that despite being "publicly humiliated," his soldiers had been "swallowing their anger [and were] . . . struggling to restrain themselves."[67] The military's outburst was exacerbated by the inadequate training and inappropriate equipment of the military units involved in the operation.

Many accounts of the military crackdown on June 3–4 vilify a particular unit, targeting one Group Army as the force that caused the majority of the bloodshed. It stands to reason that one Group Army did the bulk of the damage. One thoughtful, balanced analysis written by a participant in the student movement two years after the events explained: "If all the troops and armed police entering the capital had shot and killed people, how could anyone have dared to burn vehicles or attack the army of the people?"[68] The great majority of civilian casualties occurred in a few specific localities, lending further weight to the view that few units actually participated in the massacre. Indeed if all units had fired without hesitation, less damage might have been done to military vehicles and there might have been fewer military casualties.

The Twenty-Seventh Group Army stationed in Hubei Province is said to have carried out the bulk of the massacre.[69] Conventional wisdom has it that the bloody weekend and its aftermath marked the growing power and influence of PRC President Yang Shangkun and his clan. While there is some merit to this view (see the analysis at the end of this chapter), it has been the basis of some questionable assertions about June 4. The report that the commander of the Twenty-Seventh Group Army was Yang Shangkun's nephew, for example, was false.[70] Nor is it clear that the Twenty-Seventh Army played a leading role in the massacre. Indeed, the Thirty-Eighth Army is now emerging as the real villain. Most early accounts tended to cast the soldiers of the Thirty-Eighth as the good guys. The Thirty-Eighth was the army stationed near the capital and was generally considered to have the closest ties to Beijing inhabitants. Officers of the Thirty-Eighth had supervised military training for Beijing University students during the summer of 1988 and had continued to nurture friendships with students through the 1988–9 academic year.[71] Lending further credence to the Thirty-Eighth's positive image was the refusal of its commander, Xu Qinxian, to order his troops against the students and his subsequent court martial, already noted. According to a careful analysis written two years after the crackdown by a leading civilian participant, Gao Xin, however, it was actually soldiers of the Thirty-Eighth Group Army who fired the first shots and who did most of the killing.[72] This is supported by *The Tiananmen Papers* and corroborated by Harlan Jencks; he notes that the units involved in the bloody fighting were equipped with modern Type-69 tanks and armored cars that the Twenty-Seventh Group Army does not possess but that the Thirty-Eighth Army does.[73]

According to Gao, the Thirty-Eighth Army moved in from the west along Chang'an Avenue and first opened fire at demonstrators at Muxidi at about 11:00 P.M. on June 3.[74] According to a Ministry of State Security intelligence report of the incident, troops fired only after riot control units had been repulsed and civilians continued to hurl bricks at soldiers. Finally, troops rushed forward, chanting, "If no one attacks us, we will not attack them, but if someone attacks us, we will definitely attack them."[75] Additional bloody clashes took place at Xidan, Nanchizhi, and Zhushikou.[76] The soldiers who actually first entered Tiananmen Square and surrounded Gao and the other remaining protesters on the early morning of June 4 arrived from the east. These forces did not encounter as much resistance as units in the west that had advanced at a much slower pace. Significantly they had not encountered stiff resistance from civilians and had not opened fire yet. Gao suggests that this is why troops did not fire on the several thousand demonstrators in the square that morning and permitted them to exit peacefully.[77]

The officers and troops of the PLA had been under constant and unrelenting pressure for weeks. They were not used to being opposed by fellow Chinese, nor were they accustomed to being unable to follow orders. Even for the few who had experienced the Cultural Revolution in uniform, 1989 was rather different. Unlike in the tumultuous earlier era, the crowds in the spring of 1989 formed spontaneously and were generally well behaved and united.[78] The soldiers were first confused, then frustrated, and finally humiliated. They could not understand the greater forces at work in the Chinese capital, nor could they comprehend the exhilaration and self-confidence of the students and ordinary Chinese citizens who confronted them. PLA troops in the 1980s had no interest in politics, a low level of education, and a high degree of dissatisfaction with army life. Their predominant interest was in making money.[79] The firm but usually amiable way that the people intervened to stop the troops from following orders confounded them. As time went on, this bewilderment turned to frustration, as military units were unable to carry out even the simplest orders.

The soldiers also were confronted by increasingly ugly crowds. Troops saw their comrades injured and physically exhausted by a combination of crowd violence, freak accidents, and hot weather. Although these incidents were isolated, they tended to darken the mood both of the PLA and the public.[80] There were angry and violent confrontations between PLA and civilians well before June 3–4. The first violent scuffle took place on April 18 outside the Xinhua Gate, the main entrance to the Zhongnanhai complex that houses China's top leaders. Soldiers as well as PAP members cleared an unruly crowd outside the gate.[81] Several other serious clashes between soldiers and demonstrators occurred in mid-May. Two separate violent confrontations occurred on May 22. One took place in a village southwest of Beijing as a convoy of trucks filled with soldiers heading toward the capital was blocked by angry peasants. When soldiers broke through, fist fights erupted. Students sought unsuccessfully to halt the violence. A student at the scene said, "the citizens didn't have a good reason to hurt the soldiers."[82] PLA troops were also injured in another violent clash with civilians in Fengtai District that same day.[83] Another serious incident occurred in a southwest suburb of Beijing early on May 23. Troops and PAP personnel armed with rifles and truncheons forced their way through a crowd to enable a large convoy of trucks and tanks immobilized on the road for days to proceed to a nearby military base. Soon after the convoy had entered the installation, rock-throwing crowds stormed the camp gate. Troops armed with rocks and bottles counterattacked and dozens of injuries were reported on both sides.[84]

At least one soldier was killed in the line of duty well before June 3–4: A PLA officer apparently died in an accident in the western suburbs of Beijing on May 23. He either fell off a moving truck or was accidentally knocked under the wheels of an oncoming vehicle while engaged in crowd control. News of the officer's death spread to other military units, and he was quickly canonized as a "revolutionary hero."[85] During the latter part of May, dozens of soldiers and PAP members were also injured severely enough to be hospitalized.[86] Many were suffering from dehydration, heat stroke, or exhaustion. In the summer heat, many troops marched or jogged for miles in heavy military gear and lacked adequate water and food.[87] Gifts of food and drink from students amid bystanders likely compounded their sense of frustration and confusion over their predicament.[88]

The PLA's self-restraint and patience were wearing thin after weeks of the standoff. The crowds, although generally sympathetic and well behaved, sometimes humiliated the soldiers. People lectured, berated, and even cursed PLA troops.[89] Even during the earliest days of martial law, the level of military frustration was high. According to one colonel, his troops were deeply disturbed by the verbal abuse directed at them by some civilians on the second day of martial law. One man shouted, "You soldiers, you're all sons of bitches, devoid of any humanity!" Another man yelled, "Your sisters are being gang raped, but alas you're stuck here – quick, go home."[90] Another PLA officer told reporters on May 22 that his men could endure being deprived of water, food, and sleep, but "we cannot stand the indignities."[91] In the early morning of June 3, irate citizens rushed out onto the streets and pelted advancing troops with shoes and other objects. Crowds tore knapsacks off soldiers' backs and taunted them until troops broke up into small groups. Fearful and ashamed, some reduced to tears, the soldiers finally retreated.[92] A colonel and a major general commented sarcastically: "Later, some people said those people surrounding military vehicles were relatively 'friendly.' Their symbols of 'friendship' were bricks, stones, and liquor bottles, and even other things that couldn't be thrown."[93] Possibly the final straw came when fresh troops waiting on the outskirts of Beijing saw tired, dejected, and distraught comrades returning from unsuccessful attempts to enter the city center.

In a growing number of incidents, the crowds became less friendly, more suspicious, and even angry. The mood of the people changed because the PLA had not joined them, and they were uneasy about rumors of military and police violence against crowds. The crowds began to sense that although the military might be sympathetic to their cause, it would not abandon the authorities and join the demonstrators en masse. Many concluded that instead of being an ally, the army had become the enemy. The sense of suspicion and foreboding was heightened by a traffic accident on the evening of June 2. A speeding PAP jeep careened into a crowd, killing three persons and injuring another. Although the driver appears simply to have lost control of the vehicle, rumors swept through Beijing that the incident was a deliberately staged provocation.[94] Tension mounted in the capital, and the number of demonstrators that had dwindled during the week began to rise again. The expectations of further troop movement seemed well founded when in the early morning of Saturday, largely unarmed troops on the outskirts of Beijing attempted to enter the city center. The force was repulsed only after a violent scuffle with angry crowds. Crowds also discovered caches of weapons with out-of-uniform officers on buses attempting to enter central Beijing.[95]

Television and radio broadcasts on Saturday afternoon and evening warned residents to stay indoors. The announcement marked an escalation of the government's efforts to suppress the demonstrations, but based on the military response to date, many citizens did not believe they were in mortal danger. The people's army would never fire on the people.[96] The events of the past weeks had lulled the demonstrators into a false sense of security; the government seemed powerless against the crowds, and the army was unwilling to move against them.

Most civilians also were angry at their top leaders, who had not acknowledged officially the validity of the protesters' demands, and at the army that had not sided with them. When troops first began shooting late in the day on June 3, civilians could not believe the troops were using live ammunition. This realization provoked outrage among some who suddenly released weeks of frustration and anger and set on troops with frightening ferocity.

Many of the troops used in the Beijing crackdown were very young, eighteen and nineteen years old.[97] Some of the troops used to clear the streets of the capital displayed little discipline, were poorly trained, and badly led.[98] Certainly some of their actions were more characteristic of rampaging rebels than a disciplined infantry. There were numerous reports of troops firing wildly and randomly without provocation. Soldiers fired on medical personnel and ambulances – clearly marked as such – that were trying to aid wounded civilians.[99] Troops fired at bicyclists and pedestrians, and even into diplomatic compounds and ordinary apartment buildings, terrifying foreigners and Chinese, many of whom were not violating martial law orders but simply looking with curiosity out of the windows of their apartments.[100] Some of this behavior can be explained by the anger and frustration unleashed that fateful weekend. Soldiers had heard of comrades being injured or killed by civilians or witnessed the brutality of frenzied civilians against soldiers firsthand. Untrained in the intricacies of riot control or urban warfare, some troops panicked. Desertions may account for many of the four hundred soldiers reported missing.[101]

This inexperience and lack of training in urban warfare likely contributed to the casualty rate; many of the injuries and deaths among the troops appear to have been inflicted by fellow soldiers in the chaos of battle.[102] Eyewitnesses reported that an armored car traveling at high speed eastward along Chang'an Boulevard away from Tiananmen Square early on June 4 smashed into a truck full of soldiers, knocking it over, killing at least one soldier and injuring many others. That same evening, armored cars speeding toward the city center were tailing each other so closely that they were unable to brake without crashing into each other when the lead vehicle stopped suddenly. Many soldiers almost certainly sustained injuries from accidents like this chain collision. Troops in these and other incidents simply set ablaze and abandoned their wrecked vehicles, apparently in their haste to reach Tiananmen Square.[103]

The sheer volume of burned out military vehicles – numbering in the hundreds – is astounding.[104] Some of these metal skeletons were the handiwork of civilians, but many were actually destroyed by the soldiers themselves. Some were abandoned or destroyed by their military occupants without any apparent reason. Others were apparently abandoned by troops who deserted. But a significant number may also have been discarded as part of a scheme to wreak damage that could be blamed on the demonstrators. The CMC reportedly instructed troops to drive their vehicles to prearranged locations, set them ablaze, and withdraw. Some old armored vehicles were allegedly removed from their displays in the military museum near Muxidi, parked on the roadway outside, and set ablaze.[105]

Senior civilian and military leaders as well as PLA officers involved in the operation all insist that troops were well disciplined and obeyed orders. Many of these participants say units fired only when attacked, and only when ordered to do so. Troops first fired into the air and only when this failed to dissuade rioters did the troops fire on crowds.[106] Further, according to an internal PLA report published in 1991, troops opened fire only after being ordered to by the operational commander at 10:30 P.M. on June 3. The officer, who is not identified by name in the report, was directing operations from a helicopter hovering above the city.[107] Thus the resultant bloodshed is best viewed primarily as the outcome of a series of calculated decisions by both high-level political leaders and military officers in the field and was exacerbated by the actions of ill-disciplined troops seething with anger.

The Party Line on the Use of Deadly Force

The party line put out by senior Chinese leaders in the aftermath of June 3–4 is consistent. The heavy loss of life is regretted, but the casualties – hundreds killed and thousands injured – were unavoidable, according to officials.[108] According to many leaders, China faced a counterrevolutionary rebellion and had no choice but to resort to deadly force. Even other officials who recognized that the party faced unarmed but angry and determined protesters insist that lethal force was unavoidable because nonlethal options were simply unavailable. The PLA did not have units trained or equipped to deal with riots. Although units of the PAP were equipped with tear gas, shields, and batons, these were used only marginally. Antiriot squads were created in the early 1980s, but it appears that these units stationed in Beijing were too small and inadequately trained and equipped to have a significant effect. According to Premier Li Peng, PLA Chief of Staff Chi, and Vice Minister of Public Security Tao Siju, riot control equipment was unavailable.[109] Quite possibly riot control equipment was inaccessible or in disrepair. What is certain is that the few PAP riot control units that were deployed were ineffective in dealing with the vast crowds.[110] The police also proved incapable of dealing with the demonstrations. It should also be noted that China does produce its own tear gas; the Jing'an Corporation, with close links to the PAP, even markets tear gas and other items to foreign buyers.[111] Further, China also imports riot control gear.[112]

The evidence points in part to gross government incompetence. Although senior Chinese leaders publicly maintain that the crackdown was justified, there are clear signs from the leaders themselves that they consider June 3–4 a botched job. CCP General Secretary Jiang Zemin admitted that the authorities had erred in not maintaining an adequate force of police equipped with "non-lethal weapons."[113] Since June 1989, there has been a concerted effort to create new and more effective riot control units in major Chinese cities.[114] A telling indication of party thinking is that two of the most prominent rising stars at the national level in the immediate aftermath of June 4, the former mayor of Shanghai Jiang (as party chief) and the former mayor of Tianjin Li Ruihuan (as propaganda chief), handled the mass demonstrations in their respective cities in a sophisticated and peaceful manner.[115]

ANALYSIS

Military figures were clearly reluctant to use force in Beijing, although as the crisis continued, the soldiers became increasingly willing to crack down to end the standoff and arrest an apparent inexorable slide into chaos. It was senior party leaders, Deng in particular, who pressed for the use of military force. The solution was one that Beijing's geriatric elite had seemed prepared to use from the early days of the demonstrations. On June 9, five days after the massacre, Deng told troop commanders:

> This storm was bound to happen sooner or later.... It was just a matter of time and scale. It has turned out in our favor, for we still have a large group of veterans who have experienced many storms and have a thorough understanding of things. They were on the side of taking resolute action to counter the turmoil....
>
> The April 26 editorial of the *People's Daily* classified the problem as turmoil. The word was appropriate, but some people objected to the word and tried to amend it. But what has happened shows that the verdict was right. It was also inevitable that the turmoil would develop into a counter-revolutionary rebellion.
>
> We still have a group of senior comrades who are alive, we still have the army, and we also have a group of core cadres who took part in the revolution at various times....[116]

A comparison between the political situation at Tiananmen in 1989 and that surrounding the attempted coup d'etat in the Soviet Union in 1991 helps to explain why the Chinese military ultimately followed their orders despite their reservations. In the Soviet case, too, military units were reluctant to obey the orders of the State of Emergency Council to suppress demonstrators. In the Soviet case, however, they could cite countermanding orders from a legally constituted authority to override the original orders. Russian Federation President Boris Yeltsin and Leningrad Mayor Anatoly Sobchak emerged as clear, rival centers of loyalty who had the wherewithal to issue countermanding orders to the Red Army within their jurisdictions.[117] In the Chinese case, there emerged no such rival center of power. Party Secretary Zhao had disappeared from view; other leaders, such as Premier Li Peng and Beijing Mayor Chen Xitong, publicly sided with the Elders. In the Soviet Union, some military units went over to Yeltsin, others returned to their barracks, the effort at suppression failed, and fatalities among demonstrators were very few.[118] In the People's Republic, none of these outcomes was possible.

The People's Army or the Party's Army?

In terms of civil-military culture, the PLA felt an identity crisis. Was it the people's army or the party's army? Unlike in the countries of Eastern Europe in 1989 or the Soviet Union in 1991, in China the army proved to be loyal to the party. As a result, the sacred bond between the PLA and the Chinese people may have been irreparably damaged.[119] Since June 1989, the *Liberation Army Daily* has openly acknowledged that the public reputation of the PLA has been seriously harmed.[120] The army had long enjoyed high prestige and reverence among virtually all Chinese. Although the PLA image had been somewhat tarnished since the Cultural Revolution, it managed to retain a mystique associated with its heroic exploits against successive enemies – the Japanese, the Kuomintang, and the United States. This aura was perpetuated by "Learn from the PLA" campaigns and the army's restoration of order during the Cultural Revolution.

In the immediate aftermath of June 1989, there was a noticeable decline in the prestige of the PLA among the Chinese people and a rise in feelings of anger amid revenge directed at the army. Snipers continued to fire on troops in Beijing for days after June 3–4, and in the three-month period following the bloody crackdown there were more than 160 civilian attacks against troops stationed in Beijing, reportedly causing at least twenty-one PLA deaths.[121] Less dramatic, but equally telling, was the significant fall off in the sales of army-style hats for children that had been very popular.[122]

The nature of the PLA's doctrine, identity, and function was in a state of flux. While no longer beholden to the Maoist doctrine of People's War, the PLA had yet to conform to its Dengist "Limited War" doctrine. The evolution from the stress on a mass politically indoctrinated army to a smaller highly trained crack force was incomplete. Soldiers were displeased with the emphasis on "redness" over expertise that was trumpeted after June 1989. This went against the grain of the Dengist civil-military culture. Moreover, the switch from preoccupation with domestic security to a focus on external security was accomplished in theory but not in practice.

The increasing influence of PRC President Yang Shangkun and his younger half-brother, head of the PLA General Political Department, Yang Baibing, caused growing splits. Before the two Yangs were purged in 1992 many officers were disgruntled over what they saw as the rise of a "Yang family village." The elder Yang was seen as the dominant power on the CMC, particularly because his brother then also sat on the commission. Party Secretary Jiang, who was appointed chair in November 1989, was without sufficient stature or military experience to be more than a figurehead. In addition to serving as first vice chair of the CMC, the elder Yang also held the post of state president. Many soldiers disliked him. Retired military men, including Zhang, reportedly complained to Deng directly about Yang Shangkun's behavior.[123] Significantly, Chief of General Staff Chi made a point of categorically denying to American reporters that he was related by marriage to Yang.[124] There appeared to be strong resentment among officers toward the Yang brothers. A group of anonymous officers from the Shenyang Military Region issued a pamphlet ridiculing Yang Shangkun's classification as one of China's top thirty-three strategists in the Communist Party. The essay argued that he had never fought in a revolutionary battle or written a single book on military strategy. The honor was conferred on Yang by the CMC in November 1989. Yang, of course, was the dominant figure on the commission at the time. He was also one of only five living military figures to have merited the honor – the others being Deng, Li Xiannian, Nie, and Xu Xiangqian.[125]

Many PLA officers were not happy with the renewed emphasis on political indoctrination, party control, and the favoritism exhibited in post–June 1989 personnel appointments. All this was associated with the growing influence of regional military commanders in mid-1990, indicating that Yang Baibing was placing his own people in key positions.

The collapse of communist governments in Eastern Europe in 1989 and the disintegration of the Soviet Union in 1991 may have led some PLA officers to conclude that communism was an anachronism. The example of the Romanian army in the December 1989 revolution, which deserted Nicholae Ceausescu, might have seemed particularly relevant to some PLA officers. Chinese leaders clearly feared the spread of the "Romanian disease." In mid-1990, PRC President Yang Shangkun asked and then answered his own question on the subject: "Why did Romania collapse? The fundamental problem was that the army split up."[126] Indeed, rumors of a military revolt circulated in mid-1989.[127]

Prior to June 1989, some younger officers formed their own "salons" to debate political issues that were taboo in the stultifying atmosphere of political study sessions led by PLA commissars.[128] Certainly, younger PLA officers expressed great admiration for noncommunist foreign military heroes who became political leaders. In the aftermath of June 1989, one group established a De Gaulle Society.[129] Of more immediate concern to Chinese leaders was the discovery of secret "counterrevolutionary organizations" in several military garrisons in late 1989.[130]

Whither the Internal Security Function?

An army tends to resent being ordered to move against its own people. This is particularly true when the military's function is shifting from an emphasis on domestic security concerns to a focus on external security matters. The PLA's domestic function was supposed to have been assumed by the PAP. When this national paramilitary force failed to handle the demonstrations, the PLA was called in by default. This helps explain the deep reluctance exhibited by many soldiers to move against the demonstrators. Moreover, the employment in Beijing had significant negative effects on morale. The evidence of the decline in PLA morale, while fragmentary, is convincing. The military seems to have taken very seriously rumors that Beijing residents were trying to poison the soldiers' drinking water. And relatives of soldiers reported receiving death threats in the months following Tiananmen.[131]

CONCLUSION

The June 3–4 bloodshed was the direct result of a deliberate, calculated decision taken by Deng and supported by other senior leaders. The Elders seemed readily to conclude that (a) the demonstrations posed a grave threat to the CCP and (b) as such, merited a violent crackdown.[132] The PLA did not take its orders to move against the demonstrators lightly. After initially hesitating over unpleasant instructions and seeing no "escape clause" in the form of viable orders from an alternative center of power, the PLA reluctantly obeyed.

Moreover, after most PLA men concluded that the well-intentioned student movement had been hijacked by a small minority of troublemakers, alarm over the apparent slide of the country toward total chaos led soldiers to believe that order must be restored, even at the cost of bloodshed. It was at this point that a sudden release of anger and frustration bottled up for weeks, a lack of riot control training and equipment, combined with crowds of enraged citizens, proved an explosive and deadly mixture.

Part IV

USE OF FORCE
IN THE POST-DENG ERA

8

Show of Force: The 1995–1996 Taiwan Strait Crisis

A private visit to the United States by Taiwanese President Lee Teng-hui in June 1995 triggered a crisis in the Taiwan Strait. The crisis marked a dramatic escalation in the confrontation between the People's Republic of China (PRC) and the Republic of China on Taiwan. From August 1995 until March 1996, the People's Liberation Army (PLA) conducted a series of war games, live fire exercises, and missile tests in the vicinity of Taiwan. Beijing's rhetoric and activities raised the specter of a military conflict in East Asia over a dispute that had appeared to be at its lowest level of tensions in four decades.[1]

Was China preparing for war in 1995–6, and was the PLA leading the charge? I contend the crisis was a case of coercive diplomacy, the result of a civil-military consensus. An important distinction must be made between the terms *bellicose*, *belligerent*, and *hawkish*; the first refers to temperament, while the latter two refer to degrees of mental readiness to resort to war. A bellicose leader is warlike in mindset – that is, predisposed to resort to war in most situations. A belligerent leader is one who has crossed the mental threshold in a particular instance and is ready and eager for battle. In contrast, a hawkish leader is one who is prepared to use military means short of war – namely, saber-rattling, brinkmanship, and threats of war – to achieve a policy goal – in short, to practice coercive diplomacy. Of these terms, *hawkish* is the most accurate term to use to describe the words and deeds of Chinese soldiers. In 1995–6, the PLA favored displays of military force and threats as core elements of a policy toward Taiwan. By contrast, the words *bellicose* and *belligerent* are misleading because these give the erroneous impression that PLA leaders were spoiling for a fight in the crisis and/or were warlike by temperament.

The significance of the crisis is first explained and placed in historical context. Then the role of the PLA in the crisis is examined in some detail. Lastly, some tentative conclusions are offered.

This case seems worth studying for three reasons. First, the Taiwan Strait is perhaps the most plausible location for China to become embroiled in an armed conflict in the foreseeable future. This point was reinforced when tensions again escalated in the strait in the summer of 1999. China threatened unspecified military action, and experts stressed that these threats should be taken seriously.[2]

Yet, because the 1995–6 crisis built up and dissipated so quickly, it is tempting to ask: "Crisis, what crisis?" This would be a mistake.[3] A prominent PLA analyst in Hong Kong, in a study issued in mid-1996, after the crisis, concluded that the threat of military conflict in the Taiwan Strait would remain serious for some time.[4] Another highly respected China scholar, writing in 1998, was of the opinion that the strait has "high conflict potential."[5] More significantly, a number of studies by Chinese analysts contend that the Taiwan issue is the one dispute most likely to drag China to the brink of war in the foreseeable future.[6] Beijing also views Taiwan as the most important issue in its bilateral relationship with Washington.[7] The chill in Sino–American ties in 1999 – the accumulation of a series of prickly bilateral issues brought to a head by the accidental bombing of the PRC embassy in Belgrade in early May – is a reminder that relations between Washington and Beijing continue to be fragile. On the Chinese side, there is a firm and widespread belief among many PRC officials and citizens that the U.S. bombing of the PRC embassy in Belgrade was not a mistake but a deliberate act.[8] There is also a strong conviction that Washington is actively working to prevent unification with Taiwan.

The issue of Taiwan will not disappear. According to a senior PLA strategist writing in 1998, Hong Kong's return to China in 1997 and Macao's sched-uled return in December 1999 are parts of a "... great historical trend [that] is bound to exert a significant impact upon Taiwan's fate and future even if the Taiwan authorities refuse to recognize this."[9] The island is the ultimate prize in Beijing's quest for political control over Greater China (China plus Taiwan, Hong Kong, and Macao). Taiwan is likely to remain a central issue as China en-ters the twenty-first century because of the return of Macao to Chinese control and the outcome of Taiwan's milestone presidential election on March 18, 2000. The victor in the race was Chen Shui-bian from the Democratic Progressive Party (DPP) – an organization long committed to Taiwanese independence. The result meant the first islandwide electoral defeat for the Kuomintang (KMT) or Nationalists, who had ruled Taiwan for more than half a century. Chen's victory can only be seen as a setback for China. In the weeks leading up to the election, Chinese leaders and the official media fired salvo after salvo of verbal threats ad-monishing Taiwan not to move toward independence. The clear implication was that a vote for Chen constituted a vote for independence and the blunt message was "independence means war."[10] In fact, Chen's campaign was remarkably restrained; he advocated resuming talks with Beijing and made no mention of independence. Nevertheless, Chinese leaders remain deeply suspicious of him. Despite a muted Chinese reaction to Chen's victory in the aftermath of the vote, the future of crossstrait relations is unlikely to be smooth sailing.

Second, the recent show of force by China held considerable potential for escalation into a wider and more serious conflagration – one that could have involved the United States. The confrontation is the latest in an ongoing conflict that began in the 1940s – a holdover from a still unresolved civil war. An escalation of the 1995–6 crisis could have led to American military involvement and/or use of nuclear weaponry.

Third, the 1995–6 Strait confrontation is significant because it was the first crisis of the post–Deng Xiaoping era. While Deng was among the living during the events described, he was too sick to play any role in the decision-making.[11] His incapacitation and subsequent death in February 1997 marked the passing of the old guard of Chinese communist leaders. It signaled the last gasp of the dual role elite of the Long March generation and the emergence of a civil-military dichotomy within China's leadership. One can now speak of a clear distinction between those individuals who are soldiers and those who are civilians. Jiang Zemin and Hu Jintao, unlike Mao Zedong or Deng, have no claim to extensive military experience or expertise. This is not to say that Deng became totally irrelevant or that the Long March era leadership was completely out of the picture. Deng's name was invoked and his commitment to unification was trumpeted during the crisis. A high-level party document circulated in early 1996 prior to the March missile tests was full of quotes from Deng on the question of Taiwan. Most of these remarks were clearly quite dated, but the sternest one appeared to be of more recent vintage: "China is capable of blockading Taiwan if we consider it as necessary to solve the long term issues [in order] to serve the national interest."[12] This is very tame language for someone like Deng, who was not one to mince his words when the occasion called for tough talk. Thus it is extremely unlikely that these remarks were made during 1995 or 1996. Indeed, Deng's last significant active involvement in Taiwan policy deliberation seems to have been in July 1994, when he held a series of high-level meetings in Shanghai with senior party and military leaders.[13]

A handful of Long March era leaders did play an important role in the crisis – notably military figures. Particularly important were elderly generals Liu Huaqing and Zhang Zhen, both vice chairs of the Central Military Commission (CMC). Liu was also a member of the Chinese Communist Party's Politburo Standing Committee. But this appears to have been their last hurrah, as both Liu and Zhang have since been retired from their posts on the CMC, and Liu has been dropped from the Politburo.

THE CONTEXT

The origins of the crisis can be traced back to the victory of the Chinese Communist Party (CCP) over the KMT in the Civil War in the late 1940s. The defeated remnants of the KMT led by Chiang Kai-shek fled to Taiwan.

The United States has been intimately involved in the China–Taiwan standoff since 1950. After the CCP had taken control of most of the mainland and captured Hainan Island in April 1950, the PLA began to concentrate on the invasion of Taiwan. These preparations were aborted by the outbreak of the Korean War. In June 1950, when President Harry S. Truman decided to intervene on the Korean Peninsula, he also ordered the Seventh Fleet into the Taiwan Strait. Beijing attached great significance to the insertion of U.S. naval forces into the Strait – Mao in particular viewed this as a major event.[14] Chinese forces preparing for the invasion of Taiwan were shifted from Fujian Province, adjacent to the Strait, to Manchuria, near the border with Korea, to counter the threat posed by U.S. troops on the peninsula. Then in 1955, after the first Strait crisis, the United States and Taiwan signed a bilateral defense treaty.

While Mao and Chiang were alive, a qualitative improvement in crossstrait relations proved impossible. Only after Chiang died in 1975 and Mao passed away the following year did change become possible. When Deng had established himself as Mao's successor in late 1978, he demonstrated renewed energy and determination to recover Taiwan combined with a healthy dose of pragmatism. Whereas Mao had focused on "liberation" by military force, Deng stressed peaceful unification. Commencing on January 1, 1979, coinciding with the establishment of full diplomatic relations between Washington and Beijing, the PLA ceased its symbolic bombardment of Quemoy and Matsu. A new peace offensive was launched in 1981 by Marshal Ye Jianying, who had old KMT comrades-in-arms dating back from his days in the mid-1920s at a CCP–KMT cooperative endeavor: the Whampoa Military Academy in Guangdong Province. The core of Ye's nine-point proposal was what soon became known as the "one country, two systems" formula, whereby Taiwan could unify with the mainland while remaining autonomous and retaining its existing economic and social systems. While initially this proposal failed to elicit any tangible response from Taipei, the formula did provide the framework for a 1984 agreement between Beijing and London setting the return of Hong Kong.

Despite a legacy of rancor, China–Taiwan relations improved dramatically during the 1980s and early 1990s. Burgeoning economic interaction and crossstrait travel by individuals and groups during the 1980s evolved into direct quasiofficial negotiations between Beijing and Taipei by 1993.[15] From Beijing's perspective, following the summit between the heads of the two

quasigovernmental organs on neutral ground in Singapore, prospects for unification seemed the brightest in four decades. Unease at voices on the island
calling for independence and initiatives abroad to raise Taiwan's international
profile seemed relatively insignificant in the face of apparent continued progress
toward unification.

Still some groups in China harbored a profound distrust of KMT leader
and Taiwan President Lee and were very suspicions about U.S. motives. These
sentiments appeared to be particularly strong within the military. The rhetoric
of former or current U.S. officials seems to confirm suspicions. In July 1991, for
example, only one month after stepping down as U.S. ambassador to Beijing,
James R. Lilley spoke in support of a Taiwan separate of China during a visit
to the island. Other U.S. officials, including leading congressional members of
the U.S. foreign policy community, spoke in similar terms.[16] President Yang
Shangkun, speaking in October 1991, was adamant that "foreign forces [were]
instigating Taiwan independence." He warned, "whoever plays with fire will
perish with fire."[17] At the time Yang was the leader of the Taiwan Affairs
Leading Small Group (TALSG) and a vice chair of the CMC. A career soldier,
Yang spoke words that indicate a high level of outrage over Taiwan. Almost
identical warnings were given by Chinese leaders some four decades earlier,
prior to China's entry into Korea, and some three decades earlier, preceding
China's war with India.[18]

In late 1992, PLA leaders were enraged by the announcement by President
George Bush to sell 150 F-16 jet fighters to Taiwan.[19] The soldiers pressed
for a strong Chinese response in reports, memoranda, and high-level meetings,
including CMC, Politburo, and National People's Congress (NPC) sessions, but
Deng vetoed this. In May 1994, the National Defense University (NDU) and
Academy of Military Sciences (AMS) cohosted a conference on Taiwan policy.
Conference leaders drafted a letter to the Central Committee and the State
Council urging that Foreign Minister Qian Qichen be dismissed. The president
of the NDU and the director of the AMS reportedly blocked the letter.[20]

Further military anger was directed at U.S. pressure over the Yinhe incident in
1994.[21] In addition, U.S. adjustments in its dealings with Taiwan were perceived
by PLA leaders as marking a significant change of policy. In all these matters,
Deng reined in PLA leaders and their conservative civilian allies. He played a
key balancing role on Taiwan policy and foreign policy more generally. But by
1995, Deng was ailing and no longer actively involved.[22]

PRC President Jiang's January 1995 "Eight Point Proposal" was widely
deemed synonymous with the phrase "Chinese should not fight Chinese" and
promptly labeled conciliatory. The overall alarmist tone of Jiang's address was
overlooked, however. Jiang warned of forces on the island plotting independence

as well as "Certain foreign forces [that] have further meddled in the issue of Taiwan, interfering in China's internal affairs." Jiang intoned that Beijing had not renounced the use of force but that this was not aimed at Taiwan as such but "against the schemes of foreign forces to interfere in China's unification."[23]

THE CRISIS

The granting of a visa to President Lee of Taiwan in May 1995 to visit the United States the following month further enraged the PLA. Still the Ministry of Foreign Affairs (MFA) was restrained. The PLA focused its anger on the MFA and Foreign Minister Qian. Finally, in the wake of Lee's bombastic speech at Cornell University, military figures acted. In mid-June 1995, after Lee's triumphal return from the United States, an emergency session of Beijing's top policy-making body on Taiwan, the TALSG, was called.[24] The two civilian leaders of the TALSG, Chairman Jiang and Vice Chair (and Foreign Minister) Qian, were confronted by three irate military men insisting it was time for harsher action. Normally the body has only one military representative, Deputy Chief of General Staff Xiong Guangkai (who sits along side half a dozen civilians, including Jiang, Qian, Wang Daohan [head of Beijing's quasi-official Association for Relations across the Taiwan Strait], and Wang Zhaoguo [director of the CCP United Front Work Department]). Also present this time were the two most senior figures in the PLA, generals Liu Huaqing and Zhang, both vice chairs of the CMC. Liu at the time was also the only PLA leader on the Standing Committee of the Politburo. These military men definitely charged the atmosphere and ensured a swift change of policy.[25]

Between July 1995 and March 1996, China conducted a series of military exercises and missile tests in the vicinity of the Taiwan Strait. On July 18, 1995, Beijing announced that missile tests would be conducted targeting an area some 90 miles off the coast of northern Taiwan. Then on three consecutive days, July 21, 22, and 23, a total of six DF-15 missiles were launched from sites on the mainland (two per day). The following month, after a five-day advance warning, PLA naval vessels and aircraft conducted live-fire tests off the coast of Fujian for ten days. Further military exercises were conducted in mid-November to the south of the Strait including joint cooperation involving air, land, and sea arms of the PLA. On March 5, 1996, Beijing announced it would soon begin another round of missile tests. This time they were to be targeted at seas less than fifty miles from Taiwan's busiest ports. On March 8, three DF-15 missiles were fired from their bases on the mainland. Five days later another DF-15 missile was launched. Finally, also after advanced warning, live-fire tests and war games were conducted off the coast of Fujian to the north of the Strait and to the south of the Strait between March 12 and March 25. The maneuvers included amphibious landing exercises and aerial bombing. Some 40 naval vessels, 260 aircraft, and an estimated 150,000 troops participated.

The military exercises of the summer of 1995 were meant to signal China's displeasure at the visit of Taiwanese President Lee to the United States that June. The maneuvers and tests of March 1996 were meant to intimidate Taiwan in the lead-up to a presidential election and chasten the incumbent, President Lee, who seemed certain to be reelected (he was). The more general aim of the full show of force was to deter Taiwan from pursuing independence from China. In both instances, China was also addressing another important audience: the United States. The message for Washington was that Beijing was deadly serious about Taipei and was prepared to use force if necessary to unite Taiwan with China with or without American intervention. This message was intended to deter the United States from promoting Taiwan independence.

The Central Questions

How should China's saber-rattling be interpreted and what roles did China's military leaders play? There are a number of different, very straightforward explanations posited regarding the crisis, but none of these seems fully satisfactory.[26] There are two main nuanced and sophisticated interpretations of the crisis: China's response reflected a more belligerent, dangerous turn of policy by Beijing toward Taipei. It represented a serious escalation of tensions in the Taiwan Strait and raised the specter of war – one that could conceivably pull in the United States. This turn of events is either the result of pressure by hawkish, hardline soldiers on moderate, mild-mannered statesmen for a tougher, more aggressive response to Taiwan, or the result of a strong consensus among both civilian and military leaders in the Politburo.[27] The second interpretation is that the response was an elaborately orchestrated and scripted Chinese opera – also the result of a consensus decision by civilian and military leaders. The entire production was carefully planned and each move was clearly telegraphed well in advance to the other actors. In the minds of China's civilian and military leaders, there was little danger of actual military conflict breaking out. Leaders on both sides of the Strait recognized this was a major theatrical event with each person playing a clearly defined role. When the opera was over, matters went back to normal.[28]

What are the main assumptions implied by each interpretation? The first variant of the former interpretation, that the military was the driving force behind China's behavior, feeds into the stereotype of soldier as warmonger. The second variant of the first interpretation is that the hardline behavior was the result of a civil-military consensus forged by the powerful nationalist appeal of the Taiwan issue. The second interpretation – crisis as opera – is a cultural explanation that fits with the orthodox view of China's strategic tradition. The assumption here is that there is a Chinese cultural preference to avoid actual combat and use dramatic theatrical displays to overawe the enemy. This interpretation is consistent with the approach emphasizing that Chinese strategy and tactics since ancient times have consisted largely of seeking to win without fighting – of outwitting the opponent by ruse and stratagem instead of combat (see Chapter 2).

Which interpretation is accurate? Each appears to have a significant element of truth. The crisis does reflect a more hawkish approach but it also represents a considerable amount of posturing by individual officials and different bureaucratic actors. The missile tests and war games were undertaken in deadly earnest, but from the beginning the exercises were meant to be strictly limited to a "show of force" with absolutely no plans to escalate to actual war. In 1995–6, China was actually more bellicose toward Taiwan compared to the 1980s and early 1990s, but it was no more bellicose than it had been in the 1950s and 1960s.

A major puzzle is how to explain the hawkishness of the PLA in this instance. It seems inconsistent with the disposition of military figures in the four other cases examined in this book. Analyses of these other Chinese cases suggest that Richard Betts' findings from U.S. case studies – that soldiers tend to be no more eager, and often much less eager, than statesmen to resort to military action – hold true for China.[29]

How accurate are the accounts of bellicose Chinese military figures in the Taiwan crisis? Some experts question the reliability of these reports.[30] Tales of PLA leaders completely hijacking Taiwan policy and dictating the war games and missile tests of March 1996 in the face of considerable opposition by civilians seem far-fetched and unsubstantiated by the evidence.[31] While it does seem that the PLA was at the forefront of pushing a hardline approach on Taiwan in mid-1995, by October, a high-level consensus among civilian and military leaders had emerged that a tougher approach was needed. President Jiang, Premier Li Peng, and National People's Congress Chair Qiao Shi all separately issued very stern statements on Taiwan in mid-October 1995. According to a well-informed Hong Kong newspaper:

> It suggests that the CPC [CCP] hierarchy has reached a unanimity of views on taking an uncompromising stand toward forces favoring Taiwan independence and on dealing relentless blows at any forces trying to break Taiwan from the mainland.[32]

Most of these reports seem quite credible and consistent. Some Hong Kong newspapers have very good high-level contacts, several in the PLA. Top Chinese leaders talk to these media outlets because they can say things they are unable to say in official mainland publications.[33] Moreover, these reports are consistent with information obtained from interviews I conducted with Chinese researchers in 1998. Every civilian researcher in China with whom I spoke in 1998 agreed that the PLA was more hawkish on Taiwan than the MFA and other nonmilitary actors. Interestingly, military researchers consistently denied this was so, although most spoke more adamantly about Taiwan than did civilians. One might attribute this difference to soldiers more readily rationalizing their outbursts as posturing rather than as belligerence.

1990s PRC SOLDIERS: BELLICOSE, BELLIGERENT, OR HAWKISH?

Although there are numerous and verifiable reports of soldiers expressing hawkish views on Taiwan, it does not necessarily follow that Chinese military leaders are bellicose or belligerent. I contend that PLA figures were in part venting their frustrations, in part posturing, and in part expressing their patriotism. Three factors help explain the hawkishness of military leaders: (1) Coercive diplomacy tends to be problematic for soldiers; (2) Chinese civilian and military leaders had a clear understanding that the military exercises were strictly limited and in their minds there was little chance of escalation to actual combat; (3) the Taiwan issue evokes intensely emotional nationalism among soldiers.

Civil-Military Relations and Coercive Diplomacy

Coercive diplomacy is difficult enough for statesmen to practice without factoring in civil-military relations. In coercive diplomacy, "force is used in an exemplary, demonstrative manner, in discrete and controlled increments to induce the opponent to revise his calculations and agree to a mutually acceptable termination of the conflict."[34] For statesmen to optimize its chances of success, coercive diplomacy requires attention to both "carrot" and "stick" – that is, to demonstrate a credible threat but at the same time to offer some incentive for the other party to comply. Moreover, great care must be made to make the signals as clear as possible – to ensure that the threat of force is recognized as such and not taken as preparations for imminent attack that might escalate to open conflict. A further complication is the fact that diplomats and soldiers see coercive diplomacy from very different perspectives.[35] While both prefer a solution short of war, statesmen favor subtle signals and gradual increases in the pressure applied to an opponent in order to deter or compel them. Soldiers, in contrast, prefer to send a strong, direct, and unambiguous message promptly – a rapid, massive show of force to bring the opponent swiftly to his senses:

> ... [C]oercive diplomacy [requires] ... just enough force ... to demonstrate ... [one's resolve] to protect well defined interests and also to demonstrate the credibility of one's determination to use more force if necessary. ... [I]f threats alone do not suffice and force is actually used, it is employed in a more limited, selective way. ... [36]

The MFA's responses to Taiwanese actions and what was perceived as direct American interference was, in the PLA's view, weak and indecisive. The MFA's escalation of sanctions in the summer of 1995 seemed pathetic and ineffective; neither the cancellation of ministry-level visits between China and the United States nor the recall of Beijing's ambassador from Washington got any response. The White House had suddenly reversed itself in late May 1995 and granted Taiwanese President Lee a visa after Secretary of State Warren Christopher had insisted to his Chinese counterpart Qian a month earlier that this would not happen. The MFA had been played for a patsy, in the PLA's view. As Qian later remarked: "I was assured a visa would not be issued. Imagine what I thought and what was thought of me when the visa was granted."[37]

In June 1995, Lee went to a reunion at his alma mater, Cornell University, and gave an ebullient speech trumpeting the virtues of "the Republic of China on Taiwan." In short, his visit was hardly low key. Along with recent changes by the Clinton administration easing up on the strict rules governing contact between American officials and their Taiwanese counterparts, in Beijing's view, Lee's visit marked a significant change in U.S. policy. And, from Taipei, Lee's government seemed to launch bolder and more aggressive diplomatic initiatives aimed at giving Taiwan a higher profile on the global stage (for example, "vacation diplomacy," and offering a billion dollar donation to the United Nations in exchange for a seat). Lee's speech at Cornell seemed to confirm the concern raised by some Taiwan analysts in Beijing a year earlier of signs that the Taiwanese leader was moving further and further down the road toward independence.[38] Within Taiwan, avowed proponents of independence, the DPP in particular, grew more vocal and seemed to garner increased popular backing.

Furthermore, when viewed by the Chinese military in the light of the events of 1994–5, the conciliatory fifteen-year-old policy of "peaceful unification" seemed to bring the prospect of union between the mainland and Taiwan no closer. From the PLA's perspective, it was time to show a lot more "stick" and a lot less "carrot."

PLA leaders were particularly dissatisfied with the existing criteria for using force against Taiwan: a formal declaration of independence by Taipei and/or direct support or intervention by an outside power. Senior soldiers were instrumental in adding a third justification for resorting to war: "covert independence," or "purposeful perpetuation of a state of division" of China, including "deliberate procrastination" by Taipei in talks with Beijing. According to "an informed source," "Until the revision of the criteria for using force, the generals were frustrated that they could never legitimately start a military action since neither Lee nor other Taiwan politicians would openly declare independence."[39] This new justification for the use of force was formalized in the February 2000 White Paper on Taiwan. The document stated that China would reserve the right to use force not only in the event of a formal declaration of independence or foreign military intervention, but also if Taipei authorities "refused" to engage in negotiations with Beijing leading to unification.[40]

A Strictly Limited, Carefully Controlled Regional Operation

The military exercises were clearly defined, circumscribed in terms of location, duration, and scope. This was explicitly communicated several days in advance to Taipei and Washington.[41] The July 1995 exercises, although carefully planned, were so speedily arranged and implemented that not much advance notice was given to Taiwan or the United States. By contrast, preparations for the exercises of March 1996 were undertaken many months before, and advanced warnings were communicated that more saber-rattling could be expected. Vice Foreign Minister Liu Huaqiu was dispatched to Washington in March on an important mission to make certain that the Clinton administration was aware that China was planning only military exercises and missile tests – not a direct attack on Taiwan. Liu Huaqiu is concurrently director of the State Council's Office of Foreign Affairs and a key member of the Foreign Affairs Leading Small Group, two extremely influential bodies in Chinese foreign policy-making. He is a very senior member of Beijing's foreign policy establishment – the position he occupies has been likened to the post of the U.S. national security advisor – and his dispatch to Washington was to ensure that the Clinton administration could be confident he spoke with an authoritative voice.[42]

In order to assure strong central control, in mid-October 1995 Beijing established a Headquarters for Operations Targeting Taiwan *(dui Taiwan junshi zhihui bu)* under the command of the director of the PLA's General Staff, Zhang Wannian. Zhang reported directly to the CMC – indeed he was a vice chair of that organ. The Headquarters was responsible for directing the exercises and coordinating among the PLA services as well as the Nanjing and Guangzhou Military Regions and the East China Sea Fleet, all falling within a specially designated Nanjing "War Theater" *(zhanqu)* encompassing the entire Taiwan

Strait area.[43] Pains were also taken to ensure no direct contact with the enemy since actual hostilities were not desired. The live-fire exercises and war games, although held in the vicinity of the Taiwan Strait, were well removed from Taiwan itself. And the use of missiles was to minimize the risk of a direct confrontation between mainland and Taiwanese military forces that might lead to an exchange of fire. Of course, the use of missiles was the most provocative element of the PLA's saber-rattling, especially those missiles launched in March 1996 at the sea lanes some thirty miles off the northern port of Keelung and forty-seven miles from the busy southern port city of Kaohsiung. Still, from the PLA perspective, the missiles were almost the ideal option because they were both a clear demonstration that Beijing's threats were credible – China had the will to use force and the capability to strike Taiwan – and offered little danger of escalation. Top military leaders, including Liu Huaqing and Zhang Zhen, reportedly recommended a "significant military dimension" to China's response, including the use of missiles.[44]

Still, Chinese leaders were certainly concerned about the U.S. response; otherwise, Vice Foreign Minister Liu Huaqiu would not have been dispatched to Washington in early March 1996. This move was unprecedented in the history of the PRC and indicated the high level of importance that Beijing attached to making its intentions on Taiwan clear to Washington *and* reflected a degree of uncertainty by Beijing over the U.S. reaction to the military exercises. The muted U.S. response to the PLA exercises and missile tests of the summer of 1995 gave Chinese leaders the impression that if any response was forthcoming from Washington, it would be simply token. Assistant Secretary of Defense Joseph S. Nye visited Beijing in mid-November and Chinese officials pressed him to find out what a U.S. response to another military show of force in the Taiwan Strait might be. Nye was apparently stern but vague about possible American reactions.[45] As a result Beijing went ahead with plans for military exercises in late November 1995 and more exercises and further missile tests in March 1996. While Beijing noted the *U.S.S. Nimitz's* December passage through the Taiwan Strait, Washington's signal was ambiguous because no U.S. statement was forthcoming. Although China concluded that the United States might again send one naval battle group to the vicinity, Beijing seemed very surprised when two were dispatched. While the U.S response seemed very low key in the summer of 1995, the American response in the spring of 1996 seemed like an overreaction.[46]

The PLA did not view its actions as very dangerous or risky, especially to gauge from the muted U.S response until early 1996.[47] In fact, the aim of the exercise was to avoid actual conflict in the future by deterring Taiwan from pursing independence. The principle underlying this tactic was dubbed by military sources in Beijing as "resorting to force [in order] to press for peace."[48] Thus the harsher and more bellicose the PLA acted and talked, the more effective the exercise would be; this logic held for nuclear bravado too.[49] It is noteworthy that the most virulent and threatening rhetoric from military figures came not in the weeks surrounding the initial missile tests and live-fire exercises in the summer of 1995 but, rather, in the months leading up to the operations in the spring of 1996. Since the actions of July and August 1995 were more hastily staged and scripted – prompted by Lee's speech at Cornell – when PLA leaders were most furious, one might expect to hear the most hawkish rhetoric at this time. But the most venomous barrage of threats and condemnations came in the lead-up to March 1996 when Beijing and the PLA had months to prepare for both the exercises and to coordinate and script carefully the blasts of rhetoric. This suggests that the barrage of militant rhetoric was less an emotional diatribe expressing gut feelings and more a sequence of deliberate and well-rehearsed sound bites. The message to Taiwan was as follows: This is what you can expect if you persist in pursuing the road to independence, so stop before it is too late.

There are reports that some PLA leaders pressed for exercises and missile tests with no warnings. This seems rather implausible: Why would the military not want to give advance warning if the purpose was to intimidate Taiwan? Giving notice of the tests would only serve to heighten the level of intimidation felt by Taiwan. More credible are the reports that soldiers wanted to fire between two and eighteen more missiles during the March 1996 tests.[50] This seems plausible because in virtually every regard the military show of force that spring marked a significant escalation over the previous summer's actions – in the number of troops, ships, planes involved, and in the proximity of the missile target zones to Taiwan. The glaring exception was in the number of missiles fired: In March 1996, four DF-15 missiles were fired – two less than in the previous July. Indeed, the smaller number of missiles likely reflected a compromise between hawks and moderates.[51]

The tough talk by military figures was tempered by assurances that they did not want war with Taiwan. General Zhang Wannian, commander of the operation, insisted during the March exercises that the PLA strongly desired peaceful unification over military conquest.[52] PLA leaders did not want to fight a war they knew they could not or might not win. Therefore, the generals did not want to attack Taiwan if it could be avoided. No Chinese leader, civil or military, wanted to see a war with Taiwan. This is underlined by signs of substantial flexibility at a high-level meeting on the subject of Taiwan policy attended by all members of the Politburo Standing Committee in Beijing in May 1998; then the first crossstrait summit in five years was held in Beijing in October 1998.[53]

What the exercises of 1995–6 also reflect, however, is the PLA's interest in focusing on its new doctrine of "Limited War under High-Technology Conditions" within a meaningful, plausible, and tangible scenario. Thus military planners were presented with a golden opportunity to test the effectiveness of weaponry and combined service exercises. The seizure of Taiwan is now a central scenario for the PLA, one on which military planners can concentrate their energies.[54]

Taiwan Evokes Intensely Emotional Nationalism among Soldiers

That national unification is a deeply cherished dream by virtually all mainland Chinese is widely recognized. Taiwan, of course, is the ultimate prize for Beijing. In asserting that all Chinese are strongly nationalistic, some analysts overlook that soldiers in any country tend to be extremely patriotic, far more so than civilians.[55] PLA leaders are super patriots, fiercely supportive of unification and deeply suspicious of meddling by foreign countries in what are regarded as China's internal affairs. Perceived violations of China's territorial integrity and infringements on its sovereignty are viewed with special outrage – this is particularly true regarding Taiwan.[56]

On the subject of territorial disputes, the PLA was very angry with the MFA for downplaying the most recent squabble over the Diaoyutai or Senkaku islands (claimed by Japan and China). According to Chinese military researchers, the PLA wanted to send warships to the islands in late 1996 and early 1997 to protect activists from Hong Kong and Taiwan, but the MFA vetoed this proposal. One retired senior officer expressed to me a mixture of pride and embarrassment that Hong Kong and Taiwanese compatriots displayed far greater patriotic fervor than their mainland brethren did. Beijing was conspicuous by its silence and inaction. Indeed, some Chinese have criticized their own government for being too cowardly and overly sensitive to upsetting Japan.[57]

To understand better the hawkish stance of military leaders in the 1995–6 Taiwan Strait Crisis, it is useful to draw a parallel with the Cuban Missile Crisis of 1962. In the classic study of the crisis, *Essence of Decision*, Graham Allison depicts top American military figures as exceedingly bellicose, much more so than most of the top civilian officials.[58] U.S. soldiers tend to come off looking like the caricature of the bloodthirsty modern-day warrior portrayed in some Hollywood movies. Just as one comes away from the Cuban case with a disturbing picture of the Pentagon, so a study of the most recent Taiwan Strait Crisis presents an alarming portrait of the Chinese military high command. However, neither case is particularly representative of the dispositions of senior soldiers. This is because Cuba was a very special case for U.S. soldiers, much as Taiwan is for Chinese soldiers. Just as Cuba lies right off the U.S. mainland in the Caribbean in what has long been considered an American sphere of influence, so Taiwan, located just off the coast of mainland China, has been considered a part of Chinese territory for centuries. In 1962 the Kennedy administration viewed the interference of an outside power in Cuba, specifically the basing of Soviet missiles, as a very dangerous development – one that posed an unacceptable threat to the United States. In 1995 and 1996, China's communist leaders viewed American behavior toward Taiwan as flagrant interference in China's internal affairs, one that presented them with a grave strategic dilemma. Particularly odious in Beijing's view was the encouragement and support given to Taipei in its steps down the road to independence. An independent Taiwan backed by the United States would not only shatter China's dreams of eventual reunification, but also pose a direct security threat to the mainland.

Not only is the PLA's attitude toward Taiwan colored by intense nationalism, but it is also affected by the deep-seated belief that the military bears a special responsibility for achieving unification with Taiwan. The PLA's General Political Department has long had a Liaison Directorate *(lianluobu)* to conduct united front work. "The main target [since 1949] of its research and operations has been Taiwan."[59] In Mao's time, the PLA was on the frontline in the Taiwan Strait with the mission of liberating the last bastion of Chiang. Preparation for an invasion of the island in the early 1950s was sabotaged by U.S. intervention in the Korean War and the establishment of an American alliance with Taiwan. Throughout the 1950s, 1960s, and 1970s, the military kept up a regular barrage of the KMT-held islands of Quemoy and Matsu and grabbed the limelight in the series of crises that punctuated the first two of those three decades (1954–5, 1958, and 1962).

Furthermore, the PLA and its leaders also have been intimately involved in the post-Mao initiative to achieve a peaceful union between the mainland and Taiwan. Two key events that signaled this change from emphasizing a military solution to stressing a peaceful one involved the military. First, it was the PLA that, on January 1, 1979, ceased its shelling of the offshore islands, marking the end of an era of conflict and confrontation.[60] Second, as noted earlier, it was Marshal Ye who in September 1981 fired the first full salvo of the peaceful unification offensive toward Taiwan – what became known as the "one country, two systems" formula.

After Lee's speech at Cornell, PLA figures pressed for a quick and forceful response by Beijing. It seemed to have been the last straw. China had not vehemently protested when President Bush announced the sale of F-16s to Taiwan in 1992, and China had not strenuously objected when Lee was given a visa to visit the United States in May 1995. But the generals drew the line at

Lee's inflammatory rhetoric at Cornell.[61] In a September 1995 interview with a Hong Kong newspaper, General Liu Huaqing, at the time China's most senior soldier, stated:

In June, Li Denghui [Lee Teng-hui] went to the United States flaunting his connections with foreigners, openly forsook national interests, brazenly advocated a split, and resisted reunification. This inevitably has increased tension across the Taiwan Strait....

We... resolutely oppose any moves by foreign forces to interfere in China's internal affairs and to undermine China's reunification, and resolutely oppose the conspiracy of the Taiwan authorities of... resisting the great cause of peaceful unification of the motherland....

The People's Liberation Army of China is the powerful defender of state sovereignty and unity and will never permit any part of the territory of the motherland to be cut apart.... Our army is determined, and has the ability to smash all schemes undermining the reunification of China and practicing [of] Taiwan independence, and to triumphantly fulfill the sacred mission of safeguarding the country's territorial integrity and sovereignty.... The irresponsible policy of Li Denghui [Lee Teng-hui] will only bring disaster to the Taiwan compatriots.[62]

Moreover, it is the PLA that is most suspicious of Washington. Many soldiers are convinced that the United States is the chief instigator and supporter of the Taiwan independence movement.[63] Deputy Chief of PLA General Staff Xiong delivered a veiled threat to the United States in the course of a heated discussion with former U.S. Assistant Secretary of Defense Chas Freeman in October 1995. Freeman said he warned the Chinese officials that any PLA action against Taiwan would prompt a stern response from the United States. The Chinese military leaders at the meeting retorted that the United States didn't "have the will" to put its forces in harm's way. Xiong reportedly insisted:

... [Y]ou do not have the strategic leverage you had in the 1950s when you threatened nuclear strikes on us. You were able to do that because we could not hit back. But if you hit us now, we can hit back. So you will not make those threats. In the end you care more about Los Angeles than you do about Taipei.[64]

The remark does not appear to have been intended as a threat or to carry the weight of an official statement. Rather, according to Freeman, it was intended to make the point that the United States would be very hesitant to use nuclear weapons against China in a confrontation over Taiwan. Nevertheless, what qualifies as an off-the-record remark may offer considerable insight into the thinking of PLA senior leaders. Xiong's statement suggests that top Chinese soldiers perceive where Taiwan is concerned an "asymmetry of motivation" between China and the United States. That is, in the minds of Xiong and other top brass there is a perceived limit to what price the United States would be willing to pay to defend Taiwan. In contrast, for China no sacrifice would be too great where Taiwan is concerned. Indeed, high-level leaders told Freeman that China "would sacrifice 'millions of men' and 'entire cities' to assure the unity of China and . . . opined that the United States would not make comparable sacrifices."[65]

The depth of the PLA's suspicion about U.S. motives vis-à-vis China can be gauged from more recent examples. In the aftermath of India's surprise detonation of a nuclear device in May 1998, some military researchers in Beijing reached the conclusion that the United States had detected signs of India's preparations but remained deliberately silent in order to surprise and scare China. These researchers were highly skeptical of the U.S. claim that there had been an "intelligence failure."[66] And a year later in May 1999, many PLA figures appeared convinced that the U.S. bombing of the PRC embassy in Belgrade was no mistake.[67]

There were other factors motivating harsh rhetoric from soldiers. Military men were playing the role of hawks in part because it was expected of them and in part because it was much to their advantage to do so. The PLA as an institution is eager to put the memory of Tiananmen firmly behind it, and Taiwan provided a heaven-sent opportunity to show the military as the staunch defender of the motherland.[68] The virulent and aggressive public statements by PLA figures are plays to public opinion. Ordinary Chinese people strongly support the cause of reunification with Taiwan and most would back a military attack on Taiwan if it were rationalized as preventing Taiwan from separating from China. The massive public support for Beijing's handling of the crisis is evident from the strong approval rating that the Chinese government got for "ensuring a strong national defense" – the government's highest approval rating for all but one other issue. In a poll of Beijing residents taken in December 1995, in the midst of the Strait crisis, 64 percent of the respondents gave the government a "good" or "very good" rating in providing for national defense. This favorable assessment rose to 95 percent when the category of "fair" was included.[69] While one must be cautious of generalizing from a Beijing sample, it seems very likely that a similar approval rating existed in China's general population.

The crisis also gave the PLA a chance to show that it has a central role to play as the "stick" element in Beijing's "carrot and stick" approach to Taiwan. By vocally touting their intense patriotism, soldiers reminded China's civilian leaders of the PLA's indispensability in the serious and ongoing game of co-ercive diplomacy with Taiwan. General Ba Zhongtan, a career PLA man who had just retired as commander of the People's Armed Police, told delegates to the NPC, "At the moment, economic construction has not given enough con-sideration to the needs of national defense. . . ." He uttered these words in the immediate aftermath of the missile tests of mid-March 1996.[70] Such words were aimed at helping the PLA win a bigger defense budget or at least avoid large spending cuts.[71] It is probably not just coincidence that the public announcement of the March missile tests was made early on the morning of March 5, 1996, the same day the National People's Congress opened its new session.[72]

Individual interests also motivated hawkish and ultranationalist barrages. The saber-rattling provided officers from various military regions an opportunity to gain the attention of superiors. The commander of the Chengdu Military Region reportedly remarked that the presence of U.S. aircraft carriers in the region was "no big deal." He explained: "China and the U.S. have fought once or twice before. . . . It's the U.S. that has ended up the loser."[73] Officers and soldiers hoped that demonstrating great enthusiasm and patriotism would enhance their chances for a promotion. During the crisis, for example, the CMC reportedly was bombarded with "written requests for battle assignments" from soldiers who invariably expressed a patriotic desire to fight to prevent Taiwan from becoming independent. What was so unusual about this was both the sheer volume and the fact that ordinary rank-and-file soldiers were requesting frontline duty. Typically only officers make such requests. On the one hand, these requests reflected strong nationalistic feelings orchestrated by the central leadership itself in part to boost morale and mobilize support. On the other hand, the requests were a result of efforts by particular generals "to attract the CMC's attention" by demonstrating the depth of popular enthusiasm and political awareness of their subordinates.[74] Moreover, if by chance a military conflict arose and their units saw action, their long-term career prospects would be enhanced.[75] The shocking words of a PLA general during the crisis – "We will crush Taiwan!" *(women dapo Taiwan!)* – should be viewed in this context.[76]

CONCLUSION

PLA figures, while hawkish, were not bellicose or belligerent as some have made them out to be. Their behavior may be explained partly by soldiers' response to coercive diplomacy, partly by the military's eagerness to apply its new doctrine, and partly by the intense nationalist feelings aroused by Taiwan. The crisis reveals a distinct civil-military dichotomy in terms of perspectives. It also clearly shows a very assertive military elite. On the one hand, this case demonstrates the power and influence of the PLA; on the other hand, many of the key military figures involved in the crisis are now retired. Thus, while the crisis may have set an important precedent, without Long March era soldiers like Liu Huaqing, future PLA efforts at affecting policy may be far less effective. Although at the outset the PLA was the most enthusiastic constituency for a show of force in the Taiwan Strait, in the final analysis it was a civil-military coalition that settled on the saber-rattling. Military figures were responsible for building momentum but strong sentiment among civilian leaders resulted in a major consensus rapidly emerging.

For China's leaders, the 1995–6 Taiwan Strait Crisis stands as a largely successful instance of coercive diplomacy.[77] This conclusion seems justified because China achieved most of its goals without resorting to actual warfare: Its actions got Taipei and Washington to take China's warnings seriously and resulted in a more chastened and less boisterous Taiwanese independence movement. Coercive diplomacy fails when one of two things occurs: (a) war breaks out, or (b) the opponent fails to modify/change his behavior. In this case, war was averted, and Taiwan did moderate its words and deeds, at least for a few years – until mid-1999, when President Lee argued that Taipei–Beijing ties ought to be considered "state-to-state relations." It is more difficult to establish the precise goals of China's coercive diplomacy. However, Taiwan officials and politicians are now more aware of the need to avoid antagonizing Beijing with bravado and public relations exercises aimed at trying to trump China at every turn on the world stage.[78] Significantly, President Chen Shuibian, who took office in May 2000, has to date adopted a remarkably moderate and conciliatory stance toward Beijing. Perhaps a good measure of success in the most recent Taiwan crisis can be credited to a process of learning by Beijing on how best to manage coercive diplomacy and/or the fact that dealing with fellow Chinese minimized the potential for misreading Beijing's signals.[79]

But the effort cannot be viewed as a total success in Beijing's eyes. Only a month after the crisis, in April 1996, President William Clinton and Prime Minister Ryutaro Hashimoto signed a joint declaration committing Japan to providing logistical support and assistance to U.S. military forces in East Asia, including in the Taiwan vicinity (not specifically mentioned by name but clearly implied). While negotiations leading to this bilateral agreement were under way long before the Strait crisis, China could view this outcome only with frustration: Drawing Japan more directly into any future Strait tensions is definitely not what Beijing could view as an unqualified success.

Although the 1995–6 crisis amounted to a show of force with no intention by China to initiate actual hostilities against Taiwan, it nevertheless gives cause for concern, for four reasons. First, this crisis underlines the fact that the PLA is actively preparing to take Taiwan by military means if need be. This does not mean that an attack is imminent, or that China is capable of launching a successful invasion of Taiwan or even an effective blockade. What it does mean, however, is that the PLA is likely in time to surmount the challenge of tackling Taiwan. This is because these scenarios are consistent with current military doctrine – "Limited War under High-Technology Conditions" – and because it is concentrating its efforts in terms of force structure, training, and weapon systems development and acquisition.[80] When an organization focuses all its efforts toward achieving one task, no matter how challenging, it can get very good at this quite quickly. While armies, like all bureaucracies, as James Q. Wilson observes, can be highly resistant to change and innovation, once a new strategy has been adopted, tactics, organizational formats, and weapons systems can all be tailored remarkably swiftly to fit the required specifications.[81]

Second, the crisis provides a wake-up call that the PLA may find the idea of a preemptive attack increasingly appealing – particularly in the case of Taiwan.[82] Under the new doctrine of "Limited War," the key battle is the first one. More-over, as noted in Chapter 2, the principle of active defense *(jiji fangyu)*, which has been at the core of Chinese strategic thinking for decades, does not preclude offense. In fact, if conditions merit it, a preemptive strike may be the optimal form of "active defense."[83]

Third, the crisis highlights the preferred choice of tactics for a PLA attack on Taiwan: missiles. Using missiles as its primary weapon against Taiwan plays to China's strength.[84] While on paper China has a vast numerical superiority over Taiwan, in terms of manpower, aircraft, and naval vessels, these statistics are very misleading. It would be extremely difficult to bring into play the hundreds of thousands of soldiers needed for an invasion because China does not have the appropriate ships or landing craft in anywhere near the numbers required. This raises the specter of what has been called tongue-in-cheek the "million man swim."[85] Moreover, the PLA's dated air and naval craft are outclassed by Taiwan's more modern air wings and fleets. And many of the air and sea craft formally part of the PLA's inventory are probably inoperable, and a good portion of those that do function are in poor condition and likely capable of only limited service. Additionally, when assessing China's air capabilities, it is important to note that training for pilots is totally inadequate.[86] Thus to concentrate on demonstrating the futility of launching a full-scale invasion of Taiwan may be to risk "missing the boat," since this scenario is extremely unlikely.[87]

Missile technology is one area in which China has clear superiority over Taiwan. The threat by a senior Chinese general to former Assistant Secretary of Defense Freeman that China was prepared to launch one missile a day for thirty days at Taiwan should be taken seriously.[88] Missiles armed with conventional

190

warheads have the potential to do serious damage to Taiwan's defense capabilities. They could destroy the island's airports, grounding Taiwan's air force, or, if aimed at civilian targets or remote sparsely populated areas, they could terrorize and demoralize the 22 million inhabitants.[89] Even more alarming is the possibility of nuclear escalation.[90] While current Chinese nuclear warheads are not of an appropriate size to fit DF-15 missiles, the warheads and/or missiles could be made compatible.[91] If the alleged statement of chief MFA arms control negotiator Sha Zukang is accurate, then China has not ruled out arming these missiles with nukes. He reportedly said in August 1996 that China's "No First Use" pledge did "not apply" to Taiwan.[92] Certainly Alastair Iain Johnston's research reveals that Chinese military strategists openly discuss the use of tactical nuclear weapons.[93]

Fourth, there was a dangerous lack of clear communication between Beijing and Washington during the crisis. The result could have been an undesired escalation to direct military conflagration between two nuclear powers. The key issue for the United States was an uncertainty about just how far China was prepared to go in March 1996. Beijing believed it had made its intentions crystal clear: The object was to intimidate Taiwan and to warn the United States not to meddle in Taiwan's affairs – no actual invasion or attack was planned. Washington initially seemed asleep at the wheel – ignoring and/or downplaying the crisis and then scrambling to overcompensate in March 1996. As China's response to the May 1999 bombing of its Belgrade embassy demonstrates, the potential for misperception or misunderstanding is still there. As Warren Christopher, who served as U.S. secretary of state during the crisis, later wrote, "...the [Clinton] Administration was concerned that a simple miscalculation or misstep could lead to unintended war."[94]

9

Conclusion: Explaining China's Use of Force

CONTEMPORARY perceptions of a belligerent China and a bellicose People's Liberation Army (PLA) are heavily influenced by enduring myths about the country's strategic tradition and the relationship between the PLA and the Chinese Communist Party (CCP). In one myth, the perception of a defensive-minded, pacifist ancient culture – symbolized by the Great Wall – clashes with the new image of a more belligerent 1990s China. In the other myth, the assumption of a military completely subordinate to, or totally in synchronization with, a civilian elite in the People's Republic of China (PRC) – symbolized by the Long March – collides with the appearance of outspoken and independent-minded soldiers, claiming to speak for the Chinese nation.

In fact, China's strategic culture is neither purely pacific nor belligerent. As Chapter 2 suggests, for hundreds of years there have been two strands, a Realpolitik one and a Confucian one. These strands interact to produce an enduring Chinese "Cult of Defense" that profoundly affects China's elites. Moreover, the careful analysis of Chinese communist civil-military culture in Chapter 3 demonstrates that it has long been possible to differentiate between civilian and military leaders. Even in the earliest days of the PRC, when the politico-military leadership dominated by Mao Zedong could be described as dual role, it was possible to make certain distinctions. Then in the late twentieth century, as civil-military culture was recast under Deng Xiaoping and Jiang Zemin, the PLA became far more separate and autonomous of the CCP, revealing in the process the potency of military culture.

The impact of culture, now considered a significant factor in security studies, is best appreciated by disaggregating this dimension into distinct layers, each of which exerts a considerable influence but in ways different from each other. The Cult of Defense explains the continuity and regularity with which China uses force. The transformation of civil-military culture from that under Mao (1949

192

until the mid-1970s) to that under Jiang (since the mid-1990s) explains change in where and how China is likely to use force. Military organizational culture explains the difference in thinking between the soldier and the statesman about the way force should be employed.

This chapter reviews the nature and impact of strategic culture, civil-military culture, and military culture on China's use of force. Finally, the implications of this study are examined.

CONTINUITY: THE CULT OF DEFENSE

Chinese elites certainly view China as a defensive power, but this does not mean that China will shy away from conflict. On the contrary, China is prone to resort to force in a crisis, a consequence of the Cult of Defense identified in Chapter 2. Moreover, this Cult of Defense affects both external and internal behavior. The PLA is Janus-faced, and the use of military force is both a foreign and domestic affair.

In the twenty-first century, Chinese leaders will likely continue to view the world in Realpolitik terms while at the same time perceiving Chinese strategic culture as Confucian or pacifist and defensive-minded. Paradoxically, the Cult of Defense produces a Beijing ready to employ military force assertively against perceived external or internal threats all the while insisting that China possesses a cultural aversion to using force, doing so only defensively and solely as a last resort.

Territorial disputes are particularly important to Beijing, especially those pertaining to Taiwan and the islands in the South China Sea. Beijing has been willing to use calibrated force in Korea (1950–3), in the Taiwan Strait (1954–5, 1958, 1962, and 1995–6), against India (1962), against the USSR (1969), against Vietnam (1965–73, 1974, 1979, and 1988), and against the Philippines (since 1995).[1] In such cases, the employment of the PLA to uphold China's claims of sovereignty, while seen as offensive and/or threatening in other capitals, is viewed as purely defensive in Beijing. China has been deliberate and calculating about its use of force, issuing plenty of stern but generally rational sounding warnings and justifications. To judge by these official statements, Beijing seeks recourse to military action only as a last resort. Largely influenced by such official rhetoric and the controlled use of the military instrument, most studies of China's use of force have stressed the defensive nature and prudence of all military actions.[2] Yet, many of the PRC's military operations have entailed offensive – albeit limited – behavior beyond China's internationally recognized borders and a propensity for risk-taking.[3]

CHANGE: AN EVOLVING CIVIL-MILITARY CULTURE

Civil-military culture significantly influences where and how force is used. The evolution of civil-military culture from Mao to Deng (late 1970s to the mid-1990s) to Jiang has influenced how Chinese leaders decide to use force internally and externally. The overall continuity in the PRC's willingness to resort to force is accounted for by the interaction of the Realpolitik and Confucian strands of strategic culture. An analysis of specific cases of the use of armed force reveals that changes in civil-military culture can largely explain variation in where and how China is likely to use force. A number of scholars suggest that China's military is growing more powerful politically and/or more bellicose.[4] It may be more accurate to say that the nature of PLA power is changing and the means by which the PLA exerts this power is shifting. In the latter part of the Deng era and in the post-Deng era, military figures were far more visible and vocal, aggressively articulating their views on a variety of issues in the media and the National People's Congress. This was in significant contrast to the subtle and behind-the-scenes lobbying characteristic of the Mao era. As Chapter 4 reveals, even in the earliest days of the Maoist era, military figures demonstrated a mindset distinct from their civilian counterparts on the issue of Korea in 1950.

Civil-military culture underwent significant transformations from the Mao era to the post-Deng era. The PLA is growing increasingly differentiated and autonomous of the CCP. As a result, at the dawn of the twenty-first century, the PLA is a more distinct organizational and bureaucratic – but by no means monolithic – entity ready and capable of officially expressing its views. And over the past half century, the military does seems to have held a perspective distinct from the diplomatic establishment on matters of war and peace, and coercive diplomacy in particular. This appears to have become more pronounced over time. Civil-military consensus was easier to achieve with dual role elites in 1950 and even in 1967 and 1979. The views of dual role paramount leaders who could claim both substantive civilian and military standing were pivotal. As the national defense reforms of the Deng era took effect, as the elders of the Long March generation retired and died off, and as younger soldiers were promoted, the civil and military distinction became clearer. The functional differentiation among elites is quite striking in the 1989 and 1995–6 case studies. In the latter case, the absence of a dual role paramount leader resulted in the PLA's input having greater impact.

The doctrine has shifted from "People's War" in the Mao era to "Limited War under High-Technology Conditions" in the post-Deng era. There has been a transformation from an internal orientation with broadband duties

194

to an externally directed PLA focused on the narrow technical competencies required to wage war in the twenty-first century. The military's identity has shifted from a mass army with firm allegiance to the CCP – personified by Mao and then Deng – to an elite force with less rock-solid loyalty to the CCP.

Indeed, the PLA is likely to be distracted and divided within itself over ongoing controversial military reforms. There are different views of the future.[5] Elements within the PLA may loudly protest reforms that in their view negatively affect the army. The announcement by Jiang in July 1998 that the military should get out of business, for example, presented a major challenge. And growing unemployment in the late 1990s as state-owned enterprises went bankrupt or released personnel also affected the military, perhaps most immediately through layoffs of military spouses. Growing unemployment increases the likelihood for urban unrest and the potential for domestic deployment of the army. The momentum for the military to become a "modern" army will grow – to withdraw from the maelstrom of politics and domestic entanglements such as commercial ventures.

SOLDIERS AND THE USE OF FORCE: MILITARY CULTURE

The five case studies in this volume reveal that Chinese soldiers and statesmen hold different perceptions about how and when to use military force. Organizational culture seems influential in determining the perspective of individual figures vis-à-vis the use of force. Belying their bellicose reputation, Chinese soldiers tend to be no more hawkish than Chinese statesmen are. Indeed, frequently military leaders tend to be significantly less hawkish than their civilian counterparts. Whatever their disposition, Chinese soldiers rarely seem to be the decisive element in decisions to use force. In any event, the caution of soldiers tends to go unheeded.

In only one of the cases examined – the 1995–6 Taiwan Strait Crisis – did the thinking of PLA leaders have a significant impact on whether force was used. In this case, they were consistently more hawkish than statesmen. The term *hawkish* is used deliberately instead of *bellicose* or *belligerent* (see Chapter 8). The latter two words imply a predisposition or eagerness to resort to violence and are inaccurate in my view.

With the exception of the 1995–6 Taiwan Strait Crisis, it was the paramount leader who was the primary impetus in decisions to deploy the military both at home and abroad. Mao was the driving force behind the decisions to intervene in Korea and to send the PLA into the streets, factories, communes, and schools in the late 1960s. Deng was the prime mover in the attack launched against

Vietnam in 1979 and in the unleashing of the PLA to crush the Beijing Spring protest movement of 1989.

Generally, soldiers are more cautious and conservative than statesmen on domestic and foreign employments; however, this is less true on issues of emotional nationalism. The sentiments of Chinese soldiers in the Korea and Vietnam interventions were both influenced by a history of a close association between the PLA and the armed forces of these respective communist movements. In 1950, this history tended to reinforce sentiment to enter the war in Korea and assist old comrades-in-arms. In 1979, this history tended to reinforce sentiment among some soldiers to attack Vietnam and punish a traitorous erstwhile ally that had turned against China – a sentiment that also affected Chinese civilians. In the cases of Vietnam and Taiwan, there seems to have been a broad consensus among soldiers and statesmen that some kind of military action was required. Perhaps this was also because each case involved a "domestic" issue. In the case of Vietnam, the issue was the treatment of ethnic Chinese and territorial disputes. As for Taiwan, the issue of national unification raises the emotions of both soldiers and civilians.

The analysis here is consistent with research by other scholars about the perspectives of elite Chinese figures regarding the employment of force: Soldiers seem to be no more hawkish than their civilian counterparts. In at least three instances other than the five cases examined here – the Taiwan Strait (1958), India (1962), and Vietnam (1964–5) – it seems that at least some top soldiers opposed the use of force.[6] During the Mao and Deng eras, the opinion of China's top civilian leader appears to have carried the day, while the military view never seemed to be the determining factor in decisions to initiate actual hostilities. The 1995–6 Taiwan case study suggests this could change in the absence of a dual role paramount leader. While China's generals may remain reluctant to press for war, they can be hawkish. That is, they may engage in saber-rattling and brinkmanship, particularly on matters, such as Taiwan, that they believe threaten core issues of national sovereignty and vital strategic interests. The April 2001 collision between a Chinese F-8 fighter and a U.S. Navy EP-3 surveillance aircraft in international airspace near Hainan Island may also be viewed in this context. It appears that Chinese pilots were regularly engaged in risky flying maneuvers designed to intimidate U.S. aircrews flying routine missions near Chinese airspace. Very likely this behavior was sanctioned by the military chain of command but *without* the knowledge of top civilian leaders.[7] Any of such "shows of force" could escalate into a full-blown conflict.

The findings of this study suggest that the attitudes of Chinese soldiers and statesmen conform roughly to the pattern found by Richard Betts in his study of the attitudes of American leaders during the Cold War.[8] Betts found that military figures tended to be no more hawkish than civilian leaders and, in fact, often were more dovish. However, once a country has embarked on the path of war, soldiers, especially commanders in the theater of operations, become eager to undertake their mission. Nevertheless, on the eve of combat, officers in the field exhibit considerable caution and conservatism on strategy and tactics and on employment of maximum force. My research supports the contention by Paul H. B. Godwin that on issues of national security and foreign policy, Chinese soldiers and statesmen hold basic dispositions generally consistent with the findings of Betts.[9] This indicates the existence of a "Chinese military mind" – comparable to that identified in the United States – distinct from the thinking of Chinese civilian leaders.

Interestingly, Betts' study of U.S. crisis behavior found air force and naval commanders to be somewhat more willing to use force than army officers.[10] If we can generalize from these findings, they hold significant implications for China. The overwhelming predominance of the PLA's land component, relative to its air and naval arms, suggests that in the past the Chinese military may have been significantly less hawkish than the armed forces of other states possessing more substantial air and naval capabilities.[11] This too may be changing as China's naval and air services undergo significant modernization and enhancement of their capabilities.[12] The increasing influence of the PLA Navy is significant here. The PLA Navy seems to have a particularly strong sense of mission and appears to be a driving force behind Chinese exploration of and expansion into the South China Sea.[13]

The attitudes of soldiers and statesmen do tend to differ fundamentally on the issue of coercive diplomacy. This point is very much evident in four of the five case studies in this book. There were tensions between how civilian and military leaders viewed the way in which force should be applied. These tensions were relatively easily reconciled in all but one of the five case studies because soldiers deferred to the wishes of the paramount civilian leader. Only in the fifth and final case, Taiwan, did the generals get out in front of the civilian leadership on the necessity for using force. Nevertheless, there was widespread civil-military consensus among both political and military leaders on the appropriate action to take.

IMPLICATIONS

This study of China's use of force suggests that security studies ought to broaden the concept of culture to include the existence of multiple layers of culture: military culture, civil-military culture, as well as strategic culture. And when a state's strategic culture is being examined, researchers should be receptive to the possible presence of more than one strand and be alert for the effects of interaction between them. Moreover, when analyzing a country's strategic culture, it is important not to overlook the influence of legend, popular culture, the frequency of state-on-society and intrasocietal violence, and domestic military employments.

The Long March conception of civil-military culture is useful in understanding the origins of the party's path to power and the evolution of party-army ties in China. But this epic event is of little help in understanding politico-military interactions in China in the twenty-first century except as a reminder of the incestuous army-party ties of the previous century. The myth of the Long March will likely fade into obscurity, especially relative to the ancient splendors of China's glorious dynastic past. The exploits of the Long March generation of political and military leaders will fade as subsequent generations of leaders seek to establish and enhance great power status for China in the new century. When these leaders look back at history, the heroic trek of a ragtag band of revolutionaries will be eclipsed by their desire to recapture the glory and magnificence of ancient dynasties.

The most significant conclusion of this book is the persistence of a shared myth among Chinese decisionmakers and researchers, symbolized by the Great Wall. This fortification is essential to understanding China's contemporary strategic disposition. For many Chinese soldiers and statesmen, it represents a powerful symbol of their belief in a completely defensive Chinese strategic tradition. These elites sincerely believe that they are heirs to an ancient and enduring strategic culture that is purely defensive. This conviction will continue to move these leaders to rationalize virtually any military operation as a defensive action. Beijing seems incapable of recognizing that actions it views as purely defensive may be construed as offensive and threatening in other capitals. The implications of this final observation provide greatest cause for alarm for China's neighbors in the twenty-first century.

Notes

CHAPTER 1. INTRODUCTION

1. See, for example, Samuel P. Huntington, "The Clash of Civilizations?" *Foreign Affairs* 72 (Summer 1993):22–49; Richard K. Betts and Thomas J. Christensen, "China: Getting the Questions Right," *National Interest* 62 (Winter 2000/01):17–29; Denny Roy, "Hegemon on the Horizon?: China's Threat to East Asian Security," *International Security* 19 (Summer 1994):148–68; Richard Bernstein and Ross Munro, *The Coming Conflict with China*, New York: Alfred A. Knopf, 1997; Bill Gertz, *The China Threat: How the People's Republic of China Targets America*, Washington, DC: Regnery Publishing, 2000.
2. Arthur Waldron, "Deterring China," *Commentary* 100 (October 1995):21.
3. See, for example, Andrew J. Nathan and Robert S. Ross, *The Great Wall and the Empty Fortress: China's Search for Security*, New York: W. W. Norton, 1997, Chapter 8; David Shambaugh, "China's Military: Real or Paper Tiger?" *Washington Quarterly* 19 (Spring 1996):19–36; Karl W. Eikenberry, "Does China Threaten Asia–Pacific Regional Stability?" *Parameters* XXV (Spring 1995):82–103; Bates Gill and Michael O'Hanlon, "China's Hollow Military," *National Interest* 56 (Summer 1999):55–62.
4. See, for example, Thomas J. Christensen, "Posing Problems without Catching Up: China's Rise and Challenges for U.S. Security Policy," *International Security* 25 (Spring 2001):5–40; James Lilley and Carl Ford, "China's Military: A Second Opinion," *National Interest* 57 (Fall 1999):71–7; Mark A. Stokes, *China's Strategic Modernization: Implications for the United States*, Carlisle Barracks, PA: U.S. Army War College, September 1999.
5. Dennis J. Blasko, Philip T. Klapakis, and John F. Corbett, Jr., "Training Tomorrow's PLA: A Mixed Bag of Tricks," *China Quarterly* 146 (June 1996):522.
6. See his "Deterring China," p. 19.
7. On Taiwan, see, for example, John W. Garver, *Face Off: China, the United States, and Taiwan's Democratization*, Seattle, WA: University of Washington Press, 1997; James R. Lilley and Chuck Downs, eds., *Crisis in the Taiwan Strait*, Washington, DC: National Defense University Press, 1997. On the South China Sea, see, for example, Ian James Storey, "Creeping Assertiveness: China, the Philippines, and the South China Sea Dispute," *Contemporary Southeast Asia*

21 (April 1999):95–118; on the hawkishness of soldiers, see sources cited in footnote 44.

8. See, for example, John K. Fairbank, "Introduction," in Frank Kierman, ed., *Chinese Ways in Warfare*, Cambridge, MA: Harvard University Press, 1974, pp. 1–26.

9. Thus, I agree with Paul H. B. Godwin's assessment that "China has been willing to use coercion [since 1949]. . . . ," and "the PLA has been used with some frequency to achieve Beijing's policy objectives. . . ." See his "Soldiers and Statesmen in Conflict: Chinese Defense and Foreign Policies in the 1980s," in Samuel S. Kim, ed., *China and the World: Chinese Foreign Policy in the Post-Mao Era*, 1st ed., Boulder, CO: Westview Press, 1984, p. 216. But Godwin's judgment, while insightful, is based on the secondary literature rather than primary sources.

10. Alastair Iain Johnston, "Thinking about Strategic Culture," *International Security* 19 (Spring 1995): 45; Johnston, *Cultural Realism: Strategic Culture and Grand Strategy in Chinese History*, Princeton, NJ: Princeton University Press, 1995, p. 37. Frequently, scholars do not define what they mean by strategic culture, or their definitions tend to be extremely vague or ambiguous. See, for example, Shu Guang Zhang, *Deterrence and Strategic Culture: Chinese–American Confrontations, 1948–1958*, Ithaca, NY: Cornell University Press, 1992.

11. Leading scholars of Chinese foreign and security policy have identified strategic culture as a fruitful area of research. See, for example, Chong-pin Lin, *China's Nuclear Weapons Strategy: Tradition within Evolution*, Lexington, MA: Lexington Books, 1988; Robert S. Ross and Paul H. B. Godwin, "New Directions in Chinese Security Studies," in David Shambaugh, ed., *American Studies of Contemporary China*, Armonk, NY: M. E. Sharpe, 1993, p. 145; Samuel S. Kim, "China and the World in Theory and Practice," in Kim, ed., *China and the World*, pp. 14–15; Paul. H. B. Godwin, "Force and Diplomacy: Chinese Security in the Post–Cold War Era," in Kim, ed., *China and the World*, p. 177. For some monographs that utilize a strategic culture or cultural approach, see Zhang, *Deterrence and Strategic Culture*; Jonathan Adelman and Chih-Yu Shih, *Symbolic War: The Chinese Use of Force, 1840–1980*, Taipei: Institute for International Relations, 1993; Johnston, *Cultural Realism*.

12. My conception is similar to what Thomas Berger labels "political-military culture." Unlike Berger, however, I do not include views on the use of force – a dimension that seems clearly to fit under the rubric of strategic culture. See Berger, "Norms, Identity, and National Security in Germany and Japan," in Peter J. Katzenstein, ed., *The Culture of National Security: Norms and Identity in World Politics*, New York: Columbia University Press, 1996, pp. 325–6.

13. See, for example, Michael D. Swaine, *The Military and the Political Succession in China: Leadership, Institutions, Beliefs*, Santa Monica, CA: RAND, 1992; Michael D. Swaine, *The Role of the Chinese Military in National Security Policymaking*, Santa Monica, CA: RAND, 1996.

14. Elizabeth Kier, *Imagining War: French and British Military Doctrine between the Wars*, Princeton, NJ: Princeton University Press, 1997, p. 30. Unlike Kier, I view what has been called the "military mind" as part of the military's organizational culture. Furthermore, while each military is distinctive in the aggregate of its features, there are likely to be certain characteristics common to militaries in many countries that form part of a particular military's organizational culture. Somewhat

surprisingly, Kier excludes this dimension from her definition of "military culture." See ibid., p. 28.

15. David R. Jones, "Soviet Strategic Culture," in Carl G. Jacobsen, ed., *Strategic Culture USA/USSR*, London: St. Martin's Press, 1990, pp. 35–49; Desmond Ball, "Strategic Culture in the Asia–Pacific Region," *Security Studies* 3 (Autumn 1993):47, 62–6.

16. This type of conceptualization is suggested by Paul Kowert and Jeffrey Legro in "Norms, Identity, and Their Limits: A Theoretical Reprise," in Katzenstein, ed., *The Culture of National Security*, p. 490.

17. Gabriel Almond and Sidney Verba, the pioneers in the field, defined political culture as the "particular distribution of patterns of orientation toward political objects" within a society. *The Civic Culture*, Boston, MA: Little, Brown, 1960, p. 13. More recent scholarship views the realm of political culture as much broader than that of which Almond and Verba conceived.

18. For discussion of more contemporary understandings of political culture in the Chinese context, see Elizabeth J. Perry, "Introduction: Chinese Political Culture Revisited," in Jeffrey N. Wasserstrom and Elizabeth J. Perry, eds., *Popular Protests and Political Culture in Modern China*, 2nd ed., Boulder, CO: Westview Press, 1994, pp. 1–14.

19. See, for example, Jack L. Snyder, *The Soviet Strategic Culture: Implications for Nuclear Options*, Santa Monica, CA: RAND, 1977; Carnes Lord, "American Strategic Culture," *Comparative Strategy* 5 (1985):269–93.

20. See, for example, the collection of essays in Katzenstein, ed., *The Culture of National Security*, and in the Spring 1995 issue of *International Security*.

21. See, for example, Johnston, *Cultural Realism*; Johnston, "Cultural Realism and Strategy in Maoist China," in Katzenstein, ed., *The Culture of National Security*, pp. 216–68; Zhang, *Deterrence and Strategic Culture*.

22. Johnston, *Cultural Realism*, p. 22.

23. Arthur Waldron, *The Great Wall of China: From History to Myth*, New York: Cambridge University Press, 1990. For an example of a recent study of China's contemporary foreign policy that tends to perpetuate this myth, see Nathan and Ross, *The Great Wall and the Empty Fortress*, especially pp. 24–6.

24. Johnston, *Cultural Realism*.

25. See, for example, three recent studies: Chen Jian, *China's Road to the Korean War*, New York: Columbia University Press, 1994; Shu Guang Zhang, *Mao's Military Romanticism*, Lawrence, KS: University Press of Kansas, 1995; and Stephen M. Walt, *Revolution and War*, Ithaca, NY: Cornell University Press, 1996, pp. 310–27.

26. See, for example, Allen Whiting, *China Crosses the Yalu: The Decision to Enter the Korean War*, Stanford, CA: Stanford University Press, 1968; Allen Whiting, *The Chinese Calculus of Deterrence: India and Indochina*, Ann Arbor, MI: University of Michigan Press, 1975; Melvin Gurtov and Byung-Moo Hwang, *China under Threat: The Politics of Strategy and Diplomacy*, Baltimore, MD: Johns Hopkins University Press, 1980.

27. For the latter, see, for example, Adelman and Shih, *Symbolic War*; Lin, *China's Nuclear Weapons Strategy*; Rosita Dellios, "'How May the World Be at Peace?': Idealism as Realism in Chinese Strategic Culture," in Valerie M. Hudson, ed., *Culture and Foreign Policy*, Boulder, CO: Lynne Rienner, 1997, pp. 201–30; Nathan and

Ross, *The Great Wall and the Empty Fortress*, pp. 24–6. For the former, see, for example, Johnston, *Cultural Realism*; Johnston, "Cultural Realism"; Thomas J. Christensen, "Chinese Realpolitik," *Foreign Affairs* 75 (September/October 1996):37–52.

28. My conception of civil-military culture is closer to Morris Janowitz's depiction of the military as a subset and reflection of the larger society than Huntington's conceptualization of the military as an institution totally separate and distinct from society. See Samuel P. Huntington, *The Soldier and the State: The Theory and Politics of Civil-Military Relations*, Cambridge, MA: Belknap Press, 1957; Morris Janowitz, *The Professional Soldier: A Political and Social Portrait*, 2nd ed., New York: Free Press, 1971.

29. Berger, "Norms, Identity, and National Security in Germany and Japan," pp. 317–56.

30. Kier, *Imagining War*, p. 21.

31. See, for example, Ivan Volgyes and Dale R. Herspring, *Civil-Military Relations in Communist Systems*, Boulder, CO: Westview Press, 1978; Amos Perlmutter and William M. LeoGrande, "The Party in Uniform: Toward a Theory of Civil–Military Relations in Communist Political Systems," *American Political Science Review* 76 (December 1982):778–89.

32. See, for example, Swaine, *The Military and the Political Succession in China*.

33. See, for example, William W. Whitson with Chen-Hsia Huang, *The Chinese Military High Command, 1927–1971*, New York: Praeger, 1973; David Shambaugh, "The Soldier and the State in China: The Political Work System in the People's Liberation Army," *China Quarterly* 110 (1991):276–304; Chong-Pin Lin, "The Extramilitary Roles of the People's Liberation Army: Limits of Professionalization," *Security Studies* 1 (Summer 1992):659–89.

34. Harlan W. Jencks, *From Muskets to Missiles: Politics and Professionalism in the Chinese Army, 1945–1981*, Boulder, CO: Westview Press, 1982.

35. Andrew Charles Scobell, "Civil-Military Relations in the People's Republic of China in Comparative Perspective," Ph.D. dissertation, Columbia University, 1995.

36. On the party control model, see Eric A. Nordlinger, *Soldiers and Politics: Military Coups and Governments*, Englewood Cliffs, NJ: Prentice Hall, 1977; on the single elite model, see Perlmutter and LeoGrande, "The Party in Uniform." It should be noted that these conceptions need not necessarily be mutually exclusive.

37. See, for example, Gerald R. Segal, "The Military as a Group in Chinese Politics," in David S. G. Goodman, ed., *Groups and Politics in the People's Republic of China*, Armonk, NY: M. E. Sharpe, 1983; June Teufel Dreyer, "Civil-Military Relations in the People's Republic of China," *Comparative Strategy* 5 (1985):27–49.

38. Whitson with Huang, *The Chinese High Command*; Lucian W. Pye, *The Dynamics of Chinese Politics*, Boston, MA: Oelgeschlager, Gunn, and Hain, 1981; Segal, "The Military as a Group"; Dreyer, "Civil-Military Relations." It should be noted that some scholars do contend there is a distinct military perspective. These include Jencks, Ellis Joffe, and, to some extent, Godwin.

39. Kier, *Imagining War*.

40. Johnston, "Thinking about Strategic Culture," p. 45; David J. Elkins and Richard E. B. Simeon, "A Cause in Search of Its Effect, Or What Does Political Culture Explain?" *Comparative Politics* 11 (January 1979):128.

41. See, for example, James Q. Wilson, *Bureaucracy: What Government Agencies Do and Why They Do It*, New York: Basic Books, 1989. Different branches of the armed services can, of course, have their own distinct organizational cultures. See, for example, Carl H. Builder, *The Masks of War: American Military Styles in Strategy and Analysis*, Baltimore, MD: Johns Hopkins University Press, 1989.
42. Joseph L. Soeters, "Value Orientations in Military Academies: A Thirteen Country Study," *Armed Forces and Society* 24 (Fall 1997):7–32. On national differences between government bureaucracies, see Wilson, *Bureaucracy*, Chapter 16.
43. See, for example, Swaine, *The Role of the Chinese Military*. In the past, scholars tended to argue either that the nature and degree of PLA influence in foreign policy-making was difficult to discern or that it was "virtually nonexistent." On the former perspective, see A. Doak Barnett, *The Making of Foreign Policy in China*, Baltimore, MD: Johns Hopkins University Press, 1985, pp. 96–104; on the latter, see Segal, "The Military as a Group" (quote on p. 96). See also Gerald Segal, "The PLA and Chinese Foreign Policy Decision-Making," *International Affairs* 57 (Summer 1981):449–66.
44. In particular, military figures reportedly are the core group pressing for hardline actions against Taiwan and the United States, since the former was perceived to be aggressively pursuing independence from the mainland and the latter was viewed as actively abetting Taiwan's quest and seeking to topple the Chinese Communist Party from power. On the PLA as hawkish on Taiwan, see Ting Chen-wu, "Hawks Dominate China's Policy toward Taiwan," *Hsin Pao* (Hong Kong), March 14, 1996, p. 9, in Foreign Broadcast Information Service, *Daily Report: China*, March 21, 1996, pp. 11–13; Matt Forney," Man in the Middle," *Far Eastern Economic Review*, March 28, 1996, pp. 14–16; Kenneth Lieberthal, "A New China Strategy," *Foreign Affairs* 74 (November/December 1995):39–40. On the PLA as hawkish toward the United States, see David Shambaugh, "China's Military: Real Or Paper Tiger?" *Washington Quarterly* 19 (1996):33; Christensen, "Chinese Realpolitik." For studies that paint the PLA as hawkish on Taiwan and the United States, see Bernstein and Munro, *The Coming Conflict with China*, introduction and Chapter 1. For a study that depicts the PLA has belligerent and activist in all these areas, see John Garver, "The PLA as an Interest Group in Chinese Foreign Policy," in C. Dennison Lane, Mark Weisenbloom, and Dimon Liu, eds., *Chinese Military Modernization*, New York and Washington, DC: Kegan Paul International and AEI Press, 1996, pp. 246–81. Several scholars, however, have argued that this characterization of Chinese soldiers, at least on Taiwan, is flawed and based on unreliable sources. See June Teufel Dreyer, "The Military's Uncertain Politics," *Current History* 95 (September 1996): 258–9; Swaine, *The Role of the Chinese Military*, pp. 11–14.
45. Barry Posen, *The Sources of Military Doctrine: France, Britain, and Germany between the World Wars*, Ithaca, NY: Cornell University Press, 1984; Jack L. Snyder, *The Ideology of the Offensive: Military Decision Making and the Disasters of 1914*, Ithaca, NY: Cornell University Press, 1984. Their findings, however, have been challenged by Kier; see *Imagining War*.
46. Huntington, *The Soldier and the State*; Janowitz, *The Professional Soldier*. See also Kier, *Imagining War*.

47. Richard K. Betts, *Soldiers, Statesmen, and Cold War Crises*, 2nd ed., New York: Columbia University Press, 1991; Jong Sun Lee, "Attitudes of Civilian and Military Leaders toward War Initiation: Application of Richard Betts' Analysis of American Cases to Other Countries," Ph.D dissertation, Ohio State University, 1991, Chapter 3.
48. On growing military influence in domestic politics, see Swaine, *The Military and the Political Succession*; on the influence of the military in foreign affairs, see Swaine, *The Role of the Chinese Military*.
49. For a significant exception, see Lee, "Attitudes of Civilian and Military Leaders toward War Initiation." This is not to say that scholars do not discuss soldiers, but rather that civil-military relations are not the central focus of study. And the subject of the PLA's role in PRC decisions to use force is "murky." Ross and Godwin, "New Directions in Chinese Security Studies," p. 151.
50. See, for example, Harry Harding, *China's Foreign Relations in the 1980s*, New Haven, CT: Yale University Press, 1984; Barnett, *The Making of Foreign Policy in China*; David Shambaugh and Thomas W. Robinson, *Chinese Foreign Policy: Theory and Practice*, Oxford, UK: Clarendon Press, 1994. For some important exceptions, see Segal, "The PLA and Chinese Foreign Policy Decision-Making," Swaine, *The Role of the Chinese Military*; Godwin, "Soldiers and Statesmen," pp. 181–202.
51. Ross and Godwin, "New Direction in Security Studies," pp. 151–3.
52. See, for example, Timothy Brook, *Quelling the People: The Military Suppression of the Beijing Democracy Movement*, New York: Oxford University Press, 1992, and the studies cited in Chapter 7 of this book.
53. This topic is left to the sustained study of a handful of scholars including Dreyer, Godwin, Jencks, Joffe, Mulvenon, Shambaugh, and Swaine.
54. A prime example is the Wuhan Incident in the summer of 1967. This event has received remarkably little attention, and I am only aware of one study published in English that focuses on the military dimension: Thomas W. Robinson, "The Wuhan Incident: Local Strife and Provincial Rebellion during the Cultural Revolution," *China Quarterly* 47 (July/September 1971):413–38.
55. There is often overlap among the three approaches, and therefore some scholars are cited more than once.
56. Lin, *China's Nuclear Weapons Strategy*; Adelman and Shih, *Symbolic War*; Howard L. Boorman and Scott A. Boorman, "Strategy and National Psychology in China," *Annals of the American Academy of Political and Social Science* CLXX (1967):143–55; Scott A. Boorman, *The Protracted Game: The Wei-ch'i Model of Maoist Revolutionary Strategy*, New York: Oxford University Press, 1969; Scott A. Boorman, "Deception in Chinese Strategy," in William W. Whitson, ed., *The Military and Political Power in China in the 1970s*, New York: Praeger, 1972, pp. 313–37; Edward S. Boylan, "The Chinese Cultural Style of Warfare," *Comparative Strategy* 3 (1982):341–64; Dellios, "'How May the World Be at Peace?'" Recent, more rigorous, studies by Johnston suggest otherwise. See his *Cultural Realism* and "Cultural Realism and Strategy in Maoist China."
57. For scholarship that uses formal doctrine and official pronouncements, see Alice Langley Hsieh, *Chinese Strategy in the Nuclear Era*, Englewood Cliffs, NJ: Prentice

Hall, 1962; Ralph Powell, *Maoist Military Doctrines*, New York: American-Asian Educational Exchange, Inc., n.d.; Georges Tan Eng Bok, "Strategic Doctrine," in Gerald Segal and William T. Tow, eds., *Chinese Defence Policy*, Urbana and Chicago, IL: University of Illinois Press, 1984, pp. 3–17; Paul H. B. Godwin, "Changing Concepts of Doctrine, Strategy, and Operations in the Chinese People's Liberation Army, 1979–1987," *China Quarterly* 112 (December 1987):572–90; Godwin, "Chinese Military Strategy Revised: Local and Limited War," *Annals of the American Academy of Political and Social Science* 519 (January 1992):191–201; Godwin, "From Continent to Periphery: PLA Doctrine, Strategy and Capabilities toward 2000," *China Quarterly* 146 (June 1996):464–87; Johnston, *Cultural Realism*; Johnston, "Cultural Realism and Strategy"; Nan Li, "The PLA's Evolving Warfighting Doctrine, Strategy and Tactics, 1985–95: A Chinese Perspective," *China Quarterly* 146 (June 1996):443–63; Mark Burles and Abram N. Shulsky, *Patterns in China's Use of Force: Evidence from History and Doctrinal Writings*, Santa Monica, CA: RAND, 2000. For studies based on internal documents, see Zhang, *Deterrence and Strategic Culture*; Chen, *China's Road to the Korean War*; Thomas J. Christensen, "Threats, Assurances and the Last Chance for Peace: The Lessons of Mao's Korean War Telegrams," *International Security* 17 (Summer 1992):122–58; Christensen, *Useful Adversaries: Grand Strategy, Domestic Mobilization, and Sino-American Conflict*, Princeton, NJ: Princeton University Press, 1996.

58. Jonathan Wilkenfeld, Michael Brecher, and Sheila Moser, *Crises in the Twentieth Century*, Vol. 2: *Handbook of Foreign Policy Crises*, New York: Pergamon, 1988, p. 161. Alastair Iain Johnston, "China's Militarized Interstate Dispute Behavior 1949–1992: A First Cut at the Data," *China Quarterly* 153 (March 1998):1–30. Wilkenfeld et al. conclude that China is far more likely to use force to resolve a foreign policy crisis than the United States, Britain, and the Soviet Union. Johnston concludes that, for the period 1949–92, "China was more dispute-prone than most other major powers except for the United States." Johnston, "China's Militarized Interstate Dispute Behavior," p. 28. For a review of the literature on China's use of force, see Ross and Godwin, "New Directions in Chinese Security Studies," pp. 150–2.

59. See, for example, Steve Chan, "Chinese Conflict Calculus and Behavior: Assessment from a Perspective of Conflict Management," *World Politics* XXX (1978):391–410; Davis B. Bobrow, "Peking's Military Calculus," *World Politics* XVI (1964):287–301; Whiting, *China Crosses the Yalu*; Whiting, *The Chinese Calculus of Deterrence*; Gerald R. Segal, *Defending China*, New York: Oxford University Press, 1985; Gurtov and Hwang, *China under Threat*.

60. Christensen, "Threats, Assurances, and the Last Chance for Peace," Zhang, *Mao's Military Romanticism*; Chen, *China's Road to the Korean War*; Allen S. Whiting, "China's Use of Force, 1950–96, and Taiwan," *International Security* 26 (Fall 2001):103–31.

61. Muthiah Alagappa, "Rethinking Security," in Alagappa, ed., *Asian Security Practice*, Stanford, CA: Stanford University Press, 1988, pp. 34–8.

62. Thomas A. Fabyanic, "The Grammar and Logic of Conflict: Differing Conceptions of Statesmen and Soldiers," *Air University Review* 32 (March–April 1981): 23–31. Soldiers are those individuals who hold positions of authority in the military

hierarchy and spend most of their careers in the armed forces. Statesmen are those individuals who hold positions of authority in the party and/or state nonmilitary hierarchies and spend the majority of their careers outside of the armed forces. I have built on the definitions of Fabyanic. See ibid., especially p. 24. The disposition of individual soldiers and statesmen is determined from an analysis of their statements, speeches, writings, and behaviors.

63. Whiting, *The Chinese Calculus of Deterrence*, p. 201. Each of my cases also meet Whiting's other four criteria. They entail: (1) the perception of internal threat combined with external threat; (2) an issue of territorial security; (3) the opponent's behavior as it unfolds over a period of months; and (4) uncertainty over a relationship with a superpower adversary. Ibid., pp. 199–201.

64. Here I concur with the interpretation of Waldron, "Deterring China," p. 20.

65. Coercive diplomacy is "the use of military means in an exemplary, demonstrative manner, in discrete and controlled increments, to induce the opponent to revise his calculations and agree to a mutually acceptable termination of the conflict." Alexander l. George, David K. Hall, and William B. Simons, *The Limits of Coercive Diplomacy*, Boston, MA: Little, Brown, 1971, p. 18.

CHAPTER 2. THE CHINESE CULT OF DEFENSE

1. Thus in contrast to Alastair Iain Johnston, who identifies both strands but contends only the Realpolitik or "parabellum" strand is operative, I argue that both strands are active in influencing strategic choice. See Alastair Iain Johnston, *Cultural Realism: Strategic Culture and Grand Strategy in Chinese History*, Princeton, NJ: Princeton University Press, 1995. See also, Thomas J. Christensen, "Chinese Realpolitik," *Foreign Affairs* 75 (September/October 1996):37–52.

2. Stephen Van Evera, "The Cult of the Offense and the Origins of the First World War," *International Security* 9 (Summer 1984):58–107; Jack Snyder, "Civil-Military Relations and the Cult of the Offensive, 1914 and 1984," *International Security* 9 (Summer 1984):108–46.

3. Alastair Iain Johnston, "China's Militarized Interstate Dispute Behavior, 1949–1992: A First Cut at the Data," *China Quarterly* 153 (March 1998):1–30.

4. Strategic culture is widely recognized as a fruitful paradigm in the study of the strategies and security policies of China and other states. On strategic culture and cultural approaches generally, see Alastair Iain Johnston, "Thinking about Strategic Culture," *International Security* 19 (Spring 1995):32–64; Peter J. Katzenstein, ed., *The Culture of National Security: Norms and Identity in World Politics*, New York: Columbia University Press, 1996; on China, see Robert S. Ross and Paul H. B. Godwin, "New Directions in Chinese Security Studies," in David Shambaugh, ed., *American Studies of Contemporary China*, Armonk, NY: M. E. Sharpe, 1993, p. 145; Samuel S.Kim, "China and the World in Theory and Practice," in Kim, ed., *China and the World*, 3rd ed., Boulder, CO: Westview Press, 1994, pp. 14–15; Moh Ta-hua, "A Preliminary Study of Chinese Communist Strategic Culture," *Zhongguo dalu yanjiu* [Mainland China Studies](Taipei) 39 (May 1996):38–52. Indeed, in the case of China, cultural analyses have long dominated the study of the country's international relations and security; however, until very recently, the

term itself was not used. The first mention I can find of "strategic culture" is in Chong-Pin Lin's *Chinese Nuclear Weapons Strategy: Tradition within Evolution*, Lexington, MA: D. C. Heath, 1988.

5. See Thomas U. Berger, "Norms, Identity, and National Security in Germany and Japan," in Katzenstein, ed., *The Culture of National Security*, pp. 317–56; Peter J. Katzenstein and Nobuo Okawara, *Japan's National Security: Structures, Norms, and Policy Responses to a Changing World*, Ithaca, NY: Cornell University Press, 1993; Robert G. Herman, "Identity, Norms, and National Security: The Soviet Foreign Policy Revolution and the End of the Cold War," in Katzenstein, ed., *The Culture of National Security*, pp. 271–316.

6. Johnston, "China's Militarized Interstate Dispute Behavior"; Johnston, *Cultural Realism*; Alastair Iain Johnston, "Cultural Realism and Strategy in Maoist China," in Katzenstein, ed., *The Culture of National Security*, pp. 216–68.

7. See Mark Edward Lewis, *Sanctioned Violence in Early China*, Albany, NY: State University of New York Press, 1990.

8. Johnston, "China's Militarized Interstate Dispute Behavior," p. 11. See also Quansheng Zhao, *Interpreting Chinese Foreign Policy: The Micro-Macro Linkage Approach*, New York: Oxford University Press, 1996, Chapter 3. Despite Zhao's assertion that there was a sea change in Chinese foreign policy fundamentals between the Maoist and Dengist eras, he fails to demonstrate the impact of this alleged transformation on China's use of force. This key point is made by John Garver in his review of *Interpreting Chinese Foreign Policy* in *China Journal* 38 (July 1997):211–12.

9. You Ji, "Making Sense of War Games in the Taiwan Strait," *Journal of Contemporary China* 6 (July 1997):287–305; Andrew Scobell, "Show of Force: Chinese Soldiers, Statesmen and the 1995–1996 Taiwan Strait Crisis," *Political Science Quarterly* 115 (Summer 2000):227–46.

10. Chen Jian, *China's Road to the Korean War*, New York: Columbia University Press, 1994; Shu Guang Zhang, *Mao's Military Romanticism: China and the Korean War, 1950–1953*, Lawrence, KS: University Press of Kansas, 1995; Thomas J. Christensen, "Threats, Assurances, and the Last Chance for Peace: The Lessons of Mao's Korean War Telegrams," *International Security* 17 (Summer 1992):122–54.

11. This is also the view of Ross and Godwin, "New Directions." See also Allen S. Whiting, *China Crosses the Yalu: The Decision to Enter the Korean War*, Stanford, CA: Stanford University Press, 1968; Whiting, *The Chinese Calculus of Deterrence: India and Indochina*, Ann Arbor, MI: University of Michigan Press, 1975; Melvin Gurtov and Byung-Moo Hwang, *China under Threat: The Politics of Strategy and Diplomacy*, Baltimore, MD: Johns Hopkins University Press, 1980; Gerald R. Segal, *Defending China*, New York: Oxford University Press, 1985; Thomas E. Stolper, *China, Taiwan, and the Offshore Islands*, Armonk, NY: M. E. Sharpe, 1985; Jonathan R. Adelman and Chih-Yu Shih, *Symbolic War: The Chinese Use of Force, 1840–1980*, Taipei: Institute of International Relations, 1993.

12. Russell Spurr, *Enter the Dragon: China's Undeclared War against the U.S. in Korea, 1950–51*, New York: Henry Holt and Company, 1988; Hao Yufan and Zhai Zhihai, "China's Decision to Enter the Korean War: History Revisited," *China Quarterly* 121 (March 1990):94–115; Jonathan R. Pollack, "Korean War," in Harry Harding

and Yuan Ming, eds., *Sino–American Relations, 1945–1955: A Joint Reassessment of a Critical Decade*, Wilmington, DE: Scholarly Resources, Inc., 1989, pp. 213–37; Sergei N. Goncharov, John W. Lewis, and Xue Litai, *Uncertain Partners: Mao, Stalin and the Korean War*, Stanford, CA: Stanford University Press, 1993.

13. Christensen, "Threats, Assurances, and the Last Chance for Peace" ; Chen, *China's Road to the Korean War*; Zhang, *Mao's Military Romanticism*. Some studies stress the complex and conflicting array of factors, some favoring intervention, others opposing. See, for example, Michael H. Hunt, "Beijing and the Korean Crisis: June 1950–June 1951," *Political Science Quarterly* 107 (1992):453–78; Andrew Scobell, "Soldiers, Statesmen, Strategic Culture, and China's 1950 Intervention in Korea," *Journal of Contemporary China* 8 (1999):477–97.

14. Shu Guang Zhang, *Deterrence and Strategic Culture: Chinese–American Confrontations, 1948–1958*, Ithaca, NY: Cornell University Press, 1992; Thomas J. Christensen, *Useful Adversaries: Grand Strategy, Domestic Mobilization, and Sino–American Conflict, 1947–1958*, Princeton, NJ: Princeton University Press, 1996; Michael M. Sheng, *Battling Western Imperialism: Mao, Stalin, and the United States*, Princeton, NJ: Princeton University Press, 1997.

15. See, for example, Stephane Courtois et al., *The Black Book of Communism: Crimes, Terror, and Repression*, Cambridge, MA: Harvard University Press, 1999.

16. Theda Skocpol, "Social Revolutions and Mass Military Mobilization," *World Politics* 40 (1988):147–68; Stephen M. Walt, *Revolution and War*, Ithaca, NY: Cornell University Press, 1996.

17. John K. Fairbank, "Introduction," in Frank Kierman, ed., *Chinese Ways in Warfare*, Cambridge, MA: Harvard University Press, 1974, p. 7. However, Fairbank did note that China engaged in an entire repertoire of activities in interstate relations including war and conquest.

18. Stevan Harrell and Jonathan N. Lipman, eds., *Violence in China: Essays in Culture and Counter Culture*, Albany, NY: State University of New York Press, 1989; Lewis, *Sanctioned Violence in Early China*; James W. Tong, *Disorder under Heaven: Collective Violence in the Ming Dynasty*, Berkeley and Los Angeles, CA: University of California Press, 1991.

19. Arthur Waldron, *The Great Wall of China: From History to Myth*, New York: Cambridge University Press, 1990; Johnston, *Cultural Realism*.

20. Richard Bernstein and Ross Munro, *The Coming Conflict with China*, New York: Alfred A. Knopf, 1997; Denny Roy, "Hegemon on the Horizon?: China's Threat to East Asian Security," *International Security* 19 (Summer 1994): 149–68; Thomas J. Christensen, "China, the U.S.–Japan Alliance, and the Security Dilemma in East Asia," *International Security* 23 (Spring 1999):49–80. Bill Gertz, *The China Threat: How the People's Republic of China Targets America*, Washington, DC: Regnery Publishing, 2000.

21. United States House of Representatives Select Committee, *Report on U.S. National Security and Military/Commercial Concerns with the People's Republic of China*, 105th Congress, 2nd session, 3 vols., Christopher Cox (R-CA) chairman, Washington, DC: GPO, 1999. On the alleged spying case, see extensive coverage in the U.S. media of Chinese-American scientist Wen Ho Lee. Lee, who was originally from Taiwan, was never convicted of espionage, although he apparently

was guilty of security violations at the Los Alamos Nuclear Laboratory where he worked. For Lee's side of the story, see Wen Ho Lee with Helen Zia, *My Country versus Me: The First-Hand Account by the Los Alamos Scientist Who Was Falsely Accused of Being a Spy*, New York: Hyperion Books, 2002. On the People's Liberation Army and the Panama Canal, see Steven Mufson, "In Panama, Ports in a Storm," *Washington Post*, December 8, 1999; on the book, see John Pomfret, "China Ponders the New Rules of Unrestricted War," *Washington Post*, August 8, 1999, pp. A1, A25. See Qiao Liang and Wang Xiangsui, *Chaoxian zhan* [Unrestricted War], Beijing: Jiefangjun Wenyi Chubanshe, February 1999, and Dean B. Cheng, "Unrestricted Warfare," *Small Wars and Insurgencies* 11 (Spring 2000):122–29.

22. Hunt also notes this. See *The Genesis of Chinese Communist Foreign Policy*, New York: Columbia University Press, 1996, p. 241.

23. Joseph Fewsmith and Stanley Rosen, "The Domestic Context of Chinese Foreign Policy: Does 'Public Opinion' Matter?" in David M. Lampton, ed., *The Making of Chinese Foreign and Security Policy in the Era of Reform*, Stanford, CA: Stanford University Press, 2001, pp. 151–97.

24. These books have titles like *China Can Say No* and *Megatrends China*. A belligerent quote taken from the latter book is cited on the opening page of the introduction to Bernstein and Munro, *The Coming Conflict with China*, p. 3. For an analysis of this genre, see Matt Forney, "Patriot Games," *Far Eastern Economic Review*, October 3, 1996, pp. 22–8, and Suisheng Zhao, "Chinese Intellectuals' Quest for National Greatness and Nationalist Writing in the 1990s," *China Quarterly* 152 (December 1997):725–45.

25. Johnston, *Cultural Realism*, p. 26.

26. See, for example, Edward S. Boylan, "The Chinese Cultural Style of Warfare," *Comparative Strategy* 3 (1982):341–6.

27. See Johnston, *Cultural Realism*, Chapter 5. The quote is from p. 173.

28. See Waldron's review of *Cultural Realism* in *China Quarterly* 147 (September 1996):963.

29. See, for example, the writings of Wm. Theodore De Bary and Tu Wei-ming.

30. See, for example, Chen-Ya Tien, *Chinese Military Theory: Ancient and Modern*, Stevanage, UK: Spa Books, 1992, p. 34; S. G. Cheng, *The Chinese as a Warrior in the Light of History*, paper read before the China Society on January 27, 1916, London: East and West Ltd., n.d.; Stevan Harrell, "Introduction," in Harrell and Lipman, eds., *Violence in China*, p. 17. For a fascinating discussion and analysis of the origins of sanctioned violence in imperial China, see Lewis, *Sanctioned Violence in Early China*, especially pp. 16–19, 128–35, 222–6, 235–8.

31. Cheng, *The Chinese as a Warrior*, p. 4.

32. *Confucius: The Analects*, James Legge ed. and transl., Oxford, UK: Clarendon Press, 1893; reprint New York: Dover Publications, 1971, Bk. XII, Chapter VII (p. 254). Still, it is important to note that Confucius did rank military preparation as the least important of the three aspects.

33. Harrell, "Introduction," p. 18.

34. Johnston, *Cultural Realism*, pp. 68–73 (quote on p. 70); Lewis, *Sanctioned Violence*, pp. 235–6.

35. *Confucius: The Analects*, Bk. XVI, Chapter II (p. 310).

36. Ibid., Bk. XIII, Chapters XXIX and XXX (p. 275).

37. This is also noted by David Shambaugh, *Beautiful Imperialist: China Perceives America, 1972–1990*, Princeton, NJ: Princeton University Press, 1991, p. 82.
38. Lewis, *Sanctioned Violence*, p. 87.
39. Cheng, *The Chinese as a Warrior*, p. 4.
40. Johnston mentions in a footnote that "Confucius did not oppose military preparations, though he downplayed their role in the security of the state." See *Cultural Realism*, p. 45, n. 18.
41. On Legalism and war, see Tien, *Chinese Military Theory*, pp. 27–9; Shambaugh, *Beautiful Imperialist*, pp. 82–3. Buddhism, for example, was capable of legitimizing and spawning violence and rebellion too. See, for example, Frederick P. Brandauer, "Violence and Buddhist Idealism in the *Xiyou* Novels," in Harrell and Lipman, eds., *Violence in China*, pp. 115–48; Susan Naquin, *Millenarian Rebellion in China: The Eight Trigrams Uprising of 1813*, New Haven, CT: Yale University Press, 1970. The introduction and indigenization of Christianity also triggered violence in the form of the Taiping Rebellion. For a recent study, see Jonathan Spence, *God's Chinese Son: The Taiping Heavenly Kingdom of Hong Xiuquan*, New York: W. W. Norton, 1996.
42. Lewis, *Sanctioned Violence*, Chapter V. The quote is on p. 176 (emphasis added).
43. Ibid., pp. 196, 198.
44. Take for example, the case of the death penalty. See Andrew Scobell, "The Death Penalty under Socialism, 1917–1990: The Soviet Union, China, Cuba, and the German Democratic Republic," *Criminal Justice History* 12 (1991):189–234.
45. See Waldron's review of Johnston, *Cultural Realism*.
46. Stephen J. Morris, *Why Vietnam Invaded Cambodia: Political Culture and the Causes of War*, Stanford, CA: Stanford University Press, 1999. On the importance given to the domestic dimension of national security in many states, see Muthiah Alagappa, "Rethinking Security," in Alagappa, ed., *Asian Security Practice: Material and Ideational Influences*, Stanford, CA: Stanford University Press, 1998, pp. 34–8.
47. Johnston, *Cultural Realism*, p. 45.
48. See Joseph Esherick's review of *Cultural Realism* in *Journal of Asian Studies* 56 (August 1997):769–71. Johnston devotes an entire chapter to a theoretical justification of his conclusion of an essentially monistic Chinese strategic culture. Johnston, *Cultural Realism*, Chapter 5.
49. Hsi-sheng Ch'i, *Warlord Politics in China, 1916–1928*, Stanford, CA: Stanford University Press, 1976, pp. 180–3; James E. Sheridan, *China in Disintegration: The Republican Era in Chinese History, 1912–1989*, New York: Free Press, 1977, pp. 98–101.
50. Lewis, *Sanctioned Violence*.
51. See, for example, David Bonavia, *China's Warlords*, Hong Kong: Oxford University Press, 1995, pp. 20–5.
52. For an important exception, see Peter J. Katzenstein, *Cultural Norms and National Security: Police and Military in Postwar Japan*, Ithaca, NY: Cornell University Press, 1996. See in particular Chapters 1 and 4.
53. This is also noted by Waldron. See his review of *Cultural Realism*, pp. 963–4.

54. Lewis, *Sanctioned Violence*, Chapter 5.
55. See, for example, Tong, *Disorder under Heaven*; Elizabeth J. Perry, *Rebels and Revolutionaries in North China*, Stanford, CA: Stanford University Press, 1980; Spence, *God's Chinese Son*; and many studies of the rise of the communist movement in China.
56. Johnston examines Ming security policy with a particular focus on Chinese relations with the Mongols. Although Adelman and Shih briefly discuss civil wars, all their case studies concern China's wars with other states. See Adelman and Shih, *Symbolic War*, pp. 35–6, 47.
57. See, for example, Michael D. Swaine, *The Role of the Chinese Military in National Security Policymaking*, Santa Monica, CA: RAND, 1996, pp. 7–10.
58. See, for example, Adelman and Shih, *Symbolic War*, pp. 35–6.
59. See Arthur Waldron, *The Chinese Civil Wars, 1911–1940s*, London: St. Martin's, 1996.
60. Harrell, "Introduction," p. 1. A detailed study of collective violence in the Ming dynasty found significant and diverse occurrences of violence. The author concluded that the Ming was no more violent than other dynasties, but collective violence between societal groups in China was less common than in modern Europe. Tong, *Disorder under Heaven*, pp. 71–5.
61. Lewis, *Sanctioned Violence*, Chapters 1 and 2.
62. Ibid., p. 64.
63. Harry J. Lamley, "Lineage Feuding in Southern Fujian and Eastern Guangdong under Qing Rule," in Harrell and Lipman, eds., *Violence in China*, pp. 27–64, quote on p. 58. See also Lewis, *Sanctioned Violence*, Chapter 1; Maurice Freedman, *Chinese Lineage and Society: Fukien and Kwangtung*, London: Athlone, 1966; Elizabeth J. Perry, "Rural Violence in Socialist China," *China Quarterly* 103 (1986):414–40.
64. See, for example, John Pomfret, "Chinese Crime Rate Soars as Economic Problems Grow," *Washington Post*, January 21, 1999; Craig S. Smith, "As Crimes Rise in China, Four Germans Are Killed," *New York Times*, April 4, 2000; Craig S. Smith, "China's Efforts against Crime Make No Dent," *New York Times*, December 26, 2001.
65. Lewis, *Sanctioned Violence*, p. 209.
66. Tien, *Chinese Military Theory*, p. 32. The other righteous wars were punitive expeditions against China's neighbors, and wars of self-defense against aggressor states. See ibid.
67. This is a refinement of the "Cult of the Offensive" concept. Unlike Snyder's conception, which has bureaucratic/organizational origins, the Chinese Cult of Defense is grounded in a psychocultural mindset.
68. Zhang, *Mao's Military Romanticism*, pp. 9–11. See also Chapter 2.
69. Stuart Schram, *The Thought of Mao Tse-tung*, New York: Cambridge University Press, 1989, p. 55.
70. Lawrence Freedman cited in Carl H. Builder, *The Masks of War: American Military Styles in Strategy and Analysis*, Baltimore, MD: Johns Hopkins University Press, 1989, p. 6.
71. Quoted in Nayan Chanda, "Fear of the Dragon," *Far Eastern Economic Review*, April 13, 1995, p. 24.

72. While I am of the opinion the beliefs that constitute the Cult of Defense were also widespread in earlier decades, since the majority of my sources are from the 1980s and 1990s, I cannot state this with absolute certainty.

73. Huang Renwei, "Shilun Zhongguo zai shiji zhi jiaoguoji huanjing zhongde shenceng ci maodun" [On China's deep contradictions in the international environment at the turn of the century], *Shanghai Shehui Kexueyuan Xueshu Jikan* [Shanghai Academy of Social Sciences Quarterly Journal] 1 (1997):8–9. Implicit in two of the contradictions that Huang identifies is a rejection of any Chinese Cult of Defense. Huang points to the contradiction between China's desire to achieve national unification and the "internationalization of the Taiwan issue." He also locates a contradiction between maintaining friendly relations with China's neighbors and Beijing's territorial claims.

74. "White Paper on China's National Defense," Beijing Xinhua Domestic Service, July 27, 1998, in Foreign Broadcast Information Service *Daily Report–China* (hereafter FBIS-CHI), July 29, 1998.

75. Li Jijun, "Zhongguo junshi sixiang chuantong yu fangyu zhanlue" [Chinese traditional military thinking and defense strategy], *Zhongguo Junshi Kexue* [China Military Science, hereafter *ZGJSKX*] 4 (Winter 1997):62.

76. "Liu Huaqing on the Stand of the Military towards Taiwan," *Ta Kung Pao* (Hong Kong), September 4, 1995, in FBIS-CHI, September 7, 1995.

77. Xing Shizhong, "China Threat Theory May Be Forgotten," *Quishi* [Seeking truth] 3 (February 1996), in FBIS-CHI, February 1, 1996. See also Gao Jiquan, "China Holds High Banner of Peace," *Jiefangjun Bao* [Liberation Army Daily], June 27, 1996, in FBIS-CHI, June 27, 1996.

78. Li Jijun, "Lun zhanlue wenhua" [On strategic culture], *ZGJSKX* 1 (1997):9.

79. Ibid., p. 9; Chen Zhou, "Zhongguo xiandai jubu zhanzheng lilun yu Meiguo youxian zhanzheng lilun zhi butong" [Differences between China's theory of modern local war and America's theory of limited war], *ZGJSKX* 4 (1995), p. 46; interviews with civilian and military researchers in Beijing and Shanghai, May–June 1998 [hereafter, Interviews].

80. Wu Xinbo, "China: Security Practice of a Modernizing and Ascending Power," in Alagappa, ed., *Asian Security Practice*, pp. 121–2.

81. Wang Chang and Cui Haiming, "Deng Xiaoping de junshi sixiang chutan" [Preliminary exploration of Deng Xiaoping's military thought], in Pan Shiying, chief editor, *Dangdai Zhongguo Junshi Sixiang Jingyao* [The Essence of Contemporary Chinese Military Thinking], Beijing: Jiefangjun Chubanshe, 1992, p. 121. See also Peng Dehuai, "Junshi jianshe gaikuang" [General situation of military construction] (July 16, 1957), in *Peng Dehuai Junshi Wenxuan* [Collected Military Works of Peng Dehuai], Beijing: Zhongyang Wenxian Chubanshe, 1988, p. 588.

82. Deng Xiaoping, "Muqian de xingshi he renwu" [Present situation and tasks] (January 16, 1980) in *Deng Xiaoping Wenxuan (1975–1982)* [Selected Works of Deng Xiaoping 1975–1982], Beijing: Renmin Chubanshe, 1984, pp. 203–4.

83. Wang and Cui, "Deng Xiaoping de junshi," p. 121; interviews.

84. Wu, "China: Security Practice," pp. 152–3.

85. See the succinct discussion in Andrew J. Nathan and Robert S. Ross, *The Great Wall and the Empty Fortress: China's Search for Security*, New York: W. W. Norton, 1997, p. 5.

86. "Liu Huaqing Refutes Argument That China Poses a Threat," *Takung Pao*, September 6, 1995, in FBIS-CHI, September 8, 1995, p. 31. See also Xing, "China Threat Theory May Be Forgotten."

87. Deng, "Muqian de xingshi he renwu," pp. 203–4.

88. The importance of these concepts was stressed by Chinese researchers during interviews I conducted in May and June 1998.

89. Li Jijun, "Lun junshi zhanlue siwei" [On military strategic thinking], *ZGJSKX* 2 (1996), p. 78.

90. Gao, "China Holds High Banner of Peace."

91. Li, "Lun zhanlue wenhua," p. 10; interviews.

92. Li, "Lun junshi zhanlue siwei," p. 78; Li, "Zhongguo junshi sixiang chuantong," p. 62; interviews.

93. Li, "Zhongguo junshi sixiang chuantong," p. 63.

94. Li, "Lun zhanlue wenhua," p. 9. See also Li, "Zhongguo junshi sixiang chuantong," p. 63.

95. Li, "Lun zhanlue wenhua," p. 9.

96. Yao Youzhi, "Gudai Zhong-Xi junshi chuantong zhi bijiao" [A comparison of Chinese and Western ancient military traditions], *ZGJSKX* 3 (1995), pp. 93–4.

97. Interviews.

98. "Liu Huaqing on Stand of Military towards Taiwan."

99. Li, "Lun zhanlue wenhua," p. 10; Chen, "Zhongguo xiandai jubu zhanzheng," p. 45; Xing, "China Threat Theory May Be Forgotten"; Gao, "China Holds High Banner of Peace"; Xiong Guangkai, "Zhongguo de guofang zhengce" [China's national defense policy], *Guoji Zhanlue Yanjiu* [International Strategic Studies] 55 (January 2000):4; interviews.

100. See, for example, Zhang Liang, compiler, *The Tiananmen Papers: The Chinese Leadership's Decision to Use Force against Their Own People – in Their Own Words*, Andrew J. Nathan and Perry Link, eds., New York: PublicAffairs Press, 2001, pp. 374, 382.

101. "Huijian Yidali jizhe Naxi Polasishi de tanhua jiyao" (17 August 1980) [Summary of a talk in an interview with Italian journalist . . .] in *Xu Xiangqian Junshi Wenxuan* [Selected Military Works of Xu Xiangqian], Beijing: Jiefangjun Chubanshe, 1993, p. 305.

102. Zhang Jing and Yao Yanjin, *Jiji Fangyu Zhanlue Qianshuo* [Introduction to Active Defense Strategy], Beijing: Jiefangjun Chubanshe, 1985, p. 137.

103. Song Shilun, *Mao Zedong Junshi Sixiang de Xingcheng Jiqi Fazhan* [Formation and Development of Mao Zedong's Military Thought], Beijing: Junshi Kexue Chubanshe, 1984, p. 222.

104. See, for example, Junshi Kexueyuan Junshi Lishi Yanjiubu, ed., *Zhongguo Renmin Jiefangjun de Qishinian* [Seventy years of the Chinese People's Liberation Army], Beijing: Junshi Kexue Chubanshe, 1997, pp. 541–7, 580–2.

105. See Bruce Cummings, *Parallax Visions: Making Sense of American–East Asian Relations at the End of the Century*, Durham, NC: Duke University Press, 1999, p. 166.

106. Li Jijun, "International Military Strategy and China's Security at the Turn of the Century," *Zhongguo Pinglun* (Hong Kong), August 5, 1998, in FBIS-CHI, August 13, 1998.

107. Fan Yihua, "Shi lun Zhongguo xiandai sixiang wenhua de xing chao ji zhanlue qu...?" [On the form and strategic trend of modern thought culture in China], *ZGJSKX* 1 (1997):26.

108. See, for example, Li Zhisui, *The Private Life of Chairman Mao*, New York: Random House, 1994; Liz Sly, "A State of Paranoia," *Bulletin of the Atomic Scientists* 55 (September/October 1999):38–43. On this paranoia as a pathology distinct to communist regimes, see Nathan Leites, *The Operational Code of the Soviet Politburo*, New York: McGraw-Hill, 1951; Morris, *Why Vietnam Invaded Cambodia*.

109. On the corruption campaign, see John Schauble, "China's Communists Fear the Enemy from Within," *Sydney Morning Herald*, September 27, 2000. On threat perceptions more generally, see Sly, "A State of Paranoia," and Michael Pillsbury, ed., *China Debates the Future Security Environment*, Washington, DC: National Defense University Press, 2000.

110. Thus, the world is seen as a very dangerous place and the threat of war a constant concern. See, for example, Pan Shunnu, "War is Not Far from Us," *Jiefangjun Bao*, June 8, 1999, in FBIS-CHI, July 6, 1999.

111. Yao Yunzhu, "The Evolution of Military Doctrine of the Chinese PLA from 1985–1995," *Korea Journal of Defense Analysis* VII (Winter 1995):62–8. See also Pillsbury, *China Debates the Future Security Environment*; David Shambaugh, "China's Military Views the World: Ambivalent Security," *International Security* 24 (Winter 1999/2000):52–79.

112. For recent use of this slogan, see, for example, Gao, "China Holds High Banner of Peace."

113. Wu, "China: Security Practice," p. 133.

114. Ibid., pp. 132–5.

115. Johnston, "Cultural Realism and Strategy," pp. 231–2. The theme of just or righteous war was a significant one in many popular histories and novels that Mao – and other leaders – read. See ibid., p. 247.

116. A first strike is just only if China can claim that the attack was launched to preempt an attack being prepared by an opponent. See Peng, "Junshi jianshe gaikuang," p. 59.

117. Wang Zhiping and Li Dezhou, "Zhong-Xi gudai junshi lilun de zhexue jichu" [Philosophical foundation of Chinese and Western military theories in ancient times], *ZGJSKX* 4 (1995):30–1, 34–5; Yao, "Gudai Zhong-Xi junshi chuantong," pp. 95–6.

118. Johnston contends that the term "defense" is employed for propaganda purposes so that every military action can be labeled as defense and hence more justified than anything called "offensive." See Johnston, "Cultural Realism and Strategy," pp. 249–50, especially n. 63.

119. Paul H. B. Godwin, "Change and Continuity in Chinese Military Doctrine, 1949–1999," paper presented to the PLA Warfighting Conference sponsored by the Center for Naval Analyses held June 1999 in Washington, DC; Mao, "Problems of Strategy in China's Revolutionary War" (December 1936), in *Selected Military Writings of Mao Tse-tung*, Peking: Foreign Languages Press, 1967, p. 105; Yao, "The Evolution of Military Doctrine," pp. 77–80.

120. Peng, "Junshi jianshe gaikuang," pp. 587–8.

121. Deng quoted in Chen Zhou, "Zhongguo xiandai jubu zhanzheng lilun meiguo youxian zhanzheng lilun zhi butong," [Differences between China's theory of modern local war and America's theory of limited war], *Zhongguo Junshi Kexue* [hereafter *ZGJSKX* 4] (1995):46. See also Mi Zhenyu, "Zhongguo jiji fangyu zhan-lue fangzhen" [China's strategic guiding principle of active defense], in Shi Boke, ed., *Zhongguo Daqushi* [Megatrends China], Beijing: Hualing Chubanshe, 1996, p. 53.
122. Senior Colonel Wang Naiming, "Adhere to Active Defense and Modern People's War," in Pillsbury, ed., *Chinese Views of Future Warfare*, Washington, DC: National Defense University Press, 1997, p. 37.
123. Johnston, *Cultural Realism*, p. 102ff.
124. Jianxiang Bi, "The PRC's Active Defense Strategy: New Wars, Old Concepts," *Issues and Studies* 31 (November 1995):94.
125. Chen, "Zhongguo xiandai jubu zhanzheng," p. 46. See also Nan Li, "The PLA's Evolving Warfighting Doctrine, Strategy, and Tactics, 1985–95: A Chinese Per-spective," *China Quarterly* 146 (June 1996):443–63.
126. Peng, "Junshi jianshe gaikuang," pp. 588–90. The quotes are on pp. 588, 590.
127. For such an interpretation, depicting a broad definition of "security" with a focus on contemporary China, see Wu, "China: Security Practice," pp. 115–56.
128. Yao, "Gudai Zhong-Xi junshi chuantong," pp. 94–5.
129. For a fascinating study of the *danwei*, see Andrew G. Walder, *Communist Neo-Traditionalism: Work and Authority in Chinese Industry*, Berkeley and Los Angeles, CA: University of California Press, 1986.
130. Interviews in Beijing and Shanghai, May–June 1998.
131. Deng, "Muqian de xingshi he renwu," p. 216.
132. Guo Daohu, "Lun juyou zhongguo tese sixing zhidu" [The distinguishing features of China's institution of the death penalty], in *Mao Zedong sixiang faxue lilun lunwenxuan* [Selected papers on Mao Zedong's thought concerning legal theory], Falu Chubanshe, 1985, pp. 122–34.
133. Lynn T. White, *The Policies of Chaos: The Organizational Causes of Violence in the Chinese Cultural Revolution*, Princeton, NJ: Princeton University Press, 1989.
134. Andrew Scobell, "The Death Penalty in Post-Mao China," *China Quarterly* 123 (September 1990):503–20.
135. Deng, "Muqian de xingshi he renwu," p. 217.
136. Ibid., pp. 218–19.
137. Scobell, "The Death Penalty under Socialism."

CHAPTER 3. BRINGING IN THE MILITARY

1. David Shambaugh, "The Building of the Party State in China, 1949–1965: Bringing the Soldier Back In," in Timothy Cheek and Tony Saich, eds., *New Perspectives on State Socialism in China, 1949–1965*, Armonk, NY: M. E. Sharpe, 1996.
2. See, for example, the works of Alastair Iain Johnston, Chong-Pin Lin, and Shu Guang Zhang on the subject cited in this volume.
3. See, for example, John K. Fairbank, *The United States and China*, rev. ed., New York: Compass Books, Viking Press, 1962, p. 50; Richard J. Smith, *China's Cultural Heritage: The Ch'ing Dynasty, 1644–1912*, Boulder, CO: Westview Press, 1983,

pp. 62–63, 229, 252; Diana Lary, *Warlord Soldiers: Chinese Common Soldiers, 1911–1937*, New York: Cambridge University Press, 1985.

4. See, for example, the title page of Lary's *Warlord Soldiers* and Wei-Chin Lee's "Iron and Nail: Civil-Military Relations in the People's Republic of China," *Journal of Asian and African Studies* XXVI (1991):132–48.

5. One historian has admonished that ". . . care must be taken not to over-exaggerate the anti-military bias of Chinese culture." Edward R. McCord, *The Power of the Gun: The Emergence of Modern Chinese Warlordism*, Berkeley and Los Angeles, CA: University of California Press, 1993, p. 50.

6. Lei Bolun (pseud.), *Zhongguo wenhua yu Zhongguo de bing* [Chinese culture and the Chinese soldier], Taipei: Wanianqing, 1972; reprint, first published in the 1930s. See also Morton H. Fried, "Military Status in Chinese Society," *American Journal of Sociology* LXII (January 1952):347–57; James E. Sheridan, *China in Disintegration: The Republican Era in Chinese History, 1912–1949*, New York: Free Press, 1977, p. 98. Such fluctuation is not unusual, to judge from the experience of countries such as the United States. American soldiers, like their Chinese counterparts, have at times been held in low esteem by civilians and yet at other times have been widely respected. Morris Janowitz, *The Professional Soldier: A Social and Political Portrait*, rev. ed., New York: Free Press, 1971, p. 3. Although the status of the military improved after World War II, it declined during the Vietnam War. Most recently, the standing of the soldier rose during the administration of President Ronald Reagan (1981–9) and remains quite high as of this writing.

7. Fried, "Military Status in Chinese Society."

8. See, for example, Sheridan, *China in Disintegration*, pp. 98–101; Hsi-sheng Ch'i, *Warlord Politics in China, 1916–1928*, Stanford, CA: Stanford University Press, 1976, pp. 180–2.

9. "On the Reissue of the Three Main Rules of Discipline and the Eight Points for Attention. . . ." (October 10, 1947), *Selected Military Writings of Mao Tse-tung*, Peking: Foreign Languages Press, 1967, p. 344, n. 1.

10. Theodore H. White, *In Search of History*, New York: Harper and Row, 1978, p. 98. See also on this theme more generally, Mark Selden, *The Yenan Way in Revolutionary China*, Cambridge, MA: Harvard University Press, 1971.

11. For more on this piece, see Philip West, "The Korean War and the Criteria of Significance in Chinese Popular Culture," *Journal of American–East Asian Relations* 1 (Winter 1992):386–90.

12. The author had the opportunity to view the movie several times when it was released in 1984 and was able to witness the reaction of Chinese viewers.

13. Just as the positive images of soldiers in Chinese society were reflected in popular literature, so too the more negative images of the early 1980s were mirrored in contemporary fiction. There were various unflattering portraits of military figures evident in short stories with titles such as "General, You Cannot Do This" (published in 1979) and "General, Give Yourself a Good Bath" (published in 1981). See the discussion in Merle Goldman, *Sowing the Seeds of Democracy in China: Political Reform in the Deng Xiaoping Era*, Cambridge, MA: Harvard University Press, 1994, pp. 104–5.

14. See, for example, Thomas J. Christensen, "Chinese Realpolitik," *Foreign Affairs* 75 (September/October 1996):47.

15. On the appalling state of Banner garrisons, see Kaye Soon Im, "The Rise and Decline of the Eight Banner Garrisons in the Ch'ing Period (1644–1911): A Study of Kuang-chou, Hang-chou, and Ching-chou Garrisons," Ph.D. dissertation, University of Illinois, 1981, especially Chapter IV. On the decline of the capabilities of both the Banners and Armies of the Green Standard, see McCord, *The Power of the Gun*, pp. 19–22.
16. McCord, *The Power of the Gun*, pp. 52–5.
17. On the reforms in military education, see Richard J. Smith, "The Reform of Military Education in Late Ch'ing China, 1842–1895," *Journal of the Hong Kong Branch of the Royal Asiatic Society* 18 (1978):15–40. On the growing interest of the gentry in the late Qing, see McCord, *The Power of the Gun*, pp. 50–5.
18. McCord, *The Power of the Gun*, pp. 66–72.
19. There is considerable controversy about warlordism. While scholars are in general agreement over how to define it, they differ significantly over its origins, its starting and ending dates, and even whether warlordism is the most appropriate term. I consider warlordism to have emerged in the aftermath of 1911 and to have persisted until 1927 (although its symptoms continued to haunt China until 1949). The term *warlordism* is retained, and the roots of the phenomenon are viewed as complex and many. For some recent studies of warlordism, see Arthur Waldron, "The Warlord: Twentieth Century Chinese Understandings of Violence, Militarism, and Imperialism," *American Historical Review* 96 (October 1991):1073–1100; McCord, *The Power of the Gun*; Arthur Waldron, *From War to Nationalism: China's Turning Point, 1924–1925*, New York: Cambridge University Press, 1995; and the special issue of *Modern Asian Studies* 3 (1996) on war in modern China.
20. Indeed, Lary asks the very same question, but her answer remains unsatisfactory in my view. Lary, *Warlord Soldiers*, p. 5.
21. On modes of recruitment, see ibid., pp. 13–17; on motives, see ibid., pp. 5–6, 17–23.
22. Ibid., p. 5.
23. See Donald J. Munro, *The Concept of Man in Early China*, Stanford, CA: Stanford University Press, 1969.
24. Certainly there were significant numbers of villainous warlords who horribly mistreated their men. See Lary, *Warlord Soldiers*, Chapter 4. For portraits of some of the most prominent warlords of the period, see Sheridan, *China in Disintegration*, pp. 57–77.
25. Sheridan, *China in Disintegration*, pp. 99–102; Ch'i, *Warlord Politics in China*, pp. 181–4.
26. The term is not of Chinese origin and was imported probably in the aftermath of World War I. It was apparently the eventual founder of the Chinese Communist Party, Chen Duxiu, who introduced *junfa* into the modern Chinese political lexicon, borrowing it from the Japanese. Waldron, *From War to Nationalism*, pp. 246–8.
27. Waldron, *From War to Nationalism*, p. 246. Chen contrasts disapprovingly the reaction of these Chinese students with that of a group of Japanese students who marked the end of World War I with a banner condemning military leaders, inscribed "Down with warlords!" The reference to warlords by the students ostensibly was to the defeated German generals, but was widely understood to refer to Japanese militarists. Ibid., pp. 246–7.

28. Some scholars, in contrast, conceive of doctrine in a more rigid and deterministic fashion. See, for example, Barry R. Posen, *The Sources of Military Doctrine: France, Britain, and Germany between the Wars*, Ithaca, NY: Cornell University Press, 1984.

29. Michael H. Hunt, *The Genesis of Chinese Communist Foreign Policy*, New York: Columbia University Press, 1996, Chapters 5, 6.

30. See, for example, Chen Jian, *China's Road to the Korean War*, New York: Columbia University Press, 1994; Shu Guang Zhang, *Mao's Military Romanticism: China and the Korean War, 1950–1953*, Lawrence, KS: University Press of Kansas, 1995.

31. See, for example, the discussion in Chalmers A. Johnson, *Autopsy on People's War*, Berkeley and Los Angeles, CA: University of California Press, 1973. See also Jacques Guillermaz, "The Soldier," in Dick Wilson, ed., *Mao Zedong in the Scales of History*, New York: Cambridge University Press, 1977, pp. 117–43.

32. Johnson, *Autopsy on People's War*, Chapter 3.

33. Scott A. Boorman, *The Protracted Game: A Wei-ch'i Interpretation of Maoist Revolutionary Strategy*, New York: Oxford University Press, 1969, p. 182. See also Ralph L. Powell, *Maoist Military Doctrines*, New York: American-Asian Educational Exchange, Inc., n.d., p. 13.

34. See, for example, the recent study of Chinese foreign and military policies by Andrew J. Nathan and Robert S. Ross: *The Great Wall and the Empty Fortress: China's Search for Security*, New York: W. W. Norton, 1997.

35. Johnson, *Autopsy on People's War*, Chapter 2; Georges Tan Eng Bok, "Strategic Doctrine," in Gerald Segal and William T. Tow, eds., *Chinese Defence Policy*, Urbana and Chicago, IL: University of Illinois Press, 1984, pp. 3–17. Powell argues that Maoist doctrines were pragmatic and adaptable, but by the 1960s had become "unrealistic" and "stultifying." Powell, *Maoist Military Doctrines*, p. 28.

36. On combining guerilla warfare with conventional warfare, see "Problems of Strategy in the Guerrilla War against Japan," (May 1938), in *Selected Military Writings of Mao Tse-tung*, pp. 153–86. On the three phases of war, see "On Protracted War" (May 1938), in ibid., pp. 187–267.

37. Even veteran scholars of Chinese military history sometimes do not recognize the flexibility and broadness of People's War. Edward Dreyer, for example, criticized the set piece battles fought by communist generals in Manchuria and north China during the latter stages of the Chinese Civil War as being inconsistent with Mao's military doctrine. Edward L. Dreyer, *China at War, 1901–1949*, New York: Longman, 1995, pp. 350–5.

38. Samuel B. Griffith, "Introduction," in Sun Tzu, *The Art of War*, trans. Samuel Griffith, New York: Oxford University Press, 1963, pp. 45–6; Tan Eng Bok, "Strategic Doctrine," pp. 4–5.

39. Tan Eng Bok, "Strategic Doctrine," p. 5.

40. Boorman, *The Protracted Game*.

41. Powell, *Maoist Military Doctrines*, For an assessment of the foreign policy dimension, see Johnson, *Autopsy on People's War*. There is considerable controversy over whether any aspects of People's War remain relevant in the information age. Among those who argue for its continued relevance, it is significant that some stress the lessons of People's War for offensive strategies. Scholars at the Academy of Military Sciences, for example, reportedly spoke enthusiastically about computer

"network guerilla units" using a personal computer, a telephone line, and a modem to "cross the oceans and attack the Pentagon." "So," these researchers said, "how can one say 'the People's War will be unable to strike distant foes'?" *Ching Pao* (Hong Kong), April 1998, cited in *Inside China Mainland* (June 1998):35–6.

42. Peter Van Ness, *Revolution and Chinese Foreign Policy: Peking's Support for Wars of National Liberation*, Berkeley and Los Angeles, CA: University of California Press, 1971.

43. Johnson, *Autopsy on People's War*, Chapter 3, especially pp. 33–4, 38, 44.

44. Ibid., Chapters 7, 8.

45. John Lewis and Xue Litai, *China Builds the Bomb*, Stanford, CA: Stanford University Press, 1988; John Lewis and Xue Litai, *China's Strategic Seapower: The Politics of Force Modernization in the Nuclear Age*, Stanford, CA: Stanford University Press, 1994. See also Alice Langley Hsieh, *Communist China's Strategy in the Nuclear Age*, Englewood Cliffs, NJ: Prentice Hall, 1962.

46. Paul H. B. Godwin, "People's War Revised: Military Doctrine, Strategy and Operations," in Charles D. Lovejoy, Jr., and Bruce W. Watson, eds., *China's Military Reforms International and Domestic Implications*, Boulder, CO: Westview Press, 1984, pp. 1–13; Ellis Joffe, "People's War under Modern Conditions: A Doctrine of Modern War," *China Quarterly* 112 (December 1987):555–71. It is important to note that this doctrine had been germinating since the 1950s. See Yao Yunzhu, "The Evolution of Military Doctrine of the Chinese PLA from 1985 to 1995," *Korean Journal of Defense Analysis* VII (Winter 1995):74–5; Lewis and Xue, *China's Strategic Seapower*, p. 212.

47. See, for example, Deng Xiaoping's speeches dealing with the PLA in *Deng Xiaoping wenxuan (1975–1982)* [Selected works of Deng Xiaoping], Beijing: Renmin Chubanshe, 1983.

48. For some comprehensive studies of military modernization in the post-Mao era, see Lovejoy and Watson, eds., *China's Military Reforms*; Ellis Joffe, *The Chinese Army after Mao*, Cambridge, MA: Harvard University Press, 1987; *China Quarterly* 146 (June 1996), special issue on the PLA.

49. See Paul H. B. Godwin, "Changing Concepts of Doctrine, Strategy and Operations in the People's Liberation Army," *China Quarterly* 112 (December 1992):572–90; Paul H. B. Godwin, "Chinese Military Strategy Revised: Local and Limited War," *Annals of the American Academy of Political and Social Science* 519 (January 1992):191–201; Paul H. B. Godwin, "From Continent to Periphery: PLA Doctrine, Strategy and Capabilities toward 2000," *China Quarterly* 146 (June 1996):443–87; Yao, "The Evolution of Military Doctrine."

50. Yao, "The Evolution of Military Doctrine," pp. 70–1; Nan Li, "The PLA's Evolving Warfighting Doctrine, Strategy and Tactics, 1985–1995: A Chinese Perspective," *China Quarterly* 146 (June 1996):456–8. See also David Shambaugh, "China's Military in Transition: Politics, Professionalism, Procurement and Power Projection," *China Quarterly* 146 (June 1996):280–1.

51. John Arquilla and Solomon M. Karmel, "Welcome to the Revolution . . . in Chinese Military Affairs," *Defense Analyses* 13 (December 1997):255–70.

52. Major General Zheng Qinsheng, "Military Conflicts in the New Era," in Michael Pillsbury, ed., *Chinese Views of Future War*, Washington, DC: National Defense University Press, 1997, p. 405.

53. Alastair Iain Johnston, "China's New 'Old Thinking': The Concept of Limited Deterrence," *International Security* 20 (Winter 1995–1996):5–42; You Ji, *The Armed Forces of China*, London: I. B. Taurus, 1999, Chapter 4.

54. Lei, *Zhongguo wenhua yu Zhongguo de bing;* Paul Edward Lewis, *Sanctioned Violence in Early China*, Albany, NY: State University of New York Press, 1990, Chapters 2, 3, especially pp. 97–8; Griffith, "Introduction," pp. 30–8. See also Cheng Hsiao-shih, "Zhanguo shiqi zhengzhi junshi guanxi–jiangjun, zhengzhi yu shehui" [Politico-military relations in the Warring States period – generals, politics, and society], Taipei, manuscript, n.d. Cheng argues, however, that this transformation occurred before the Warring States era in the latter part of the Spring and Autumn period. See his "Chunqiu shiqi de zhengjun guanxi" [Politico-military relations in the Spring and Autumn period], Taipei: Academia Sinica, 1994.

55. "Problems of War and Strategy (November 6, 1938)," *Selected Military Writings of Mao Tse-tung*, p. 274.

56. Lei, *Zhongguo wenhua yu Zhongguo de bing*.

57. See, for example, Frederick C. Teiwes, *Leadership, Legitimacy, and Conflict in China: From a Charismatic Mao to the Politics of Succession*, Armonk, NY: M. E. Sharpe, 1984, Chapter III, especially pp. 96, 98, 123–34.

58. Song Renqiong, "Chairman Mao Refused to Be the Grand Marshal," *Minzhu yu Fazhi* (December 1993), pp. 8–9; Shiping Zheng, *Party vs. State in Post-1949 China: The Institutional Dilemma*, New York: Cambridge University Press, 1997, p. 111.

59. William W. Whitson with Chen-hsia Huang, *The Chinese High Command: A History of Communist Military Politics, 1927–1971*, New York: Praeger, 1973, pp. 518–19.

60. Kenneth G. Lieberthal, *Governing China*, New York: W. W. Norton, 1995, Chapter 7.

61. On this trend in the warlord era, see Lucian W. Pye, *Warlord Politics: Conflict and Coalition in the Modernization of Republican China*, New York: Praeger, 1971, p. 138, table 8.3 on p. 144.

62. The exception to the rule is PLA veteran Yu Qiuli. Yu became involved in oil production and economic planning; appointed minister of petroleum industry in 1959, he was later selected to head the State Planning Commission. In the early 1980s, however, he was relieved of economic policy-making duties and returned to the PLA as director of the General Political Department. See Kenneth Lieberthal and Michel Oksenberg, *Policy Making in China: Leaders, Structures, and Processes*, Princeton, NJ: Princeton University Press, 1988, Chapter 5, especially pp. 84–5, 264–5. On the role of the PLA in foreign policy-making, see Lu Ning, *The Dynamics of Foreign-Policy Decisionmaking in China*, Boulder, CO: Westview Press, 1997.

63. See, for example, Monte R. Bullard, *China's Political–Military Evolution: The Party and the Military in the PRC, 1960–1984*, Boulder, CO: Westview Press, 1985. Another more recent study also highlights the overlap or "blending" between the CCP and the PLA. See Fang Zhu, *Gun Barrel Politics: Party–Army Relations in Mao's China*, Boulder, CO: Westview Press, 1998.

64. "Problems of Strategy in China's Revolutionary War (December 1936)," in *Selected Military Writings of Mao Tse-tung*, p. 88.

65. Harlan W. Jencks, "Watching China's Military: A Personal View," *Problems of Communism* XXXV (May–June 1986):77; Zheng, *Party vs. State in Post-1949 China*, p. 111.

66. Wang Changyan and Cui Haiming, "Deng Xiaoping de junshi sixiang chutan" [Preliminary exploration of Deng Xiaoping's military thinking], in Pan Shiying, ed., *Dangdai Zhongguo junshi sixiang jingyao* [Essence of contemporary Chinese military thinking], Beijing: Jiefangjun Chubanshe, 1992, p. 110.

67. See, for example, Fried, "Military Status in Chinese Society," pp. 353–4; Sheridan, *China in Disintegration*, pp. 100–1; McCord, *The Power of the Gun*, p. 50.

68. Lewis, *Sanctioned Violence in Early China*, pp. 200–10.

69. Samuel P. Huntington, *The Soldier and the State: The Theory and Politics of Civil-Military Relations*, Cambridge, MA: Belknap Press, 1957.

70. See, for example, S. E. Finer, *The Man on Horseback: The Role of the Military in Politics*, rev. ed., Harmondsworth, UK: Penguin Books, 1975; Eric A. Nordlinger, *Soldiers in Politics: Military Coups and Governments*, Englewood Cliffs, NJ: Prentice Hall, 1977.

71. Lewis, *Sanctioned Violence in Early China*, Chapter 3, especially pp. 121–33 (quote on p. 97). See also Griffith, "Introduction," pp. 1–38.

72. A. Doak Barnett, *Uncertain Passage: China's Transition to the Post-Mao Era*, Washington, DC: Brookings Institution Press, 1974, p. 71.

73. Soldiers becoming statesmen is not unusual. In the United States, for example, there is a positive tradition of military leaders becoming paramount political leaders. That the accession of a war hero to the office of president of the United States arouses little concern among Americans is attributable to the successful civilianization of these individuals. Military leaders like George Washington and Ulysses S. Grant made the transition from general to president smoothly, assuming their civilian identity and functioning much as their civilian successors had (Huntington, *The Soldier and the State*, pp. 157–61). It helped significantly that political leaders and social groups did not view America's small peacetime military as posing any threat to civilian supremacy.

74. See, for example, Finer, *The Man on Horseback*.

75. Whitson with Huang, *The Chinese High Command*, pp. xxiv, 16, 376. Whitson and Huang purposefully refrain from calling him a military figure in the latter reference.

76. Deng, *Deng Xiaoping wenxuan*; Beijing Xinhua Domestic Service, November 29, 1989, in Foreign Broadcast Information Service, *Daily Report: China* (hereafter FBIS-CHI), November 30, 1989, p. 21.

77. June Teufel Dreyer, "Deng Xiaoping: Soldier," *China Quarterly* 135 (September 1993):536–50.

78. Alfred Stepan's writings on military politics, for example, disregard questions of loyalty. See his *The Military in Politics: Changing Patterns in Brazil*, Princeton: Princeton University Press, 1971; *Rethinking Military Politics: Brazil and the Southern Cone*, Princeton, NJ: Princeton University Press, 1988. A major study by Eric Nordlinger makes virtually no mention of loyalty as an important variable; indeed the term is not even listed in the index. See his *Soldiers in Politics*.

79. Loyalty is a key concept and dynamic in understanding and explaining the behavior and disposition of members of all organizations. See, for example, the classic study by Albert O. Hirschman, *Exit, Voice, Loyalty: Responses to Decline*

in Firms, Organizations and States, Cambridge, MA: Harvard University Press, 1970.

80. See, for example, Edward A. Shils and Morris Janowitz, "Cohesion and Disinte-gration in the Wehrmacht in World War II," *Public Opinion Quarterly* 12 (Summer 1948):280–315; Morris Janowitz, *Sociology and the Military Establishment*, 3rd ed., Beverly Hills, CA: Sage, 1974, Chapter 4.

81. See, for example, Omer Bartov, *Hitler's Army: Soldiers, Nazis, and War in the Third Reich*, New York: Oxford University Press, 1991. Bartov highlights the strong identification many German soldiers in World War II formed with Nazi ideology and the intense loyalty many felt toward Adolf Hitler. While Bartov's research challenges the findings of Shils and Janowitz cited in footnote 80 and he persuasively argues that "primary group" loyalties among German troops on the Eastern Front were weak, Bartov nevertheless acknowledges the importance of a soldier's loyalties to his primary group for good morale and combat motivation. See ibid., Chapter 2. Although Shils and Janowitz concluded the identification of German soldiers with "secondary symbols" was weak, they nevertheless stressed that soldiers also tended to hold "an intense and personal devotion to Adolph Hitler . . . throughout the war." "Cohesion and Disintegration," p. 305. For most German soldiers, this devotion to Hitler was an abstract one fused with their allegiance to the German state.

82. Lawrence A. Schneider, *A Madman of Ch'u: The Chinese Myth of Loyalty and Dissent*, Berkeley and Los Angeles, CA: University of California Press, 1980 (quote on p. 1).

83. See, for example, the works of Joffe, Jencks, and Whitson with Huang cited in this chapter.

84. Amos Perlmutter, *The Military and Politics in Modern Times*, New Haven, CT: Yale University Press, 1977, p. 15, and Chapter 1, especially table 1.1 on p. 16.

85. See, for example, Huntington, *The Soldier and the State*; Janowitz, *The Professional Soldier*; Bengt Abrahamsson, *Military Professionalization and Political Power*, Beverly Hills, CA: Sage Publications, 1972; Alfred Stepan, "The New Profession-alism of Internal Warfare and Military Role Expansion," in Stepan, ed., *Authoritar-ian Brazil: Origins, Policies, and Future*, New Haven, CT: Yale University Press, 1973, pp. 47–65; Nordlinger, *Soldiers in Politics*.

86. Amos Perlmutter and William M. LeoGrande, "The Party in Uniform: Toward a Theory of Civil-Military Relations in Communist Political Systems," *American Political Science Review* 76 (December 1982):778–89.

87. See, for example, Gerald Segal and John Phipps, "Why Communist Armies Defend Their Parties," *Asian Survey* XXX (October 1990):959–76.

88. Harlan W. Jencks, *From Muskets to Missiles: Politics and Professionalism in the Chinese Army, 1945–1981*, Boulder, CO: Westview Press, 1982, pp. 30, 266.

89. David Mozingo, "The Chinese Army and the Communist State," in Victor Nee and David Mozingo, eds., *State and Society in Contemporary China*, Ithaca, NY: Cornell University Press, 1983, p. 91.

90. Paul H. B. Godwin, "Professionalism and Politics in the Chinese Armed Forces: A Reconceptualization," in Dale R. Herspring and Ivan Volgyes, eds., *Civil-Military Relations in Communist Systems*, Boulder, CO: Westview Press, 1978, pp. 229–30. Godwin argues that the PLA is embroiled in a "conflict over [military] ethics." If one examines his definition of *ethics* however, it becomes clear that a crucial aspect

of these ethics is loyalty or, more specifically, the competing loyalties to the party, state, and the people.

91. See, for example, Jonathan D. Pollack, "Structure and Process in the Chinese Military System," in Kenneth G. Lieberthal and David M. Lampton, eds., *Bureaucracy, Politics, and Decisionmaking in Post-Mao China*, Berkeley and Los Angeles, CA: University of California Press, 1992, pp. 151–80.
92. See the works of Parris Chang and Lucian Pye. See also June Teufel Dreyer, "Civil-Military Relations in the People's Republic of China," *Comparative Strategy* 5 (1985):27–49; Eberhard Sandschneider, "Military and Politics in the PRC," in June Teufel Dreyer, ed., *Chinese Defense and Foreign Policy*, New York: Paragon House, 1989, pp. 331–50.
93. The classic work that develops this thesis is Whitson with Huang, *The Chinese High Command*.
94. *Deng Xiaoping wenxuan (1975–1982)*, p. 1; "Resolution on Certain Questions in the History of Our Party since the Founding of the People's Republic," adopted by the Sixth Plenum of the Eleventh Central Committee, cited in Xinhua (Beijing), June 30, 1981, in FBIS-CHI, July 1, 1981, p. K27.
95. Here I am paraphrasing Richard J. Latham's insightful observation. See his "China's Party-Army Relations after June 1989: A Case for Miles' Law?" in Richard H. Yang, Peter Kien-hong Yu, and Andrew N. Yang, eds., *China's Military: The PLA in 1990/1991*, Boulder, CO: Westview Press, 1991, p. 112.
96. Ralph L. Powell, *The Rise of Chinese Military Power, 1895–1912*, Princeton, NJ: Princeton University Press, 1956, p. 32.
97. Ibid., p. 4ff.
98. Cited in Stephen R. MacKinnon, "The Peiyang Army: Yuan Shih-k'ai and the Origins of Modern Chinese Warlordism,' *Journal of Asian Studies* XXXII (May 1973):405.
99. Stanley Spector, *Li Hung-chang and the Huai Army: A Study in Nineteenth Century Regionalism*, Seattle, WA: University of Washington Press, 1964, p. 318.
100. Sun saw this as a critical reason for the success of the Russian Revolution. Speech to the Whampoa cadets in 1924, "Zongli xunci," in Guomin Geming Zhongyang Junshi Zhengzhi Xuexiao, ed., *Huangpu Congshu* [Whampoa materials], n. p.: Guomin Gemingjun Zongsilingbu, Junxuchu, June 1927, pp. 2–3.
101. F. F. Liu, *A Military History of Modern China, 1924–1949*, Princeton, NJ: Princeton University Press, 1956, pp. 11–12; Roderick MacFarquhar, "The Whampoa Military Academy," *Papers on China*, Harvard University East Asia Regional Studies Seminar 9 (August 1955):159–61; Richard B. Landis, "Training and Indoctrination at the Whampoa Academy," in F. Gilbert Chan and Thomas H. Etzold, eds., *China in the 1920s: Nationalism and Revolution*, New York: New Viewpoints, 1976, pp. 80–5.
102. Fairbank, *The United States and China*, p. 236.
103. MacFarquhar, "The Whampoa Military Academy," p. 158.
104. The emergence of this "technically trained and patriotically inspired new officer class" is also noted by Fairbank. See *The United States and China*, p. 195. Certainly, other Chinese military schools had sought to promote an overarching vision;

indeed, some stressed a broader concept of Chinese nationalism beyond provincial loyalties. Donald S. Sutton, *Provincial Militarism in the Chinese Republic: The Yunnan Army, 1905–25*, Ann Arbor, MI: University of Michigan Press, 1980, pp. 45–51.

105. "Zongli xunsi," pp. 1–12. These themes also pervaded the lectures of other prominent leaders. For transcripts of these lectures, see Guomin, *Huangpu congshu*. For a good summary and content analysis of the lectures of Chiang and Liao Zhongkai, see Landis, "Training and Indoctrination."

106. Donald A. Jordan, *The Northern Expedition: China's National Revolution of 1926–1928*, Honolulu, HI: University of Hawaii Press, 1976.

107. Ibid., pp. 239–50, 291.

108. Cheng Hsiao-shih, *Party-Military Relations in Taiwan and the PRC: The Paradoxes of Control*, Boulder, CO: Westview Press, 1990, pp. 22–3. Perhaps the most significant difference between KMT and CCP indoctrination efforts was the exclusion and inclusion respectively of the rank and file. The communist leadership saw the value in extending the concept to include ordinary foot soldiers, something that the Kuomintang seemed to see no reason to do.

109. Landis, "Training and Indoctrination," p. 79.

110. Ibid., p. 76; MacFarquhar, "The Whampoa Military Academy," p. 163.

111. Liu, *A Military History*, pp. 81–3.

112. Guangdong Geming Lishi Bowuguan, compiler, *Huangpu junxiao shiliao* [Historical materials of the Whampoa Academy], n.p.: Guangdong Renmin Chubanshe, 1982, p. 93.

113. MacFarquhar, "The Whampoa Military Academy," pp. 159–60; Liu, *A Military History*, p. 10.

114. Liu, *A Military History*, p. 10. The same lip service to political loyalties and attention to personal loyalty to the leader was essentially true of the better warlord armies. See, for example, James E. Sheridan, *Chinese Warlord: The Career of Feng Yu-hsiang*, Stanford, CA: Stanford University Press, 1966, pp. 123–4.

115. Whitson with Huang, *The Chinese High Command*, pp. 9–22, 50.

116. Jane L. Price, "Revolution, Nation-Building, and Chinese Communist Leadership Education during the Sino–Japanese War," in Joshua A. Fogel and William T. Rowe, eds., *Perspectives on a Changing China*, Boulder, CO: Westview Press, 1971, pp. 197–8, 216.

117. Price, "Revolution, Nation-Building," p. 199.

118. Michael D. Swaine, *The Chinese Military and Political Succession: Leadership, Institutions, Beliefs*, Santa Monica, CA: RAND, 1992.

119. See David Shambaugh, "China's Commander-in-Chief: Jiang Zemin and the PLA," in C. Dennison Lane, Mark Weisenbloom, and Dimon Liu, eds., *Chinese Military Modernization*, New York and Washington, DC: Kegan Paul International and American Enterprise Institute Press, 1996, pp. 209–45.

120. For more on this incident and why it qualifies as a military coup, see Andrew Scobell, "Military Coups in the People's Republic of China: Failure, Fabrication, or Fancy?" *Journal of Northeast Asian Studies* XIV (Spring 1995):25–46. The author has been unable to confirm any other successful military coup attempts and only one other unsuccessful attempt – in September 1971.

121. Xinhua reports in Chinese and English both on November 12, 1989, and cited in FBIS-CHI, November 13, 1989, pp. 36–7.
122. *Jiefangjun Bao* [hereafter *JFJB*], June 27, 1990, in FBIS-CHI, July 11, 1990, p. 42. At least one other scholar has noted Deng's conflation of PLA loyalty to the party, state, and people. See Jeremy T. Paltiel, "PLA Allegiance on Parade: Civil-Military Relations in Transition," *China Quarterly* 143 (September 1995):787. On the point more generally, see ibid., pp. 785–8.
123. "Law of the People's Republic of China on National Defense," Beijing Xinhua Domestic Service in Chinese, March 18, 1997, cited in FBIS-CHI, March 23, 1997.
124. Beijing Xinhua Domestic Service in Chinese, April 28, 1997, in FBIS-CHI, May 1, 1997.
125. *JFJB*, November 6, 1992, in FBIS-CHI, November 13, 1992, pp. 42–3.
126. Max Weber, *The Theory of Social and Economic Organization*, A. M. Henderson and Talcott Parsons, eds. and trans., reprint of 1947 ed., New York: Free Press, 1964, p. 336.
127. Andrew Scobell, "After Deng, What?: Reconsidering the Prospects for a Democratic Transition in China," *Problems of Post-Communism* 44 (September–October 1997):26; interviews in Beijing and Shanghai, May–June 1998. See also Swaine, *The Chinese Military and Political Succession, C*hapter 8; David Shambaugh, "China's Post-Deng Military Leadership: New Faces, New Trends," discussion paper, Stanford, CA: Asia/Pacific Research Center, Stanford University, June 1998, p. 6.
128. Bruce Gilley, *Tiger on the Brink: Jiang Zemin and China's New Elite*, Berkeley and Los Angeles, CA: University of California Press, 1998, pp. 164–7, 225–7.
129. Ibid., pp. 253–4, 257–8. For a less positive assessment of Jiang's relationship with the PLA, see Lo Ping, "Zhu Rongji Rescues Jiang Zemin from a Siege in the Army," *Cheng Ming* (Hong Kong), December 1, 1998, in FBIS-CHI, December 8, 1998.
130. Willy Wo-Lap Lam, *The Era of Jiang Zemin*, Singapore: Prentice Hall, 1999, pp. 204–7; John W. Garver, "The PLA as an Interest Group in Foreign Policy," in Lane, Weisenbloom, and Liu, eds., *Chinese Military Modernization*, pp. 252–4; Melvin Gurtov and Byong-Moo Hwang, *China's Security: The New Roles of the Military*, Boulder, CO: Lynne Rienner, 1998, pp. 43–4.
131. See, for example, Tai Ming Cheung, "The Influence of the Gun: China's Central Military Commission and Its Relationship with the Military, Party and State Decision-Making Systems," in David M. Lampton, ed., *The Making of Chinese Foreign and Security Policy in the Era of Reform*, Stanford, CA: Stanford University Press, 2001, pp. 61–90.
132. Joseph Heinlein, "The Ground Forces," in William W. Whitson, ed., *The Military and Political Power in China in the 1970s*, New York: Praeger, 1972, pp. 156–7.
133. Nathan and Ross, *The Great Wall and the Empty Fortress*, p. 139.
134. Edward L. Dreyer, "Military Continuities: The PLA and Imperial China," in Whitson, ed., *The Military and Political Power*, pp. 3–24.
135. Smith, *China's Cultural Heritage*, pp. 62–3.
136. *Renmin Ribao, Hongqi*, and *JFJB*, all July 1, 1971, in *Survey of China Mainland Press*, nos. 709–10, August 3–9, 1971, and quoted in Paul Elmquist, "The Internal Role of the Military," in Whitson, ed., *The Military and Political Power*, p. 270. See

also Harvey W. Nelson, "Regional and Paramilitary Ground Forces," pp. 135–52; Harry Harding, Jr., "The Making of Chinese Military Policy," p. 364. Nelson and Harding are in Whitson, ed., *The Military and Political Power.*

137. Chong-Pin Lin, "The Extramilitary Roles of the People's Liberation Army in Modernization: Limits of Professionalization," *Security Studies* 1 (Summer 1992): 659–89.

138. On the military as entrepreneur, see, inter alia, James Charles Mulvenon, *Soldiers of Fortune: The Rise and Fall of the Chinese Military-Business Complex*, Armonk, NY: M. E. Sharpe, 2000; Tai Ming Cheung, "China's Entrepreneurial Army: The Structure, Activities, and Economic Returns of the Military Business Complex," in Lane, et al., eds., *Chinese Military Modernization*, pp. 168–97; Gurtov and Hwang, *China's Security*, Chapter 6. On weapon sales, see John Wilson Lewis, Hua Di, and Xue Litai, "Beijing's Defense Establishment: Solving the Arms-Export Enigma," *International Security* 15 (Spring 1991):87–109.

139. Seth Faison, "China's Chief Tells Army to Give Up Its Commerce," *New York Times*, July 23, 1998; John Pomfret, "Jiang Tells Army to End Trade Role," *Washington Post*, July 23, 1998.

140. Mark Magnier, "Chinese Military Still Embedded in the Economy," *Los Angeles Times*, January 9, 2000; Mulvenon, *Soldiers of Fortune.*

141. Kuang Tong-chou, "Premier Promises to Increase Military Funding to Make Up for 'Losses' ... ," *Sing Tao Jih Pao* (Hong Kong), July 24, 1998, in FBIS-CHI, July 24, 1998.

142. See James Mulvenon, "China: Conditional Compliance," in Muthiah Alagappa, ed., *Coercion and Governance: The Declining Political Role of the Military in Asia*, Stanford, CA: Stanford University Press, 2001, pp. 329–31; Craig S. Smith, "China Sends Its Army Money, and Taiwan a Signal," *New York Times*, March 11, 2001.

143. Adam Roberts, "The British Armed Forces and Politics: A Historical Perspective," in Cynthia H. Enloe and Ursula Semin-Panzer, eds., *The Military, the Police and Domestic Order: British and Third World Experiences*, London: Richardson Institute for Conflict and Peace Research, 1976, p. 9. The author's remark may refer only to Great Britain, but this is not clear. Whatever the intent, the comment seems relevant to most countries.

144. Morris Janowitz, *Military Institutions and Coercion in the Developing Nations*, Chicago, IL: University of Chicago Press, 1977, Part I.

145. David H. Bayley, "The Police and Political Development in Europe," in Charles Tilly, ed., *The Formation of National States in Western Europe*, Princeton, NJ: Princeton University Press, 1975, pp. 328–79; Robert M. Fogelson, *Big City Police*, Cambridge, MA: Harvard University Press, 1977, pp. 16–17.

146. Janowitz, *Military Institutions*, pp. 39–43.

147. Ibid., pp. 44–6.

148. This typology is derived from ibid., pp. 27–9.

149. Alison Dray-Novey, "Spatial Order and Police in Imperial Beijing," *Journal of Asian Studies* 52 (November 1993):903–5.

150. See, for example, Richard J. Smith, "Chinese Military Institutions in the Mid-Nineteenth Century, 1850–1860," *Journal of Asian History* 8 (1974):122–61. The Banner garrisons were also supposed to serve as a check on the political reliability

of the Green Standard forces. Im, "The Rise and Decline of the Eight Banner Garrisons in the Ch'ing," p. 12.

151. John L. Rawlinson, *China's Struggle for Naval Development, 1839–1995*, Cambridge, MA: Harvard University Press, 1967, p. 13.

152. Powell, *The Rise of Chinese Military Power*, p. 36.

153. Unless otherwise noted, the information in this section is from Frederic Wakeman, Jr., "Models of Historical Change: The Chinese State and Society, 1839–1989," in Kenneth Lieberthal, Joyce Kallgren, Roderick MacFarquhar, and Frederic Wakeman, eds., *Perspectives on Modern China: Four Anniversaries*, Armonk, NY: M. E. Sharpe, 1991, pp. 68–102.

154. On the development of a modern-type police organization in Beijing, see David Strand, *Rickshaw Beijing: City People and Politics in the 1920s*, Berkeley and Los Angeles, CA: University of California Press, 1989, Chapter 4.

155. See, for example, Andrew J. Nathan, *China's Transition*, New York: Columbia University Press, 1997, pp. 45, 47.

156. Wang Cunzhu, "Persist in Performing Domestic Functions of the People's Army," *JFJB*, March 27, 1990, cited in FBIS-CHI, April 25, 1990, p. 35.

157. Harvey W. Nelson, *The Chinese Military System: An Organizational Study of the Chinese People's Liberation Army*, Boulder, CO: Westview Press, 1977, p. 31.

158. Tai Ming Cheung, "The People's Armed Police: First Line of Defense," *China Quarterly* 146 (June 1996):525–6.

159. Ibid., pp. 526–7.

160. On the history of the force prior to the 1980s, see ibid., pp. 525–7. According to Nelson, the force was abolished during the mid-1960s. See Nelson, "Regional and Paramilitary Ground Forces," pp. 141–2. Sources conflict on the actual date of the establishment of these organs in the early 1980s. Tai Ming Cheung provides different dates. Initially he reported the PAP was established in 1982. See "Strong Arm of the Law," *Far Eastern Economic Review*, January 17, 1991, p. 17. He later gives the date as 1983. See Cheung "The People's Armed Police," pp. 535–47. Wakeman gives the dates for the establishment of both the PAP and Ministry of State Security (MSS) as 1983. See his "Models of Historical Change," pp. 91–2. It seems that the first PAP unit was formed in 1982, but the force did not become a nationwide one until the following year. See "The People's Armed Police," *China News Analysis* 1482 (April 1, 1993):1–9. For a more recent study, see Murray Scot Tanner, "The Institutional Lessons of Disaster: The People's Armed Police after Tiananmen," in James C. Mulvenon and Andrew N. D. Yang, eds., *The PLA as Organization*, Santa Monica, CA: RAND, 2002.

161. Cheung, "Strong Arm of the Law," p. 17.

162. Cited in Joffe, *The Chinese Army after Mao*, p. 153.

163. Cheung, "The People's Armed Police," p. 527.

164. Ibid.; Cheung, "Strong Arm of the Law."

165. Cheung, "The People's Armed Police," pp. 527, 538.

166. Nicholas Eftimiades, *Chinese Intelligence Operations*, Annapolis, MD: Naval Institute Press, 1994, Part II.

167. Nathan also notes this. See *China's Transition*, pp. 47–8.

168. Wakeman makes a similar point. See "Models of Historical Change," p. 91.

169. "Looking towards Modernization by the Mid-21st Century," *Beijing Review*, April 1–7, 1991, p. 24.
170. Wang, "Persist in Performing Domestic Functions," p. 36.
171. Chi Haotian, "Create a New Situation in Which the Army Is Managed According to Law . . . ," *JFJB*, June 27, 1990, in FBIS-CHI, July 11, 1990, p. 41.
172. *Renmin Luntan*, August 5, 1992, cited in FBIS-CHI, December 17, 1992, pp. 34–6. Quotes on p. 35.
173. Chi Haotian, "Create a New Situation. . . ."; RTHK Radio (Hong Kong), September 15, 1992, in FBIS-CHI, September 15, 1992, p. 37.
174. *Zhonghua Renmin Gongheguo jieyanfa* [Law on martial law of the People's Republic of China], Beijing: Falu Chubanshe, 1996, articles 8, 21, and 31; "Law of the People's Republic of China on National Defense" (article 22), cited in Xinhua Beijing Domestic Service, March 18, 1997, in FBIS-CHI, March 24, 1997; "China's White Paper on National Defense Xinhua Beijing Domestic Service," July 27, 1998, in FBIS-CHI, July 28, 1998; *2000 nian Zhongguo de guofang* [China's National Defense Year 2000], Beijing: Guowuyuan Xinwen Bangongshi, October 2000. See also Andrew Scobell, "The Meaning of Martial Law for the PLA and Internal Security in China after Deng," paper presented to the RAND/CAPS Conference "New Reforms in the PLA," held June 21–4, 2001, Washington, DC.
175. Murray Scot Tanner, "Cracks in the Wall: China's Eroding Coercive State," *Current History* 100 (September 2001):246.
176. Cheung, "Strong Arm of the Law," pp. 16–17; Zuo Ni, "Jiang Zemin, Li Peng Sign Order on Expanding Police Forces. . . . ," *Cheng Ming*, March 1, 1995, in FBIS-CHI, April 27, 1995, pp. 27–8.
177. Joffe, *The Chinese Army after Mao*, Chapter 4.
178. See, for example, Wang and Cui, "Deng Xiaoping de junshi sixiang chutan," p. 130.
179. James C. Mulvenon, *Professionalization of the Senior Chinese Officer Corps: Trends and Implications*, Santa Monica, CA: RAND, 1997, p. 73.

CHAPTER 4. LIPS AND TEETH: CHINA'S DECISION TO INTERVENE IN KOREA

1. Scholars can now utilize participant autobiographies and participant interviews. Moreover, there are numerous scholarly monographs, articles on party and military history, and collections of telegrams and speeches all published in China.
2. Bin Yu, "What China Learned from Its 'Forgotten War' in Korea," in Xiaobing Li, Allen R. Millett, and Bin Yu, eds. and trans., *Mao's Generals Remember Korea*, Lawrence, KS: University Press of Kansas, 2001, pp. 9–29.
3. See, inter alia, Chen Jian, *China's Road to the Korean War*, New York: Columbia University Press, 1994; Sergei N. Goncharov, John W. Lewis, and Xue Litai, *Uncertain Partners: Stalin, Mao, and the Korean War*, Stanford, CA: Stanford University Press, 1993; Shu Guang Zhang, *Mao's Military Romanticism: China and the Korean War, 1950–1953*, Lawrence, KS: University Press of Kansas, 1995.
4. This is not to say that there has not been any coverage of the perspectives of specific Chinese elite figures. Rather, it means that the study of individual views (other than Mao's) toward Chinese intervention in Korea was not until 1999 (when an earlier version of this chapter appeared) the focus of an article or monograph published

in English. For a strategic culture approach that focuses exclusively on Mao, see Alastair Iain Johnston, "Cultural Realism and Strategy in Maoist China," in Peter J. Katzenstein, ed., *The Culture of National Security*, New York: Columbia University Press, 1996.

5. Allen S. Whiting, *China Crosses the Yalu: The Decision to Enter the Korean War*, Stanford, CA: Stanford University Press, 1968; John Gittings, *The World and China, 1922–1972*, New York: Harper and Row, 1974, Chapter 9; Lawrence S. Weiss, "Storm around the Cradle: The Korean War and the Early Years of the People's Republic, 1949–1953," Ph.D. dissertation, Columbia University, 1981, Chapter 3; Melvin Gurtov and Byung-Moo Hwang, *China under Threat*, Baltimore, MD: Johns Hopkins University Press, 1982, Chapter 2; Gerald Segal, *Defending China*, London: Oxford University Press, 1985, Chapter 6; Jonathan D. Pollack, "The Korean War and Sino–American Relations," in Harry Harding and Yuan Ming, eds., *Sino–American Relations, 1945–1955: A Joint Reassessment of a Critical Decade*, Wilmington, DE: Scholarly Resources, Inc., 1989, pp. 213–37. See also Jonathan R. Adelman and Chih-Yu Shih, *Symbolic War: China's Use of Force, 1840–1980*, Taipei: Institute of International Relations, 1993, Chapter 10, which, although published in 1993, is based on older secondary sources.

6. Thomas J. Christensen, "Threats, Assurances, and the Last Chance for Peace: Lessons of Mao's Korean War Telegrams," *International Security* 17 (Summer 1992):122–54; Chen, *China's Road to the Korean War*; Zhang, *Mao's Military Romanticism*; Michael M. Sheng, "Beijing's Decision to Enter the Korean War: A Reappraisal and New Documentation," *Korea and World Affairs* 19 (Summer 1995):294–313; Allen S. Whiting, "China's Use of Force, 1950–96," *International Security* 26 (Fall 2001):106–8. The study by Goncharov, Lewis, and Xue depicts a reluctant Mao pulled into supporting Kim Il Sung's plan to unify the Koreas by force. However, following the Inchon landings in mid-September 1950, these same authors characterize Mao as being the strongest proponent of China crossing the Yalu. According to Goncharov, Lewis, and Xue, Mao was "the most avid advocate of intervention" on the Politburo. *Uncertain Partners*, p. 193. For an exception that stresses the indecisiveness of Beijing, see Hai-Wen Li, "How and When Did China Decide to Enter the Korean War?" trans. Jian Chen, *Korea and World Affairs* XVIII (Spring 1994):83–98.

7. A noteworthy exception is the analysis of Jong Sun Lee. This perceptive study, however, is based on a limited array of mostly secondary sources. See Lee, "Attitudes of Civilian and Military Leaders toward War Initiation: Application of Richard Betts' Analysis of American Cases to Other Countries," Ph.D dissertation, Ohio State University, 1991, Chapter 3.

8. One of the most nuanced, comprehensive, and circumspect analyses of China's decision to intervene appears in William Stueck, *The Korean War: An International History*, Princeton, NJ: Princeton University Press, 1995, pp. 98–103.

9. See, for example, Whiting, *China Crosses the Yalu*; Christensen, "Threats, Assurances, and the Last Chance for Peace."

10. Chen, *China's Road to the Korean War*, pp. 110–11, 134.

11. Xu Yan, *Diyici jiaoliang: KangMei yuanChao de lishi huiyi yu fansi* [The first trial: A historical retrospective and review of the resist America and aid Korea war], n.p.: Zhongguo Guangbo Dianshi Chubanshe, 1990, pp. 19–20; Chai Chengwen

and Zhao Yongtian, *Banmendian tanpan* [Panmunjom negotiations], Beijing: Jiefangjun Chubanshe, 1989, pp. 77–8.

12. Whiting, *China Crosses the Yalu.*
13. Chen, *China's Road to the Korean War*, p. 13.
14. Zhang Xi, "Peng Dehuai shouming shuaiyuan kangMei yuanChao de qianqian houhou" [The complete story of Peng Dehuai's appointment to lead the resist America, aid Korea war], *Zhonggong dangshi ziliao* 31 (1989):111–59; Michael H. Hunt, "Beijing and the Korea Crisis, June 1950–June 1951," *Political Science Quarterly* 107 (1992):475–8. But one cannot assert that had the United States heeded China's warnings, or at least taken the possibility of Chinese intervention more seriously, China would not have intervened. Mao had decided that if China intervened, the ultimate aim would be nothing less than the complete expulsion of UNC troops from the peninsula. Hope of a cease-fire or negotiated settlement in late 1950 after China intervened was based on the erroneous assumption that the lull in fighting in November was a deterrent signal to the UNC. See Christensen, "Threats, Assurances."
15. This is clear not only from most accounts, but also from the contents of telegrams sent by Mao, including those sent to Soviet leader Joseph Stalin. See Mao Zedong, *Jianguo yilai Mao Zedong wengao* [Mao Zedong's manuscripts since the founding of the Republic], Vol. 1, *September 1949–December 1950*, Beijing: Zhongyang Lishi Wenjian Chubanshe, 1987; for English translations of key telegrams, see Mao Zedong, "Mao's Dispatch of Chinese Troops to Korea: Forty-Six Telegrams, July–October 1950," trans. Li Xiaobing, Wang Xi, and Chen Jian, *Chinese Historians* V (Spring 1992):63–86.
16. Zhang, "Peng Dehuai shouming," p. 119.
17. Nie Rongzhen, *Inside the Red Star: The Memoirs of Marshal Nie Rongzhen*, trans. Zhong Renyi, Beijing: New World Press, 1988, p. 635; Pollack, "The Korean War," p. 219; Chen Jian, "China's Changing Aims during the Korean War, 1950–1951," *Journal of American-East Asian Relations* 1 (Spring 1992):23.
18. The two-day sequence version is from Zhang, "Peng Dehuai shouming," pp. 123–5; Chen, "China's Changing Aims," p. 17; Hunt, "Beijing and the Korean Crisis," p. 460. Another account gives the dates as October 4 and 5. See Hong Xuezhi, *KangMei yuanChao zhanzheng huiyi* [Memoirs of the war to resist America and aid Korea], Beijing: Jiefangjun Wenyi Chubanshe, 1990, pp. 18–19. Other reports say Mao decided on October 2. Chai Chengwen and Zhao Yongtian, *Kang-Mei yuanChao jishi* [Chronicle of the resist America, aid Korea war], Beijing: Zhonggong Dangshi Ziliao Chubanshe, 1987, p. 56. The significance of October 2 is further underlined by the fact that it was also on this date that Mao sent a telegram to Stalin informing him of China's intention to intervene militarily in Korea.
19. Zhang, "Peng Dehuai shouming," pp. 140–2.
20. Chen, "China's Changing Aims," pp. 21–2; Zhang, "Peng Dehuai shouming," pp. 148–9.
21. Zhai Zhihai and Hao Yufan, "China's Decision to Enter the Korean War: History Revisited," *China Quarterly* 121 (March 1990):111.
22. Zhang, "Peng Dehuai shouming," pp. 149–51; Hong, *KangMei yuanChao*, p. 24; Chen, "China's Changing Aims," pp. 21–2.

23. Shu Guang Zhang, "In the Shadow of Mao: Zhou Enlai and New China's Diplomacy," in Gordon A. Craig and Francis L. Loewenheim, eds., *The Diplomats, 1939–1979*, Princeton, NJ,: Princeton University Press, 1994, pp. 346–7, 352–5.

24. Although Zhou varied in the harshness of his terminology, his tone is consistent. Thus, for example, his speech printed in *Renmin Ribao* on September 30, 1950, is far more virulent than his remarks to Panikkar in the early morning hours of October 3. *Zhou Enlai waijiao wenxuan* [Selected diplomatic works of Zhou Enlai], Beijing: Zhongyang Wenxian Chubanshe, 1990, pp. 24–5. His tough tone on Korea is traceable to at least late August from the report he gave to the Central Military Commission at that time. Chen, *China's Road to the Korean War*, pp. 149–50.

25. Qiao Guanhua, one of Zhou's colleagues in the Ministry of Foreign Affairs, insists that Zhou was a hawk on Korea. While the source for this characterization is not wholly reliable, his depiction of Zhou is entirely consistent with the other sources cited previously. See Russell Spurr, *Enter the Dragon: China's Undeclared War against the U.S. in Korea, 1950–51*, New York: Henry Holt and Company, 1988, p. xx. Zhou's strong, sometimes harsh words could have been an effort to stave off any accusation that he was soft on American imperialism, but Zhou's words on Korea are consistent with his Hobbesian outlook on the world. See Dick Wilson, *Zhou Enlai: A Biography*, New York: Viking, 1984, pp. 189–91, 295, 300. It is also possible that Zhou could have supported intervention to side with Mao in order to avoid incurring the chairman's wrath. Indeed Zhou's political longevity was due in large part to siding expediently with Mao on many issues. See Roderick MacFarquhar, *The Origins of the Cultural Revolution*, Vol. 1, *Contradictions among the People, 1956–1957*, New York: Columbia University Press, 1974, pp. 7–9; Zhang, "In the Shadow of Mao." However, Zhou did not seem to shy away from disagreeing with Mao when he felt strongly about an issue. Wilson, *Zhou Enlai*, pp. 297–8.

26. Bo Yibo, *Ruogan zhongda juece yu shijian de huigu*, [Reflections on certain important decisions and events], Vol. 1, Beijing: Zhonggong Zhongyang Dangxiao Chubanshe, 1991, p. 43.

27. Chai and Zhao, *Banmendian tanpan*, pp. 77–8.

28. Carsun Chang, *The Third Force in China*, New York: Bookman Associates, 1952, p. 286.

29. Chen, *China's Road to the Korean War*, p. 281, n. 78.

30. Zhang, "In the Shadow of Mao," p. 354.

31. In the first phase, the army would be cut from 5.4 million to 4.0, and then down to 3 million during the second phase. Xu, *Diyici jiaoliang*, p. 13; Zhai and Hao, "China's Decision to Enter the Korean War," p. 99. Certainly this is best viewed as a "restructuring" of the PLA. Chen, *China's Road to the Korean War*, pp. 95–6. This demobilization was initiated in order to economize and respond to China's changing security needs at the end of the Civil War on the mainland and during the preparations for the invasion of Taiwan. Goncharov, Lewis, and Xue, *Uncertain Partners*, pp. 148, 152. While this should not be interpreted as a step toward Chinese disarmament, nor should it be read as preparation for war with the United States, as one scholar suggests. Chen, *China's Road to the Korean War*, p. 96.

32. Pollack, "The Korean War," pp. 218, 220. Hunt, "Beijing and the Korean Crisis," pp. 460–1. See also Zhai and Hao, "China's Decision to Enter the Korean War," p. 104.
33. Hu Guangzheng, "Yingming de juece, weida de chengguo – lun kangMei yuan-Chao zhanzheng de chubing canzheng juece" [Brilliant policy decision, great achievements – on the policy decision to dispatch troops to fight the resist America, aid Korea war], *Dangshi yanjiu* 1 (February 1983):34; Zhang, "Peng Dehuai shou-ming," p. 132.
34. Zhang, "Peng Dehuai shouming," p. 136.
35. Xu, *Diyici jiaoliang*, p. 20.
36. Gurtov and Hwang, *China under Threat*, p. 55; Weiss, "Storm around the Cradle," pp. 80–2; Segal, *Defending China*, p. 105.
37. Chen Yun, *Chen Yun wenxuan, 1949–1956* [Selected works of Chen Yun, 1949–1956], Beijing: Renmin Chubanshe, 1982, pp. 111–12. David Bachman argues that Chen was less than enthusiastic about the war but not strongly opposed. See David Bachman, *Chen Yun and the Chinese Political System*, Chinese Research Monograph No. 29, Berkeley, CA: Institute of East Asian Studies and Center for Chinese Studies, University of California, 1985, p. 34. Red Guard documents insist that Chen was against intervention. One charged, "Chen Yun took the attitude that to fight the war of resistance against the Americans and continue with economic construction was absolutely incompatible." Cited in Gittings, *The World and China*, pp. 182–3. See also Weiss, "Storm around the Cradle," p. 81. Given the limited evidence, however, a definitive answer cannot be given.
38. Bo stresses the persuasiveness of Mao and Zhou. While not explicitly revealing his own thinking, his account of the decision-making process strongly implies that he and others were won over by these convincing advocates of intervention. See *Ruogan zhongda jueche*, pp. 43–4.
39. Chang, *The Third Force*, p. 286.
40. Segal, *Defending China*, pp. 105–6; Weiss, "Storm around the Cradle," pp. 81–2.
41. Frederick C. Teiwes, *Politics at Mao's Court: Gao Gang and Party Factionalism in the Early 1950s*, Armonk, NY: M. E. Sharpe, 1990, p. 307, n. 39. Teiwes cites a 1955 report given by Deng. Zhai and Hao also contend that Gao opposed intervention in Korea. See "China's Decision to Intervene in Korea," p. 105. A 1967 Red Guard document also alleges this. See Union Research Institute, *The Case of Peng Teh-huai, 1959–1968*, Hong Kong: Union Research Institute, 1968, p. 154. Two other accounts suggest otherwise. According to one anonymous high-level communist source, Gao backed the decision to intervene. See Chang, *The Third Force*, p. 286. Reportedly, an aide to Peng heard Gao remark in early September 1950, "[On Korea] I fully support him [Mao]." Spurr, *Enter the Dragon*, p. 85.
42. Zhang, "Peng Dehuai shouming," pp. 120–1. Another account by a British journalist citing interviews with Chinese military officials, although differing in details, supports this view of Peng's thinking. See Spurr, *Enter the Dragon*, pp. 63–9.
43. Pollack, "The Korean War," p. 218.
44. Peng Dehuai, *Peng Dehuai zishu* [Peng Dehuai's own account], Beijing: Renmin Chubanshe, 1981, pp. 257–8. The term *biyao* is translated as "necessary" in the

English version of Peng's reminiscences but this does not capture the emphatic tone that is implied in the Chinese. See Peng Dehuai, *Memoirs of a Chinese Marshal: The Autobiographical Notes of Peng Dehuai (1898–1974)*, trans. Zheng Longpu, Beijing: Foreign Languages Press, 1984, pp. 473–4; Hong, *KanMei yuanChao*, pp. 18–19. Yao Xu gives different dates (October 5 and 6, not October 4 and 5), but the rest of his account jibes with the other accounts cited here. Yao Xu, "KangMei yuanChao de yingming juece" [The wise policy decision to resist America and aid Korea], *Dangshi yanjiu* 5 (October 1980):8. See also Pollack, "The Korean War," p. 218.

45. Zhang, "Peng Dehuai shouming," pp. 133–5. Nie simply recalls that "At the [October 4] meeting, he [Peng] firmly supported Comrade Mao Zedong's proposal to dispatch troops to Korea." Nie, *Inside the Red Star*, p. 636. Nie's account probably has the date wrong and also does not note the deliberation that went into the decision. Some other accounts do not mention this either. See, for example, Hu Guangzheng, "Yingming de juece, weida de chengguo," *Dangshi yanjiu* (February 1983), p. 37; and Xu, *Diyici jiaoliang*, p. 23. Red Guard pamphlets accused Peng of opposing the Korea decision, but this is not corroborated by any post–Cultural Revolution source. Cited in Gittings, *The World and China*, pp. 182–3; Weiss, "Storm around the Cradle," p. 81. According to one post-Mao account, this allegation is "completely false." Hu, "Yingming de juece," p. 37. Perhaps, aside from the obvious effort at character assassination, this charge has some basis in reality since, as the analysis here indicates, Peng was not enthusiastic about intervention until after some serious soul-searching on the night of October 4–5, 1950.

46. Zhang, "Peng Dehuai shouming," pp. 133–4.

47. Hong, *KangMei yuanChao*, p. 19.

48. Zhang, "Peng Dehuai shouming," pp. 136–7; Chen, *China's Road to the Korean War*, pp. 183–4.

49. Roderick MacFarquhar, *The Origins of the Cultural Revolution*, Vol. 2, *The Great Leap Forward, 1958–1960*, New York: Columbia University Press, 1983, pp. 193–5; Frederick C. Teiwes, "Peng Dehuai and Mao Zedong," *Australian Journal of Chinese Affairs* 16 (July 1986):81–98.

50. Peng, *Memoirs of a Chinese Marshal*, pp. 473–4.

51. See, for example, Yang Chengwu, *Yang Chengwu huiyilu* [Memoirs of Yang Chengwu], Beijing: Jiefangjun Chubanshe, 1990, pp. 338, 356; Nie Rongzhen, *Nie Rongzhen huiyilu* [Memoirs of Nie Rongzhen], Beijing: Jiefangjun Chubanshe, 1984, p. 736; Liu Zhen, *Liu Zhen huiyilu* [Memoirs of Liu Zhen], Beijing: Jiefangjun Chubanshe, 1990, p. 381.

52. See, for example, Bruce Cummings, *Origins of the Korean War*, Vol. 2: *The Roaring of the Cataract: 1947–1950*, Princeton, NJ: Princeton University Press, 1990, Chapter 11; Chen, *China's Road to the Korean War*, pp. 106–9.

53. In fact, the eight-character slogan in the campaign to rally support for the war took the element of patriotism even further, linking it to the protection of one's family: *KangMei yuanChao; baojia, weiguo* [Resist America, aid Korea; protect your family, defend your country].

54. Nie, *Inside the Red Star*, pp. 633–4.

55. K. M. Panikkar, *In Two Chinas: Memoirs of a Diplomat*, London: Allen and Unwin, 1955; reprint ed., Westport, CT: Hyperion Press, 1981, p. 108. Nie, *Inside the Red*

Star, p. 637. One scholar, on the basis of this conversation, labels Nie a proponent of intervention. Weiss, "Storm around the Cradle," p. 82.

56. Gittings, *The World and China*, p. 184.

57. "The Korean war situation was a matter of prime importance, and Zhu De, He Long, Luo Ronghuan, Nie Rongzhen, Ye Jianying, Li Xiannian, and other comrades paid me visits and much of the contents of our conversations were on this situation." Xu Xiangqian, *Lishi de huigu* [Reflections on history], Vol. 3, Beijing: Jiefangjun Chubanshe, 1987, p. 798.

58. Pollack, "The Korean War," p. 223.

59. Xu, *Diyici jiaoliang*, pp. 23–4; Chai and Zhao, *Banmendian tanpan*, p. 83; Zhai and Hao, "China's Decision to Enter the Korean War," p. 105; Nie, *Inside the Red Star*, p. 636; Chen, *China's Road to the Korean War*, pp. 153, 185.

60. The belief that Lin served as commander of the CPV was once widely accepted as fact because many of the Chinese units in Korea were from the Fourth Field Army. Lin had commanded this army, and captured CPV troops listed Lin as their commander-in-chief. See Jurgen Domes, *Peng Te-huai: The Man and the Image*, Stanford, CA: Stanford University Press, 1985, p. 61. On Lin as an advocate of intervention, see William W. Whitson with Chen-Hsia Huang, *The Chinese High Command: Military Politics, 1927–1971*, New York: Praeger, 1973, p. 329. On Lin as the first commander of the CPV see ibid., and June Teufel Dreyer, *China's Political System: Modernization and Tradition*, 2nd ed., Boston, MA: Allyn and Bacon, 1996, p. 194. The latter account states that after major battlefield reverses, a "new" CPV commander was appointed: Peng. While the author does not specifically name the "first" commander, by implication it must be Lin.

61. Lin Qinshan, *Lin Biao zhuan* [Biography of Lin Biao], Vol. 1, Beijing: Zhishi Chubanshe, 1988, p. 71; Chen, *China's Road to the Korean War*, pp. 173–4. There is some controversy about this. Hunt argues that the choice of Lin is strange because Mao and Lin had a history of conflict over military strategy during the Civil War. Hunt, "Beijing and the Korean Crisis," p. 462, n. 29.

62. Lin, *Lin Biao zhuan*, Vol. 1, pp. 71–2.

63. Su was a logical choice since he had been reassigned to command the NEFDA created several months earlier. But he was ruled out, also because of ill health. Zhang, "Peng Dehuai shouming," pp. 125–6, 135.

64. Chai and Zhao, *Banmendian tanpan*, p. 78.

65. Zhang, "Peng Dehuai shouming," p. 126.

66. Goncharov, Lewis, and Xue, *Uncertain Partners*, p. 167. There was considerable concern among Chinese leaders that the United States might use the bomb either on the Korean Peninsula or against cities and/or military installations in China itself. Proponents of intervention downplayed this possibility, arguing that the bomb was unsuitable for use in Korea and that the United States would be unwilling to risk triggering a nuclear response from the Soviet Union. These arguments seem to have calmed the fears. Ibid., pp. 164–7, 182.

67. Quote cited in ibid., p. 167. See also Xu, *Diyici jiaoliang*, pp. 23–4.

68. Xu, *Diyici jiaoliang*, pp. 23–4.

69. Chai and Zhao, *Banmendian tanpan*, p. 83; Zhang, "Peng Dehuai shouming," pp. 135, 143; Hu, "Yingming de juece," p. 37; Yao, "KangMei yuanChao," p. 8; Hong, *KangMei yuanChao*, p. 19. Hong's source is Peng, who had a strong personal

and professional rivalry with Lin and therefore good reason to imply that Lin was faking illness.

70. Certainly this is very possible. Nie remarked that the whole episode was "most peculiar" *(qiguai dehen)*, insisting he had "never seen him [Lin] so frightened of anything." *Nie Rongzhen huiyilu*, p. 736. In any event, by the 1960s – if not before – Lin appears to have become a hypochondriac. See the bizarre account by one of Lin's secretaries: Zhang Yunsheng, *Maojiawan jishi: Lin Biao mishu huiyilu* [Maojiawan account: The memoirs of Lin Biao's secretary], Beijing: Chunqiu Chubanshe, 1988.

71. See, for example, Lin, *Lin Biao zhuan*, Vol. 1, p. 65ff.

72. Ibid., Vol. 1, pp. 68–73, 77–8.

73. Zhang, "Peng Dehuai shouming," pp. 126, 135.

74. Frederick C. Teiwes, *Leadership, Legitimacy, and Conflict in China: From a Charismatic Mao to the Politics of Succession*, Armonk, NY: M. E. Sharpe, 1984, pp. 30, 106; MacFarquhar, *Origins of Cultural Revolution*, Vol. 2, pp. 245–6. Nie suffered from stress and overwork, collapsing in late 1952. He remained acting chief of general staff, however, until near the end of the Korean War, when he formally resigned the post to recuperate properly. Nie resumed work again in late 1956, only after three years of treatment. See Nie, *Inside the Red Star*, pp. 618, 659. Furthermore, according to one source, Mao wanted Su to command the CPV but had to discount him because Su was seriously ill and recuperating in Qingdao. Zhang, "Peng Dehuai shouming," p. 125.

75. Lin, *Lin Biao zhuan*, Vol. 1, p. 74.

76. Cummings, *Origins of the Korean War*, Vol. 2, pp. 726–9. Ye allegedly voiced grave concerns about intervening in Korea from midsummer 1950 and warned Mao that mobilizing a force of sufficient strength to be effective in Korea would take months rather than weeks, as the chairman believed. Spurr, *Enter the Dragon*, pp. 59–60, 63–4, 66–7.

77. Spurr, *Enter the Dragon*, pp. 53–65.

78. Whiting, *China Crosses the Yalu*, p. 21.

79. James Chieh Hsiung, *Ideology and Practice: The Evolution of Chinese Communism*, New York: Praeger, 1970, p. 172.

80. Zhang, "Peng Dehuai shouming," pp. 118–19.

81. Hong, *KangMei yuanChao*, pp. 8–9.

82. Ibid., p. 15.

83. Ibid., pp. 16–18.

84. Ibid., p. 19.

85. Zhang, "Peng Dehuai shouming," p. 144.

86. Liu, *Liu Zhen huiyilu*, pp. 337–8, 342.

87. Ibid., p. 337.

88. Chai and Zhao, *Banmendian tanpan*, p. 78.

89. Hong, *KangMei yuanChao*, pp. 21–2.

90. Zhang, "Peng Dehuai shouming," p. 157.

91. Mao, *Jianguo yilai*, p. 567; Mao, "Mao's Dispatch of Chinese Troops to Korea," p. 75.

92. Zhang, "Peng Dehuai shouming," pp. 157–8; Chen, *China's Road to the Korean War*, p. 208.

93. Hong, *KangMei yuanChao*, Chapter 3; Zhang, "Peng Dehuai shouming," p. 159.

94. However, Lee also concludes erroneously, based on limited data, that civilians were equally if not more dovish. Lee, "Attitudes of Civilian and Military Leaders toward War Initiation," pp. 65–67.
95. See, for example, Goncharov, Lewis, and Xue, *Uncertain Partners*, p. 182.

CHAPTER 5. "SUPPORT THE LEFT": PLA INTERVENTION IN THE
CULTURAL REVOLUTION

1. See, for example, Ellis Joffe, "The Chinese Army in the Cultural Revolution: The Politics of Intervention," *Current Scene* (Hong Kong) VIII (December 7, 1970):1–25; Ellis Joffe, "The Chinese Army after the Cultural Revolution: The Effects of Intervention," *China Quarterly* 55 (July–September 1973):450–77; Harvey W. Nelson, *The Chinese Military System: An Organizational Study of the Chinese People's Liberation Army*, Boulder, CO: Westview Press, 1977, Chapters 2, 4. On Wuhan, see Thomas W. Robinson, "The Wuhan Incident: Local Strife and Provincial Rebellion during the Cultural Revolution," *China Quarterly* 47 (July/September 1971): 413–38; Fang Zhu, *Gun Barrel Politics: Party–Army Relations in Mao's China*, Boulder, CO: Westview Press, 1998, Chapters 5, 6.
2. Ellis Joffe, *The Chinese Army after Mao*, Cambridge, MA: Harvard University Press, 1987, p. 19; "Decision on Certain Questions of Party History since the Founding of the People's Republic," Xinhua, June 30, 1981, cited in Foreign Broadcast Information Service, *Daily Report: China*, July 1, 1981, p. K17. For an important exception, see Li Ke and Chi Shengzhang, *"Wenhua Dageming" zhong de Renmin Jiefangjun* [The People's Liberation Army during the "Great Cultural Revolution"], Beijing: Zhonggong Danshi Ziliao, 1989.
3. The most important party document issued since the Cultural Revolution, the 1981 "Decision on Questions of Party History," merely acknowledges the role played by the PLA in restoring order. Meanwhile, the most widely available history of the Cultural Revolution era provides only a single mention of the involved role of the PLA. See Yan Jiaqi and Gao Gao, *Zhongguo "wenge" shinian shi* [A history of China's ten-year "cultural revolution"], n.p.: Zhongguo Wenti Yanjiu Chubanshe, n.d., p. 294.
4. This sensitivity is also very evident in analyses of who was technically in overall control in 1989 in Beijing while martial law was in force. Chinese scholars insist that the military was never in absolute control. Rather, there was joint military and civilian supervision at all times. See, for example, the sources quoted in Andrew Scobell, "The Meaning of Martial Law for the PLA and Internal Security in China after Deng," paper presented to the RAND/CAPS Conference "New Reforms in the PLA," held in Washington, DC, June 21–4, 2001.
5. On the origins of the movement, see Roderick MacFarquhar, *The Origins of the Cultural Revolution*, 3 vols., New York: Columbia University Press, 1974–97. For good coverage and analysis of the Cultural Revolution, see Hong Yung Lee, *The Politics of the Chinese Cultural Revolution: A Case Study*, Berkeley and Los Angeles, CA: University of California Press, 1978; Harry Harding, "The Chinese State in Crisis, 1966–1969," *The Cambridge History of China*, Vol. 15, *The People's Republic*, Part 2, *Revolutions within the Chinese Revolution, 1966–1982*, New York: Cambridge University Press, 1991, pp. 107–217; Lynn T White, III, *The Policies of*

Chaos: The Organizational Causes of Violence in China's Cultural Revolution, Princeton, NJ: Princeton University Press, 1989; Wang Shaoguang, *Failure of Charisma: The Cultural Revolution in Wuhan*, Hong Kong: Oxford University Press, 1995. Wang Nianyi, *1949–1989 nian de Zhongguo*, Vol. 3, *Da dongluan de niandai* [China in 1949–1989: decade of great turmoil], Henan Renmin Chubanshe, 1988 [hereafter *Da dongluan de niandai*]. While the movement was primarily an urban one, the Cultural Revolution did affect rural China, particularly areas proximate to cities and towns. For a fascinating study of this dimension, see Richard Baum, "The Cultural Revolution in the Countryside: Anatomy of a Limited Rebellion," in Thomas W. Robinson, ed., *The Cultural Revolution in China*, Berkeley and Los Angeles, CA: University of California Press, 1971, pp. 367–476.

6. For more on the meaning and implications of such groups in a society, including Cultural Revolution–era China, see Andrew Scobell and Brad Hammitt, "Goons, Gunmen, and Gendarmerie: Toward Reconceptualization of Paramilitary Formations," *Journal of Political and Military Sociology* 26 (Winter 1998): 37–50.

7. Gao Yuan, *Born Red: A Chronicle of the Cultural Revolution*, Stanford, CA: Stanford University Press, 1987, p. 94.

8. Jin Qiu, *The Culture of Power: The Lin Biao Incident and the Cultural Revolution*, Stanford, CA: Stanford University Press, 1999, pp. 87–90.

9. *Selections from China Mainland Magazines Supplement* 15 (May 8, 1967):36.

10. Zhengzhi Xueyuan Zhonggong Dangshi Jiaoyanshi, ed., *Zhongguo Gongchandang liushinian dashi jianjie* [A survey of major events in sixty years of Chinese Communist Party history], (hereafter *Liushinian dashi*), Beijing: Guofang Daxue Chubanshe, 1986, p. 550.

11. Zhang Yunsheng, *Maojiawan jishi: Lin Biao mishu huiyilu* [Maojiawan account: the memoirs of Lin Biao's secretary], Beijing: Chunqiu Chubanshe, 1988, p. 78; Ralph L. Powell and Chong-kun Yoon, "Public Security and the PLA," *Asian Survey* XII (December 1972): 1087.

12. *Liushinian dashi*, p. 554.

13. Nelson, *The Chinese Military System*, pp. 27–31.

14. *Liushinian dashi*, p. 550. See Mao's formal approval of the decision in *Jianguo yulai Mao Zedong wengao* [Manuscripts of Mao Zedong since the founding of the Republic], Vol. 12, *1966 January–1968 December*, Beijing: Zhongyang Wenxian Chubanshe, 1998, p. 199. See also Mao's letter to Lin Biao, which makes the same point. Jerome Ch'en, ed., *Mao Papers: Anthology and Bibliography*, New York: Oxford University Press, 1970, p. 134.

15. Marshal Xu's account of the creation of the eight-point order portrays himself as the hero, while depicting Marshal Lin as the feeble, bumbling sycophant of Mao. In fact, Xu gives the clear impression that it was Xu alone who originally formulated the order and got other military leaders to go along with him. See Xu Xiangqian, *Lishi de huigu* [Recollections of history], Vol. 3, Beijing: Jiefangjun Chubanshe, 1987, pp. 827–31. For a version that does not single out Xu, see Yan and Gao, *Zhongguo "wenge,"* p. 138. For a more complete analysis, see Hu Changshui, "Zhongyang Junwei 'Batiao mingling' de chansheng" [Formulation of the "eight-point order" by the Central Military Commission], *Zhonggong Dangshi Yanjiu* [Research on history of the Chinese Communist Party] 6 (1991):53–9. See also Zhang, *Maojiawan*, p. 78;

Jianguo yilai Mao Zedong wengao 12: 203–6. Mao added another point so that the final directive contained eight points instead of seven.

16. For analysis of the 1971 "coup" and assessment of Lin's role, see Jin, *The Culture of Power*; Andrew Scobell, "Military Coups in the People's Republic of China: Failure, Fabrication, or Fancy?" *Journal of Northeast Asian Studies* XIV (Spring 1995): 25–46.

17. See, for example, the account of his secretary, Zhang, *Maojiawan*, as well as Jin, *The Culture of Power*.

18. See Frederick C. Teiwes and Warren Sun, *The Tragedy of Lin Biao: Riding the Tiger during the Cultural Revolution, 1966–1971*, Honolulu, HI: University of Hawaii Press, 1996; Jin, *The Culture of Power*.

19. Teiwes and Sun, *The Tragedy of Lin Biao*, pp. 52–3 (quote on p. 52). See also Jin, *The Culture of Power*.

20. On Xu's acknowledgement of Lin's commitment to keeping order in the PLA, see Hu, "Zhongyang Junwei 'Batiao Mingling,'" p. 58; on Xu as the primary force behind the eight-point order, see ibid., pp. 57–9; on Lin's active involvement, see ibid., and Teiwes and Sun, *The Tragedy of Lin Biao*, p. 73; on the quote by Lin, see Xu, *Lishi de huigu* 3:828

21. Zhang, *Maojiawan*, pp. 84–5.

22. Ibid.

23. Xinhua, December 12, 1967, cited by Baum, "The Cultural Revolution in the Countryside," p. 426.

24. Zhang, *Maojiawan*, pp. 86–7.

25. Ibid., pp. 89–90.

26. *Liushinian dashi*, pp. 550–1; Nie Rongzhen, *Inside the Red Star: The Memoirs of Marshal Nie Rongzhen*, trans. Zhong Renyi, Beijing: New World Press, 1988, p. 740.

27. *Liushinian dashi*, pp. 550–1.

28. Nie, *Inside the Red Star*, p. 740.

29. *Liushinian dashi*, p. 552.

30. Ibid., p. 552.

31. Ibid., p. 551.

32. Ibid.

33. Nie, *Inside the Red Star*, p. 741.

34. Ibid., p. 742.

35. *Liushinian dashi*, pp. 551–2.

36. Ibid., p. 552.

37. Ibid., p. 550.

38. "Order of the Military Commission of the CCP Central Committee" (April 6, 1967), cited in *Current Background* 852 (May 6, 1968):115–16.

39. Powell and Yoon, "Public Security," p. 1089; Feng Jicai, *Voices from the Whirlwind: An Oral History of the Chinese Cultural Revolution*, New York: Random House, 1991, p. 89.

40. Feng, *Voices from the Whirlwind*, p. 89.

41. Powell and Yoon, "Public Security," p. 1087, n. 25.

42. Nelson, *The Chinese Military System*, pp. 126–37.

43. Lee, *The Politics of the Cultural Revolution*, p. 247.

44. Yan and Gao, *Zhongguo "wenge,"* p. 268; Chen Zaidao, *Chen Zaidao huiyilu*, [Memoirs of Chen Zaidao] 2 vols., Beijing: Jiefangjun Chubanshe, 1988–91, 2: 341–2.
45. Chen, *Chen Zaidao huiyilu*, 2:335–8.
46. Zhang, *Maojiawan*, pp. 125–7.
47. Yan and Gao, *Zhongguo "wenge,"* p. 268; Chen, *Chen Zaidao huiyilu*, 2:341, 343.
48. Chen, *Chen Zaidao huiyilu*, 2: 341–5.
49. According to one account, Mao and the other leaders arrived as an entourage on July 13. See Wang Shaoguang, *Failure of Charisma*, p. 149. The does not seem to have been the case. They all appear to have arrived on July 14 at different times. Zhou arrived by air from Beijing at 2:30 A.M.; Wang and Xie arrived separately from Sichuan, and Mao left Beijing on July 13 by special train arriving the next day in Wuhan. See Wang Nianyi, *Da dongluan de niandai*, p. 261; Zhonggong Zhongyang Wenyi Yanjiushi, compiler, *Zhou Enlai nianpu* [Chronology of Zhou Enlai], Vol. 3: *1966–1976*, Beijing: Zhongyang Wenxian Chubanshe, 1997, p. 170; Yan and Gao, *Zhongguo "wenge,"* p. 264; Chen, *Chen Zaidao huiyilu*, 2:316–17; Li Zhisui, *The Private Life of Chairman* Mao, trans. Tai Hung–chao, New York: Random House, 1994, pp. 488–91.
50. *Zhou Enlai nianpu, 1949–1976*, 3:170–1; Chen, *Chen Zaidao huiyilu*, 2: 319–22.
51. Chen, *Chen Zaidao huiyilu*, 2:322–3. Yan and Gao state that Zhou was also at this meeting. *Zhongguo "wenge,"* p. 265.
52. Chen, *Chen Zaidao huiyilu*, 2:332–3.
53. Yan and Gao, *Zhongguo "wenge,"* p. 268.
54. Chen, *Chen Zaidao huiyilu*, 2:338–9.
55. Chen, *Chen Zaidao huiyilu*, 2:334–9. See also Yan and Gao, *Zhongguo "wenge,"* pp. 266–8.
56. Wang Shaoguang, *Failure of Charisma*, p. 154.
57. Thomas Robinson argues that Chen Zaidao was probably in Lin's loyalty network. Robinson, "The Wuhan Incident," pp. 421–3.
58. Xu wrote the foreword to the first volume of Chen Zaidao's memoirs, which were published in 1988. Chen, *Chen Zaidao huiyilu*, 1: foreword.
59. Chen, *Chen Zaidao huiyilu*, 2:313; Yan and Gao, *Zhongguo "wenge,"* pp. 270–1.
60. Yan and Gao, *Zhongguo "wenge,"* p. 269.
61. The process, nevertheless, was slow and conditions did not fully stabilize for several weeks. See Robinson, "The Wuhan Incident," pp. 427–33.
62. Wang Nianyi, *Da dongluan de niandai*, pp. 265–6; Li Ke and Chi Shengzhang, *"Wenhua Dageming" zhong*, p. 52.
63. Lee, *The Politics of the Cultural Revolution*, p. 247. See also Yan and Gao, *Zhongguo "wenge,"* p. 270.
64. *Jianguo yilai Mao Zedong wengao*, 12:380.
65. *Survey of China Mainland Press Supplement* (hereafter SCMPS) 198 (August 18, 1967):8.
66. Powell and Yoon, "Public Security," pp. 1088–9; Zhang, *Maojiawan*, pp. 128–9.
67. See, for example, "Letter from the Central Committee of the Chinese Communist Party to Revolutionary Workers and Staff and Revolutionary Cadres in Industrial

and Mining Enterprises throughout the Country," dated March 18, 1967, in *Peking Review* 13 (March 24, 1967):5–6; "Notice on Suggestions on Questions Concerning Consultations about the Three Supports, Two Militaries" and "Decision on a Number of Questions Concerning the Three Supports, Two Militaries," both issued by the Central Committee, August 21, 1967, cited in *Liushinian dashi*, p. 550.

68. *Liushinian dashi*, p. 555. On October 7, Beijing issued "An Important Directive of Chairman Mao's Inspection Tour of the North, South-Central, and Eastern Regions." Although Mao declared that the "overall situation throughout the country is good," he urged that "struggle be conducted through reasoning rather than through force." Ibid.

69. Ross Terrill, *Mao: A Biography*, New York: Harper and Row, 1980, p. 328.

70. Nelson, *The Chinese Military System*, p. 37.

71. *Renmin ribao* [People's daily], March 30, 1968, cited in Terrill, *Mao*, p. 328.

72. Zhang, *Maojiawan*, pp. 131–2.

73. Thomas W. Robinson, "Chou En–lai and the Cultural Revolution in China," in Robinson, ed., *The Cultural Revolution in China*, pp. 227–9. For a more recent and scathing critique of Zhou's role in this period, see Yongyi Song, "The Role of Zhou Enlai in the Cultural Revolution: A Contradictory Image from Diverse Sources," *Issues and Studies* 37 (March/April 2001):1–28.

74. See Robinson, "Chou En–lai and the Cultural Revolution," pp. 165–312; *Zhou Enlai nianpu*, Vol. 3.

75. *Deng Xiaoping wenxuan (1975–1982)* [Selected works of Deng Xiaoping, 1975–1982], Beijing: Renmin Chubanshe, 1983, p. 336.

76. *Zhongfa* 288, cited in *Survey of China Mainland Press* (hereafter *SCMP*) 4026 (September 22, 1967):1–2.

77. "Important Talk Given by Comrade Chiang Ch'ing on Sept. 5. . . . ," *SCMP* 4069 (November 29, 1967):5.

78. "Chiu-Peng-Lo Chan-pao" [Drag out Peng and Luo combat news] (Canton) 3 (February 19, 1968), in *SCMP* 4139 (March 15, 1968):5. No date is given for Xie's speech but it was probably delivered in December 1967 or January 1968.

79. Powell and Yoon, "Public Security," pp. 1093–5.

80. "Decision on Certain Questions of Party History since the Founding of the People's Republic," *Xinhua*, June 30, 1981, cited in FBIS-CHI, July 1, 1981, p. K17.

81. Lee, *The Politics of the Cultural Revolution*, pp. 182–3.

82. "Hsu Shih-yu's Talk at a Group Discussion at the Third Plenum of the Eleventh CCP Central Committee," *Issues and Studies* XVI (May 1980):78.

83. Lee, *The Politics of the Cultural Revolution*, p. 142.

84. Ezra Vogel, *Canton under Communism: Programs and Politics in a Provincial Capital, 1949–1968*, New York: Harper Torch Books, 1971, p. 324; Jurgen Domes, *China after the Cultural Revolution: Politics between Two Party Congresses*, trans. Annette Berg and David Goodman, Berkeley and Los Angeles, CA: University of California Press, 1977, p. 11.

85. Liang Heng and Judith Shapiro, *Son of the Revolution*, New York: Vintage Books, 1984, p. 155.

86. Vogel, *Canton under Communism*, pp. 331–2.

87. Lee, *The Politics of the Cultural Revolution*, p. 160.

88. Elizabeth J. Perry and Li Xun, *Proletarian Power: Shanghai in the Cultural Revolution*, Boulder, CO: Westview Press, 1997, pp. 126–7, 140–1, 161–2.
89. Zhang, *Maojiawan*, pp. 129–30.
90. Wang Shaoguang, *Failure of Charisma*, pp. 161–2; *Liushinian dashi*, p. 554.
91. "Important Talk Given by Comrade Chiang Ch'ing," p. 5.
92. Lin Qingshan, *Lin Biao zuan* [Biography of Lin Biao], 2 vols., Beijing: Zhishi Chubanshe, 1988, 1: Chapter 10.
93. Anne F. Thurston, *Enemies of the People*, New York: Alfred A. Knopf, 1987, pp. 135–6.
94. Nelson, *The Chinese Military System*, p. 137; Gao, *Born Red*, p. 206ff.
95. Lee, *The Politics of the Cultural Revolution*, p. 250; Nelson, *The Chinese Military System*, pp. 38, 137.
96. Zhang, *Maojiawan*, p. 131.
97. Domes, *China after the Cultural Revolution*, p. 12.
98. Vogel, *Canton under Communism*, pp. 335–6.
99. See Jurgen Domes, "The Role of the Military in the Formation of Revolutionary Committees 1967–68," *China Quarterly* 44 (October/December 1970):112–45; Li and Chi, *"Wenhua Dageming" zhong*, pp. 245–6.
100. Harlan W. Jencks, "The Chinese People's Liberation Army: 1949–1989," in David S. G. Goodman and Gerald Segal, eds., *China at Forty: A Mid–Life Crisis*, Oxford, UK: Clarendon Press, 1989, pp. 93–6; Nelson, *The Chinese Military System*, p. 43.
101. Samuel P. Huntington, *Political Order in Changing Societies*, New Haven, CT: Yale University Press, 1968, Chapter 4.
102. S. E. Finer, *The Man On Horseback: The Role of the Military in Politics*, 2nd ed., Harmondsworth, UK: Penguin Books, 1975.
103. Shiping Zheng, *Party vs. State in Post-1949 China: The Institutional Dilemma*, New York: Cambridge University Press, 1997, pp. 139–40.
104. "Hsu Shih-yu's Talk," p. 79.
105. Alfred Stepan, "The New Professionalism of Internal Warfare and Military Role Expansion," in Stepan, ed., *Authoritarian Brazil: Origins, Policies, Future*, New Haven, CT: Yale University Press, 1973, pp. 47–65.
106. Edgar Snow, *The Long Revolution*, New York: Random House, 1972, p. 103.
107. Eric A. Nordlinger, *Soldiers in Politics: Military Coups and Governments*, Englewood Cliffs, NJ: Prentice Hall, 1977, pp. 54–5, 90–1.
108. Perry and Li, *Proletarian Power*, pp. 161–2.
109. On challenges to the military's monopoly of force, see Nordlinger, *Soldiers in Politics*, pp. 48, 75–8; on threats to the corporate interests of the military, see ibid., and Andrew Scobell, "Politics, Professionalism, and Peace–keeping: An Analysis of the 1987 Military Coup in Fiji," *Comparative Politics* 26 (January 1994):187–99.
110. Snow, *The Long Revolution*, p. 103.
111. Scobell and Hammitt, "Goons, Gunmen, and Gendarmerie."

CHAPTER 6. HALF-HEARTED COERCIVE DIPLOMACY: CHINA'S 1979
ATTACK ON VIETNAM

1. However, some unnamed "foreign military experts" reportedly predicted there would be no war. Hong Kong Agence France Presse in English, January 21, 1979, in

Foreign Broadcast Information Service, *Daily Report: People's Republic of China* (hereafter FBIS-CHI), January 22, 1979, p. A7. And Vietnam's leaders might have convinced themselves, after months of stern Chinese pronouncements but no action, that China might be all bark and no bite.

2. For some accounts and analyses of the war, see Jonathan R. Adelman and Chih-Yu Shih, *Symbolic War: The Chinese Use of Force, 1984–1980*, Taipei: Institute for International Relations, 1993, Chapter 14; King C. Chen, *China's War With Vietnam, 1979: Issues, Decisions, Implications*, Stanford, CA: Hoover Institution Press, 1987; Harlan Jencks, "China's 'Punitive' War on Vietnam," *Asian Survey* 19 (August 1979): 801–15; James Mulvenon, "The Limits of Coercive Diplomacy: The 1979 Sino–Vietnam Border War," *Journal of Northeast Asian Studies* XVI (Fall 1995):68–88; Edgar O'Balance, *The Wars in Vietnam, 1954–1980*, New York: Hippocrene Books, 1981, Chapter 16; Douglas Pike, "Communist vs. Communist in Southeast Asia," *International Security* 4 (Summer 1979):20–38; Gerald Segal, *Defending China*, New York: Oxford University Press, 1985, Chapter 12; Daniel Tretiak, "China's Vietnam War and Its Consquences," *China Quarterly* 80 (December 1979):740–67; Herbert Yee, "The Sino–Vietnamese Border War," *China Report* 16 (January–February 1980):15–32. For some Chinese accounts, see Junshi Kexueyuan Junshi Lishi Yanjiubu, *Zhongguo Renmin Jiefangjun de qishi nian* [Seventy years of China's People's Liberation Army], Beijing: Junshi Kexueyuan Chubanshe, 1997, pp. 609–16; Jiang Jiannong, chief ed., *Zhongnanhai sandai lingdao jiti yu gongheguo* [The third generation of collective leadership in Zhongnanhai], Vol. 2: *Junshi shilu* [Record of military affairs], Beijing: Zhongguo Jingji Chubanshe, 1998, pp. 313–26. For a Vietnamese perspective, see Nguyen Manh Hung, "The Sino–Vietnamese Conflict: Power Play among Communist Neighbors," *Asian Survey* XIX (November 1979): 1037–52.

3. A number of studies highlight the international dimensions and factors leading to the conflict. See, for example, Robert S. Ross, *The Indochina Tangle: China's Vietnam Policy, 1975–1979*, New York: Columbia University Press, 1988; Nayan Chanda, *Brother Enemy: The War after the War*, New York: Harcourt Brace Jovanovich, 1986; Steven J. Hood, *Dragons Entangled: Indo-China and the China–Vietnam War*, Armonk, NY: M. E. Sharpe, 1992.

4. For a notable exception, see Chen, *China's War with Vietnam.*

5. See Chen Jian, *Mao's China and the Cold War*, Chapel Hill, NC: University of North Carolina Press, 2001, Chapters 5, 8; Quansheng Zhao, *Interpreting Chinese Foreign Policy: The Micro-Macro Approach*, New York: Oxford University Press, 1996, pp. 43–4.

6. On the first use of the Cuba analogy, see *On Vietnam's Expulsion of Chinese Residents*, Peking: Foreign Languages Press, 1978, p. 131, cited in Chanda, *Brother Enemy*, p. 258. An article in the CCP theoretical journal *Hongqi*'s first issue of 1979 also used the analogy, and Deng Xiaoping also used this phrase at a press conference in Washington on January 31, 1979. See, respectively, "Red Flag on SRV's National Chauvinism....," Beijing Xinhua Domestic Service, January 3, 1979, in FBIS-CHI, January 4, 1979, p. A13; "SRV Needs Lessons," Beijing Xinhua in English, February 1, 1979, in FBIS-CHI, February 1, 1979, p. A8. On China's particular concern with the Soviet threat, see Ross, *The Indochina Tangle.*

7. On Vietnam's efforts to improve ties with the United States, see Chanda, *Brother Enemy*, Chapter 9.
8. Ibid., pp. 234–5.
9. Ibid., pp. 245, 257–8.
10. Ibid., pp. 231–4.
11. This is the figure quoted by Beijing. See, for example, *Zhongguo Renmin Jiefangjun de qishi nian*, p. 610. The number is consistent with figures quoted by non-Chinese sources.
12. See the analysis in Chanda, *Brother Enemy*, pp. 243–344.
13. On the Hoa, see Chanda, *Brother Enemy*; Hood, *Dragons Entangled*, Chapter 6.
14. Chanda, *Brother Enemy*, pp. 242–3.
15. Ibid., pp. 244–5.
16. For more on the territorial disputes, see Pao-min Chang, *The Sino–Vietnamese Territorial Dispute*, Washington Papers no. 118, New York: Praeger, 1986; Hood, *Dragons Entangled*, Chapter 5.
17. Nguyen, "The Sino–Vietnamese Conflict," p. 1049.
18. Chanda, *Brother Enemy*, pp. 259–60, citing a report in the Japanese press. Another source told Chanda that the Politburo made the decision in early July. Ibid., p. 261. That the decision was made in May seems more likely. However, one key reference work has no record of a Politburo meeting during the spring or summer of 1978. See Kenneth G. Lieberthal and Bruce J. Dickson, eds., *A Research Guide to Central Party and Government Meetings in China, 1949–1986*, Armonk, NY: M. E. Sharpe, 1989, pp. 252–6. Of course, this does not mean that no such meeting took place.
19. The information in this paragraph is taken from the text of a talk given by the vice chair of the Overseas Chinese Affairs Office of the State Council to provincial officials in Guangzhou in early June 1978. The speech was published by a Taiwan source. While the conduit and context of the information merit caution, the content and tone of the speech are consistent with other reports on China's policy toward Vietnam, including the source cited by Chanda. "State Council Official Comments on PRC Policy toward SRV," cited in Hong Kong Agence France Presse in English, February 8, 1979, in FBIS-CHI, February 9, 1979, p. E1 (emphasis added).
20. On the move as a "test," see Ross, *The Indochina Tangle*, pp. 183–5; on the move as publicity stunt, see Chanda, *Brother Enemy*, pp. 245–7.
21. Ross, *The Indochina Tangle*, pp. 155–67, 170–1.
22. Chanda, *Brother Enemy*, pp. 261–2, 322–3.
23. Ibid., pp. 325–7.
24. Chen, *China's War with Vietnam*, pp. 85–7. For a summary of the work conference, see Lieberthal and Dickson, *A Research Guide*, pp. 258–9.
25. This is also noted by Segal, *Defending China*, p. 214.
26. Chanda, *Brother Enemy*, pp. 259–61.
27. Ross, *The Indochina Tangle*, conclusion.
28. Chanda, *Brother Enemy*, p. 323; Chen, *China's Vietnam War*, pp. 88–91.
29. "SRV Needs Lessons," p. A8.
30. See, for example, Deng's remarks to a steady stream of foreign officials: the Secretary General of the Organization of American States (Hong Kong Agence France Presse in English, February 19, 1979, in FBIS-CHI, February 21, 1979, p. A4), the President of the European Economic Community Commission (Hong Kong

Agence France Presse in English, February 23, 1979, in FBIS-CHI, February 26, 1979, p. A1), and the head of Japan's Kyodo News Service ("Deng Welcomes UN Call for PRC, SRV Pullouts," Tokyo Kyodo in English, February 26, 1979, in FBIS-CHI, February 26, 1979, pp. A5–A6). See also editorials in *Renmin Ribao*, February 18, 1979 (quoted by Beijing Xinhua in English, February 17, 1979, and cited in FBIS-CHI, February 21, 1979, pp. A11–A12); *Jiefangjun Bao*, February 19, 1979 (quoted by Beijing Xinhua Domestic Service, February 18, 1979 and cited in FBIS-CHI, February 21, 1979, pp. A13–A14).

31. An explicit parallel with the Indian and Soviet border wars was made in a central CCP document read to foreign experts working in Beijing. See "AFP Highlights General Atmosphere in Beijing, Elsewhere," Paris Agence France Presse in English, February 21, 1979, in FBIS-CHI, February 22, 1979, p. E2. China's leaders seemed to view the conflict with India as their model – evident from such things as Deng's direct reference to the earlier conflict in his remarks to the head of the Kyodo new service about the Vietnam war ("Deng Welcomes UN Call for PRC, SRV Pullouts," p. A6), and the pointed remarks of a Chinese diplomat to his French counterpart in Manila on February 12, 1979 (Chanda, *Brother Enemy*, p. 355).

32. Segal, *Defending China*, pp. 213–14. Despite this, several scholars insist that the same pattern is evident for Vietnam too. See Yee, "The Sino–Vietnamese Border War," pp. 21–2; Tretiak, "China's Vietnam War," p. 750.

33. An official protest delivered to Vietnam's embassy in Beijing by the PRC Ministry of Foreign Affairs delivered on December 13, 1979, stated:

> The Vietnam Government should understand that there is a limit to China's forbearance and restraint towards its armed provocations against China and encroachments upon Chinese territory. If the Vietnamese authorities should persist in their course and continue to encroach upon Chinese territory . . . they must be held responsible for the consequences arising therefrom (Peking Domestic Service, December 13, 1978, in FBIS-CHI, December 13, 1978, p. A12).

This statement was followed by an even harsher editorial in the *Renmin Ribao* two weeks later (quoted later in this chapter).

The CCP's theoretical journal *Hongqi*'s January 1979 issue, by contrast, was extremely muted and nonthreatening in an article on Vietnam. It stated that "The sympathy and support of the Chinese people . . . are on the side of Kampuchea [Cambodia]." Moreover it strongly implied that any Chinese assistance forthcoming would be extremely limited and unlikely to make a dramatic difference: "The Kampuchean people's struggle against Soviet and Vietnamese aggression will be protracted, tortuous and fierce" ("Red Flag on SRV's National Chauvinism . . . ," p. A14).

Even more dramatic is the contrast between the wording of an official protest delivered to the Vietnamese embassy in Beijing on February 10 by the Ministry of Foreign Affairs and the earlier one dated December 13, 1978. The former document was very subdued, simply stating: "The Vietnamese authorities must stop their military provocations against China; otherwise they must be held responsible for all the consequences arising therefrom" (Beijing Xinhua in English, February 10, 1979, in FBIS-CHI, February 12, 1979, p. A7).

34. For the Chinese perspective, see Dangdai Zhongguo Waijiao Bianji Weiyuanhui, *Dangdai Zhongguo Waijiao* [Foreign Relations of Contemporary China], Beijing: Zhongguo Shehui Kexue Chubanshe, 1990, p. 286.
35. Deng told the head of the Kyodo news agency during the Vietnam conflict that he could not give a specific deadline for the cessation of hostilities because "Vietnam is stronger than India." "Deng Welcomes UN Call for PRC, SRV Pullouts," p. A6.
36. Chanda, *Brother Enemy*, pp. 348–9.
37. See the memoirs of the top U.S. foreign policy officials at the time: Cyrus Vance, *Hard Choices: Critical Years in American Foreign Policy*, New York: Simon and Schuster, 1983; Zbigniew Brzezinski, *Power and Principle: Memoirs of the National Security Advisor, 1977–1981*, New York: Farrar, Straus, and Giroux, 1983.
38. See, for example, Mulvenon, "The Limits of Coercive Diplomacy," p. 84, n. 49.
39. Jencks, "China's 'Punitive' War on Vietnam," pp. 808, 813; Dangdai Zhongguo Kongjun Bianjibu, compiler, *Dangdai Zhongguo Kongjun* [The Air Force of Contemporary China], Beijing: Zhongguo Shehui Kexue Chubanshe, 1989, pp. 636–9.
40. For a brief summary of the meeting, see Lieberthal and Dickson, *A Research Guide*, p. 262.
41. Beijing Xinhua in English, January 19, 1979, in FBIS-CHI, January 22, 1979, pp. A8–A10.
42. "Deng Discusses Asia with Indian Journalists," Paris AFP in English, February 14, 1979, in FBIS-CHI, February 15, 1979, p. A7. See also Yee, "The Sino–Vietnamese Border War," p. 22; Jencks, "China's 'Punitive' War on Vietnam," p. 805.
43. Chanda, *Brother Enemy*, p. 357.
44. On consensus among leaders, see Segal, *Defending China*, p. 224; on divisions among leaders, see "AFP Highlights General Atmosphere in Beijing, Elsewhere," p. E3.
45. Cited in "State Council Official Comments on PRC Policy toward SRV," p. E2.
46. For some interesting analysis of Deng's sense of his own identity and status within the Chinese communist movement, see Ruan Ming, *Deng Xiaoping: Chronicle of an Empire*, Nancy Liu, Peter Rand, and Lawrence R. Sullivan, trans., Boulder, CO: Westview Press, 1994, pp. 55–6. Deng almost certainly saw himself as a gifted strategist. As the chief architect of the war against Vietnam, he felt personally insulted by the criticism of the war by a young dissident named Wei Jingsheng in a poster pasted on Democracy Wall in the spring of 1979. See ibid.
47. See Carol Lee Hamrin, "Competing 'Policy Packages' in Post-Mao China," *Asian Survey* XXIV (May 1984):495–8; Chanda, *Brother Enemy*, p. 329.
48. Michel Oksenberg, "A Decade of Sino–American Relations," *Foreign Affairs* 61 (1982):187.
49. For clear evidence of Deng's abiding interest in defense reform, see the numerous pieces on this topic in *Deng Xiaoping wenxuan (1975–1982)* [Selected works of Deng Xiaoping (1975–1982)], Beijing: Renmin Chubanshe, 1983.
50. Chen, *China's War with Vietnam*, pp. 87–8.
51. Wang defies simple categorization and is sometimes considered a military man.
52. Chanda argues that Wang was a messenger sent to inform Pol Pot that direct Chinese intervention in Cambodia was unlikely to be forthcoming (Chanda, *Brother Enemy*, p. 326). Given the composition of the delegation, it must be viewed as a fact-finding

mission to enable the Politburo to make an informed decision about China's best course of action. Indeed, this is the way Chanda seems to view it on the following page (ibid., p. 327).

53. Chen, *China's War with Vietnam*, p. 86.
54. Chanda, *Brother Enemy*, p. 326.
55. Beijing Xinhua in English, February 11, 1979, in FBIS-CHI February 12, 1979, p. A7.
56. March 5, 1979, *Yomuri Shimbun*, cited in Hamrin, "Competing 'Policy Packages,'" p. 503.
57. See Hamrin, "Competing 'Policy Packages,'" p. 503; Hamrin, "Elite Politics and the Development of China's Foreign Relations," in Thomas W. Robinson and David Shambaugh, eds., *Chinese Foreign Policy: Theory and Practice*, Oxford, UK: Clarendon Press, 1994, p. 102.
58. "Zai Zhongyang gongzuo huiyi shang de jianghua" [Talk at a central work conference] (April 5, 1979), in *Li Xiannian wenxuan* [Selected works of Li Xiannian], Beijing: Renmin Chubanshe, 1989, p. 351.
59. King Chen contends that if Hua had been in the driver's seat in February 1979, he would have never permitted the attack to take place. See *China's War with Vietnam*, p. 153.
60. "State Council Official Comments on PRC Policy toward Vietnam," p. E2.
61. Chen, *China's War with Vietnam*, p. 94.
62. Ruan, *Deng Xiaoping*, p. 58.
63. Tretiak, "China's Vietnam War," pp. 752–3.
64. Chen, *China's War with Vietnam*, p. 113.
65. See Agence France Presse Taipei, August 3, 1979, cited in Hamrin, "Competing 'Policy Packages,'" pp. 502–3. See also Lieberthal and Dickson, *A Research Guide*, p. 263 (Meeting no. 426).
66. Gerald Segal, "The PLA and Chinese Foreign Policy Decision-Making," *International Affairs* 57 (Summer 1981):463–4. This conclusion is based on deduction and inference due to a lack of hard evidence. Segal's working assumption is that the PLA did not play a key role in the decision to launch the attack.
67. Chanda, *Brother Enemy*, p. 260.
68. This is according to Geng. See Chen, *China's War with Vietnam*, pp. 85–6.
69. Chen, *Mao's China and the Cold War*, pp. 123–38.
70. Chanda, *Brother Enemy*, p. 232.
71. "Zai Zhongyang Junshi Wei shouyu jing mo danwei he ge ren rongyu chenghao mingming dahui shang de jianghua" (October 13, 1979), in *Xu Shiyou Huiyilu* [Memoirs of Xu Shiyou], Beijing: Jiefangjun Chubanshe, 1986, p. 623.
72. Chen, *China's War with Vietnam*, p. 86.
73. Beijing Xinhua in English, January 17, 1979, in FBIS, January 18, 1979, p. A19.
74. "Huijian Yidali jizhe Naxi Pilaosi shi de jianghua jiyao," *Xu Xiangqian junshi wenxuan* [Selected works of Xu Xiangqian], Beijing: Jiefangjun Chubanshe, 1993, p. 305.
75. "Zai Zhongyang Junwei Renmin Wuzhuang Weiyuanhui diyi huiyi shang de jianghua" (March 27, 1979), in *Xu Xiangqian junshi wenxuan*, p. 271.
76. Ibid., pp. 273–4.

77. Dangdai Zhongguo Renwu Zongji Congshu Bianjubu, ed., *Xu Xiangqian zhuan* [Biography of Xu Xiangqian], Beijing: Dangdai Zhongguo Chubanshe, 1991, pp. 608, 549.

78. Geng Biao, *Geng Biao huiyilu* [Memoirs of Geng Biao], Beijing: Jiefangjun Chubanshe, 1991, pp. 554–64. Geng was transferred from the PLA to the Ministry of Foreign Affairs in the late 1940s. For the next quarter of a century, he served as People's Republic of China's ambassador to Switzerland, Denmark, Finland, Pakistan, Burma, and Albania. But by the late 1970s, he was reappointed to the CMC, and in the early 1980s he was named as minister of national defense. Ibid., pp. 559–61.

79. Belgrade Tanjug in English, February 21, 1979, in FBIS-CHI, February 23, 1979, p. A11.

80. Chen, *China's War with Vietnam*, pp. 85–7.

81. Xinhua, November 1, 1978, cited in FBIS-CHI, November 2, 1978, p. E3, quoted in Hamrin, "Competing 'Policy Packages,'" pp. 497–8.

82. "Zai qingqu Zhonghua Renmin Gongheguo chengli sanshi zhounian dahui shang de jianghua" (September 29, 1979), *Ye Jianying xuanji* [Selected works of Ye Jianying], Beijing: Renmin Chubanshe, 1996, pp. 550–1.

83. *Gongren Ribao*, February 4, 1981, cited in Hamrin, "Competing 'Policy Packages,'" p. 509.

84. According to Beijing, the numbers of armed provocations by Vietnam are as follows, 1974: 121; 1975, 439; 1976, 986; 1977, 752; 1978, "more than 1, 100." In the six-month period from September 1978 through early February 1979, there were reportedly 162 violations of Chinese territory and some 300 border troops were killed or injured by Vietnamese attacks during 1978 (*Zhongnanhai sandai*, 2:308–9). Segal wisely cautions against accepting these figures uncritically (*Defending China*, p. 215). Indeed it is always advisable to be skeptical of Chinese statistics. However, in this case, there are good reasons for accepting them as fairly reliable, and the Chinese version of events as fairly accurate although almost certainly prone to exaggeration. First, both Chinese and Vietnamese reports of border tensions have been generally consistent with each other. Beijing reported that Vietnamese incursions became more frequent in late August 1978 and grew more serious in November and December. Vietnam did not allege Chinese border violations until late October 1978 and did not call them serious until February 1979. Second, Chinese allegations of Vietnamese actions are rather detailed and specific, and the number of reported border incidents claimed by Beijing at the time is consistent with figures quoted by Chinese sources two decades later. Third, China had little reason to want to provoke a large-scale Vietnamese attack on China before the PLA was properly positioned to deal with such a contingency. Chang, *The Sino-Vietnamese Territorial Dispute*, pp. 48–9. For consistency in statistics, compare Chinese figures from February 1979 (Tretiak, "China's Vietnam War," p. 741) with figures used in a 1998 source (*Zhongnanhai sandai*, 2:308–9).

85. On the "asymmetry of motivation," see Mulvenon, "The Limits of Coercive Diplomacy," pp. 75–7; on the absence of incentives for Vietnam to take the desired action, and the loud background "noise," see ibid., pp. 74–5, 80.

86. Beijing New China News Agency in English, December 24, 1978, in FBIS-CHI, December 26, 1978, p. A16.

87. Yee, "The Sino–Vietnamese Border War," p. 18.
88. "Jianchi Sixiang jiben yuanze" [Uphold the four cardinal principles] (March 30, 1979), in *Deng Xiaoping wenxuan*, p. 146. This point was also made by Segal, *Defending China*, p. 218.
89. Yee, "The Sino–Vietnamese Border War," p. 19.
90. Roger Garside, *Coming Alive: China after Mao*, New York: Mentor Books, 1982, p. 204.
91. "Jianchi Sixiang jiben yuanze," p. 146.
92. One scholar calls it "Deng Xiaoping's War." Chen, *China's War with Vietnam*, p. 152.
93. S. K. Ghosh, "Deng Xiaoping Steps Down from Military Leadership," *China Report* XVI (March–April 1980):3–4.
94. See Chen, *China's War with Vietnam*, pp. 96–100; Ellis Joffe, *The Chinese Army after Mao*, Cambridge, MA: Harvard University Press, 1987, pp. 77–80.
95. Joffe, *The Chinese Army after Mao*, pp. 57–8.
96. "Jingjian jundui, tigao zhandouli" [Streamline the army and raise its combat-effectiveness] (March 12, 1980), *Deng Xiaoping wenxuan*, pp. 248, 253.
97. On the bad blood between Deng and Xu Shiyou, see Richard Baum, *Burying Mao: Chinese Politics in the Age of Deng Xiaoping*, Princeton, NJ: Princeton University Press, 1994, p. 88; Jurgen Domes, *The Government and Politics of the PRC: A Time of Transition*, Boulder, CO: Westview Press, 1985, pp. 171–2.
98. See Alastair Iaian Johnston, "Party Rectification in the People's Liberation Army, 1983–1987," *China Quarterly* 112 (December 1987):591–630, especially pp. 602–3.
99. Yee, "The Sino–Vietnamese Border War," p. 17.
100. Baum, *Burying Mao*, p. 80. Baum mistakenly interprets this criticism as directed at Deng.
101. W. J. F. Jenner, *The Tyranny of History: The Roots of China's Crisis*, London: Allen Lane, 1992, p. 58.
102. "AFP Highlights General Atmosphere in Beijing, Elsewhere," p. E3.
103. Chanda, *Brother Enemy*, pp. 361–2.
104. Author's interviews with researchers in Beijing and Shanghai, May and June 1998; author's conversations, Kunming, 1984–5. On the origins of the phrase cited in the text, see Chapter 3.
105. See, for example, Hong Kong AFP in English, February 18, 1979, in FBIS-CHI, February 22, 1979, p. E1. The same point is also made by Segal, *Defending China*, p. 224; Tretiak, "China's Vietnam War," p. 751; Yee, "The Sino–Vietnamese Border War," p. 20.
106. Beijing Domestic Service, February 20, 1979, cited in FBIS-CHI, February 22, 1979, p. E2.
107. Thomas A. Fabyanic, "The Grammar and Logic of Conflict: The Differing Conceptions of Statesmen and Soldiers," *Air University Review* 32 (March–April 1981): 23–31.
108. Alexander George, "The Development of Doctrine and Strategy," in Alexander George, David K. Hall, and William E. Simons, *The Limits of Coercive Diplomacy: Laos, Cuba, and Vietnam*, Boston, MA: Little, Brown and Company, 1971, p. 18.
109. Hong Kong AFP, February 27, 1979, cited in FBIS-CHI, February 27, 1979, p. A7.

110. See, for example, Chen *China's War with Vietnam*, p. 95.
111. "Deng Discusses Asia with Indian Journalists," p. A7.
112. "Deng Welcomes UN Call for PRC, SRV Pullouts," p. A5.
113. For the classic articulation of the "military mind," see Samuel P. Huntington, *The Soldier and the State: The Theory and Politics of Civil-Military Relations*, Cambridge, MA: Belknap Press, 1957, Chapter 3; Richard K. Betts, *Soldiers, Statesmen, and Cold War Crises*, 2ⁿᵈ ed., New York: Columbia University Press, 1991.
114. R. Bates Gill, *Chinese Arms Transfers: Purposes, Patterns, and Prospects in the New World Order*, New York: Praeger, 1992, p. 54. See also pp. 55, 192; Appendix 2 on p. 215; Appendix 3 on p. 217; Appendix 4 on p. 219.
115. Direct and massive military intervention by China in Cambodia would have been a far more ambitious and aggressive act than the limited strike on Vietnam.
116. Tretiak, "China's Vietnam War," pp. 757–8; Segal, *Defending China*, p. 225; Joffe, *The Chinese Army after Mao*, p. 34; Baum, *Burying Mao*, p. 80; Lu Ning, *The Dynamics of Foreign-Policy Decisionmaking in China*, Boulder, CO: Westview Press, 1997, p. 157.
117. Segal, *Defending China*, pp. 223–4. It should be noted that one analyst argues that the war did have a huge impact domestically in terms of the road not taken. Specifically, he contends that the war caused Deng to shift the focus of his reform from democratizing China to constructing a new "totalitarian empire." See Ruan, *Deng Xiaoping*. This seems implausible, however. See my review of Ruan's book in *China Information* XI (July 1996):162–5.

CHAPTER 7. WHY THE PEOPLE'S ARMY FIRED ON THE PEOPLE: BEIJING, 1989

1. See, for example, Zhang Liang (pseud.), compiler, *The Tiananmen Papers: The Chinese Leadership's Decision to Use Force against Their Own People – In Their Own Words*, Andrew J. Nathan and Perry Link, eds., New York: PublicAffairs, 2001; the Chinese version, Zhang Liang, compiler, *Zhongguo "liu si" zhenxiang* [China "June 4": The true story], 2 vols., n.p.: Mingjing Chubanshe, 2001; Yi Mu and Mark V. Thompson, *Crisis at Tiananmen: Reform and Reality*, San Francisco, CA: China Books, 1989; *Problems of Communism* 38 (September–October 1989) (entire issue); Amnesty International, *People's Republic of China: Preliminary Findings on the Killings of Unarmed Civilians, Arbitrary Arrests and Summary Executions since June 3, 1989*, New York: Amnesty International Publications, 1989 (hereafter *Preliminary Findings*). On the military's role, see June Teufel Dreyer "China after Tiananmen: The Role of the PLA," *World Policy Journal* 4 (Fall 1989):6–17; Dreyer, "The People's Liberation Army and the Power Struggle of 1989," *Problems of Communism* 38 (September–October 1989): 41–8 (hereafter "Power Struggle of 1989"); Harlan W. Jencks, "The Military in China," *Current History* 88 (September 1989):265–8, 291–3; Jencks, "The Losses in Tiananmen Square," *Air Force Magazine* 72 (November 1989): 62–6; Michael T. Byrnes, "The Death of a People's Army," in George Hicks, ed., *The Broken Mirror: China after Tiananmen*, Harlow, Essex, UK: Longman Group, 1990, pp. 132–51; Gao Xin, "'Liu san' zhiye: shui kai qiang?" [The evening of June 3: Who fired?], *Zhongguo zhi chun* [China Spring] 97 (June 1991):6–10; Richard H. Yang, Peter Kien-hong Yu,

and Andrew N. Yang, eds., *China's Military: The PLA in 1990/1991*, Boulder, CO: Westview Press, 1991; Timothy Brook, *Quelling the People: The Military Suppression of the Beijing Democracy Movement*, New York: Oxford University Press, 1992; Andrew Scobell, "Why the People's Army Fired on the People," in Roger V. Des Forges, Luo Ning, and Wu Yen-bo, eds., *Chinese Democracy and the Crisis of 1989: Chinese and American Reflections*, Albany, NY: State University of New York Press, 1993, pp. 191–221.

2. Ironically, an important aspect of Deng's political reforms was a reinvigoration of the bureaucracy. Older officials were encouraged to retire and younger, more energetic ones were promoted.

3. On how the Chinese referred to this group, see John P. Burns, "China's Governance: Political Reform in a Turbulent Environment," *China Quarterly* 119 (September 1989):483–4. Nathan also dubs this group "the Elders." See Andrew J. Nathan, "Introduction: The Documents and Their Significance," *The Tiananmen Papers*.

4. *Cheng Ming*, March 1, 1989, in Foreign Broadcast Information Service, *Daily Report: China* (hereafter FBIS-CHI), March 3, 1989, pp. 22–5; and ibid., April 1, 1989, in FBIS-CHI, April 3, 1989, pp. 39–41.

5. Harlan W. Jencks, "Civil-Military Relations in China: Tiananmen and After," *Problems of Communism* 40 (May–June 1991):28.

6. On Deng's role in the April 26 editorial, see *The Tiananmen Papers*, pp. 71–5. For the text of the April 26 editorial, see "Quarterly Chronicle and Documentation," in *China Quarterly* 119 (September 1989):717–19.

7. Alan P. L. Liu, "Aspects of Beijing's Crisis Management: The Tiananmen Square Demonstration," *Asian Survey* XXX (May 1990):512–13. While Liu uses what he labels "crisis management" to analyze the episode, he examines, in effect, coercive diplomacy in a domestic setting.

8. *New York Times* (hereafter *NYT*), May 28, 1989.

9. On efforts by the leadership at coercive diplomacy, see Liu, "Aspects of Beijing's Crisis Management," pp. 512–14.

10. These comments were made in interviews conducted before June 1989, but were not published until a year later. *Ming Pao*, March 6, 1990, in FBIS-CHI, March 6, 1990, pp. 30–1; Jencks, "Civil-Military Relations in China," p. 26.

11. Zhongguo Xinwenshe, May 18, 1989, in FBIS-CHI, May 18, 1989, pp. 38–9.

12. See, for example, Beijing television, May 19–20, 1989, in FBIS-CHI, May 22, 1989, pp. 9–13; Li Peng's interview in *Die Welt* (Hamburg), November 20, 1989 (hereafter "Li Peng interview"), in FBIS-CHI, November 22, 1989, p. 26.

13. *Cheng Ming*, June 1, 1989, in FBIS-CHI, May 31, 1989, p. 70. PLA and PAP units in Beijing reportedly had been on full alert since April 18, and on April 20 the CMC ordered thousands of PLA troops to Beijing. See, respectively, *Cheng Ming*, May 1, 1989, in FBIS-CHI, May 2, 1989, p. 28; *The Tiananmen Papers*, p. 47. On April 20, two other Elders, Peng Zhen and Wang Zhen, reportedly expressed alarm at the unrest and seemed to favor a harsh crackdown on the protesters. *The Tiananmen Papers*, pp. 45–6.

14. See "Quarterly Chronicle and Documentation," *China Quarterly* 119 (September 1989) (hereafter "Deng's Speech"): 725.

15. See "Beijing Mayor's Address to NPC Standing Committee on Background to the 4th June Massacre," in "Quarterly Chronicle and Documentation," *China Quarterly*

120 (December 1989):919–46 (hereafter "Mayor's Address"); Andrew Nathan, "Chinese Democracy in 1989: Continuity and Change," *Problems of Communism* 38 (September–October 1989):26–7.

16. Zhongguo Xinwenshe and *Renmin Ribao*, both May 20, 1989, in FBIS-CHI, May 22, 1989, pp. 21–3; *Wen Wei Po*, June 25, 1989, in FBIS-CHI, June 26, 1989, p. 34; Yi and Thompson, *Crisis at Tiananmen*, pp. 64–6.

17. Technically the declaration imposed martial law only on "parts" of the capital, but as far as soldiers and civilians were concerned, the entire municipality was affected. For a detailed analysis of the imposition of martial law in 1989, see Andrew Scobell, "The Meaning of Martial Law for the PLA and Internal Security in China after Deng," presented to the CAPS/RAND conference "New Reforms in the PLA," held in Washington, DC, June 21–4, 2001. For the martial law announcement, see Beijing television, May 20, 1989, in FBIS-CHI, May 22, 1989, p. 26.

18. For the text of the martial law orders issued on May 20, 1989, see "Quarterly Chronicle and Documentation," *China Quarterly* 119 (September 1989):723–4.

19. On the meeting, see *The Tiananmen Papers*, pp. 184–93, 204–11; Mu Wang, "Zhongnanhai gaoceng douzheng zhenxiang" [The real high-level struggle at Zhongnanhai], *Ching Pao Monthly*, June 1989, p. 23; *South China Morning Post* (hereafter *SCMP*), May 23, 1989, in FBIS-CHI, May 23, 1989, p. 42; AFP, May 22, 1989, in FBIS-CHI, May 22, 1989, pp. 20–1; Nicholas D. Kristof, "China Update: How the Hardliners Won," *New York Times Magazine*, November 12, 1989, p. 95. Deng was also the prime mover behind the decision to impose martial law in Lhasa in early March, although this decision reflected unanimity among both the "retired" Elders and the formal officeholders. On the March decision, see Agence France Presse (Hong Kong), May 22, 1989, in FBIS-CHI, May 22, 1989, p. 21; Zhongguo Xinwenshe, March 7, 1989, in FBIS-CHI, March 8, 1989, p. 17; *Far Eastern Economic Review* (hereafter *FEER*), March 19, 1989, p. 10.

20. Lucian Pye, "Tiananmen and Chinese Political Culture: The Escalation of Confrontation from Moralizing to Revenge," *Asian Survey* 30 (April 1990):331–47.

21. For Li Xiannian's quote, see *The Tiananmen Papers*, p. 205; on concerns about civil war, see Deng's remarks on June 2, 1989, ibid., p. 359.

22. Kyodo News Agency, May 22, 1989, in FBIS-CHI, May 22, 1989, p. 4. According to another version, the marshals also telephoned Deng on May 21 to express their opposition to the use of force. *Hong Kong Standard* (hereafter *HKS*) and *Wen Wei Po*, both May 22, 1989, both in FBIS-CHI, May 22, 1989, pp. 4–5.

23. Beijing radio, May 21, 1989, in FBIS-CHI, May 22, 1989, pp. 51–2.

24. *SCMP*, May 23, 1989, in FBIS-CHI, May 23, 1989, pp. 41–2; *Ming Pao*, May 22, 1989, in FBIS-CHI, May 22, 1989, pp. 5–6. Qin, however, seems to have supported the imposition of martial law at the key May 18 meeting. *The Tiananmen Papers*, p. 210. Of course, both are possible: that Qin came out in favor of martial law, and that he expressed opposition to PLA troops using force against unarmed civilians.

25. On Zhao's "mistakes," see "Mayor's Address."

26. *Asiaweek*, June 9, 1989. Deng told military leaders on June 9 that a "rebellious clique" wanted to "overthrow our state and the party." See "Deng's Speech," p. 725.

27. Michel Oksenberg, Lawrence R. Sullivan, and Marc Lambert, eds., *Beijing Spring, 1989: Confrontation and Conflict: The Basic Documents*, Armonk, NY: M. E. Sharpe, 1990, p. 360, n. 5.

28. See *Hsin Wan Pao*, May 17, 1989, in FBIS-CHI, May 17, 1989, p. 57; AFP, May 23, 1989, in FBIS-CHI, May 24, 1989, p. 29.
29. Personal communication, Mr. Harry Wells, formerly of the Hong Kong police and a riot control expert.
30. Melanie Manion, "Introduction: Reluctant Duelists: The Logic of the 1989 Protests and Massacre," in Oksenberg, Sullivan, and Lambert, eds., *Beijing Spring*, pp. xxxix–xl, especially, n. 89.
31. This point is also made by Manion. See "Introduction," p. xl. "[O]nly the PLA could have cowered the opposition so completely." Byrnes, "The Death of a People's Army," p. 138.
32. *The Tiananmen Papers*, pp. 354–62.
33. Ibid., pp. 366–9.
34. Ibid., p. 368; "Mayor's Address," p. 940; Shi Wei, "What Happened in Beijing?" in *The June Turbulence*, Beijing: New Star Publishers, 1989, p. 43; *HKS*, June 5, 1989, in FBIS-CHI, June 5, 1989, p. 10; *Ming Pao*, June 12, 1989, in FBIS-CHI, June 12, 1989, pp. 19–20.
35. "Minutes of the Politburo meeting of June 3," in *The Tiananmen Papers*, pp. 368–70.
36. *Cheng Ming*, October 1, 1990, in FBIS-CHI, October 5, 1990, p. 15. Yang Shangkun told the enlarged Politburo Standing Committee on June 3 that Deng had directed that Tiananmen Square be cleared. *The Tiananmen Papers*, pp. 369–70.
37. Various sources claim that the crackdown was championed by Yang Shangkun, Li Peng, or Qiao. *Ming Pao*, June 5, 1989, in FBIS-CHI, June 5, 1989, p. 79; *Ta Kung Pao*, June 4, 1989, in FBIS-CHI, June 5, 1989, p. 23.
38. *The Tiananmen Papers*, p. 370. Manion, "Introduction," p. xxxix.
39. On Yang Shangkun's words, see *The Tiananmen Papers*, p. 370; on Nathan's assessment, ibid., p. 365; for the orders given to the PLA, ibid., p. 370.
40. *China Daily*, June 5, 1989, in FBIS-CHI, June 5, 1989, pp. 76–7.
41. *Ta Kung Pao*, June 4, 1989, in FBIS-CHI, June 5, 1989, p. 23.
42. Byrnes, "The Death of a People's Army," p. 143.
43. *Der Spiegel* (in German), June 5, 1989, in FBIS-CHI, June 7, 1989, pp. 29–30.
44. *NYT*, June 4, 1989, pp. 1, 20.
45. "Main Points of Yang Shangkun's Secret Speech," in *Ming Pao*, May 29, 1989, in FBIS-CHI, May 30, 1989, pp. 18–19. *The Tiananmen Papers* corroborate the claim that retired marshals Nie and Xu supported the imposition of martial law. See *The Tiananmen Papers*, pp. 264–5.
46. See the text of these letters in Zhonggong Zhongyang Xuanchuan Bu, ed., *Jianjue yonghu dangzhongyang juece, jianjue pingxi fangeming baoluan* [Resolutely support the policy of the central party authorities, resolutely suppress the counterrevolutionary rebellion], Beijing: Renmin Chubanshe, 1989, pp. 62–4. At least one of the letters (Nie's) was broadcast on local radio. See Xinhua News Agency, June 12, 1989, in FBIS-CHI, June 13, 1989, p. 16.
47. "Main Points of Yang Shangkun's Secret Speech," p. 20. This point is also supported by *The Tiananmen Papers*, p. 210.
48. Xinhua News Agency, June 9, 1989, in FBIS-CHI, June 13, 1989, p. 17.
49. *U.S. News and World Report* (hereafter *USN&WR*), March 12, 1990, p. 54.

50. Gerald Segal, "The Military as a Group in Chinese Politics," in David S. G. Goodman, ed., *Groups and Politics in the People's Republic of China*, Armonk, NY: M. E. Sharpe, 1984, p. 94. Even Segal, who argues that the PLA cannot be identified as a "group actor" in Chinese politics, still acknowledges that the military tends to be united on this question.
51. Dreyer, "Power Struggle of 1989," p. 47.
52. Jencks, "Civil-Military Relations in China," pp. 14–15, 16.
53. Gao, "'Liusan'zhiye," p. 6.
54. *The Tiananmen Papers*, pp. 213, 239–40; Jencks, "Civil-Military Relations in China," p. 16.
55. For these rumors, see *SCMP*, *Ta Kung Pao*, *Ming Pao*, Kyodo News Agency, *Wen Hui Pao*, all June 6, 1989, in FBIS-CHI, June 6, 1989, pp. 25–8; Hong Kong television June 6, 1989, *Ming Pao*, *Ta Kung Pao*, and *Wen Wei Po*, all June 7, 1989, in FBIS-CHI, June 7, 1989, pp. 26–8; *Washington Post* (hereafter *WP*), June 6, 1989, pp. A1, A14; *Wall Street Journal* (hereafter *WSJ*), June 7, 1989, p. A28; *NYT*, June 9, 1989, p. A11.
56. Commercial Radio (Hong Kong) and *SCMP*, both June 5, 1989, in FBIS-CHI, June 5, 1989, p. 52; *Ming Pao*, June 6, 1989, in FBIS-CHI, June 6, 1989, pp. 17–18.
57. This is the conclusion of most experts. For assessments of the evidence, see Dreyer, "Power Struggle of 1989," p. 45; Jencks, "The Military in China," p. 267. Tai Ming Cheung concludes a few clashes occurred, but he does not cite any evidence. See *FEER*, October 5, 1989, p. 69. Brook also concludes that there was some fighting between military units, but admits to finding "no hard evidence." *Quelling the People*, p. 187.
58. Dreyer, "China after Tiananmen," p. 65; *SCMP*, June 10, 1989, in FBIS-CHI, June 12, 1989, p. 16; *Ming Pao*, June 7, 1989, in FBIS-CHI, June 7, 1989, p. 25.
59. *The Tiananmen Papers*, p. 239. Military units from at least six different provinces were ordered to Beijing. *Zhongguo "liu si" zhenxiang*, 2:558–9. See also Jencks, "The Losses in Tiananmen Square," p. 65; Jencks, "The Military in China," p. 267; Kyodo News Agency, May 23, 1989, in FBIS-CHI, May 24, 1989, p. 19; *NYT*, June 7, 1989, p. A8; *Yangcheng Wanbao* (Guangzhou), July 8, 1989, in FBIS-CHI, August 1, 1989, pp. 55–6.
60. Jencks, "Civil-Military Relations in China," pp. 25–6.
61. Jencks, "The Military in China," p. 267.
62. *FEER*, February 1, 1990, p. 22; *The Tiananmen Papers*, pp. 239–40.
63. *FEER*, June 14, 1990, p. 32.
64. Jencks, "Civil-Military Relations in China," p. 22.
65. Jencks, "The Losses in Tiananmen Square," p. 64.
66. Jencks, "Civil-Military Relations in China," p. 15.
67. *The Tiananmen Papers*, p. 369.
68. Gao, "'Liusan' zhi ye," p. 11.
69. Dreyer, "Power Struggle of 1989," p. 45; *SCMP*, June 6, 1989, in FBIS-CHI, June 6, 1989, p. 27; *Economist*, June 10, 1989, pp. 19–21.
70. Jencks, "Civil-Military Relations in China," p. 26.
71. *Ming Pao*, April 30, 1989, in FBIS-CHI, May 1, 1989, p. 18.
72. Gao, "'Liusan' zhi ye."

73. According to official military accounts of the operation, the 38th was the "vanguard" Group Army. *The Tiananmen Papers*, pp. 372, 389–91. See also Jencks, "The Losses in Tiananmen Square," p. 65.
74. Gao, "'Liusan' zhi ye," p. 7; corroborated in *The Tiananmen Papers*, p. 372.
75. *The Tiananmen Papers*, p. 374; *Zhongguo "liu si" zhenxiang*, 2:932. Troops chanted the same mantra as they cleared Tiananmen Square on the morning of June 4. *The Tiananmen Papers*, p. 387.
76. Gao, "'Liusan' zhi ye," p. 8.
77. Ibid., p. 10.
78. For some accounts that stress the uniqueness of 1989, see *WP*, June 6, 1989, p. A17; Jonathan D. Spence, *The Search for Modern China*, New York: W. W. Norton, 1990, p. 741.
79. See the results of a poll. Zhang Wenrui, Yang Yuwen, and Liu Bangguo, "The Great Changes and New Characteristics in the Composition of Our Troops," *Qingnian Yanjiu*, June 6, 1986, translated in *Chinese Law and Government* 20 (Summer 1987):102–17.
80. Dreyer, "Power Struggle of 1989," pp. 42, 45.
81. *Financial Times* (London), April 19, 1989, p. 1; *Cheng Ming*, May 1, 1989, in FBIS-CHI, May 2, 1989, p. 28. Most accounts do not mention that troops were involved.
82. *WP*, May 23, 1989, p. A18.
83. Xinhua New Agency, May 23, 1989, in FBIS-CHI, May 24, 1989, pp. 39–40.
84. *SCMP*, May 23, 1989, in FBIS-CHI, May 23, 1989, p. 41.
85. Beijing radio, May 24, 1989, in FBIS-CHI, May 25, 1989, p. 25; Beijing television, May 29, 1989, in FBIS-CHI, May 29, 1989, p. 56.
86. Hundreds of PAP and public security personnel were also injured. See Xinhua New Agency, May 25, 1989, in FBIS-CHI, May 26, 1989, p. 6; Beijing television, May 28, 1989, in FBIS-CHI, May 31, 1989, p. 57; Shi Wei, "Why Impose Martial Law in Beijing?" in *The June Turbulence*, p. 37.
87. Xinhua News Agency, May 24, 1989, in FBIS-CHI, May 25, 1989, p. 36; Tanjug (Belgrade), June 3, 1989, in FBIS-CHI, June 5, 1989, p. 27; "State Council Spokesman Yuan My Held a Press Conference. . . . ," in *The June Turbulence* (hereafter "State Council Spokesman"), pp. 11–12; *Preliminary Findings*, p. 5.
88. See, for example, *WP*, May 21, 1989, p. A1; *Beijing Review*, June 5–11, 1989, p. 13.
89. *Renmin Ribao*, May 23, 1989, in FBIS-CHI, May 25, 1989, p. 40; *Wen Wei Po*, May 25, 1989, in FBIS-CHI, May 25, 1989, p. 25; Dreyer, "Power Struggle of 1989," p. 46.
90. *Jieyan yiri (jingxuan ben)* [A day under martial law – volume of selections], Beijing: Jiefanjun Wenyi Chubanshe, 1990, p. 28. There are many other examples in this volume. These accounts by the troops themselves seem realistic, plausible, matter-of-fact, free of propaganda, and often consistent with civilian eyewitness accounts.
91. *Wen Wei Po*, May 25, 1989, in FBIS-CHI, May 25, 1989, p. 25.
92. Scott Simmie and Bob Nixon, *Tiananmen Square*, Seattle, WA: University of Washington Press, 1989, pp. 171–72; Shi, "What Happened in Beijing?" p. 42.
93. *Jieyan yiri*, p. 223.
94. Yi and Thompson, *Crisis at Tiananmen*, pp. 78–81. Although the vehicle involved had police license plates at the time of the accident, it was allegedly on loan

to Chinese state television. See *Renmin Ribao*, overseas edition, June 10, 1989, p. 1.

95. *Preliminary Findings*, p. 5. The weapons may have been deliberately left for civilians to obtain and use – thus providing an excuse for the PLA to use deadly force against the protesters. See Huan Guocang, "The Events of Tiananmen Square," *Orbis* 33 (Fall 1989):497. More likely, however, the military sought secretly to move weapons to supply unarmed troops who were infiltrating the city center. See Kristof, "China Update," p. 71.

96. This was the pervasive feeling of people in the streets at the time according to most published accounts and reports given to the author by eyewitnesses. See, for example, Yi and Thompson, *Crisis at Tiananmen*, p. 81; Gao, "'Liusan' zhi ye," p. 7.

97. "Deng's Speech," p. 726.

98. Dreyer calls the soldiers "misfits." See *WSJ*, June 7, 1989, p. A28.

99. *Preliminary Findings*, pp. 16–17.

100. See, for example, *WSJ*, June 8, 1989, pp. A1, A16; *Preliminary Findings*, pp. 12–17.

101. On the alleged shortage of riot control gear, see *WP*, July 7, 1989, pp. A1, A27. On the lack of riot control training, see Jencks, "The Military in China," p. 267. On desertions, see Hong Kong radio, June 3, 1989, in FBIS-CHI, June 5, 1989, p. 28. As of June 6, four hundred officers and enlisted men were reportedly missing. See "State Council Spokesman," p. 5.

102. Many PLA deaths were probably from "friendly fire." See Gerald Segal, "The Future of the People's Liberation Army," in Paul Beaver, ed., *China in Crisis: The Role of the Military*, London: Jane's Information Group, 1989, p. 38. Of course, death from friendly fire is not uncommon in warfare.

103. *Preliminary Findings*, pp. 8–9, 14–15.

104. According to a Martial Law Enforcement Command bulletin of June 4, "More than 500 army trucks were torched." See *The Tiananmen Papers*, p. 384. See also *Financial Times*, June 6, 1989, p. 6.

105. *Pai Hsing*, November 16, 1989, in FBIS-CHI, November 28, 1989, pp. 30–1.

106. See, for example, the excerpt from a Martial Law Enforcement Command bulletin of June 3 in *The Tiananmen Papers*, pp. 372–3. "Li Peng Interview," p. 26; Chi's statement in *USN&WR*, March 12, 1990, p. 54.

107. Cited in *SCMP*, July 19, 1991, p. 11.

108. Li Peng stated at a Politburo Standing Committee meeting on June 6 that "about 200" civilians and a total of thirty-six PLA and PAP troops died. He also said that more than two thousand civilians and five thousand PLA troops were injured. *The Tiananmen Papers*, p. 421. Li Ximing told a Politburo meeting on June 9 that 218 civilians and twenty-three PLA soldiers had died, and about two thousand civilians and five thousand PLA were injured. *The Tiananmen Papers*, p. 436. Chen Xitong stated that two hundred died and three thousand were injured. See "Mayor's Address," p. 944. Yuan Mu reported three hundred deaths. See "State Council Spokesman," p. 5. Kristof estimates as many as one thousand people died. See *NYT*, June 3, 1990, p. 20. Amnesty International estimated that up to one thousand people died. See *Preliminary Findings*, p. 22.

109. For Li Peng's remarks, see *WP*, July 7, 1989, pp. A1, A27; for those by Chi and Tao, see *USN&WR*, March 12, 1990, p. 54.

110. See, for example, the Ministry of State Security intelligence report excerpted in *The Tiananmen Papers*, p. 374; *Preliminary Findings*, pp. 6, 19; and *WP*, June 4, 1989, pp. A1, A34.

111. Personal communication, Mr. Harry Wells.

112. At least one shipment was seized in Hong Kong en route to China. *HKS*, May 25, 1989, in FBIS-CHI, May 25, 1989, p. 67.

113. *Beijing Review*, June 25–July 1, 1990, p. 13.

114. Central News Agency (Taipei), March 9, 1990, in FBIS-CHI, March 14, 1990, p. 22; *Wen Wei Po*, March 17, 1990, in FBIS-CHI, March 20, 1990, p. 33.

115. *Pai Hsing*, November 16, 1989, in FBIS-CHI, November 22, 1989, p. 21.

116. "Deng's Speech," p. 725.

117. *NYT*, August 28, 1991, p. A10.

118. William E. Odom, *The Collapse of the Soviet Military*, New Haven, CT: Yale University Press, 1998, Chapter 14.

119. Jencks, "The Military in China," p. 293.

120. See, for example, *Jiefangjun Bao*, February 8, 1990, in FBIS-CHI, March 2, 1990, pp. 23–5.

121. November 16, 1989, *China Daily* report, cited in Byrnes, "The Death of a People's Army," p. 147; *Tang Tai* (Hong Kong), May 12, 1990, in FBIS-CHI, May 18, 1990, pp. 16–17.

122. *NYT*, October 29, 1989, "Week in Review" section, p. 2.

123. *Cheng Ming*, December 1, 1989, in FBIS-CHI, December 7, 1989, p. 56.

124. *USN&WR*, March 12, 1990, p. 54.

125. Xinhua News Agency, November 29, 1989, in FBIS-CHI, November 30, 1989, p. 26; *Cheng Ming*, March 2, 1990, in FBIS-CHI, March 2, 1990, p. 10.

126. *Cheng Ming*, October 1, 1990, in FBIS-CHI, October 5, 1990, p. 14.

127. *NYT*, June 14, 1989, p. A17.

128. *Tang Tai*, January 6, 1990, in FBIS-CHI, January 9, 1990, p. 2.

129. Dr. Huan Guocang, personal communication.

130. *Cheng Ming*, January 1, 1990, in FBIS-CHI, January 2, 1990, pp. 22–3.

131. Dreyer, "Power Struggle of 1989," p. 46.

132. This also seems to be the conclusion of Liu. See "Aspects of Beijing's Crisis Management."

CHAPTER 8. SHOW OF FORCE: THE 1995–1996 TAIWAN STRAIT CRISIS

1. For some studies of the crisis, see John W. Garver, *Face Off: China, the United States, and Taiwan's Democratization*, Seattle, WA: University of Washington Press, 1997; You Ji, "Making Sense of War Games in the Taiwan Strait," *Journal of Contemporary China* 6 (1997):287–305; Suisheng Zhao, ed., *Across the Taiwan Strait: Mainland China, Taiwan, and the 1995–1996 Crisis*, New York: Routledge, 1999; Patrick Tyler, *A Great Wall: Six Presidents and China*, New York: Public Affairs, 1999, pp. 19–43; Andrew Scobell, "Show of Force: Chinese Soldiers, Statesmen and the 1995–1996 Taiwan Strait Crisis," *Political Science Quarterly* 115 (Summer 2000):227–46; Robert S. Ross, "The 1995–96 Taiwan Strait Confrontation: Coercion, Credibility, and the Use of Force," *International Security* 25 (Fall 2000):87–123.

2. See, for example, Michael Laris and Steven Mufson, "China Mulls Use of Force off Taiwan, Experts Say," *Washington Post*, August 13, 1999.

3. Andrew Nien-Dzu Yang, "Crisis, What Crisis? – Lessons of the 1996 Tension and the ROC View of Security in the Taiwan Strait," in Jonathan D. Pollack and Richard H. Yang, eds., *In China's Shadow: Regional Perspectives on Chinese Foreign Policy and Military Development*, Santa Monica, CA: RAND, 1998, pp. 143–53.

4. See the summary of the study's findings cited in *Defense News*, August 26–September 1, 1996, p. 8.

5. Allen S. Whiting, "Chinese Foreign Policy: Retrospect and Prospect," in Samuel S. Kim, ed., *China and the World: Chinese Foreign Policy Faces the New Millennium*, Boulder, CO: Westview Press, 1998, pp. 289–92. See also Chong-Pin Lin, "The Military Balance in the Taiwan Strait," *China Quarterly* 146 (June 1996):577–95; Richard Bernstein and Ross H. Munro, *The Coming Conflict with China*, New York: Alfred A. Knopf, 1997, pp. 19, 186.

6. Fan Zhenjiang, "China's Defense Policy into the Twenty-First Century," *Guofang Daxue xuebao* [National Defense University Journal] 1 (March 10, 1997):6. Another military researcher highlights Taiwan as an area of serious conflict potential. See Lt. Gen. Mi Zhenyu, "China's Strategic Guiding Principle of Active Defense," in Shi Bike, ed., *Zhongguo daqushi* [Megatrends China], Beijing: Hualing Chubanshe, 1996, pp. 58–9. According to an influential civilian academic, Taiwan is "East Asia's greatest potential hot spot." See Zheng Wenmu, "The Main Points of China's International Political [situation] in the Twenty-First Century," in ibid., p. 46. Taiwan is also a central scenario for China's military forecasters and planners as the next war. See, for example, Xiao Bing and Qing Bo, *Zhongguo jundui neng fou da ying xia yi chang zhanzheng* [Will China's army win the next war?], Chongqing: Xinan Shifan Daxue Chubanshe, 1993, Chapter 3. See also the analysis and excerpts translated in Ross H. Munro, "Eavesdropping on the Chinese Military: Where It Expects War – Where It Doesn't," *Orbis* 38 (Summer 1994):355–72.

7. According to one group of military researchers, "After the end of the Cold War Taiwan has been increasingly used by the United States as an extremely important chess piece to contain China." See *Zhongmei guanxi de fazhan bianhua ji qi qushi* [Changing developments and trends in China–U.S. relations], chief ed. Zhu Chenghu, Nanjing: Jiangsu Renmin Chubanshe, 1998, p. 194. Taiwan of course has always been a central issue in U.S.–China relations. "The greatest obstacle to the normalization of relations between the two countries was the Taiwan question." See Zi Zhongyun, "Foreword," in *Mei-Tai guanxi sishi nian, 1949–1989* [Forty years of U.S.–Taiwan relations], Beijing: Renmin Chubanshe, 1991, p. 1.

8. See Willy Wo-Lap Lam, "Urgent US Action Needed to Soothe Beijing and Prevent Collapse of Ties," and Matthew Miller, "Belgrade Bombing: Marchers Try to Break Down Consulate Door," both in *South China Morning Post*, May 10, 1999. For an excellent overview of U.S.–China relations since 1989, see David M. Lampton, *Same Bed, Different Dreams: Managing U.S.–China Relations, 1989–2000*, Berkeley and Los Angeles, CA: University of California Press, 2001.

9. Li Jijun, "This Century's Strategic Heritage and Next Century's Strategic Trend," *Jiefangjun Bao*, July 28, 1998, in Foreign Broadcast Information Service, *Daily Report: China* (hereafter FBIS-CHI), July 28, 1998.

10. See, for example, "Taiwan Independence Means War," *Jiefangjun Bao*, March 6, 2000.

11. Lu Ning, *The Dynamics of Foreign-Policy Decisionmaking in China*, Boulder, CO: Westview Press, 1997, p. 9.

12. "Document Cites Deng Remarks on Taiwan Blockade," *Hong Kong Standard*, February 13, 1996, cited in FBIS-CHI, February 13, 1996, p. 11.

13. Garver, *Face Off*, p. 59. See also Li Qiqing, "Deng Meets Chen; They Reach 8 Point Understanding," *Cheng Ming*, September 1, 1994, in FBIS-CHI, September 6, 1994, pp. 37–8.

14. See, for example, Shu Guang Zhang, *Deterrence and Strategic Culture: Chinese and American Confrontations, 1949–1958*, Ithaca, NY: Cornell University Press, 1992, pp. 73–8.

15. On this dynamic, see Ralph N. Clough, *Reaching across the Taiwan Strait: People to People Diplomacy*, Boulder, CO: Westview Press, 1993.

16. Andrew Scobell, "Taiwan as Macedonia?: Strait Tensions as a Syndrome," *Studies in Conflict and Terrorism* XXI (April–June 1998):194–9.

17. "Yang Shangkun's Speech," *Renmin Ribao*, October 10, 1991, in FBIS-CHI, October 15, 1991, p. 33.

18. This parallel is noted by Whiting. See "Chinese Nationalism and Foreign Policy after Deng," *China Quarterly* 142 (June 1995):303.

19. On this case specifically and the PLA influence more generally, see John W. Garver, "The PLA as an Interest Group in Chinese Foreign Policy," in C. Dennison Lane, Mark Weisenbloom, and Dimon Liu eds., *Chinese Military Modernization*, New York and Washington, DC: Kegan Paul International and AEI Press, 1996, pp. 246–81; Whiting, "Chinese Nationalism and Foreign Policy after Deng."

20. See Garver, *Face Off*, p. 58. See also Lo Ping, "Notes on a Northern Journey: CPC Military Attacks the MFA," *Cheng Ming*, July 1, 1994, in FBIS-CHI, July 26, 1994, pp. 14–15.

21. Whiting, "Chinese Nationalism and Foreign Policy after Deng," p. 314.

22. Garver, *Face Off*, pp. 52–9.

23. "Jiang Zemin's Eight Point Proposal," Beijing Xinhua Domestic, January 30, 1995, in FBIS-CHI, January 30, 1995, pp. 85–6.

24. For the background and significance of the TALSG, see Michael D. Swaine, "Chinese Decision-Making Regarding Taiwan, 1979–2000," in David M. Lampton, ed., *The Making of Chinese Foreign and Security Policy in the Era of Reform, 1978–2000*, Stanford, CA: Stanford University, 2001, pp. 289–336.

25. Ting Chen-wu, "Hawks Dominate China's Policy toward Taiwan," *Hsin Pao*, March 14, 1996, in FBIS-CHI, March 21, 1996, pp. 12–13. The policy change had to be endorsed by the Politburo and the overall military response was determined by the CMC. Jiang made a self-criticism at a June meeting of the Central Military Commission, taking responsibility for mistakes in Beijing's policy toward Taiwan. David Shambaugh, "China's Commander-in-Chief: Jiang Zemin and the PLA," in Lane et al. eds., *China's Military Modernization*, p. 210.

26. See the special section of *China Journal* 36 (July 1996). For a critique of these explanations, see Scobell, "Taiwan as Macedonia?" pp. 183–4.

27. For one of the best articulations of this interpretation, see Mel Gurtov and Byong-Moo Hwang, *China's Security: The New Roles of the Military*, Boulder, CO: Lynne

Rienner, 1998, pp. 274–9. The authors argue that both points are relevant. That is, firstly, the military became outraged and took the initiative in pressing for a harsh response, and then a general consensus among all top leaders emerged that a tough military response was required.

28. You Ji, an academic based in Australia, and several perceptive analysts this author spoke with on Taiwan and in China in 1998, posit such an interpretation. See You, "Making Sense of War Games"; this author's interviews in Beijing, Shanghai, and Taipei, May–June 1998.

29. See the revised edition of the classic study originally published in 1977 by Harvard University Press: Richard K. Betts, *Soldiers, Statesmen, and Cold War Crises*, 2nd ed., New York: Columbia University Press, 1991.

30. Michael D. Swaine, *The Role of the Chinese Military in National Security Policy-making*, Santa Monica, CA: RAND, 1996, pp. 11–14; June Teufel Dreyer, "The Military's Uncertain Politics," *Current History* 95 (September 1996):258–9.

31. Swaine, "Chinese Decision-Making Regarding Taiwan, 1979–2000," pp. 319–27. On the military calling all the shots in March 1996, see, for example, Willy WoLap Lam, "'Hardline Generals' Takeover the Taiwan Affairs Office," *South China Morning Post*, March 12, 1996, in FBIS-CHI, March 13, 1996; Lam, "'Relentless Expansion' of Army Power Viewed," *South China Morning Post*, March 20, 1996, in FBIS-CHI, March 21, 1996. It should be noted that I am challenging not the reliability of accounts of specific incidents but rather the sensationalistic interpretation of their overall significance. On allegations of deep differences of opinion over the show of force in the Taiwan Strait in March 1996, see Thomas J. Christensen, "Chinese Realpolitik," *Foreign Affairs* 75 (September/October 1996):47.

32. Leng Mou, "CPC to Conduct Missile Tests in Taiwan Strait: Jiang, Li, Qiao Sternly Warn against Taiwan Independence," *Kuang Chiao Ching* (Hong Kong), November 1, 1995, in FBIS-CHI, November 29, 1995, p. 94. On the consensus of opinion on this approach generally, see You, "Making Sense of Wargames"; Gurtov and Hwang, *China's Security*.

33. The Hong Kong newspaper *Hsin Pao* is particularly well connected to the PLA. Garver, *Face Off*, p. 171, n. 17. On the utility and reliability of Hong Kong media reports on the PLA in the crisis, see ibid., pp. 109, 171, n. 15.

34. Alexander George, "The Development of Doctrine and Strategy," in Alexander George, David K. Hall, and William E. Simons, *The Limits of Coercive Diplomacy: Laos, Cuba, and Vietnam*, Boston, MA: Little, Brown and Company, 1971, p. 18.

35. Thomas A. Fabyanic, "The Grammar and Logic of Conflict: Differing Conceptions of Statesmen and Soldiers," *Air University Review* 32 (March–April 1981): 23–31.

36. George, "The Development of Doctrine and Strategy," p. 18.

37. *New York Times*, July 29, 1995.

38. See, for example, Li Jiaquan, "Where Are the Chinese People's Feelings?" *Renmin ribao* [People's Daily], June 17, 1994. I am grateful to Ramon Myers for bringing this article to my attention.

39. Willy Wo-Lap Lam, "'Covert Independence Movement' Justifies Invasion," *South China Morning Post*, November 28, 1995, in FBIS-CHI, November 29, 1995, pp. 92–3.

40. "The One China Principle and the Taiwan Issue," Xinhua in English, February 21, 2000, in FBIS-CHI, February 21, 2000.

41. You, "Making Sense of War Games," p. 301.
42. For an account of Liu Huaqiu's meetings with U.S. officials in January 1996, see Barton Gellman, "U.S. and China Nearly Came to Blows in 1996," *Washington Post*, June 21, 1998. On Liu Huaqiu's power and influence in Beijing's foreign policy establishment, see Swaine, *The Role of the Military*, pp. 25–6.
43. Jen Hui-wen, "CPC Specially Sets Up Headquarters to Plan Military Exercises Targeting Taiwan," *Hsin Pao*, December 22, 1995, cited in FBIS, January 2, 1996, p. 37; Lam, "'Covert Independence Movement' Justifies Invasion," p. 93.
44. Swaine, "Chinese Decision-Making Regarding Taiwan," p. 323.
45. Garver, *Face Off*, pp. 85–6.
46. See also the analysis of Garver, *Face Off*, Chapter 10. As Robert Sutter of the Congressional Research Service put it in March 1996, "We went seven months with China in the Taiwan Strait area acting as if we didn't care." Cited in Julian Baum and Matt Forney, "Cross Purposes," *Far Eastern Economic Review*, March 21, 1996, p. 14.
47. This is not to say these moves were completely without risk of escalation into actual war. As Garver soberly points out, "This situation [the crisis] could have led to a war that neither side initially wanted or intended." *Face Off*, p. 110.
48. Jen Hui-wen, "Communist China Meticulously Plans Simulated Offensive Exercises Targeted at Taiwan," *Hsin Pao* (Hong Kong), December 1, 1995, in FBIS-CHI, December 20, 1995.
49. You Ji and Garver also make this point. See, respectively, "Making Sense of War Games," pp. 300–1; *Face Off*, p. 63. On the nuclear coercion dimension of this, see *Face Off*, p. 132.
50. Richard D. Fisher, Jr., "China's Missiles over the Taiwan Strait: A Political and Military Assessment," in James R. Lilley and Chuck Downs, eds., *Crisis in the Taiwan Strait*, Washington, DC: National Defense University Press, 1997, p. 174.
51. Swaine, "Chinese Decision-Making Regarding Taiwan, 1979–2000," p. 326.
52. Speech to participants in the March 1996 military exercises, quoted in *Ta Kung Pao*, March 27, 1996, cited by You, "Making Sense of War Games," p. 301.
53. Interviews in Beijing and Shanghai, May–June 1998. On the emergence of a more moderate and flexible line on Taiwan, see Bruce Gilley and Julian Baum, "What's in a Name?: For China, an Offer It Thinks Taiwan Can't Refuse," *Far Eastern Economic Review*, May 7, 1998, pp. 26–7.
54. See, for example, Nan Li, "The PLA's Evolving Warfighting Doctrine, Strategy, and Tactics, 1985–1995: A Chinese Perspective," *China Quarterly* 146 (June 1996), and the insights, in late 1998, of a "recently retired senior PRC leader" responsible for China's Taiwan policy. See Robert Sutter, "Taiwan–Mainland China Talks: Competing Approaches and Implications for U.S. Policy," report for Congress, Washington, DC: Congressional Research Service, 1998, p. 3.
55. For some significant exceptions, see Allen S. Whiting, "The PLA and China's Threat Perceptions," *China Quarterly* 146 (June 1996):606–7; and Garver, *Face Off*, p. 51.
56. This is also noted by Christensen, "Chinese Realpolitik," pp. 46–7.
57. Interviews in Beijing and Shanghai, May–June 1998. See also Matt Forney, Sebastian Moffett, and Gary Silverman, "Ghosts of the Past," *Far Eastern Economic*

Review, October 10, 1996, p. 24. Beijing was also concerned about domestic protests getting out of control.

58. Graham T. Allison, *Essence of Decision: Explaining the Cuban Missile Crisis,* Boston, MA: Little, Brown and Company, 1971, Chapter 6.

59. Lu, *The Dynamics of Foreign-Policy Decisionmaking,* pp. 123–4.

60. Junshi Kexueyuan Junshi Lishi Yanjiubu, ed., *Zhongguo Renmin Jiefang Jun liushinian dashiji (1927–1987)* [Chinese People's Liberation Army: Sixty year record of major events (1927–1987)], Beijing: Juneshi Kexue Chubanshe, 1988, p. 689.

61. Ting, "Hawks Dominate China's Policy toward Taiwan," pp. 12–13. See also Lam, "'Covert Independence Movement,'" pp. 92–3.

62. *Ta Kung Pao,* September 4, 1995, cited in FBIS-CHI, September 7, 1995, p. 32.

63. See, for example, Garver, "The PLA as an Interest Group in Chinese Foreign Policy," pp. 259–72.

64. Ambassador Chas Freeman, "Did China Threaten to Bomb Los Angeles?" *Proliferation Brief* 4 (March 22, 2001), available at www.ceip.org/files/publications/proliferationbrief404.asp? from=pubtype; Allen S. Whiting, "China's Use of Force, 1950–1996, and Taiwan," *International Security* 26 (Fall 2001):129–30; Patrick E. Tyler, "As China Threatens Taiwan, It Makes Sure the U.S. Listens," *New York Times,* January 24, 1996. See also Gellman, "U.S. and China Nearly Came to Blows." In each source, the quote is worded slightly differently. I have used the version that appears in the article authored by Freeman. While Freeman has refused to reveal his source, the U.S. intelligence community has concluded it was Xiong who made this incendiary remark. See Gellman, "U.S. and China Nearly Came to Blows." Freeman insists the comment was not made as a threat. Was Xiong speaking strictly as an individual, or did his bombastic choice of words reflect high-level thinking? Garver thinks the latter is true; either this was approved by the Politburo or the CMC. *Face Off,* p. 129. Assistant Secretary of State Winston Lord argued the former. Lord told CNN that the rhetoric was "not official" and represented "psychological warfare." *Face Off,* p. 131.

65. Tyler, "As China Threatens Taiwan."

66. Interviews in Beijing and Shanghai, May–June 1998.

67. On this belief among generals and other officials, see Lam, "Urgent US Action Needed to Soothe Beijing." On this belief within Chinese society, see Miller, "Marchers Try to Break Down Consulate Door."

68. Christensen, "Chinese Realpolitik," p. 47.

69. The highest approval rating was for "implementing family planning"; 77 percent of the respondents said the government was doing a "good" or "very good" job of this (this rose to 96 percent if the category of "fair" was included). In comparison, the percentages of the sample agreeing that the government did a good or very good job of "providing welfare to the needy" and "maintaining societal order" were 23 percent and 22 percent respectively. Yang Zhong, Jie Chen, and John M. Scheb II, "Political Views from Below: A Survey of Beijing Residents," *PS: Political Science and Politics* XXX (September 1997):479. There is no way to determine how much the strong approval rating on defense policy was influenced by Beijing's handling of the Strait crisis.

70. Lam, "'Relentless Expansion' of Army Power Viewed."

71. You, "Making Sense of War Games," p. 295.
72. This point is also made by Fisher. See "China's Missiles over the Taiwan Strait," p. 174.
73. Lam, "'Relentless Expansion' of Army Power Viewed."
74. "Chinese Military Has Strong Desire to Attack Taiwan, Grass Roots Soldiers Also Send Petitions Asking for Battle Assignments," *Tungfang Jihpao* (Hong Kong), January 3, 1996, in FBIS-CHI, January 8, 1996.
75. This point is also made by Garver. See *Face Off*, p. 51.
76. Interviews in Taipei, May 1998.
77. Swaine, "China's Decision-Making Regarding Taiwan," pp. 326–7. For a more circumspect evaluation of China's performance, see Garver, *Face Off*, Chapter 14. Although Garver does not consider this case a major success of coercive diplomacy, significantly, he does conclude that the brinkmanship was seen as a major victory in Beijing's eyes. *Face Off*, p. 156.
78. Interviews in Taipei, May 1998.
79. I am grateful to Ramon Myers for suggesting this latter point to me. If this point has validity – and I believe it does – it begs the question of why earlier instances of coercive diplomacy by Beijing in the Taiwan Strait were not more successful. Several factors seem important in explaining the different outcomes of the earlier cases, including the fact that in the 1950s China's "stick" was not big enough and there was no obvious "carrot" for Taiwan. In short, forty years ago Beijing was neither adept at or capable of practicing the diplomatic and military dimensions of effective coercive diplomacy.
80. Tai Ming Cheung, "Chinese Military Preparations against Taiwan over the Next 10 Years," in Lilley and Downs, eds., *Crisis in the Taiwan Strait*, p. 52.
81. James Q. Wilson, *Bureaucracy: What Government Agencies Do and Why They Do It*, New York: Basic Books, 1989, pp. 5–6, 14–18. Wilson's case in point is the German military and its preparations to attack France at the outset of World War II. I am grateful to Karl Eikenberry for drawing my attention to Wilson's insights.
82. Cheung, "Chinese Military Preparations against Taiwan," p. 60.
83. See, for example, Mi, "China's Strategic Guiding Principle of Active Defense," pp. 53–4. See also Li, "The PLA's Evolving Warfighting Doctrine."
84. Fisher, "China's Missiles over the Taiwan Strait," pp. 186–7; Cheung, "Chinese Military Preparations against Taiwan," pp. 55, 60; Eric McVadon, "PRC Exercises, Doctrine, and Tactics toward Taiwan: The Naval Dimension," in Lilley and Downs, eds., *Crisis in the Taiwan Strait.*, pp. 269–72. See also Bruce Gilley, "Operation Mind Games," *Far Eastern Economic Review*, May 28, 1998, pp. 31–2; Julian Baum, "Defense Dilemma," *Far Eastern Economic Review*, May 28, 1998, p. 33. See also Mark A. Stokes, *China's Strategic Modernization: Implications for the United States*, Carlisle Barracks, PA: U.S. Army War College, September 1999, pp. 136–40. At least one analyst anticipated this kind of use of missiles by Beijing. See Chong-Pin Lin, "The Role of the People's Liberation Army in the Process of Reunification: Exploring the Possibilities," in Richard H. Yang, chief editor, *China's Military: The PLA in 1992/1993*, Boulder, CO: Westview Press, 1993, p. 170.
85. McVadon, "PRC Exercises, Doctrine, and Tactics," pp. 249–76.
86. On these issues, see Harlan W. Jencks, "Wild Speculations on the Military Balance in the Taiwan Strait," and Kenneth W. Allen, "PLAAF Modernization: An

Assessment," both in Lilley and Downs, eds., *Crisis in the Taiwan Strait*, pp. 131–65, 217–47.

87. For some studies that focus on the invasion scenario, see David A. Shlapak, David T. Orletsky, and Barry A. Wilson, *Dire Strait?: Military Aspects of the China–Taiwan Confrontation and Options for U.S. Policy*, Santa Monica, CA: RAND, 2000; Michael O'Hanlon, "Why China Cannot Conquer Taiwan," *International Security* 25 (Fall 2000):51–86. See also Michael O'Hanlon and Bates Gill, "China's Hollow Military," *National Interest* 56 (Summer 1999):58–9.

88. Tyler, "As China Threatens Taiwan."

89. I am indebted to Harry Rowen for making this important point about the threat posed by conventional missiles.

90. For some discussion of this possibility, see Jencks, "Wild Speculations," pp. 151–4.

91. For a fascinating account and analysis of China's missile program, see John Wilson Lewis and Hua Di, "China's Ballistic Missile Programs: Technologies, Strategies, Goals," *International Security* 17 (Fall 1992):4–40. On the DF-15, see pp. 34–26, and Table 1 on p. 11.

92. Quoted in Richard K. Betts and Thomas J. Christensen, "China: Getting the Questions Right," *National Interest* 62 (Winter 2000/01):19; Fisher, "China's Missiles over the Taiwan Strait," pp. 167, 200.

93. Alastair Iain Johnston, "China's New 'Old Thinking': The Concept of Limited Deterrence," *International Security* 20 (Winter 1995–6):5–42. For a further analysis of the nuclear dimension of the latest Taiwan Strait crisis, see Garver, *Face Off*, Chapter 12.

94. Warren Christopher, *In the Stream of History: Shaping Foreign Policy for a New Era*, Stanford, CA: Stanford University Press, 1998, p. 427.

CHAPTER 9. CONCLUSION: EXPLAINING CHINA'S USE OF FORCE

1. For a recent comprehensive analysis, see Allen S. Whiting, "China's Use of Force, 1950–96, and Taiwan," *International Security* 26 (Fall 2001):103–31. For Korea, the 1979 Vietnam conflict, and the latest Taiwan Strait Crisis, see the relevant chapters of this book. On the earlier Strait crises, see Thomas E. Stolper, *China, Taiwan, and the Offshore Islands*, Armonk, NY: M. E. Sharpe, 1985; Shu Guang Zhang, *Deterrence and Strategic Culture: Chinese and American Confrontations, 1948–1958*, Ithaca, NY: Cornell University Press, 1992; on India and Indochina in the 1960s and early 1970s, see Allen S. Whiting, *The Chinese Calculus of Deterrence: India and Indochina*, Ann Arbor, MI: University of Michigan Press, 1975; on Vietnam in 1974 and 1988, see Quansheng Zhao, *Interpreting China's Foreign Policy: The Micro–Macro Linkage Approach*, New York: Oxford University Press, 1996, pp. 42–6; on the USSR in 1969, see Thomas Robinson, "China Confronts the Soviet Union: Warfare and Diplomacy on China's Inner Asian Frontiers," in Roderick MacFarquhar and John K. Fairbank, eds., *Cambridge History of China*, Vol. 15: *The People's Republic*, Part 2: *Revolutions within the Chinese Revolution 1966–1982*, New York: Cambridge University Press, 1991, pp. 218–301; on the 1995 clashes with the Philippines, see, for example, Marichu Villanueva, "Senators Fear 'Full-Blown' War over Spratlys," *Manila Standard*, February 18, 1995. See also Rigoberto Tiglao, Andrew Sherry, Nate Thayer, and Michael Vatikiotis, "'Tis

the season," *Far Eastern Economic Review*, December 24, 1998, pp. 18–20. Manila continues to take this last case extremely seriously.

2. See, for example, Whiting, *The Chinese Calculus of Deterrence*; Gerald Segal, *Defending China*, New York: Oxford University Press, 1995; Melvin Gurtov and Byung-Moo Hwang, *China under Threat*, Baltimore, MD: Johns Hopkins University Press, 1980.

3. Whiting, "China's Use of Force, 1950–96, and Taiwan," p. 130.

4. Michael D. Swaine, *The Role of the Chinese Military in National Security Policymaking*, Santa Monica, CA: RAND, 1996; Ross Munro and Richard Bernstein, *The Coming Conflict with China*, New York: Alfred A. Knopf, 1997.

5. Michael Pillsbury, ed., *China Debates the Future Security Environment*, Washington, DC: National Defense University Press, 2000; Andrew Scobell, "Playing to Win: Chinese Army Building in the Era of Jiang Zemin," *Asian Perspective* 25 (2001):73–105.

6. On Taiwan, see Segal, *Defending China*, p. 134; on India, see ibid., pp. 153–4; Gurtov and Hwang, *China under Threat*, pp. 169–70.

7. For an analysis of what the crisis reveals about civil-military interactions in China, see James Mulvenon, "Civil-Military Relations and the EP-3 Crisis: A Content Analysis," *China Leadership Monitor* 1 (Winter 2002) available at: www.chinaleadershipmonitor.org/20011/20011JM1.html

8. See Betts, *Soldiers, Statesmen, and Cold War Crises*, 2nd ed., New York: Columbia University Press, 1991. This pattern has also been found in some but not all other countries. See Jong Sun Lee, "Attitudes of Civilian and Military Leaders towards War Initiation: Application of Richard Betts' Analysis of American Cases to Other Countries," Ph.D dissertation, Ohio State University, 1991.

9. Paul H. B. Godwin, "Soldiers and Statesmen: Chinese Defense and Foreign Policies in the 1990s," in Samuel S. Kim, ed., *China and the World: New Directions in Chinese Foreign Relations*, 2nd ed., Boulder, CO: Westview Press, 1989, pp. 181–202.

10. Commanders in the air force and, to a lesser extent, those in the navy tend to be less reticent to commit forces to combat than those in the army. Betts, *Soldiers, Statesmen, and Cold War Crises*, pp. 116–42.

11. As of the late 1990s, some three-quarters of PLA manpower was concentrated in the ground forces. See You Ji, *The Armed Forces of China*, London: I.B. Tauris, 1999, pp. 28–9. This assertion and statistic are not meant to suggest for a moment that the PLA Air Force or PLA Navy are inconsequential. On the contrary, they are quite significant. For a recent study of the air service, see Kenneth W. Allen, Glenn Krumel, and Jonathan D. Pollack, *China's Air Force Enters the 21st Century*, Santa Monica, CA: RAND, 1995; for a recent study of the navy, see Bernard D. Cole, *The Great Wall at Sea: China's Navy Enters the Twenty-First Century*, Annapolis, MD: Naval Institute Press, 2001.

12. On China's energetic program of weapons purchases, see Bates Gill and Taeho Kim, *China's Arms Acquisitions from Abroad: A Quest for "Superb and Secret Weapons,"* Oxford, UK: Oxford University Press, 1995.

13. John W. Garver, "China's Push through the South China Sea: The Intersection of Bureaucratic and National Interests," *China Quarterly* 132 (December 1992):999–1028. See also Lu Ning, *The Dynamics of Foreign-Policy Decisionmaking in China*, Boulder, CO: Westview Press, 1997, pp. 124–7.

Bibliography

2000 Zhongguo de guofang [China's national defense 2000], Beijing: Guowuyuan Xinwen Bangongshi, October 2000.

Abrahamsson, Bengt, *Military Professionalization and Political Power*, Beverly Hills, CA: Sage Publications, 1972.

Adelman, Jonathan, and Chih-Yu Shih, *Symbolic War: The Chinese Use of Force, 1840–1980*, Taipei: Institute for International Relations, 1993.

"AFP Highlights General Atmosphere in Beijing, Elsewhere," Paris Agence France Presse in English, February 21, 1979, in Foreign Broadcast Information Service; *Daily Report: China* (hereafter FBIS-CHI), February 22, 1979, p. E2.

Alagappa, Muthiah, "Rethinking Security," in Alagappa, ed., *Asian Security Practice: Material and Ideational Influences*, Stanford, CA: Stanford University Press, 1998.

Allen, Kenneth W., "PLAAF Modernization: An Assessment," in James Lilley and Chuck Downs, eds., *Crisis in the Taiwan Strait*, Washington, DC: National Defense University Press, 1997, pp. 217–47.

Allen, Kenneth W., Glenn Krumel, and Jonathan D. Pollack, *China's Air Force Enters the 21ˢᵗ Century*, Santa Monica, CA: RAND, 1995.

Allison, Graham T., *Essence of Decision: Explaining the Cuban Missile Crisis*, Boston, MA: Little, Brown and Company, 1971.

Almond, Gabriel, and Sidney Verba, *The Civic Culture*, Boston, MA: Little, Brown, 1960.

Amnesty International, *People's Republic of China: Preliminary Findings on the Killings of Unarmed Civilians, Arbitrary Arrests and Summary Executions since June 3, 1989*, New York: Amnesty International Publications, 1989.

Arquilla, John, and Solomon M. Karmel, "Welcome to the Revolution . . . in Chinese Military Affairs," *Defense Analyses* 13 (December 1997):255–70.

Bachman, David, *Chen Yun and the Chinese Political System*, Chinese research monograph no. 29, Berkeley, CA: Institute of East Asian Studies and Center for Chinese Studies, University of California, 1985.

Ball, Desmond, "Strategic Culture in the Asia-Pacific Region," *Security Studies* 3 (Autumn 1993): 44–77.

Barnett, A. Doak, *Uncertain Passage: China's Transition to the Post-Mao Era*, Washington, DC: Brookings Institution Press, 1974.

―――, *The Making of Foreign Policy in China*, Baltimore, MD: Johns Hopkins University Press, 1985.

Bartov, Omer, *Hitler's Army: Soldiers, Nazis, and War in the Third Reich*, New York: Oxford University Press, 1991.

Baum, Julian, "Defense Dilemma," *Far Eastern Economic Review*, May 28, 1998, p. 33.

Baum, Julian, and Matt Forney, "Cross Purposes," *Far Eastern Economic Review*, March 21, 1996, p. 14.

Baum, Richard, "The Cultural Revolution in the Countryside: Anatomy of a Limited Rebellion," in Thomas W. Robinson, ed., *The Cultural Revolution in China*, Berkeley and Los Angeles, CA: University of California Press, 1971, pp. 367–476.

―――, *Burying Mao: Chinese Politics in the Age of Deng Xiaoping*, Princeton, NJ: Princeton University Press, 1994.

Bayley, David H., "The Police and Political Development in Europe," in Charles Tilly, ed., *The Formation of National States in Western Europe*, Princeton, NJ: Princeton University Press, 1975, pp. 328–79.

"Beijing Mayor's Address to NPC Standing Committee on Background to the 4th June Massacre," in "Quarterly Chronicle and Documentation," *China Quarterly* 120 (December 1989):919–46.

Berger, Thomas U., "Norms, Identity, and National Security in Germany and Japan," in Peter J. Katzenstein, ed., *The Culture of National Security: Norms and Identity in World Politics*, New York: Columbia University Press, 1996, pp. 317–56.

Bernstein, Richard, and Ross Munro, *The Coming Conflict with China*, New York: Alfred A. Knopf, 1997.

Betts, Richard K., *Soldiers, Statesmen, and Cold War Crises*, 2nd ed., New York: Columbia University Press, 1991.

Betts, Richard K., and Thomas J. Christensen, "China: Getting the Questions Right," *National Interest* 62 (Winter 2000/01):17–29.

Bi Jianxiang, "The PRC's Active Defense Strategy: New Wars, Old Concepts," *Issues and Studies* 31 (November 1995):59–97.

Blasko, Dennis J., Philip T. Klapakis, and John F. Corbett, Jr., "Training Tomorrow's PLA: A Mixed Bag of Tricks," *China Quarterly* 146 (June 1996):488–524.

Bo Yibo, *Ruogan zhongda juece yu shijian de huigu* [Reflections on certain important decisions and events] Vol. 1, Beijing: Zhonggong Zhongyang Dangxiao Chubanshe, 1991.

Bobrow, Davis B., "Peking's Military Calculus," *World Politics* XVI (1964):287–301.

Bonavia, David, *China's Warlords*, Hong Kong: Oxford University Press, 1995.

Boorman, Howard L., and Scott A. Boorman, "Strategy and National Psychology in China," *The Annals of the American Academy of Social and Political Science* CLXX (1967):143–55.

Boorman, Scott A., *The Protracted Game: The Wei-ch'i Model of Maoist Revolutionary Strategy*, New York: Oxford University Press, 1969.

―――, "Deception in Chinese Strategy," in William W. Whitson, ed., *The Military and Political Power in China in the 1970s*, New York: Praeger, 1972, pp. 313–37.

Boylan, Edward S., "The Chinese Cultural Style of Warfare," *Comparative Strategy* 3 (1982):341–64.

Brandauer, Frederick P., "Violence and Buddhist Idealism in the *Xiyou* Novels," in Jonathan N. Lipman and Stevan Harrell, eds., *Violence in China: Essays in Culture and Counter Culture*, Albany, NY: State University of New York Press, 1989, pp. 115–48.

Brook, Timothy, *Quelling the People: The Military Suppression of the Beijing Democracy Movement*, New York: Oxford University Press, 1992.

Brzezinski, Zbigniew, *Power and Principle: Memoirs of the National Security Advisor, 1977–1981*, New York: Farrar, Straus, and Giroux, 1983.

Builder, Carl H., *The Masks of War: American Military Styles in Strategy and Analysis*, Baltimore, MD: Johns Hopkins University Press, 1989.

Bullard, Monte R., *China's Political–Military Evolution: The Party and the Military in the PRC, 1960–1984*, Boulder, CO: Westview Press, 1985.

Burles, Mark, and Abram N. Shulsky, *Patterns in China's Use of Force: Evidence from History and Doctrinal Writings*, Santa Monica, CA: RAND, 2000.

Burns, John P., "China's Governance: Political Reform in a Turbulent Environment," *China Quarterly* 119 (September 1989):481–518.

Byrnes, Michael T., "The Death of a People's Army," in George Hicks, ed., *The Broken Mirror: China after Tiananmen*, Harlow, Essex, UK: Longman Group, 1990, pp. 132–51.

Chai Chengwen and Zhao Yongtian, *KangMei yuanChao jishi* [Chronicle of the resist America, aid Korea war], Beijing: Zhonggong Dangshi Ziliao Chubanshe, 1987.

———, *Banmendian tanpan* [Panmunjom negotiations], Beijing: Jiefangjun Chubanshe, 1989.

Chan, Steve, "Chinese Conflict Calculus and Behavior: Assessment from a Perspective of Conflict Management," *World Politics* XXX (1978):391–410.

Chanda, Nayan, *Brother Enemy: The War after the War*, New York: Harcourt Brace Jovanovich, 1986.

———, "Fear of the Dragon," *Far Eastern Economic Review*, April 13, 1995.

Chang, Carsun, *The Third Force in China*, New York: Bookman Associates, 1952.

Chang Pao-min, *The Sino–Vietnamese Territorial Dispute*, Washington papers no. 118, New York: Praeger, 1986.

Chen, Jerome, ed., *Mao Papers: Anthology and Bibliography*, New York: Oxford University Press, 1970.

Chen Jian, "China's Changing Aims during the Korean War, 1950–1951," *Journal of American–East Asian Relations* 1 (Spring 1992):8–41.

———, *China's Road to the Korean War*, New York: Columbia University Press, 1994.

———, *Mao's China and the Cold War*, Chapel Hill, NC: University of North Carolina Press, 2001.

Chen, King C., *China's War with Vietnam, 1979: Issues, Decisions, Implications*, Stanford, CA: Hoover Institution Press, 1987.

Chen Yun, *Chen Yun wenxuan, 1949–1956* [Selected works of Chen Yun, 1949–1956], Beijing Renmin Chubanshe, 1982.

Chen Zaidao, *Chen Zaidao huiyilu* [Memoirs of Chen Zaidao], 2 vols., Beijing: Jiefangjun Chubanshe, 1988–91.

Chen Zhou, "Zhongguo xiandai jubu zhanzheng lilun yu Meiguo youxian zhanzheng lilun zhi butong" [Differences between China's theory of modern local war and America's theory of limited war], *Zhongguo Junshi Kexue* (hereafter *ZGJSKX*) 4 (1995):43–7.

Cheng, Dean B., "Unrestricted Warfare," *Small Wars and Insurgencies* 11 (Spring 2000):122–9.

Cheng Hsiao-shih, *Party–Military Relations in Taiwan and the PRC: The Paradoxes of Control*, Boulder, CO: Westview Press, 1990.

Cheng Hsiao-shih, "Chunqiu shiqi de zhengjun guanxi" [politico-military relations in the Spring and Autumn period], Taipei: Academia Sinica, 1994.

Cheng Hsiao-shih, "Zhanguo shiqi zhengzhi junshi guanxi – jiangjun, zhengzhi yu shehui" [Politico–military relations in the Warring States Period – generals, politics, and society], Taipei: manuscript, n.d.

Cheng, S. G., *The Chinese as a Warrior in the Light of History*, paper read before the China Society on January 27, 1916, London: East and West Ltd., n.d.

Cheung, Tai Ming, "Strong Arm of the Law," *Far Eastern Economic Review*, January 17, 1991, p. 17.

———, "China's Entrepreneurial Army: The Structure, Activities, and Economic Returns of the Military Business Complex," in C. Dennison Lane, Mark Weisenbloom, and Dimon Liu, eds., *Chinese Military Modernization*, New York and Washington, DC: Kegan Paul International and AEI Press, 1996, pp. 168–97.

———, "The People's Armed Police: First Line of Defense," *China Quarterly* 146 (June 1996):535–47.

———, "Chinese Military Preparations against Taiwan over the Next 10 Years," in Lilley and Downs, eds., *Crisis in the Taiwan Strait*, 1997.

———, "The Influence of the Gun: China's Central Military Commission and Its Relationship with the Military, Party, and State Decision-Making Systems," in David M. Lampton, ed., *The Making of Chinese Foreign and Security Policy in the Era of Reform*, Stanford, CA: Stanford University Press, 2001, pp. 61–90.

Chi Haotian, "Why We Cracked Down," *U.S. News and World Report*, March 12, 1990, p. 54.

———, "Create a New Situation in Which the Army Is Managed According to Law . . . ," *Jiefangjun Bao*, June 27, 1990, in FBIS-CHI, July 11, 1990, pp. 41–5.

Ch'i, Hsi-sheng, *Warlord Politics in China, 1916–1928*, Stanford, CA: Stanford University Press, 1976.

"China's White Paper on National Defense," Xinhua Beijing Domestic Service, July 27, 1998, in FBIS-CHI, July 28, 1998.

"Chinese Military Has Strong Desire to Attack Taiwan, Grass Roots Soldiers Also Send Petitions Asking for Battle Assignments," *Tungfang Jihpao*, Hong Kong, January 3, 1996, in FBIS-CHI, January 8, 1996, pp. 41–2.

"Chiu-Peng-Lo Chan-pao" [Drag out Peng and Luo combat news] (Canton), no. 3 (February 19, 1968), in *Survey of China Mainland Press* (hereafter *SCMP*), no. 4139 (March 15, 1968):5.

Christensen, Thomas J., "Threats, Assurances, and the Last Chance for Peace: Lessons of Mao's Korean War Telegrams," *International Security* 17 (Summer 1992):22–154.

———, "Chinese Realpolitik," *Foreign Affairs* 75 (September/October 1996):37–52.

———, *Useful Adversaries: Grand Strategy, Domestic Mobilization, and Sino–American Conflict, 1947–1958*, Princeton, NJ: Princeton University Press, 1996.

———, "China, the U.S.–Japan Alliance, and the Security Dilemma in East Asia," *International Security* 23 (Spring 1999):49–80.

_____, "Posing Problems without Catching Up: China's Rise and the Challenges for U.S. Security Policy," *International Security* 25 (Spring 2001):5–40.

Christopher, Warren, *In the Stream of History: Shaping Foreign Policy for a New Era*, Stanford, CA: Stanford University Press, 1998.

Clough, Ralph N., *Reaching across the Taiwan Strait: People to People Diplomacy*, Boulder, CO: Westview Press, 1993.

Cole, Bernard D., *The Great Wall at Sea: China's Navy Enters the Twenty-First Century*, Annapolis, MD: Naval Institute Press, 2001.

Courtois, Stephane et al., *The Black Book of Communism: Crimes, Terror, and Repression*, Cambridge, MA: Harvard University Press, 1999.

Cumings, Bruce, *Origins of the Korean War, Vol. 2: The Roaring of the Cataract: 1947–1950*, Princeton, NJ: Princeton University Press, 1990.

_____, *Parallax Visions: Making Sense of American–East Asia Relations at the End of the Century*, Durham, NC: Duke University Press, 1999.

Dangdai Zhongguo Kongjun Bianjibu, compiler, *Dangdai Zhongguo Kongjun* [The air force of contemporary China], Beijing: Zhongguo Shehui Kexue Chubanshe, 1989.

Dangdai Zhongguo Renwu Zhuanji Congshu Bianjubu, ed., *Xu Xiangqian zhuan* [Biography of Xu Xiangqian], Beijing: Dangdai Zhongguo Chubanshe, 1991.

Dangdai Zhongguo Waijiao Bianji Weiyuanhui, *Dangdai Zhongguo Waijiao* [Foreign relations of contemporary China], Beijing: Zhongguo Shehui Kexue Chubanshe, 1990.

"Decision on Certain Questions of Party History since the Founding of the People's Republic," Xinhua, June 30, 1981, cited in FBIS-CHI, July 1, 1981.

Dellios, Rosita, "'How May the World Be at Peace?': Idealism as Realism in Chinese Strategic Culture," in Valerie M. Hudson, ed., *Culture and Foreign Policy*, Boulder, CO: Lynne Rienner, 1997, pp. 201–30.

"Deng Discusses Asia with Indian Journalists," Paris AFP in English, February 14, 1979, in FBIS-CHI, February 15, 1979, p. A7.

Deng Xiaoping wenxuan (1975–1982) [Selected works of Deng Xiaoping, 1975–1982], Beijing: Renmin Chubanshe, 1983.

"Document Cites Deng Remarks on Taiwan Blockade," *Hong Kong Standard*, February 13, 1996, cited in FBIS-CHI, February 13, 1996, p. 11.

Domes, Jurgen, "The Role of the Military in the Formation of Revolutionary Committees 1967–68," *China Quarterly* 44 (October/December 1970):112–45.

_____, *China after the Cultural Revolution: Politics between Two Party Congresses*, trans. Annette Berg and David Goodman, Berkeley and Los Angeles, CA: University of California Press, 1977.

_____, *The Government and Politics of the PRC: A Time of Transition*, Boulder, CO: Westview Press, 1985.

_____, *Peng Te-huai: The Man and the Image*, Stanford, CA: Stanford University Press, 1985.

Dray-Novey, Alison, "Spatial Order and Police in Imperial Beijing," *Journal of Asian Studies* 52 (November 1993):885–922.

Dreyer, Edward L., "Military Continuities: The PLA and Imperial China," in William W. Whitson, ed., *The Military and Political Power in China in the 1970s*, New York: Praeger, 1972, pp. 3–24.

_____, *China at War, 1901–49*, New York: Longman, 1995.

Dreyer, June Teufel, "Civil-Military Relations in the People's Republic of China," *Comparative Strategy* 5 (1985):27–49.

———, "China after Tiananmen: The Role of the PLA," *World Policy Journal* 4 (Fall 1989):6–17.

———, "The People's Liberation Army and the Power Struggle of 1989," *Problems of Communism* 38 (September–October 1989):41–8.

———, "Deng Xiaoping: The Soldier," *China Quarterly* 135 (September 1993):536–50.

———, *China's Political System: Modernization and Tradition*, 2nd ed., Boston, MA: Allyn and Bacon, 1996.

———, "The Military's Uncertain Politics," *Current History* 95 (September 1996): 254–9.

Eftimiades, Nicholas, *Chinese Intelligence Operations*, Annapolis, MD: Naval Institute Press, 1994.

Eikenberry, Karl D., "Does China Threaten Asia-Pacific Regional Stability?" *Parameters* XXV (Spring 1995):82–103.

Elkins, David J., and Richard E. B. Simeon, "A Cause in Search of Its Effect, Or What Does Political Culture Explain?" *Comparative Politics* 11 (January 1979):127–45.

Elmquist, Paul, "The Internal Role of the Military," in William W. Whitson, ed., *The Military and Political Power in China in the 1970s*, New York: Praeger, 1972, pp. 269–90.

Esherick, Joseph, review of *Cultural Realism* in *Journal of Asian Studies* 56 (August 1997):769–71.

Fabayanic, Thomas A., "The Grammar and Logic of Conflict: Differing Conceptions of Statesmen and Soldiers," *Air University Review* 32 (March–April 1981):23–31.

Fairbank, John K., *The United States and China*, rev. ed., New York: Compass Books, Viking Press, 1962.

———, "Introduction," in Frank A. Kierman, ed., *Chinese Ways in Warfare*, Cambridge, MA: Harvard University Press, 1974, pp. 1–26.

Faison, Seth, "China's Chief Tells Army to Give Up Its Commerce," *New York Times*, July 23, 1998.

Fan Yinhua, "Shi lun Zhongguo xiandai sixiang wenhua de xing chaoji zhanlue qu . . ." [On the form and strategic trend of modern thought culture in China], *ZGJSKX* 38 (1997):21–7.

Fan Zhenjiang, "China's Defense Policy into the Twenty-First Century," *Guofang Daxue xuebao* [National Defense University Journal] 1 (March 10, 1997):3–7, 12.

Feng Jicai, *Voices from the Whirlwind: An Oral History of the Chinese Cultural Revolution*, New York: Random House, 1991.

Fewsmith, Joseph, and Stanley Rosen, "The Domestic Context of Chinese Foreign Policy: Does 'Public Opinion' Matter?" in David M. Lampton, ed., *The Making of Chinese Foreign and Security Policy in the Era of Reform*, Stanford, CA: Stanford University Press, 2001, pp. 151–97.

Finer, S. E., *The Man on Horseback: The Role of the Military in Politics*, rev. ed., Harmondsworth, UK: Penguin Books, 1975.

Fisher, Richard D., Jr., "China's Missiles over the Taiwan Strait: A Political and Military Assessment," in Lilley and Downs, eds., *Crisis in the Taiwan Strait*, pp. 167–216.

Fogelson, Robert M., *Big City Police*, Cambridge, MA: Harvard University Press, 1977.

Forney, Matt, "Man in the Middle," *Far Eastern Economic Review*, March 28, 1996, pp. 14–16.
———, "Patriot Games," *Far Eastern Economic Review*, October 3, 1996, pp. 22–8.
Forney, Matt, Sebastian Moffett, and Gary Silverman, "Ghosts of the Past," *Far Eastern Economic Review*, October 10, 1996, p. 24.
Freedman, Maurice, *Chinese Lineage and Society: Fukien and Kwangtung*, London: Athlone, 1966.
Freeman, Chas, "Did China Threaten to Bomb Los Angeles?" *Proliferation Brief* 4 (March 22, 2001), accessed at http://www.ceip.org/files/publications/proliferationbrief404.asp?from=pubtype.
Fried, Morton H., "Military Status in Chinese Society," *American Journal of Sociology* LXII (January 1952):347–57.
Frolic, B. Michael, *Mao's People: Sixteen Portraits of Life in Revolutionary China*, Cambridge, MA: Harvard University Press, 1980.
Gao Jiquan, "China Holds High Banner of Peace," *Jiefangjun Bao* [Liberation Army Daily], June 27, 1996, in FBIS-CHI, June 27, 1996.
Gao Xin, "'Liu san' zhiye: shui kai qiang?" [The evening of June 3: Who fired?], *Zhongguo zhi chun* [China Spring] 97 (June 1991):6–10.
Gao Yuan, *Born Red: A Chronicle of the Cultural Revolution*, Stanford, CA: Stanford University Press, 1987.
Garside, Roger, *Coming Alive: China after Mao*, New York: Mentor Books, 1982.
Garver, John W., "China's Push through the South China Sea: The Intersection of Bureaucratic and National Interests," *China Quarterly* 132 (December 1992):999–1028.
———, "The PLA as an Interest Group in Chinese Foreign Policy," in C. Dennison Lane, Mark Weisenbloom, and Dimon Liu, eds., *Chinese Military Modernization*, New York and Washington, DC: Kegan Paul International and AEI Press, 1996, pp. 246–81.
———, *Face Off: China, the United States, and Taiwan's Democratization*, Seattle, WA: University of Washington Press, 1997.
———, Review of Zhao Quansheng, *Interpreting China's Foreign Policy*, in *China Journal* 38 (July 1997):211–12.
Gellman, Barton, "U.S. and China Nearly Came to Blows in 1996," *Washington Post*, June 21, 1998.
Geng Biao, *Geng Biao huiyilu* [Memoirs of Geng Biao], Beijing: Jiefangjun Chubanshe, 1991.
George, Alexander L., David K. Hall, and William B. Simons, *The Limits of Coercive Diplomacy*, Boston, MA: Little, Brown, 1971.
Gertz, Bill, *The China Threat: How the People's Republic of China Targets America*, Washington, DC: Regnery, 2000.
Ghosh, S. K., "Deng Xiaoping Steps Down from Military Leadership," *China Report* XVI (March–April 1980):3–4.
Gill, R. Bates, *Chinese Arms Transfers: Purposes, Patterns, and Prospects in the New World Order*, New York: Praeger, 1992.
Gill, Bates, and Taeho Kim, *China's Arms Acquisitions from Abroad: A Quest for "Superb and Secret Weapons,"* Oxford: Oxford University Press, 1995.
Gill, Bates, and Michael O'Hanlon, "China's Hollow Military," *National Interest* 56 (Summer 1999):55–62.

Gilley, Bruce, "Operation Mind Games," *Far Eastern Economic Review*, May 28, 1998, pp. 31–2.

——, *Tiger on the Brink: Jiang Zemin and China's New Elite*, Berkeley and Los Angeles, CA: University of California Press, 1998.

Gilley, Bruce, and Julian Baum, "What's in a Name?: For China, an Offer It Thinks Taiwan Can't Refuse," *Far Eastern Economic Review*, May 7, 1998, pp. 26–7.

Gittings, John, *The World and China, 1922–1972*, New York: Harper and Row, 1974.

Godwin, Paul H. B., "Professionalism and Politics in the Chinese Armed Forces: A Reconceptualization," in Dale R. Herspring and Ivan Volgyes, eds., *Civil-Military Relations in Communist Systems*, Boulder, CO: Westview Press, 1978, pp. 219–40.

——, "People's War Revised: Military Doctrine, Strategy and Operations," in Charles D. Lovejoy, Jr., and Bruce W. Watson, eds., *China's Military Reforms: International and Domestic Implications*, Boulder, CO: Westview Press, 1984, pp. 1–13.

——, "Soldiers and Statesmen in Conflict: Chinese Defense and Foreign Policies in the 1980s," in Samuel S. Kim, ed., *China and the World: Chinese Foreign Policy in the Post-Mao Era*, 1st ed., Boulder, CO: Westview Press, 1984.

——, "Changing Concepts of Doctrine, Strategy, and Operations in the Chinese People's Liberation Army, 1979–1987," *China Quarterly* 112 (December 1987): 572–90.

——, "Soldiers and Statesmen: Chinese Defense and Foreign Policies in the 1990s," in Samuel S. Kim, ed., *China and the World: New Directions in Chinese Foreign Relations*, 2nd ed., Boulder, CO: Westview Press, 1989, pp. 181–202.

——, "Chinese Military Strategy Revised: Local and Limited War," *Annals of the American Academy of Political and Social Science* 519 (January 1992):191–201.

——, "Force and Diplomacy: Chinese Security in the Post–Cold War Era," in Kim, ed., *China and the World*, 3rd ed., Boulder, CO: Westview Press, 1994.

——, "From Continent to Periphery: PLA Doctrine, Strategy and Capabilities toward 2000," *China Quarterly* 146 (June 1996):464–87.

——, "Change and Continuity in Chinese Military Doctrine, 1949–1999," paper presented to "PLA Warfighting Conference," sponsored by Center for Naval Analyses, June 1999, in Washington, DC.

Goldman, Merle, *Sowing the Seeds of Democracy in China: Political Reform in the Deng Xiaoping Era*, Cambridge, MA: Harvard University Press, 1994.

Goncharov, Sergei N., John W. Lewis, and Xue Litai, *Uncertain Partners: Stalin, Mao, and the Korean War*, Stanford, CA: Stanford University Press, 1993.

Griffith, Samuel B., "Introduction," in Sun Tzu, *The Art of War*, trans. Samuel B. Griffith, New York: Oxford University Press, 1963, pp. 1–38.

Guangdong Geming Lishi Bowuguan, compiler, *Huangpu junxiao shiliao* [Historical materials of the Whampoa Academy], n.p.: Guangdong Renmin Chubanshe, 1982.

Guillermaz, Jacques, "The Soldier," in Dick Wilson, ed., *Mao Zedong in the Scales of History*, New York: Cambridge University Press, 1977, pp. 117–43.

Guo Daohu, "Lun juyou Zhongguo tese sixing zhidu" [The distinguishing features of China's institution of the death penalty] in *Mao Zedong sixiang faxue lilun lunwen xuan* [Selected papers on Mao Zedong's thought concerning legal theory], Beijing Falu Chubanshe, 1985, pp. 122–34.

Guomin Geming Zhongyang Junshi Zhengzhi Xuexiao, ed., *Huangpu congshu* [Whampoa materials], n.p.: Guomin Genmingjun Zongsilingbu, Junxuchu, June 1927.

Gurtov, Melvin, and Byung-Moo Hwang, *China under Threat: The Politics of Strategy and Diplomacy*, Baltimore, MD: Johns Hopkins University Press, 1980.

_____, *China's Security: The New Roles of the Military*, Boulder, CO: Lynne Rienner, 1998.

Hamrin, Carol Lee, "Competing 'Policy Packages' in Post-Mao China," *Asian Survey* XXIV (May 1984):487–518.

_____, "Elite Politics and Development of China's Foreign Relations," in Thomas W. Robinson and David Shambaugh, eds., *Chinese Foreign Policy: Theory and Practice*, Oxford, UK: Clarendon Press, 1994, pp. 70–109.

Harding, Harry, Jr., "The Making of Chinese Military Policy," in William W. Whitson, ed., *The Military and Political Power in China in the 1970s*, New York: Praeger, 1972, pp. 361–85.

_____, ed., *China's Foreign Relations in the 1980s*, New Haven, CT: Yale University Press, 1984.

_____, "The Chinese State in Crisis, 1966–1969," *The Cambridge History of China*, Vol. 15, *The People's Republic*, Part 2, *Revolutions within the Chinese Revolution, 1966–1982*, New York: Cambridge University Press, 1991, pp. 107–217.

Harrell, Stevan, "Introduction," in Jonathan N. Lipman and Harrell, eds., *Violence in China: Essays in Culture and Counter Culture*, Albany, NY: State University of New York Press, 1989.

Heinlein, Joseph, "The Ground Forces," in William W. Whitson, ed., *The Military and Political Power in China in the 1970s*, New York: Praeger, 1972, pp. 153–70.

Herman, Robert G., "Identity, Norms, and National Security: The Soviet Foreign Policy Revolution and the End of the Cold War," in Peter J. Katzenstein, ed., *The Culture of National Security: Norms and Identity in World Politics*, New York: Columbia University Press, 1996, pp. 271–316.

Herspring, Dale R., and Ivan Volgyes, *Civil-Military Relations in Communist Systems*, Boulder, CO: Westview Press, 1978.

Hirschman, Albert O., *Exit, Voice, Loyalty: Responses to Decline in Firms, Organizations and States*, Cambridge, MA: Harvard University Press, 1970.

Hong Xuezhi, *KangMei yuanChao zhanzheng huiyi* [Memoirs of the war to resist America and aid Korea], Beijing: Jiefangjun Wenyi Chubanshe, 1990.

Hood, Steven J., *Dragons Entangled: Indo-China and the China–Vietnam War*, Armonk, NY: M. E. Sharpe, 1992.

Hsieh, Alice Langley, *Chinese Strategy in the Nuclear Era*, Englewood Cliffs, NJ: Prentice Hall, 1962.

Hsiung, James Chieh, *Ideology and Practice: The Evolution of Chinese Communism*, New York: Praeger, 1970.

"Hsu Shih-yu's Talk at a Group Discussion at the Third Plenum of the Eleventh CCP Central Committee," *Issues and Studies* XVI (May 1980):78–80.

Hu Changshui, "Zhongyang Junwei 'Batiao mingling' de chansheng" [Formulation of the "Eight Point Order" by the Central Military Commission], *Zhonggong Dangshi Yanjiu* [Research on history of the Chinese Communist Party], no. 6 (1991): 53–9.

Hu Guangzheng, "Yingming de juece, weida de chengguo – lun kangMei yuanChao zhanzheng de chubing canzheng juece" [Brilliant policy decision, great achievements – on the policy decision to dispatch troops to fight the resist America, aid Korea war], *Dangshi yanjiu* 1 (February 1983).

Bibliography

Huan Guocang, "The Events of Tiananmen Square," *Orbis* 33 (Fall 1989):487–500.

Huang Renwei, "Shilun Zhongguo zai shiji zhi jiao guoji huanjing zhongde shenceng ci maodun" [On China's deep contradictions in the international environment at the turn of the century], *Shanghai Shehui Kexueyuan Xueshu Jikan* [Shanghai Academy of Social Sciences Quarterly Journal] 1 (1997): 5–13.

Hunt, Michael H., "Beijing and the Korea Crisis, June 1950–June 1951," *Political Science Quarterly* 107 (1992):453–78.

————, *The Genesis of Chinese Communist Foreign Policy*, New York: Columbia University Press, 1996.

Huntington, Samuel P., *The Soldier and the State: The Theory and Politics of Civil-Military Relations*, Cambridge, MA: Belknap Press, 1957.

————, *Political Order in Changing Societies*, New Haven, CT: Yale University Press, 1968.

————, "The Clash of Civilizations?" *Foreign Affairs* 72 (Summer 1993):22–49.

Im, Kaye Soon, "The Rise and Decline of the Eight Banner Garrisons in the Ch'ing Period (1644–1911): A Study of Kuang-chou, Hang-chou, and Ching-chou Garrisons," Ph.D. dissertation, University of Illinois, 1981.

"Important Talk Given by Comrade Chiang Ch'ing on Sept. 5....," *SCMP* 4069 (November 29, 1967):5.

Janowitz, Morris, *The Professional Soldier: A Social and Political Portrait*, rev. ed., New York: Free Press, 1971.

————, *Sociology and the Military Establishment*, 3rd ed., Beverly Hills, CA: Sage, 1974.

————, *Military Institutions and Coercion in the Developing Nations*, Chicago: University of Chicago Press, 1977.

Jen Hui-wen, "Communist China Meticulously Plans Simulated Offensive Exercises Targeted at Taiwan," *Hsin Pao*, Hong Kong, December 1, 1995, in FBIS-CHI-95–236.

————, "CPC Specially Sets Up Headquarters to Plan Military Exercises Targeting Taiwan," *Hsin Pao*, December 22, 1995, cited in FBIS-CHI, January 2, 1996, p. 37.

Jencks, Harlan, "China's 'Punitive' War on Vietnam," *Asian Survey* 18 (August 1979):801–15.

————, *From Muskets to Missiles: Politics and Professionalism in the Chinese Army, 1945–1981*, Boulder, CO: Westview Press, 1982.

————, "Watching China's Military: A Personal View," *Problems of Communism* XXV (May–June 1986):71–8.

————, "The Chinese People's Liberation Army: 1949–1989," in David S. G. Goodman and Gerald Segal, eds., *China at Forty: A Mid-Life Crisis*, Oxford, UK: Clarendon Press, 1989.

————, "The Military in China," *Current History* 88 (September 1989):265–8, 291–3.

————, "The Losses in Tiananmen Square," *Air Force Magazine* 72 (November 1989): 62–6.

————, "Civil-Military Relations in China: Tiananmen and After," *Problems of Communism* 40 (May–June 1991):14–29.

————, "Wild Speculations on the Military Balance in the Taiwan Strait," in Lilley and Downs, eds., *Crisis in the Taiwan Strait*, pp. 136–66.

Jenner, W. J. F., *The Tyranny of History: The Roots of China's Crisis*, London: Allen Lane, 1992.

Jiang Jiannong, chief ed., *Zhongnanhai sandai lingdao jiti yu gongheguo* [The third generation of collective leadership in Zhongnanhai], Vol. 2, *junshi shilu* [record of military affairs], Beijing: Zhongguo Jingji Chubanshe, 1998.

"Jiang Zemin's Eight Point Proposal," Beijing Xinhua Domestic, January 30, 1995, in FBIS-CHI, January 30, 1995, pp. 85–6.

Jieyan yiri (Jingxuan ben) [A day under martial law – volume of selections], Beijing: Jiefanjun Wenyi Chubanshe, 1990.

Jin Qiu, *The Culture of Power: The Lin Biao Incident and the Cultural Revolution*, Stanford, CA: Stanford University Press, 1999.

Joffe, Ellis, "The Chinese Army in the Cultural Revolution: The Politics of Intervention," *Current Scene* (Hong Kong) VIII (December 7, 1970):1–25.

———, "The Chinese Army after the Cultural Revolution: The Effects of Intervention," *China Quarterly* 55 (July–September 1973):450–77.

———, *The Chinese Army after Mao*, Cambridge, MA: Harvard University Press, 1987.

———, "People's War under Modern Conditions: A Doctrine of Modern War," *China Quarterly* 112 (December 1987):555–71.

Johnson, Chalmers A., *Autopsy on People's War*, Berkeley and Los Angeles, CA: University of California Press, 1973.

Johnston, Alastair Iain, "Party Rectification in the People's Liberation Army, 1983–1987," *China Quarterly* 112 (December 1987):591–630.

———, *Cultural Realism: Strategic Culture and Grand Strategy in Chinese History*, Princeton, NJ: Princeton University Press, 1995.

———, "Thinking about Strategic Culture," *International Security* 19:4 (Spring 1995):32–64.

———, "China's New 'Old Thinking': The Concept of Limited Deterrence," *International Security* 20 (Winter 1995–6):5–42.

———, "Cultural Realism and Strategy in Maoist China," in Peter J. Katzenstein, ed., *The Culture of National Security: Norms and Identity in World Politics*, New York: Columbia University Press, 1996, pp. 216–68.

———, "China's Militarized Interstate Dispute Behavior, 1949–1992: A First Cut at the Data," *China Quarterly* 153 (March 1998):1–30.

Jones, David R., "Soviet Strategic Culture," in Carl G. Jacobsen, ed., *Strategic Culture USA/USSR*, London: St. Martin's Press, 1990, pp. 35–49.

Jordan, Donald A., *The Northern Expedition: China's National Revolution of 1926–1928*, Honolulu, HI: University of Hawaii Press, 1976.

Junshi Kexueyuan Junshi Lishi Yanjiubu, ed., *Zhongguo Renmin Jiefangjun liushinian dashiji (1927–1987)* [Chinese People's Liberation Army – sixty-year record of major events (1927–1987)], Beijing: Junshi Kexue Chubanshe, 1988.

———, *Zhongguo Renmin Jiefangjun de qishi nian* [Seventy years of the Chinese People's Liberation Army], Beijing: Junshi Kexue Chubanshe, 1997.

Kier, Elizabeth, *Imagining War: French and British Military Doctrine between the Wars*, Princeton, NJ: Princeton University Press, 1997.

Kim, Samuel S., "China and the World in Theory and Practice," in Kim, ed., *China and the World: Chinese Foreign Relations in the Post Cold War Era*, 3rd ed., Boulder, CO: Westview Press, 1994.

Kowert, Paul, and Jeffrey Legro, "Norms, Identity, and Their Limits: A Theoretical Reprise," in Peter J. Katzenstein, ed., *The Culture of National Security: Norms and Identity in World Politics*, New York: Columbia University Press, 1996, pp. 451–97.

Kristof, Nicholas D., "China Update: How the Hardliners Won," *New York Times Magazine*, November 12, 1989, pp. 38–41, 66–71.

Kuang Tong-chou, "Premier Promises to Increase Military Funding to Make Up for 'Losses' . . . ," *Sing Tao Jih Pao* (Hong Kong), July 24, 1998, in FBIS-CHI, July 24, 1998.

Lam, Willy Wo-Lap, "'Covert Independence Movement' Justifies Invasion," *South China Morning Post*, November 28, 1995.

———, "'Hardine Generals' Takeover the Taiwan Affairs Office," *South China Morning Post*, March 12, 1996.

———, "'Relentless Expansion' of Army Power Viewed," *South China Morning Post*, March 20, 1996.

———, *The Era of Jiang Zemin*, Singapore: Prentice Hall, 1999.

———, "Urgent US Action Needed to Soothe Beijing and Prevent Collapse of Ties," *South China Morning Post*, May 10, 1999.

Lamley, Harry J., "Lineage Feuding in Southern Fujian and Eastern Guangdong under Qing Rule," in Jonathan V. Lipman and Stevan Harrell, eds., *Violence in China: Essays in Culture and Counter Culture*, Albany, NY: State University of New York Press, 1989, pp. 27–64.

Lampton, David M., *Same Bed, Different Dreams: Managing U.S.–China Relations, 1989–2000*, Berkeley and Los Angeles, CA: University of California Press, 2001.

Landis, Richard B., "Training and Indoctrination at the Whampoa Academy," in F. Gilbert Chan and Thomas H. Etzold, eds., *China in the 1920s: Nationalism and Revolution*, New York: New Viewpoints, 1976, pp. 73–93.

Lary, Diana, *Warlord Soldiers: Chinese Common Soldiers, 1911–1937*, New York: Cambridge University Press, 1985.

Latham, Richard J., "China's Party–Army Relations after June 1989: A Case for Miles' Law?" in Richard H. Yang, Peter Kien-hong Yu, and Andrew N. Yang, eds., *China's Military: The PLA in 1990/1991*, Boulder, CO: Westview Press, 1991.

"Law of the People's Republic of China on National Defense," Beijing Xinhua Domestic Service in Chinese, March 18, 1997, cited in FBIS-CHI, March 24, 1997.

Lee, Hong Yung, *The Politics of the Chinese Cultural Revolution: A Case Study*, Berkeley and Los Angeles, CA: University of California Press, 1978.

Lee, Jong Sun, "Attitudes of Civilian and Military Leaders toward War Initiation: Application of Richard Betts' Analysis of American Cases to Other Countries," Ph.D dissertation, Ohio State University, 1991.

Lee, Wei-Chin, "Iron and Nail: Civil-Military Relations in the People's Republic of China," *Journal of Asian and African Studies* XXVI (1991):132–48.

Lee, Wen Ho, with Helen Zia, *My Country versus Me: The First-Hand Account by the Los Alamos Scientist Who Was Falsely Accused of Being a Spy*, New York: Hyperion Books, 2002.

Legge, James, ed. and trans., *Confucius: The Analects*, Oxford, UK: Clarendon Press, 1893; reprint New York: Dover Publications, 1971.

Lei Bolun (pseud.), *Zhongguo wenhua yu Zhongguo de bing* [Chinese culture and the Chinese soldier], Taipei: Wannianqing, 1972.

Leites, Nathan, *The Operational Code of the Politburo*, New York: McGraw-Hill, 1951.

Leng Mou, "CPC to Conduct Missile Tests in Taiwan Strait: Jiang, Li, Qiao Sternly Warn against Taiwan Independence," *Kuang Chiao Ching*, Hong Kong, November 1, 1995, in FBIS-CHI, November 29, 1995, p. 94.

"Letter from the Central Committee of the Chinese Communist Party to Revolutionary Workers and Staff and Revolutionary Cadres in Industrial and Mining Enterprises Throughout the Country," dated March 18, 1967, *Peking Review* 13 (March 24, 1967): 5–6.

Lewis, John Wilson, and Hua Di, "China's Ballistic Missile Programs: Technologies, Strategies, Goals," *International Security* 17 (Fall 1992):4–40.

Lewis, John Wilson, Hua Di, and Xue Litai, "Beijing's Defense Establishment: Solving the Arms-Export Enigma," *International Security* 15 (Spring 1991):87–109.

Lewis, John Wilson, and Xue Litai, *China Builds the Bomb*, Stanford, CA: Stanford University Press, 1988.

———, *China's Strategic Seapower: The Politics of Force Modernization in the Nuclear Age*, Stanford, CA: Stanford University Press, 1994.

Lewis, Mark Edward, *Sanctioned Violence in Early China*, Albany, NY: State University of New York Press, 1990.

Li Chen, ed., *Zhongguo junshi jiaoyu shi* [A history of military education in China], Taibei: Zhongyang Wenwu Gongyingshe, 1983.

Li Hai-Wen, "How and When Did China Decide to Enter the Korean War?" trans. Chen Jian, *Korea and World Affairs* XVIII (Summer 1994):83–98.

Li Jiaquan, "Where are the Chinese People's Feelings?" *Renmin ribao* [People's Daily], June 17, 1994.

Li Jijun, "Lun junshi zhanlue siwei" [On military strategic thinking], *ZGJSKX* 2, (1996):75–81.

———, "Lun zhanlue wenhua" [On strategic culture], *ZGJSKX* 1 (1997):8–15.

———, "Zhongguo junshi sixiang chuantong yu fangyu zhanlue" [Chinese traditional military thinking and defense strategy], *ZGJSKX* 4 (Winter 1997):62–64.

———, "This Century's Strategic Heritage and Next Century's Strategic Trend," *Jiefangjun Bao*, July 28, 1998, in FBIS-CHI, July 28, 1998.

———, "International Military Strategy and China's Security at the Turn of the Century," *Zhongguo Pinglun* (Hong Kong), August 5, 1998, in FBIS-CHI, August 13, 1998.

Li Ke and Hao Shengzhang, *"Wenhua Dageming" zhong de Renmin Jiefangjun* [The People's Liberation Army during the "Great Cultural Revolution"], Beijing: Zhonggong Danshi Ziliao, 1989.

Li, Nan, "The PLA's Evolving Warfighting Doctrine, Strategy and Tactics, 1985–1995: A Chinese Perspective," *China Quarterly* 146 (June 1996):443–63.

"Li Peng Interview," in *Die Welt* (Hamburg), November 20, 1989, in FBIS-CHI, November 22, 1989.

Li Qiqing, "Deng Meets Chen; They Reach 8 Point Understanding," *Cheng Ming*, September 1, 1994, in FBIS-CHI, September 6, 1994, pp. 37–8.

Li Xiannian wenxuan [Selected works of Li Xiannian], Beijing: Renmin Chubanshe, 1989.

Li Zhisui, *The Private Life of Chairman Mao*, trans. Tai Hung-chao, New York: Random House, 1994.

Liang Heng and Judith Shapiro, *Son of the Revolution*, New York: Vintage Books, 1984.

Lieberthal, Kenneth G., *Governing China*, New York: W. W. Norton, 1995.

_____, "A New China Strategy," *Foreign Affairs* 74 (November/December 1995): 35–49.

Lieberthal, Kenneth G., and Bruce J. Dickson, eds., A *Research Guide to Central Party and Government Meetings in China, 1949–1986*, Armonk, NY: M. E. Sharpe, 1989.

Lieberthal, Kenneth, and Michel Oksenberg, *Policy Making in China: Leaders, Structures, and Processes*, Princeton, NJ: Princeton University Press, 1988.

Lilley, James R., and Chuck Downs, eds., *Crisis in the Taiwan Strait*, Washington, DC: National Defense University Press, 1997.

Lilley, James R., and Carl Ford, "China's Military: A Second Opinion," *National Interest* 57 (Fall 1999):71–7.

Lin, Chong-Pin, *China's Nuclear Weapons Strategy: Tradition within Evolution*, Lexington, MA: Lexington Books, 1988.

_____, "The Extramilitary Roles of the People's Liberation Army: Limits of Professionalization," *Security Studies* 1 (Summer 1992):659–89.

_____, "The Role of the People's Liberation Army in the Process of Reunification: Exploring the Possibilities," in Richard H. Yang, chief ed., *China's Military: The PLA in 1992/1993*, Boulder, CO: Westview Press, 1993.

_____, "The Military Balance in the Taiwan Strait," *China Quarterly* 146 (June 1996):577–95

Lin Qingshan, *Lin Biao Zhuan* [Biography of Lin Biao], 2 vols., Beijing: Zhishi Chubanshe, 1988.

Liu, Alan P. L., "Aspects of Beijing's Crisis Management: The Tiananmen Square Demonstration," *Asian Survey* XXX (May 1990): 505–21.

Liu, F. F., *A Military History of Modern China, 1924–1949*, Princeton, NJ: Princeton University Press, 1956.

"Liu Huaqing on the Stand of the Military towards Taiwan," *Ta Kung Pao* (Hong Kong), September 4, 1995, in FBIS-CHI, September 7, 1998.

"Liu Huaqing Refutes Argument That China Poses a Threat," *Ta Kung Pao*, September 6, 1995, in FBIS-CHI, September 8, 1995, p. 31.

Liu Zhen, *Liu Zhen huiyilu* [Memoirs of Liu Zhen], Beijing: Jiefangjun Chubanshe, 1990.

Lo Ping, "Notes on a Northern Journey: CPC Military Attacks the MFA," *Cheng Ming*, July 1, 1994, in FBIS-CHI, July 26, 1994, pp. 14–15.

_____, "Zhu Rongji Rescues Jiang Zemin from a Siege in the Army," *Cheng Ming*, December 1, 1998, in FBIS-CHI, December 8, 1998.

"Looking Towards Modernization by the Mid-21st Century," *Beijing Review* (April 1–7, 1991):24.

Lord, Carnes, "American Strategic Culture," *Comparative Strategy* 5 (1985):269–93.

Lovejoy, Charles D., and Bruce W. Watson, eds., *Chinese Military Reforms: International and Domestic Implications*, Boulder, CO: Westview Press, 1984.

Lu Ning, *The Dynamics of Foreign-Policy Decisionmaking in China*, Boulder, CO: Westview Press, 1997.

MacFarquhar, Roderick, "The Whampoa Military Academy," *Papers on China* (Harvard University East Asia Regional Studies Seminar) 9 (August 1955):146–72.

MacFarquhar, Roderick, *The Origins of the Cultural Revolution*, Vol. 1: *Contradictions among the People, 1956–1957*, New York: Columbia University Press, 1974.

_____, *The Origins of the Cultural Revolution*, Vol. 2: *The Great Leap Forward, 1958–1960*, New York: Columbia University Press, 1983.

_____, *The Origins of the Cultural Revolution*, Vol. 3: *The Coming of the Cataclysm, 1961–1966*, New York: Columbia University Press, 1997.

MacKinnon, Stephen R., "The Peiyang Army: Yuan Shih-k'ai and the Origins of Modern Chinese Warlordism," *Journal of Asian Studies* XXXII (May 1973): 405–23.

Magnier, Mark, "Chinese Military Still Embedded in the Economy," *Los Angeles Times*, January 9, 2000.

"Main Points of Yang Shangkun's Secret Speech," *Ming Pao*, May 29, 1989, in FBIS-CHI, May 30, 1989.

Manion, Melanie, "Introduction: Reluctant Duelists: The Logic of the 1989 Protests and Massacre," in Michel Oksenberg, Lawrence R. Sullivan, and Marc Lambert, eds., *Beijing Spring, 1989: Confrontation and Conflict: The Basic Documents*, Armonk, NY: M. E. Sharpe, 1990.

Mao Zedong, *Selected Military Writings of Mao Tse-tung*, Peking: Foreign Languages Press, 1967.

_____, *Jianguo yilai Mao Zedong wengao* [Mao Zedong's manuscripts since the founding of the Republic], Vol. 1: *September 1949–December 1950*, Beijing: Zhongyang Wenxian Chubanshe, 1987.

_____, "Mao's Dispatch of Chinese Troops to Korea: Forty-Six Telegrams, July–October 1950," trans. Li Xiaobing, Wang Xi, and Chen Jian, *Chinese Historians* V (Spring 1992):63–86.

_____, *Jianguo yilai Mao Zedong wengao* [Manuscripts of Mao Zedong since the founding of the Republic], Vol. 12: *1966 January–1968 December*, Beijing: Zhongyang Wenxian Chubanshe, 1998.

McCord, Edward A., *The Power of the Gun: The Emergence of Modern Chinese Warlordism*, Berkeley and Los Angeles, CA: University of California Press, 1993.

McVadon, Eric, "PRC Exercises, Doctrine, and Tactics toward Taiwan: The Naval Dimension," in Lilley and Downs, eds., *Crisis in the Taiwan Strait*, pp. 249–76.

Mi Zhenyu, "Zhongguo jiji fangyu zhanlue fangzhen" [China's strategic guiding principle of active defense], in Shi Bike, ed., *Zhongguo daqushi* [Megatrends China], Beijing: Hualing Chubanshe, 1996, pp. 52–9.

Miller, Matthew, "Belgrade Bombing: Marchers Try to Break Down Consulate Door," *South China Morning Post*, May 10, 1999.

Mo Ta-hua, "A Preliminary Study of Chinese Communist Strategic Culture," *Zhongguo Dalu Yanjiu* [China Mainland Studies] (Taipei) 39 (May 1996):38–52.

Morris, Stephen J., *Why Vietnam Invaded Cambodia: Political Culture and the Causes of War*, Stanford, CA: Stanford University Press, 1999.

Mozingo, David, "The Chinese Army and the Communist State," in Victor Nee and David Mozingo, eds., *State and Society in Contemporary China*, Ithaca, NY: Cornell University Press, 1983, pp. 89–105.

Mu Wang, "Zhongnanhai gaoceng douzheng zhenxiang" [The real high-level struggle at Zhongnanhai], *Ching Pao Monthly*, June 1989, pp. 18–25.

Mufson, Steven, "In Panama, Ports in a Storm," *Washington Post*, December 8, 1999.

Mulvenon, James, "The Limits of Coercive Diplomacy: The 1979 Sino–Vietnam Border War," *Journal of Northeast Asian Studies* XVI (Fall 1995):68–88.

———, *Professionalization of the Senior Chinese Officer Corps: Trends and Implications*, Santa Monica, CA: RAND, 1997.

———, "China: Conditional Compliance," in Muthiah Alagappa, ed., *Coercion and Governance: The Declining Political Role of the Military in Asia*, Stanford, CA: Stanford University Press, 2001, pp. 317–35.

———, *Soldiers of Fortune: The Rise and Fall of the Chinese Military–Business Complex*, Armonk, NY: M. E. Sharpe, 2001.

———, "Civil-Military Relations and the EP-3 Crisis: A Content Analysis," *China Leadership Monitor* 1 (Winter 2002), available at www.chinaleadershipmonitor.org/29911/20011JM1.htm.

Munro, Donald J., *The Concept of Man in Early China*, Stanford, CA: Stanford University Press, 1969.

Munro, Ross. H., "Eavesdropping on the Chinese Military: Where It Expects War – Where It Doesn't," *Orbis* 38 (Summer 1994):355–72.

Naquin, Susan, *Millenarian Rebellion in China: The Eight Trigrams Uprising of 1813*, New Haven, CT: Yale University Press, 1970.

Nathan, Andrew, "Chinese Democracy in 1989: Continuity and Change," *Problems of Communism* 38 (September–October 1989):17–29.

———, *China's Transition*, New York: Columbia University Press, 1997.

Nathan, Andrew J., and Robert S. Ross, *The Great Wall and the Empty Fortress: China's Search for Security*, New York: W. W. Norton, 1997.

Nelson, Harvey, "Regional and Paramilitary Ground Forces," in William Whitson, ed., *The Military and Political Power in China in the 1970s*, New York Praeger, 1972, pp. 135–52.

———, *The Chinese Military System: An Organizational Study of the Chinese People's Liberation Army*, Boulder, CO: Westview Press, 1977.

Nguyen, Manh Hung, "The Sino–Vietnamese Conflict: Power Play among Communist Neighbors," *Asian Survey* XIX (November 1979):1037–52.

Nie Rongzhen, *Nie Rongzhen Huiyilu* [Memoirs of Nie Rongzhen], Beijing: Jiefangjun Chubanshe, 1984.

———, *Inside the Red Star: The Memoirs of Marshal Nie Rongzhen*, trans. Zhong Renyi, Beijing: New World Press, 1988.

Nordlinger, Eric A., *Soldiers and Politics: Military Coups and Governments*, Englewood Cliffs, NJ: Prentice Hall, 1977.

O'Balance, Edgar, *The Wars in Vietnam, 1954–1980*, New York: Hippocrene Books, 1981.

O'Brien, Anita M., "Military Academies in China, 1885–1915," in Joshua A. Fogel and William T. Rowe, eds., *Perspectives on a Changing China: Essays in Honor of Professor C. Martin Wilbur on the Occasion of His Retirement*, Boulder, CO: Westview Press, 1979.

Odom, William E., *The Collapse of the Soviet Military*, New Haven, CT: Yale University Press, 1998.

O'Hanlon, Michael, "Why China Cannot Conquer Taiwan," *International Security* 25 (Fall 2000):51–86.

Oksenberg, Michel, "A Decade of Sino–American Relations," *Foreign Affairs* 61 (Fall 1982):175–95.

Oksenberg, Michel, Lawrence R. Sullivan, and Marc Lambert, eds., *Beijing Spring, 1989: Confrontation and Conflict: The Basic Documents*, Armonk, NY: M. E. Sharpe, 1990.

"The One China Principle and the Taiwan Issue," Xinhua, February 21, 2000, in FBIS-CHI, February 21, 2000.

"Order of the Military Commission of the CCP Central Committee" (April 6, 1967), cited in *Current Background* 852 (May 6, 1968):115–16.

Paltiel, Jeremy T., "PLA Allegiance on Parade: Civil–Military Relations in Transition," *China Quarterly* 143 (September 1995):784–800.

Pan Shunu, "War Is Not Far from Us," *Jiefangjun Bao*, June 8, 1999, in FBIS-CHI, July 6, 1999.

Panikkar, K. M., *In Two Chinas: Memoirs of a Diplomat*, London: Allen and Unwin, 1955; reprint ed., Westport, CT: Hyperion Press, 1981.

Peng Dehuai, *Peng Dehuai zishu* [Peng Dehuai's own account], Beijing: Renmin Chubanshe, 1981.

———, *Memoirs of a Chinese Marshal: The Autobiographical Notes of Peng Dehuai (1898–1974)*, trans. Zheng Longpu, Beijing: Foreign Languages Press, 1984.

———, *Peng Dehuai junshi wenxuan* [Collected military works of Peng Dehuai], Beijing: Zhongyang Wenxian Chubanshe, 1988.

"The People's Armed Police," *China News Analysis* 1482 (April 1, 1993):1–9.

"People's Republic of China National Defense Law," cited in Beijing Xinhua Domestic Service, March 18, 1997, in FBIS-CHI, March 24, 1997.

Perlmutter, Amos, *The Military and Politics in Modern Times*, New Haven, CT: Yale University Press, 1977.

Perlmutter, Amos, and William M. LeoGrande, "The Party in Uniform: Toward a Theory of Civil-Military Relations in Communist Political Systems," *American Political Science Review* 76 (December 1982):778–89.

Perry, Elizabeth J., *Rebels and Revolutionaries in North China*, Stanford, CA: Stanford University Press, 1980.

———, "Rural Violence in Socialist China," *China Quarterly* 103 (1986):414–40.

———, "Introduction: Chinese Political Culture Revisited," in Jeffrey N. Wasserstrom and Perry, eds., *Popular Protests and Political Culture in Modern China*, 2nd ed., Boulder, CO: Westview Press, 1994, pp. 1–14.

Perry, Elizabeth J., and Li Xun, *Proletarian Power: Shanghai in the Cultural Revolution*, Boulder, CO: Westview Press, 1997.

Pike, Douglas, "Communist vs. Communist in Southeast Asia," *International Security* 4 (Summer 1979):20–39.

Pillsbury, Michael, ed., *Chinese Views of Future Warfare*, Washington, DC: National Defense University Press, 1997.

———, ed., *China Debates the Future Security Environment*, Washington, DC: National Defense University Press, 2000.

Pollack, Jonathan, "The Korean War and Sino–American Relations," in Harry Harding and Yuan Ming, eds., *Sino–American Relations, 1945–1955: A Joint Reassessment of a Critical Decade*, Wilmington, DE: Scholarly Resources, Inc., 1989, pp. 213–37.

―――, "Structure and Process in the Chinese Military System," in Kenneth G. Lieberthal and David M. Lampton, eds., *Bureaucracy, Politics, and Decision-Making in Post-Mao China*, Berkeley and Los Angeles, CA: University of California Press, 1992, pp. 151–80.

Pomfret, John, "Jiang Tells Army to End Trade Role," *Washington Post*, July 23, 1998.

―――, "Chinese Crime Rate Soars as Economic Problems Grow," *Washington Post*, January 21, 1999.

―――, "China Ponders the New Rules of Unrestricted War," *Washington Post*, August 8, 1999.

Posen, Barry, *The Sources of Military Doctrine: France, Britain, and Germany between the World Wars*, Ithaca, NY: Cornell University Press, 1984.

Powell, Ralph, *Maoist Military Doctrines*, New York: American–Asian Educational Exchange, Inc., n.d.

―――, *The Rise of Chinese Military Power, 1895–1912*, Princeton, NJ: Princeton University Press, 1956.

Powell, Ralph L., and Chong-kun Yoon, "Public Security and the PLA," *Asian Survey* XVII (December 1972):1082–1100.

Price, Jane L., "Revolution, Nation-Building, and Chinese Communist Leadership Education during the Sino–Japanese War," in Joshua A. Fogel and William T. Rowe, eds., *Perspectives on a Changing China*, Boulder, CO: Westview Press, 1979, pp. 197–216.

Pye, Lucian W., *Warlord Politics: Conflict and Coalition in the Modernization of Republican China*, New York: Praeger, 1971.

―――, *The Dynamics of Chinese Politics*, Boston, MA: Oelgeschlager, Gunn, and Hain, 1981.

―――, "Tiananmen and Chinese Political Culture: The Escalation of Confrontation from Moralizing to Revenge," *Asian Survey* 30 (April 1990):331–47.

Qiao Liang, and Wang Xiangsui, *Chaoxian zhan* [Unrestricted warfare], Beijing: Jiefangjun Wenyi Chubanshe, February 1999.

Rawlinson, John L., *China's Struggle for Naval Development, 1839–1895*, Cambridge, MA: Harvard University Press, 1967.

"Red Flag on SRV's National Chauvinism. . . . ," Beijing Xinhua Domestic Service, January 3, 1979, in FBIS-CHI, January 4, 1979, p. A13.

"Resolution on Certain Questions in the History of Our Party since the Founding of the People's Republic," adopted by the Sixth Plenum of the Eleventh Central Committee, cited in Xinhua (Beijing), June 30, 1981, in FBIS-CHI, July 1, 1981.

Roberts, Adam, "The British Armed Forces and Politics: A Historical Perspective," in Cynthia H. Enloe and Ursula Semin-Panzer, eds., *The Military, the Police and Domestic Order: British and Third World Experiences*, London: Richardson Institute for Conflict and Peace Research, 1976.

Robinson, Thomas W., "The Wuhan Incident: Local Strife and Provincial Rebellion during the Cultural Revolution," *China Quarterly* 47 (July/September 1971): 413–38.

―――, "Chou En-lai and the Cultural Revolution in China," in Robinson, ed., *The Cultural Revolution in China*, Berkeley and Los Angeles, CA: University of California Press, 1971, pp. 165–312.

―――, "China Confronts the Soviet Union: Warfare and Diplomacy on China's Inner Asian Frontiers," in Roderick MacFarquhar and John K. Fairbank, eds.,

Cambridge History of China, Vol. 15: *The People's Republic*, Part 2: *Revolutions within the Chinese Revolution, 1966–1982*, New York: Cambridge University Press, 1991, pp. 218–301.

Robinson, Thomas W., and David Shambaugh, eds., *Chinese Foreign Policy: Theory and Practice*, Oxford, UK: Clarendon Press, 1994.

Ross, Robert S., *The Indochina Tangle: China's Vietnam Policy, 1975–1979*, New York: Columbia University Press, 1988.

————, "The 1995–96 Taiwan Strait Confrontation: Coercion, Credibility, and the Use of Force," *International Security* 25 (Fall 2000):87–129.

Ross, Robert S., and Paul H. B. Godwin, "New Directions in Chinese Security Studies," in David Shambaugh, ed., *American Studies of Contemporary China*, Armonk, NY: M. E. Sharpe, 1993, pp. 138–60.

Roy, Denny, "Hegemon on the Horizon?: China's Threat to East Asian Security," *International Security* 19 (Summer 1994):148–68.

Ruan Ming, *Deng Xiaoping: Chronicle of an Empire*, trans. Nancy Liu, Peter Rand, and Lawrence R. Sullivan, Boulder, CO: Westview Press, 1994.

Sandschneider, Eberhard, "Military and Politics in the PRC," in June Teufel Dreyer, ed., *Chinese Defense and Foreign Policy*, New York: Paragon House, 1989, pp. 331–50.

Sawyer, Ralph D., trans., *The Seven Military Classics of Ancient China*, Boulder, CO: Westview Press, 1993.

Schauble, John, "China's Communists Fear the Enemy Within," *Sydney Morning Herald*, September 27, 2000.

Schneider, Lawrence A., *A Madman of Ch'u: The Chinese Myth of Loyalty and Dissent*, Berkeley and Los Angeles, CA: University of California Press, 1980.

Schram, Stuart, *The Thought of Mao Tse-tung*, New York: Cambridge University Press, 1989.

Scobell, Andrew, "The Death Penalty in Post-Mao China," *China Quarterly* 123 (September 1990):503–20.

————, "The Death Penalty under Socialism: The Soviet Union, China, Cuba and the German Democratic Republic, 1917–1990," *Criminal Justice History* 12 (1991):189–234.

————, "Why the People's Army Fired on the People," in Roger V. Des Forges, Luo Ning, Wu Yen-bo, eds., *Chinese Democracy and the Crisis of 1989: Chinese and American Reflections*, Albany, NY: State University of New York Press, 1993, pp. 191–221 (originally published as "Why the People's Army Fired on the People: The Chinese Military and Tiananmen," *Armed Forces and Society* 18 [Winter 2002]: 193– 213).

————, "Politics, Professionalism, and Peacekeeping: An Analysis of the 1987 Military Coup in Fiji," *Comparative Politics* 26 (January 1994):187–99.

————, "Civil-Military Relations in the People's Republic of China in Comparative Perspective," Ph.D. dissertation, Columbia University, 1995.

————, "Military Coups in the People's Republic of China: Failure, Fabrication, or Fancy?" *Journal of Northeast Asian Studies* XIV (Spring 1995):25–46.

————, review of Ruan Ming, *Deng Xiaoping: Chronicle of an Empire*, in *China Information* XI (July 1996):162–5.

————, "After Deng, What?: Reconsidering the Prospects for a Democratic Transition in China," *Problems of Post-Communism* 44 (September–October 1997):22–31.

———, "Taiwan as Macedonia?: The Strait Crisis as a Syndrome," *Studies in Conflict and Terrorism* 21 (1998):181–216.

———, "Show of Force: Chinese Soldiers, Statesmen, and the 1995–1996 Taiwan Strait Crisis," *Political Science Quarterly* 115 (Summer 2000):227–47.

———, "Playing to Win: Chinese Army Building in the Era of Jiang Zemin," *Asian Perspective* 25 (2001):73–105.

———, "The Meaning of Martial Law for the PLA and Internal Security in China after Deng," paper presented to the RAND/CAPS Conference "New Reforms in the PLA," held June 2001, Washington, DC.

———, "The Chinese Cult of Defense," *Issues and Studies* 37 (September/October 2001):100–27.

Scobell, Andrew, and Brad Hammitt, "Goons, Gunmen, and Gendarmerie: Toward Reconceptualization of Paramilitary Formations," *Journal of Political and Military Sociology* 26 (Winter 1998):37–50.

Segal, Gerald, "The PLA and Chinese Foreign Policy Decision-Making," *International Affairs* 57 (Summer 1981):449–66.

———, "The Military as a Group in Chinese Politics," in David S. G. Goodman, ed., *Groups and Politics in the People's Republic of China*, Armonk, NY: M. E. Sharpe, 1984, pp. 83–101.

———, *Defending China*, New York: Oxford University Press, 1985.

———, "The Future of the People's Liberation Army," in Paul Beaver, ed., *China in Crisis: The Role of the Military*, London: Jane's Information Group, 1989.

Segal, Gerald, and John Phipps, "Why Communist Armies Defend Their Parties," *Asian Survey* XXX (October 1990):959–76.

Selden, Mark, *The Yenan Way in Revolutionary China*, Cambridge, MA: Harvard University Press, 1971.

Shambaugh, David, *Beautiful Imperialist: China Perceives America, 1972–1990*, Princeton, NJ: Princeton University Press, 1991.

———, "The Soldier and the State in China: The Political Work System in the People's Liberation Army," *China Quarterly* 110 (1991):276–304.

———, "China's Commander-in-Chief: Jiang Zemin and the PLA," in C. Dennison Lane, Mark Weisenbloom, and Dimon Liu, eds., *Chinese Military Modernization*, New York and Washington, DC: Kegan Paul International and American Enterprise Institute Press, 1996, pp. 209–45.

———, "China's Military in Transition: Politics, Professionalism, Procurement and Power Projection," *China Quarterly* 146 (June 1996):265–98.

———, "China's Military: Real or Paper Tiger?" *Washington Quarterly* 19 (Spring 1996):19–36.

———, "The Building of the Party-State in China, 1949–1965: Bringing the Soldier Back In," in Timothy Cheek and Tony Saich, eds., *New Perspectives on State Socialism in China*, Armonk, NY: M. E. Sharpe, 1997, pp. 125–50.

———, "China's Post-Deng Military Leadership: New Faces, New Trends," discussion paper, Stanford, CA: Asia/Pacific Research Center, June 1998.

———, "China's Military Views the World: Ambivalent Security," *International Security* 24 (Winter 1999/2000):52–79.

Sheng, Michael M., "Beijing's Decision to Enter the Korean War: A Reappraisal and New Documentation," *Korea and World Affairs* 19 (Summer 1995):294–313.

———, *Battling Western Imperialism: Mao, Stalin, and the United States*, Princeton, NJ: Princeton University Press, 1997.

Sheridan, James E., *Chinese Warlord: The Career of Feng Yu-hsiang*, Stanford, CA: Stanford University Press, 1966.

———, *China in Disintegration: The Republican Era in Chinese History, 1912–1949*, New York: Free Press, 1977.

Shi Wei, "What Happened in Beijing?" in *The June Turbulence in Beijing*, Beijing: New Star Publishers, 1989, pp. 38–48.

———, "Why Impose Martial Law in Beijing?" in *The June Turbulence in Beijing*, Beijing: New Star Publishers, 1989, pp. 21–37.

Shils, Edward A., and Morris Janowitz, "Cohesion and Disintegration in the Wehrmacht in World War II," *Public Opinion Quarterly* 12 (Summer 1948):280–315.

Shlapak, David A., David T. Orletsky, and Barry A. Wilson, *Dire Strait: Military Aspects of the China–Taiwan Confrontation and Options for U.S. Policy*, Santa Monica, CA: RAND, 2000.

Simmie, Scott, and Bob Nixon, *Tiananmen Square*, Seattle, WA: University of Washington Press, 1989.

Skocpol, Theda, "Social Revolutions and Mass Mobilization," *World Politics* XL (January 1988):147–68.

Smith, Craig S., "As Crimes Rise in China, Four Germans Are Killed," *New York Times*, April 4, 2000.

———, "China Sends Its Army Money and Taiwan a Signal," *New York Times*, March 11, 2001.

———, "China's Efforts against Crime Make No Dent," *New York Times*, December 26, 2001.

Smith, Richard J., "Chinese Military Institutions in the Mid-Nineteenth Century, 1850–1860," *Journal of Asian History* 8:2 (1974):122–61.

———, "The Reform of Military Education in Late Ch'ing China, 1842–1895," *Journal of the Hong Kong Branch of the Royal Asiatic Society* 18 (1978):15–40.

———, *China's Cultural Heritage: The Ch'ing Dynasty, 1644–1912*, Boulder, CO: Westview Press, 1983.

Snow, Edgar, *The Long Revolution*, New York: Random House, 1972.

Snyder, Jack L., *The Soviet Strategic Culture: Implications for Nuclear Options*, Santa Monica, CA: RAND, 1977.

———, *The Ideology of the Offensive: Military Decision Making and the Disasters of 1914*, Ithaca, NY: Cornell University Press, 1984.

———, "Civil-Military Relations and the Cult of the Offensive, 1914 and 1984," *International Security* 9 (Summer 1984):108–46.

Soeters, Joseph L., "Value Orientations in Military Academies: A Thirteen Country Study," *Armed Forces and Society* 24 (Fall 1997):7–32.

Song Renqiong, "Chairman Mao Refused to Be the Grand Marshal," *Minzhu yu Fazhi* (December 1993), pp. 8–9.

Song Shilun, *Mao Zedong junshi sixiang de xingcheng jiqi fazhan* [Formation and development of Mao Zedong's military thought], Beijing: Junshi Kexue Chubanshe, 1984.

Song Yongyi, "The Role of Zhou Enlai in the Cultural Revolution: A Contradictory Image From Diverse Sources," *Issues and Studies* 37 (April/May 2001): 1–28.

Spector, Stanley, *Li Hung-chang and the Huai Army: A Study in Nineteenth Century Regionalism*, Seattle, WA: University of Washington Press, 1964.

Spence, Jonathan D., *The Search for Modern China*, New York: W. W. Norton, 1990.

———, *God's Chinese Son: The Taiping Heavenly Kingdom of Hong Xiuquan*, New York: W. W. Norton, 1996.

Spurr, Russell, *Enter the Dragon: China's Undeclared War against the U.S. in Korea, 1950–1951*, New York: Henry Holt, 1988.

"State Council Official Comments on PRC Policy toward SRV," cited in Hong Kong Agence France Presse in English, February 8, 1979, in FBIS-CHI, February 9, 1979, p. E1.

"State Council Spokesman Yuan Mu Held a Press Conference," in *The June Turbulence in Beijing*, Beijing: New Star Publishers, 1989, pp. 4–20.

Stepan, Alfred, *The Military in Politics: Changing Patterns in Brazil*, Princeton, NJ: Princeton University Press, 1971.

———, "The New Professionalism of Internal Warfare and Military Role Expansion," in Stepan, ed., *Authoritarian Brazil: Origins, Policies, and Future*, New Haven, CT: Yale University Press, 1973, pp. 47–65.

———, *Rethinking Military Politics: Brazil and the Southern Cone*, Princeton, NJ: Princeton University Press, 1988.

Stokes, Mark A., *China's Strategic Modernization: Implications for the United States*, Carlisle Barracks, PA: U.S. Army War College, September 1999.

Stolper, Thomas E., *China, Taiwan, and the Offshore Islands*, Armonk, NY: M. E. Sharpe, 1985.

Storey, Ian James, "Creeping Assertiveness: China, the Philippines, and the South China Sea Dispute," *Contemporary Southeast Asia* 21 (April 1999):95–118.

Strand, David, *Rickshaw Beijing: City People and Politics in the 1920s*, Berkeley and Los Angeles, CA: University of California Press, 1989.

Stueck, William, *The Korean War: An International History*, Princeton, NJ: Princeton University Press, 1995.

Sutter, Robert, "Taiwan – Mainland China Talks: Competing Approaches and Implications for U.S. Policy," report for Congress, Washington, DC: Congressional Research Service, 1998.

Sutton, Donald S., *Provincial Militarism and the Chinese Republic: The Yunnan Army, 1905–25*, Ann Arbor, MI: University of Michigan Press, 1980.

Swaine, Michael D., *The Military and Political Succession in China: Leaders, Structures, and Beliefs*, Santa Monica, CA: RAND, 1992.

———, *The Role of the Chinese Military in National Security Policymaking*, Santa Monica, CA: RAND, 1996.

———, "Chinese Decision-Making Regarding Taiwan, 1979–2000," in David M. Lampton, ed., *The Making of Chinese Foreign and Security Policy in the Era of Reform*, Stanford, CA: Stanford University Press, 2001, pp. 289–336.

Tan Eng Bok, Georges, "Strategic Doctrine," in Gerald Segal and William T. Tow, eds., *Chinese Defence Policy*, Urbana and Chicago, IL: University of Illinois Press, 1984, pp. 3–17.

Tanner, Murray Scot, "Cracks in the Wall: China's Eroding Coercive State," *Current History* 100 (September 2001):243–9.

Bibliography

Tanner, Murray Scot, "The Institutional Lessons of Disaster: The People's Armed Police after Tiananmen," in James C. Mulvenon and Andrew N. D. Yang, ed., *The PLA as Organization*, Santa Monica, CA: RAND, 2002, pp. 587–635.

Teiwes, Frederick C., *Leadership, Legitimacy, and Conflict in China: From a Charismatic Mao to the Politics of Succession*, Armonk, NY: M. E. Sharpe, 1984.

———, "Peng Dehuai and Mao Zedong," *Australian Journal of Chinese Affairs* 16 (July 1986):81–98.

———, *Politics at Mao's Court: Gao Gang and Party Factionalism in the Early 1950s*, Armonk, NY: M. E. Sharpe, 1990.

Teiwes, Frederick C., and Warren Sun, *The Tragedy of Lin Biao: Riding the Tiger during the Cultural Revolution, 1966–1971*, Honolulu, HI: University of Hawaii Press, 1996.

Terrill, Ross, *Mao: A Biography*, New York: Harper and Row, 1980.

Thurston, Anne F., *Enemies of the People*, New York: Alfred A. Knopf, 1987.

Tien Chen-Ya, *Chinese Military Theory: Ancient and Modern*, Stevanage, UK: Spa Books, 1992.

Tiglao, Rigoberto, Andrew Sherry, Nate Thayer, and Michael Vatikiotis, "'Tis the Season," *Far Eastern Economic Review*, December 24, 1998, pp. 18–20.

Ting Chen-wu, "Hawks Dominate China's Policy toward Taiwan," *Hsin Pao*, March 14, 1996, in FBIS-CHI, March 21, 1996, pp. 11–13.

Tong, James W., *Disorder under Heaven: Collective Violence in the Ming Dynasty*, Berkeley and Los Angeles, CA: University of California, 1991.

Tretiak, Daniel, "China's Vietnam War and Its Consequences," *China Quarterly* 80 (December 1979):740–67.

Tyler, Patrick E., "As China Threatens Taiwan, It Makes Sure the U.S. Listens," *New York Times*, January 24, 1996.

———, *A Great Wall: Six Presidents and China*, New York: PublicAffairs, 1999.

Union Research Institute, *The Case of Peng Teh-huai, 1959–1968*, Hong Kong: Union Research Institute, 1968.

United States House of Representatives Select Committee, *U.S. National Security and Military/Commercial Concerns with the People's Republic of China*, 105th Congress, 2nd session, Washington, DC: GPO, 1999.

Van Evera, Stephen, "The Cult of the Offense and the Origins of the First World War," *International Security* 9 (Summer 1984):58–107.

Van Ness, Peter, *Revolution and Chinese Foreign Policy: Peking's Support for Wars of National Liberation*, Berkeley and Los Angeles, CA: University of California Press, 1971.

Vance, Cyrus, *Hard Choices: Critical Years in American Foreign Policy*, New York: Simon and Schuster, 1983.

Villanueva, Marichu, "Senators Fear 'Full-Blown' War over Spratlys," *Manila Standard*, February 18, 1995.

Vogel, Ezra, *Canton under Communism: Programs and Politics in a Provincial Capital, 1949–1968*, New York: Harper Torch Books, 1971.

Wakeman, Jr., Frederic, "Models of Historical Change: The Chinese State and Society, 1839–1989," in Kenneth Lieberthal, Joyce Kallgren, Roderick MacFarquhar, and Frederic Wakeman, eds., *Perspectives on Modern China: Four Anniversaries*, Armonk, NY: M. E. Sharpe, 1991, pp. 68–102.

Walder, Andrew G., *Communist Neo-Traditionalism: Work and Authority in Chinese Industry*, Berkeley and Los Angeles, CA: University of California Press, 1986.

Waldron, Arthur, *The Great Wall of China: From History to Myth*, New York: Cambridge University Press, 1990.

———, "The Warlord: Twentieth Century Chinese Understandings of Violence, Militarism, and Imperialism," *American Historical Review* 96 (October 1991):1073–1100.

———, *From War to Nationalism: China's Turning Point, 1924–1925*, New York: Cambridge University Press, 1995.

———, "Deterring China," *Commentary* 100 (October 1995):17–21.

———, *The Chinese Civil Wars, 1911–1940s*, London: St. Martin's, 1996.

———, review of *Cultural Realism* in *China Quarterly* 147 (September 1996):962–4.

Walt, Stephen M., *Revolution and War*, Ithaca, NY: Cornell University Press, 1996.

Wang Changyan and Cui Haiming, "Deng Xiaoping de junshi sixiang chutan" [Preliminary exploration of Deng Xiaoping's military thought], in Pan Shiying, ed., *Dangdai Zhongguo junshi sixiang jingyao* [Essence of contemporary Chinese military thinking], Beijing: Jiefangjun Chubanshe, 1992, pp. 92–135.

Wang Cunzhu, "Persist in Performing Domestic Functions of the People's Army," *JFJB*, March 27, 1990, cited in FBIS-CHI, April 25, 1990, p. 35.

Wang Naiming, "Adhere to Active Defense and Modern People's War," in Michael Pillsbury, ed., *Chinese Views of Future Warfare*, Washington, DC: National Defense University Press, 1997, pp. 37–44.

Wang Nianyi, *1949–1989 nian de Zhongguo* [China in 1949–1989], Vol. 3: *Da dongluan de niandai* [Decade of great turmoil], Zhengzhou: Henan Renmin Chubanshe, 1988.

Wang Shaoguang, *Failure of Charisma: The Cultural Revolution in Wuhan*, Hong Kong: Oxford University Press, 1995.

Wang Zhiping, and Li Dezhou, "Zhong-Xi gudai junshi lilun de zhexue jichu" [Philosophical foundation of Chinese and Western military theories in ancient times], *ZGJSKX* 4 (1995):30–5.

Weber, Max, *The Theory of Social and Economic Organization*, A. M. Henderson and Talcott Parsons, eds. and trans., reprint of 1947 ed., New York: Free Press, 1964.

Weiss, Lawrence S., "Storm around the Cradle: The Korean War and the Early Years of the People's Republic, 1949–1953," Ph.D. dissertation, Columbia University, 1981.

West, Philip, "The Korean War and the Criteria of Significance in Chinese Popular Culture," *Journal of American–East Asian Relations* 1 (Winter 1992):383–408.

White, Lynn T., III, *The Policies of Chaos: The Organizational Causes of Violence in China's Cultural Revolution*, Princeton, NJ: Princeton University Press, 1989.

White, Theodore H., *In Search of History*, New York: Harper and Row, 1978.

"White Paper on China's National Defense," Xinhua Domestic Service, July 27 1998, in FBIS-CHI, July 29, 1998.

Whiting, Allen S., *China Crosses the Yalu: The Decision to Enter the Korean War*, Stanford, CA: Stanford University Press, 1968.

———, *The Chinese Calculus of Deterrence: India and Indochina*, Ann Arbor, MI: University of Michigan Press, 1975.

———, "Chinese Nationalism and Foreign Policy after Deng," *China Quarterly* 142 (June 1995): 295–316.

———, "The PLA and China's Threat Perceptions," *China Quarterly* 146 (June 1996): 606–7.

————, "Chinese Foreign Policy: Retrospect and Prospect," in Samuel S. Kim, ed., *China and the World: Chinese Foreign Policy Faces the New Millennium*, Boulder, CO: Westview Press, 1998, pp. 287–308.

————, "China's Use of Force, 1950–96, and Taiwan," *International Security* 26 (Fall 2001):103–31.

Whitson, William W., with Chen-Hsia Huang, *The Chinese High Command: Military Politics, 1927–1971*, New York: Praeger, 1973.

Wilkenfeld, Jonathan, Michael Brecher, and Sheila Moser, *Crises in the Twentieth Century*, Vol. 2: *Handbook of Foreign Policy Crises*, New York: Pergamon, 1988.

Wilson, Dick, *Zhou Enlai: A Biography*, New York: Viking, 1984.

Wilson, James Q., *Bureaucracy: What Government Agencies Do and Why They Do It*, New York: Basic Books, 1989.

Wu Xinbo, "China: Security Practice of a Modernizing and Ascending Power," in Muthiah Alagappa, ed., *Asian Security Practice: Material and Ideational Influences*, Stanford, CA: Stanford University Press, 1998.

Xiao Bing, and Qing Bo, *Zhongguo jundui neng fou da ying xia yi chang zhanzheng* [Will China's army win the next war?], Chongqing: Xinan Shifan Daxue Chubanshe, 1993.

Xing Shizhong, "China Threat Theory May Be Forgotten," *Quishi* [Seeking truth] 3 (February 1996), in FBIS-CHI, February 1, 1996.

Xiong Guangkai, "Zhongguo de guofang zhengce" [China's national defense policy], *Guoji zhanlue yanjiu* [International strategic studies] 55 (January 2000):1–3.

Xu Shiyou, *Xu Shiyou Huiyilu* [Memoirs of Xu Shiyou], Beijing: Jiefangjun Chubanshe, 1986.

Xu Xiangqian, *Lishi de huigu* [Reflections on history], Vol. 3, Beijing: Jiefangjun Chubanshe, 1987.

————, *Xu Xiangqian junshi wenxuan* [Selected military works of Xu Xiangqian], Beijing: Jiefangjun Chubanshe, 1993.

Xu Yan, *Diyici jiaoliang: kangMei yuanChao de lishi huiyi yu fansi* [The first trial: A historical retrospective and review of the resist America and aid Korea war], n.p.: Zhongguo Guangbo Dianshi Chubanshe, 1990.

Yan Jiaqi, and Gao Gao, *Zhongguo "wenge" shinian shi* [A history of China's ten-year cultural revolution], n.p.: Zhongguo Wenti Yanjiu Chubanshe, n.d.

Yang, Andrew Nien-Dzu, "Crisis, What Crisis?: Lessons of the 1996 Tension and the ROC View of Security in the Taiwan Strait," in Jonathan D. Pollack and Richard H. Yang, eds., *In China's Shadow: Regional Perspectives on Chinese Foreign Policy and Military Development*, Santa Monica, CA: RAND, 1998, pp. 143–53.

Yang Chengwu, *Yang Chengwu huiyilu* [Memoirs of Yang Chengwu], Beijing: Jiefangjun Chubanshe, 1990.

Yang, Richard H., Peter Kien-hong Yu, and Andrew N. Yang, eds., *China's Military: The PLA in 1990/1991*, Boulder, CO: Westview Press, 1991.

"Yang Shangkun's Speech," *Renmin ribao* [People's Daily], October 10, 1991, in FBIS-CHI, October 15, 1991.

Yao Xu, "KangMei yuanChao de yingming juece" [The wise policy decision to resist America and aid Korea], *Dangshi yanjiu* 5 (October 1980): 5–14.

Yao Youzhi, "Gudai Zhong-Xi junshi chuantong zhi bijiao" [Comparison of Chinese and Western ancient military traditions], *ZGJSKX* 3 (1995):93–100.

Bibliography

Yao Yunzhu, "The Evolution of Military Doctrine of the Chinese PLA from 1985 to 1995," *Korean Journal of Defense Analysis* VII (Winter 1995):57–80.

Ye Jianying xuanji [Selected works of Ye Jianying], Beijing: Renmin Chubanshe, 1996.

Yee, Herbert, "The Sino–Vietnamese Border War," *China Report* 16 (January–February 1980):15–32.

Yi Mu, and Mark V. Thompson, *Crisis at Tiananmen: Reform and Reality*, San Francisco, CA: China Books, 1989.

You Ji, "Making Sense of War Games in the Taiwan Strait," *Journal of Contemporary China* 6 (1997):287–305.

———, *The Armed Forces of China*, London: I. B. Tauris, 1999.

Yu Bin, "What China Learned from Its 'Forgotten War' in Korea," in Xiaobing Li, Allen R. Millett, and Bin Yu, eds. and trans., *Mao's Generals Remember Korea*, Lawrence, KS: University Press of Kansas, 2001, pp. 2–29.

Yue Daiyun, and Carolyn Wakeman, *To The Storm: The Odyssey of a Revolutionary Chinese Woman*, Berkeley and Los Angeles, CA: University of California Press, 1985.

Zhai Zhihai and Hao Yufan, "China's Decision to Enter the Korean War: History Revisited," *China Quarterly* 121 (March 1990):94–115.

Zhang Jing and Yao Yanjin, *Jiji fangyu zhanlue qianshuo* [Introduction to active defense strategy], Beijing: Jiefangjun Chubanshe, 1985.

Zhang Liang, compiler, *The Tiananmen Papers: The Chinese Leadership's Decision to Use Force against Their Own People – In Their Own Words*, Andrew J. Nathan and Perry Link, eds., New York: PublicAffairs, 2001.

———, compiler, *Zhongguo "liu si" zhenxiang* [China "June 4": The true story], 2 vols., n.p.: Mingjing Chubanshe, 2001.

Zhang Liyun, "Cong Beiyang wubei xuetang dao Baoding lujun junguan xuexiao" [From the Beiyang military school to the Baoding military academy], in Hebeisheng Zhengxie Wenli Ziliao Yanjiu Weiyuanhui and Baodingshi Zhengxie Wenshi Ziliao Yanjiu Weiyuanhui, compilers, *Baoding lujun junguan xuexiao*, n.p.: Hebei Renmin Chubanshe, 1987.

Zhang, Shu Guang, *Deterrence and Strategic Culture: Chinese–American Confrontations, 1948–1958*, Ithaca, NY: Cornell University Press, 1992.

———, "In the Shadow of Mao: Zhou Enlai and New China's Diplomacy," in Gordon A. Craig and Francis L. Loewenheim, eds., *The Diplomats, 1939–1979*, Princeton, NJ: Princeton University Press, 1994, pp. 337–70.

———, *Mao's Military Romanticism: China and the Korean War, 1950–1953*, Lawrence, KS: University Press of Kansas, 1995.

Zhang Wenrui, Yang Yuwen, and Liu Bangguo, "The Great Changes and New Characteristics in the Composition of Our Troops," *Qingnian Yanjiu*, June 6, 1986, translated in *Chinese Law and Government* 20 (Summer 1987):102–17.

Zhang Xi, "Peng Dehuai shouming shuaiyuan kangMei yuanChao de qianqian houhou" [The complete story of Peng Dehuai's appointment to lead the resist America, aid Korea War], *Zhonggong dangshi ziliao* 31 (1989):111–59.

Zhang Yunsheng, *Maojiawan jishi: Lin Biao mishu huiyilu* [The Maojiawan story: Memoirs of Lin Biao's secretary], Beijing: Chunqiu Chubanshe, 1988.

Zhao Quansheng, *Interpreting China's Foreign Policy: A Micro-Macro Linkage Approach*, New York: Oxford University Press, 1996.

Zhao Suisheng, "Chinese Intellectuals' Quest for National Greatness and Nationalist Writing in the 1990s," *China Quarterly* 152 (December 1997):725–45.

————, ed., *Across the Taiwan Strait: Mainland China, Taiwan, and the 1995–1996 Crisis*, New York: Routledge, 1999.

Zheng Qinsheng, "Military Conflicts in the New Era," in Pillsbury, ed., *Chinese Views of Future War*, pp. 399–407.

Zheng, Shiping, *Party vs. State in Post-1949 China: The Institutional Dilemma*, New York: Cambridge University Press, 1997.

Zheng Wenmu, "21 Shiji Zhongguo guoji zhengzhi jiao dian" [The main points of China's international political situation in the 21st century], in Shi Bike, ed., *Zhongguo daqushi* [Megatrends China], Beijing: Hualing Chubanshe 1996, pp. 28–34.

Zhengzhi Xueyuan Zhonggong Dangshi Jiaoyanshi, ed., *Zhongguo Gongchandang liushinian dashi jianjie* [A survey of major events in sixty years of Chinese Communist Party history], Beijing: Guofang Daxue Chubanshe, 1986.

Zhong Yang, Jie Chen, and John M. Scheb II, "Political Views from Below: A Survey of Beijing Residents," *PS: Political Science and Politics* XXX (September 1997): 478–82.

Zhongfa 288, cited in *Survey of China Mainland Press* 4026 (September 22, 1967):1–2.

Zhonggong Zhongyang Wenyi Yanjiushi, compiler, *Zhou Enlai nianpu* [Chronology of Zhou Enlai], Vol. 3: *1966–1976*, Beijing: Zhongyang Wenxian Chubanshe, 1997.

Zhonggong Zhongyang Xuanchuan Bu, ed., *Jianjue yonghu dangzhongyang juece, jianjue pingxi fangeming baoluan* [Resolutely support the policy of the central party authorities, resolutely suppress the counterrevolutionary rebellion], Beijing: Renmin Chubanshe, 1989.

Zhonghua Renmin Gongheguo Jieyanfa [Martial law of the People's Republic of China], Beijing: Falu Chubanshe, 1996.

Zhou Enlai Nianpu, 1949–1976 [Zhou Enlai chronology, 1949–1976], Beijing: Zhongyang Wenxian Chubanshe, 1997, 3 volumes.

Zhou Enlai waijiao wenxuan [Selected diplomatic works of Zhou Enlai], Beijing: Zhongyang Wenxian Chubanshe, 1990.

Zhu Chenghu, chief ed., *Zhongmei guanxi de fazhan bianhua ji qi qushi* [Changing developments and trends in China–U.S. relations], Nanjing: Jiangsu Renmin Chubanshe, 1998.

Zhu, Fang, *Gun Barrel Politics: Party–Army Relations in Mao's China*, Boulder, CO: Westview Press, 1998.

Zi Zhongyun, "Foreword," *in Mei-Tai guanxi sishi nian, 1949–1989* [Forty years of U.S.–Taiwan relations], Beijing: Renmin Chubanshe, 1991.

Zuo Ni, "Jiang Zemin, Li Peng Sign Order on Expanding Police Forces....," *Cheng Ming*, March 1, 1995, in FBIS-CHI, April 27, 1995, pp. 27–8.

Index

format (*see* civil-military culture)
Four Cardinal Principles 147
Freeman, Chas. 186–7, 190, 261
Fu Quanyou 73
function (*see* civil-military culture)

Gang of Four 63, 97, 115, 129, 149
Gao Gang 82, 84, 90–1, 232
Garver, John W. 28, 199, 203, 207, 225, 256, 258–64
Geng Biao 126, 133, 138, 247
George, Alexander 141, 206, 248, 259
Godwin, Paul H. B. xiii, 58, 197, 200, 204–7, 214, 219, 222, 264
Great Wall xi–xii, 2, 4, 31, 53, 192, 198
Green Standard (Armies of the) 43, 67, 69, 217, 226–7
Gu Gui 73
Gu Mu 100
Guan Feng 100, 107
Guan Yu (God of War) 44–5
Gurtov, Melvin (and Byung-Moo Hwang) xi, 201, 207, 229, 232, 258, 264

Han Nianlong 126
He Long 44, 62, 89, 110, 234
hegemony (hegemonism) 30
Hoa (ethnic Chinese in Vietnam) 121–2, 124, 135, 243
Hong Kong xiii, 29–30, 42, 153, 172, 174, 178, 184, 256
Hong Xuezhi 89–91, 149, 155–6, 230, 233–5
Hu Jintao, 6, 173
Hu Qili 148, 151
Hu Yaobang 124, 146
Hua Guofeng 52, 56, 63, 129, 130–1, 137–8, 143, 246
Huan Guocang 255–6
Huang, Chen-Hsia (*see* Whitson, William W.)
Hughes, Christopher xiii
Huntington, Samuel P., 57, 199, 202–3, 221–2, 241, 249
Hwang, Byung-Moo (*see* Gurtov, Melvin)

identity (*see* civil-military culture)
India
  nuclear tests (1998) 187
  Sino–Indian War (1962) 32, 125–6, 175, 193, 196, 244, 263
  intrastate violence 23–5
Islam 21

Janowitz, Morris 68, 202–3, 216, 222, 226
Japan 1, 16, 85, 92, 151, 184, 189
  Anti-Japanese War (1937–45) 70, 86
  Sino–Japanese War (1894–95) 42–4, 62
Jencks, Harlan W. 159, 202, 204, 221–2, 241–2, 245, 249–50, 253, 255–6, 262–3
Jiang Qing 97–101, 103, 106–8, 113
Jiang Zemin xi, 6–7, 9–10, 52, 59, 63–7, 75–6, 164, 166, 173, 175–6, 178, 192–5, 258
Joffe, Ellis xiii, 202, 204, 219, 222, 227–8, 236, 248
Johnston, Alastair Iain xiii, 4, 9, 19–20, 22–3, 34–5, 39, 191, 200–2, 204–7, 209–11, 214–15, 220, 229, 248, 263
just war 20, 25, 28, 34, 211, 214

Kang Sheng 70, 100
Kangda (Anti-Japanese Political and Military University) 62–3
Khmer Rouge 120–1, 123–4, 129, 131, 134–5
Kier, Elizabeth 5, 200, 202–3
Kim, Samuel xii, 200, 206, 264
Korea
  Korean Peninsula 43, 80–1, 84, 174
  Korea, North 33, 80, 120
  Korea, South 80, 151
  Korean War (1950–3) 10, 16–17, 32, 35, 42, 79–93, 119, 140–1, 174–5, 185, 195–6, 234, 263
Kuomintang (KMT) 42, 46–7, 60–2, 70, 165, 172, 174–5, 185, 224

Taiwan
  island of xiii, 11, 30, 43, 81, 89,
    172–90, 193, 196, 203, 243, 257,
    262
  Taiwan Affairs Leading Small Group
    (TALSG) 175–6
  Taiwan Strait Crises
    1954–5: 48, 185, 193
    1958: 185, 193, 196
    1962: 185, 193
    1995–6: 1, 10–11, 32, 65, 171–91,
    193, 195–7, 262–3
Tan, Zhenlin 100–1
Tao Siju 163
Tiananmen
  (Tiananmen) Papers 159, 249–56
  (Tiananmen) Square 36, 96, 146–7,
    149–52, 154, 159, 162
  Tiananmen (Square) Massacre (1989)
    xii, 32, 42, 63, 72–3, 144–67,
    187, 196, 252
Tibet 49, 72

United States 1, 7, 11, 28, 32, 35, 46, 48,
  79–80, 84, 88, 114, 120, 125–6,
  165, 171, 173–8, 180–2, 185–8,
  191, 203, 221, 230, 234
use of force (*see* culture, strategic; *see
  also specific cases*)

Van Evera, Stephen 15, 26, 206
Vietnam 32, 114, 119–27, 142, 243–4,
  247
  Vietnam War (1964–73) 193,
    196
  Vietnam War (1974, 1988) 193
  Vietnam War (1979) 10, 32, 42,
    119–43, 196, 245, 263

Waldron, Arthur 1, 4, 20, 39, 45, 199,
  201, 206, 208–11, 217
Wang Daohan 176
Wang Dongxing 124, 129, 245
Wang Li 101, 103–7, 113, 239
Wang Shanrong 132
Wang Zhaoguo 176
Wang Zhen 134, 145–6, 250

warlord (warlordism) 45, 62, 217
  warlord era 43–5, 217
Warring States period 16, 21, 25, 51, 54
Weber, Max 64–5
Wei Guoqing 109, 132
Weiqi (Go, Chinese chess) 47–8, 218
Wells, Harry 252, 256
Whampoa Academy 60–2, 174, 223
White Papers (China)
  on defense (1998) 28–9, 32, 34, 74
  on defense (2000) 34, 74
  on defense (2002) 34
  on Taiwan (2000) 181
Whiting, Allen S. xi, xiii, 201, 205–7,
  229, 235, 257–8, 260–1, 263–4
Whitson, William W. (and Chen-Hsia
  Huang) 52, 55, 62, 202, 204,
  220–5, 234
Wilson, James Q. 190, 203, 262
Worker's Daily 134
*Wreaths of Flowers at the Foot of the Tall
  Mountains* 42
Wu Faxian 105
Wu Xiuquan 134
Wuhan Incident (1967) 102–7, 113, 204

Xiao Jingguang 134
Xiao Ke 150
Xie Fuzhi 100, 103–6, 108, 239–40
Xing Shizhong 29, 212–13
Xinjiang 49, 72
Xiong Guangkai 66, 176, 186–7, 213,
  261
Xu Qinxian 156–7, 159
Xu Shiyou 108, 112, 127, 132, 139, 246,
  248
Xu Xiangqian 32, 61, 86–8, 97–8, 100–1,
  105, 110–13, 127, 133, 138–9,
  150, 155, 166, 213, 234, 237–8,
  246–7, 252
Xue Litai (*see* Lewis, John W.)

Yang Baibing 166
Yang Chengwu 97
Yang Dezhi 127, 132, 150
Yang Shangkun 66, 73, 145, 148, 152,
  155, 158, 166, 175, 252, 258

Other books in the series (continued from page iii)

Yung-chen Chiang, *Social Engineering and the Social Sciences in China, 1919–1949*

Joseph Fewsmith, *China Since Tiananmen: The Politics of Transition*

Mark W. Frazier, *The Making of the Chinese Industrial Workplace: State, Revolution, and Labor Management*

Thomas G. Moore, *China in the World Market: Chinese Industry and International Sources of Reform in the Post-Mao Era*

Stephen C. Angle, *Human Rights and Chinese Thought: A Cross-Cultural Inquiry*

For EU product safety concerns, contact us at Calle de José Abascal, 56–1°,
28003 Madrid, Spain or eugpsr@cambridge.org.

www.ingramcontent.com/pod-product-compliance
Ingram Content Group UK Ltd.
Pitfield, Milton Keynes, MK11 3LW, UK
UKHW042152130625

459647UK00011B/1294